NOTTINGHAMSHIRE IN THE EIGHTEENTH CENTURY

A STUDY OF LIFE AND LABOUR UNDER THE SQUIREARCHY

J. D. CHAMBERS, Ph.D.
Emeritus Professor of Economic and Social History,
The University, Nottingham.

SECOND EDITION

FRANK CASS & CO. LTD.
1966

First published in 1932
by P. S. King and Son, Ltd.

This edition published by
Frank Cass & Co. Ltd.
10 Woburn Walk, London, W.C.1

First edition 1932
Second edition 1966

Printed in Great Britain by
Thomas Nelson (Printers) Ltd., London and Edinburgh.

NOTTINGHAMSHIRE IN THE EIGHTEENTH CENTURY

INTRODUCTION TO THE SECOND EDITION

The Experience of Regional Economic Growth

SINCE the appearance of this book in 1932, the regional historiography of which it is part has been developed in a number of new directions. In particular, valuable light has been thrown on the problems of transport and communications[1], on the history of the industries of hosiery and lace[2], and on the establishment of factory production in spinning[3]. The remarkable innovations of Sir Francis Willoughby at Wollaton, including the use of boring rods and horse-driven pumping machinery which made the area a disseminating centre of mining techniques, and the varied forms of enterprise in the Derbyshire metallurgical industries, have received careful attention in published and unpublished researches[4]. The fluctuations of the harvests have been made the subject of an article of wide general significance[5]; and the passage of the region as a whole from a traditional agrarian society through the early phases of industrialisation has been presented in the context of demographic change under agricultural, industrial and urban conditions of growth[6]. If to these are added the studies of increased agricultural production by yeoman and gentleman farmers from the turn of the seventeenth century in the neighbouring counties of Leicestershire and Lincolnshire[7], and the critical assessment recently undertaken of the transition from paternalism to laissez-faire as seen in the work of Nottinghamshire poor law reformers in the early nineteenth century[8], we have a coverage in time as well as space, in ideas as well as in "entities with a metrical aspect", which brings into manageable focus most of the factors of regional change in this critical period.

That is not to say that the whole field has been covered or that final judgements can yet be given; there is much to be done on the demographic side, perhaps particularly on the fluctuating tide of population growth from the early seventeenth century and the related changes in family size and structure; the sources of change in social attitudes and policy, rooted, probably in religious and philosophical thought, have hardly been touched upon; little has been done in the immediate area dealt with in this book on the improvements in techniques (apart from enclosure) which enabled agricultural production to outstrip population growth from the middle of the seventeenth century with incalculable results on the internal market for industrial goods; and, of course, the incommensurable factor of internal and external trade has been left out of account altogether. Nevertheless, with these provisos, the various studies mentioned can be treated as a collective whole which comprehends most of the influences at work in regional development, and their mere existence within the given limits of time and space invites the question to what extent, if at all, an underlying pattern can be discerned among them. Somewhere in their interplay may be found not only clues to the problem of the phenomenal economic development of the region, but also to a truer assessment of the highly charged social environment, marked, as it was, by Luddism, a Nottinghamshire export, and Chartism, of which Nottinghamshire provided many active centres; in short, a better understanding both of the mechanism and also the spirit of change in this climactic period of transition, the watershed between the old world and the new. A search for such clues has its dangers, but so long as it abjures dogmatism and points to better solutions by others of the problems of the period, it has its uses; and with this in mind, an attempt is made to draw together in barest outline some of the results of these independent but regionally related studies in what remains of this Introduction.

In the first place, this present volume provides the social background from which the process of industrialisation emerged and matured. It shows a society in which the landed gentry were left supreme by the decline in the sixteenth and seventeenth centuries of the Church and the Crown; and the supremacy which they exercised by right of wealth and legal authority, they enhanced by enterprise and leadership in most departments of the regional economic life. It should also not be forgotten that they provided the essential framework of the unpaid bureaucracy which was responsible for police, relief of the poor and road repair, and at the same time they promoted, by means of legacies and benefactions, forms of education appropriate to a society that regarded the acquisition of wealth as the reward of a well-spent life[9]. They also assumed a heavy burden of taxation in the form of the land tax, which in the period of low prices before 1750, must be accounted a factor in the decline of the small landowner and the consolidation of large estates. The race went to the strong; but the strong did not notably abuse their strength.

An important characteristic of their administration was that they permitted the maximum degree of freedom consonant with the maintenance of public order; no effective police force existed and the military forces of the state were rarely, if ever, called on until the last turbulent years of the century. The cement of society was not physical force but the magic of hereditary degree, and this blessed sanction could be acquired through the accumulation as well as the the inheritance of wealth, above all, landed wealth. Such accumulation was made easier by the slow erosion of centralised control, e.g. in regard to enclosure, apprenticeship, wage fixing, which, if maintained, might have placed obstacles in the way of enterprise. Agricultural improvements were facilitated by private enclosure, which, in spite of the shrill protests of conservatives like Dr. Thoroton, went on in village after village where the soil lent itself to a quick response to the market, so that by 1700 probably one third of the area of the county—especially in the grazing and dairying areas in the Trent Valley and the Vale of Belvoir—was already enclosed. The instruments by which this was done were discreetly embodied in the proceedings of Chancery and the Court of the Exchequer where they have remained, until recently, as immune from the attentions of the historian as they were from the scrutiny of members of Parliament[10]. Similarly, the machinery for bureaucratic control of industry was allowed slowly to lapse without being officially dismantled, so that local authorities could exercise their powers of coercion when it suited them, e.g. against vagrants, unmarried mothers and unemployable strangers, while retaining the reality of free mobility of able-bodied labour. Far from being "imprisoned" in their parishes, as Adam Smith tells us, working men and women moved fast enough, if only to the next parish, to drive to distraction the modern demographer who may try to catch up with them; and though legislative restriction on the employment of un-apprenticed workmen could still be invoked, it was never allowed to interfere with the expansion of new forms of industry on the basis of cheap labour.

These institutional loopholes for the advance of laissez-faire were widened by the passage of entrepreneurs of all social ranks, including the leaders of the local aristocracy. Both before and after the Civil War, the nobility and gentry of Nottinghamshire and Derbyshire advanced their fortunes by investment in coal, iron, copper and lead on a surprisingly massive scale[11]. In agriculture, the varying qualities of the soil were being adapted from the early seventeenth century to the type of farming for which they were especially suited, the heavy clays of the Vale of Belvoir lending themselves to conversion to pasture for cattle and sheep; the lighter soils of the Trent Valley to dairying, and the margins of the sandy area of Sherwood Forest to experiments in root crops and to large-scale plantations for timber by aristocratic lessees of the Crown. At the same time, the traditional corn lands of the Keuper marl clays were not immune to the forces of progressive change, even while retaining the archaic pattern of the three field strip farming, as the re-organization of Laxton in the 1720's shows[12]. There was a ceaseless process of capital accumulation at work, deriving mainly from the steady changeover from copyhold to leasehold and the raising of rents when leases fell in, but also through improvements in land use on enclosed farms where it was possible to practise the most advanced forms of husbandry, i.e. convertible husbandry and the growing of roots, though the question of how far these new methods of land use were carried out in the county still awaits investigation.

Whatever direction the advance of agriculture took, it inevitably led to the increase in the size of farming units and hastened the polarisation of rural society between wealthy squires and tenants—the "landed interest"—and the labouring poor who, being for the most part without land, were deemed to have no "interest" in the land; but it differentiated in favour of the abler tenants who were not only encouraged but were sought out by the more enterprising landlords to their mutual advantage; when times were bad, they were helped by rent and tax remissions and by direct landlord investment, e.g. in buildings, and they shared in the rising profits of their joint enterprise when times were good. This unique form of partnership which had grown up between them and under which so much of the soil of England was farmed, was such as to reconcile the interests of the landed interest with the economic needs of the nation and to build up in course of time an agricultural system which provided a fund of investment, e.g. for building and transport, and for development of the extractive industries. By raising real wages, as a result of rising agricultural production and productivity, it also had the effect of enlarging the market for the products of industy. The gradual fall of agricultural prices from about 1660 (in spite of the reduction of arable acreage in the ley farming areas) and the substantial volume of exports under the Corn Bounty Acts, are eloquent witnesses to the silent break-through of productivity which the landed interest had achieved before the upward turn of prices from about 1750. It was now the turn of the old open-field areas, the traditional corn lands of England, to share in the advance, and a spate of enclosure acts, fluctuating in volume with the movement of prices, made possible the conquest, in course of time, of virtually the whole arable area of the county by the turnip and clover with their appropriate rotations; and the Keuper marl villages of central Nottinghamshire and the great areas of waste in the west and north of the county rapidly took on the patch-work pattern which they wear today and which the "pasture areas" had acquired a century before.

The rising profits of farming which brought the traditional arable areas into the current of agrarian change seem also to have exercised an influence on the development of transport by stimulating the movement of coal from the pits along the Nottinghamshire-Derbyshire border to meet the growing demand in the agricultural centres to the east and south of the county.[13] Parallel with the spate of enclosure acts was a spate of turnpike acts, and the east-west pattern which they form on the map, together with the evidence relating to the formation of the turnpike trusts themselves, confirms the supposition that the demands of the expanding towns and villages of the interior of the county could no longer be met by the age-old traffic of coal carried by the Trent. In the whole of England there were 93 turnpikes between 1750 and 1754, and in Nottinghamshire, during the five years between 1753–8, nearly twice as many miles of road were turnpiked as in the previous twenty-five years. In 1755 the first survey was made for a canal to join the Trent at Shardlow and the Weaver in Cheshire, and a second was made in 1758 on behalf of Earl Gowan and Lord Anson. The driving force was the demand for coal—for domestic use, for manufacturing processes and brewing, perhaps expecially for building the new houses of brick and tile that were rising up in town and country as the new phase in the rebuilding of England gathered force.

This underswell of agrarian and commercial activity bore on its surface more tangible signs of economic change. By the end of the seventeenth century, the industry of framework knitting had taken root in many towns and villages of the region, its location being largely determined by the existence of cheap labour supplies in areas where population growth was encouraged by abundance of land for settlement or by the absence of institutional checks, such as the rigid control of settlement by landlords and parish officers[14]. The capital of merchant hosiers in London strengthened the Midlands hosiery industry, and the London merchant, Sir Thomas Lombe, through the agency of his brother John, and the Derby engineer, George Sorocold, transplanted the silk-throwing industry of Lombardy to an island in the Derwent in his massive silk mill built 1717–19 at the cost, it is said, of £30,000[15]. Local and London capital combined with cheap labour and native skill to found a new region of the textile industry, a region that was shortly to lay claim to a priority in the chronology of factory production that has received less attention than it deserves.

From what has been said, it will be seen that population growth is included among the factors making for the economic development of the region. It played a part in the supply of cheap labour, but there is also evidence that it provided a stimulus to economic expansion through the effective demand which the rising population was able to make upon the domestic market. As is shown in Chapter IX, even the poorest labourers in the first half of the eighteenth century enjoyed a margin above bare subsistence, and except for the small arable farmers in the period of exceptionally low prices between 1730–50—the "Agricultural Depression"—their social betters appear to have enjoyed a high level of prosperity. The rate of increase of population thus to some extent determined the size of the internal market, and since, by their organisation and tradition, both industry and agriculture were responsive to market influence, a change in the rate of population growth might be expected to have repurcussions on the general level of economic activity. This, indeed, appears to have been the case. There seems no doubt that the upward movement of population followed a fluctuating not a uniform trend, and there is evidence to suggest that these fluctuations were not without effect upon the movement of the regional economy as a whole.

The last decades of the seventeenth century and the early decades of the eighteenth century were marked by substantial balances of births over deaths in most of the parishes examined, and by 1725 the population of the region may well have been between 30% and 40% higher than in 1670, most of the growth having taken place between 1690 and 1720[16]. During this period of population growth there is evidence of rapid advance in hosiery manufacture and silk throwing, of substantial activity in iron and agriculture, and it is marked by the first phase in the widening of the bottle neck of Midland transport, the opening of the Derwent to navigation in 1719 and the turnpiking of the Nottinghamshire section of the Great North Road in 1725.

From the middle 1720's, most of these forms of activity appear to have been relatively quiescent; from this time to the middle forties, there is little in the way of advance to report anywhere but perhaps something in the way of retreat[17]. At the same time, the forward movement of population was actually reversed in the 1720's as a result of heavy epidemics, especially in the fatal years 1727–9, the virulence of which was disproportionate to the physical causes in the shape of harvest failures and weather conditions to which they could be attributed; and though the recovery was rapid, there were further set-backs in 1736 and 1741–2. There was one industrial innovation of great importance, however: the use by a Nottingham stockinger of cotton yarn for the manufacture of hosiery in 1730. This was to prove a portentous event in the industrial history of the town; but its potentialities were not realised until the late 1750's when Jedediah Strutt's invention of the Derby Rib machine (1758) marked a turning point in the fortunes of the whole regional textile industry. If a single invention could be said to have triggered off a phase of the Industrial Revolution, this is the one. It was itself a product of other men's ideas and was therefore a symptom as well as a cause of the fever of invention that marked those years, a fever that culminated in the migration of Hargreaves and Arkwright to Nottingham in 1768 and the formation of the epoch-making partnership between Strutt and Arkwright in 1771. In that year they moved to Derbyshire and began the creation of those industrial communities along the banks of the Derwent which are now the object of pilgrimage by those who wish to see the handiwork of the pioneers of industrialism recognisably as they left it nearly two centuries ago.

The direct impact of Strutt, Arkwright and Hargreaves on the local textile industry has been made the subject of important studies by Mr. S. D. Chapman, but space permits of only two comments to be made here: first, the part played by Hargreaves in initiating an intermediate form of factory production suitable for installation in isolated farm communities as far afield as Tideswell and Edale and other centres of the Peak of Derbyshire, and second, the extent to which local leaders of enterprise were drawn from the merchanting side of the hosiery industry, consisting originally of mercers, drapers and grocers, with offices in Nottingham for the marketing of hosiery in London. They formed an urban élite, with close cultural links through their association with dissenting chapels, and particularly, the Unitarian Chapel on High Pavement under the distinguished leadership of George Walker, F.R.S., friend of Price, Priestley and Adam Smith. On sixty-six occasions between 1700 and 1800[18], the mayor of the town was drawn from the membership of this remarkable community and of the leading textile innovators of whom we have knowledge, only three were outside it. One was Robert Hall, the famous bleacher and cotton spinner of Basford, product of one of the "commercial academies" of the town, a student of Lavoisier, Scheele, Berthollet and Black, and reputedly the first manufacturer in England to introduce the use of chlorine in bleaching. He was a leading Wesleyan and widely known for his benevolence and good relations with his workpeople.

As for Arkwright himself, the establishment of ten massive spinning establishments in Nottinghamshire and Derbyshire alone between 1769 and 1784 is evidence of the impact of his explosive energy on the local scene; the Strutts, father and son, built five before the end of the century, and others—the Evans's, the Robinsons, the Dennisons—followed in their wake so that by 1800 there were a hundred power mills in cotton spinning alone in the Midlands (excluding Glossop) of which no less than 31 were strung out along the Derwent, 23 were in Nottingham and South Nottinghamshire, 10 in Mansfield and North Nottinghamshire, 14 in other parts of the Trent Valley, 8 in the Dove Valley and 14 in various more distant locations of the Midlands. The Arkwright method of spinning was also successfully applied to worsted, and by the end of the century there were 18 worsted mills in the Midland region[19]. The random seeds sown by William Lee, the mysterious clergyman of Calverton, who invented the stocking frame in 1589, and Slater the stockinger of Bellargate, who made the first pair of cotton hose in 1730[20], had yielded a fabulous harvest.

Such was the general pattern of regional economic change in the first three quarters of the eighteenth century: an acceleration of expansion in industry, transport, agriculture, and inland trade, to the early 1720's; a falling off in the rate of expansion in all these branches until the 1740's, followed by an upward movement on all sides on such a scale as to presage the advent of a new age. On the side of population, the crucial factor seems to have been the failure of the cycle of epidemics to materialise in the 1760–70 decade. The rate of growth in the Nottinghamshire villages may have declined during those years compared to the three previous decades; but the position was incomparably better than in 1680–90 and 1720–30 when the village population suffered a substantial net reduction. As for Nottingham itself, apart from sporadic and insignificant surpluses of burials over baptisms, it was now growing by almost continuous natural increase of births over deaths as well as by migration from outside. Unnoticed by contemporaries or by later historians, the demographic revolution had proclaimed itself in the silent witness of the urban parish registers, and from 1745 the town took its place, along with the villages, as a self-recruiting source of continuous population growth.

This is an intriguing pattern of economic change and it would be tempting to try to transpose it to the general trend of the national economy itself. But the proviso must be borne in mind that the regional experience of acceleration and deceleration of advance in conjuction with changing rates of population growth may be exceptional and unrepresentative; and the analysis undertaken by Professor A. H. John of the factors, both internal and external, that affected the national economy during the period suggests that it was[21]. To Professor John, the pattern is a steady upward trend, accelerating in the last quarter of the century. To the authors of *British Economic Growth 1685–1959*[22] it is an undulating movement marked by a dip in the second quarter, a decided upward thrust in the third—the "little Industrial Revolution" as it has been called—to be followed, after a pause during the war with the American colonies, by the break-through to sustained economic growth.

In this argument, one region only has had its say; but it was, in many ways, a representative one, and, whatever the reasons, a new era both in demographic and economic growth was discernible by the late 1750's. The terms of trade between farm and workshop were now moving in favour of the former and on a substantially increased output; agricultural prices were slowly rising; the "Agricultural Depression" was over, and conditions were present for renewed investment in roads, enclosures, canals, in new buildings and improvements of all kinds, and in mechanical devices to meet that particular form of demand which had outstripped the limits of existing technical resources, i.e. the demand for cotton yarn for woven and knitted goods; and the agent of this general stimulation of the economy appears to have been the rise of population in conjunction with a new wave of prosperity in agriculture. If the Industrial Revolution is to be dated from the coming of factory spinning of cotton, Nottingham, because of its consumption of cotton yarn for hosiery, was the first town to experience it.

At the same time, the labour situation was poised for a new trend in per capita production. Nottingham was not the only town where working men were in a fever to float on the tide of technological opportunity. Some of them, according to Gravenor Henson, lost their reason as a result of their frustrated exertions; but all of them were subject to the stimulus from another quarter, from the growing pressure of competition on the part of increasing numbers of young people who had been spared for industry by a fall of the urban death rate in the generation following the disasters of 1727–9, 1736 and 1740–2. Moreover, the drive to preserve a rising standard of life was enhanced by the growing recognition on the part of publicists and employers of the positive relation between high wages and output[23], and an increasing supply of labour coincided with a growing awareness on the part of entrepreneurs of the importance of the human aspect of labour relations. Both Hargreaves and Arkwright organised "works outings"; and Arkwright's workmen sang beery songs in his honour in the inn which he built for them[24] at Cromford. Except in the two cases reported by Robert Blincoe, even the treatment of parish apprentices in the new cotton mills is now seen to have been less black than it has been painted[25]; and the worst evils of the time prove to have been the consequence, not of the irresponsible exercise of power by the new factory owners, the most important of whom were humane and sometimes radical leaders of the local society[26], but of the inherent weaknesses of obsolete economic organisation, e.g. the framework knitting industry, in an age of mass production for an expanding but fluctuating market. In the new industries both the motivation of labour and the techniques of management were being directed for the first time towards the goals of higher output, a factor that cannot be measured but that should by no means be ignored in assessing the forces of change in these critical years.

Unfortunately, these happy portents of harmonious social development within a changing economic environment were to go unfulfilled. Within a generation there was a change of social climate, the significance of which has hardly yet been realised and in which Nottinghamshire played a notable part. The systematic sabotage by the Nottinghamshire Luddites from 1811 to 1817 and the influence exerted by the famous poor law reformers, the Rev. Robert Lowe, the Rev. J. T. Becher and especially Captain George Nicholls (overseer of Southwell between 1818–20) was a reflection of the free market in labour, the transition from paternalism to laissez-faire, which had become the dominant fact in social relations in the last decades of the eighteenth century. The change can best be illustrated by the wide difference of spirit and intention that lay between the two poor law enactments of 1782—Gilbert's Act, which virtually guaranteed a basic minimum to the unemployed worker in the form of work or maintenance in his own home—and the Poor Law Amendment Act of 1834, which offered him the workhouse test. Moreover, the greatest social invention of the age, the friendly society, a form of mutual insurance to meet the exigencies of ill health and old age, created by the wage earners themselves and widely recognised in the last years of the eighteenth century as the appropriate counterpart in social policy to the effects of the free market in labour[27], was ignored by the policy makers in spite of the promptings of the Prime Minister himself. In 1795, in the year of Speenhamland (which itself implied a rudimentary redistribution of income through family allowances),

William Pitt, disciple of Adam Smith but not yet of Malthus, advocated not only family allowances but compulsory membership of friendly societies: "Making relief where there are a number of children a matter of right and an honour . . . and making them (sic) subscribe to friendly societies"[28].

These hopeful possibilities withered under the impact of twenty years of anti-Jacobin war and the remorseless logic of Malthus and Ricardo; and the "hidden hand of self interest" was left to contribute to the interests of all without the aid of these anticipatory elements of the welfare state. From this time, the harsh asperities of the free market in labour were to be left as a self-regulating mechanism for correcting the maldistribution of capital and labour[29], a decision for which the Nottinghamshire reformers had a considerable measure of responsibility. By 1818, the Rev. Robert Lowe, overseer at Bingham, had invented the principle of "less eligibility", and by 1821 Captain George Nicholls, overseer at Southwell, was writing to the *Nottingham Journal* of the "terror of a well regulated workhouse" as the correct medicine for able-bodied pauperism, a kind of institution, he said, which "would be looked to with dread by our labouring classes, and the reproach for being an inmate passed from father to son"[30]. An ardent disciple of Malthus and Ricardo and a dedicated disciplinarian of the poor at Southwell, he made a deep impression on the authors of the Report of 1834, but they failed to notice the important part played in the reduction of the poor rates by the expansion of the local economy as a result of the boom in the lace industry and, hardly less important, the continued prosperity of agriculture, which enabled the local gentry to adopt a remarkably cooperative attitude in the anti-pauper campaign. However, on the strength of his spurious claim to have solved the problem of able-bodied pauperism in the area of Southwell, Nicholls was made one of the three Poor Law Commissioners to enforce the panacea of the workhouse test throughout the land. His work in Nottinghamshire has been subjected to close scrutiny by Dr. J. D. Marshall with results that entirely confirm the verdict recently pronounced by Dr. Blaug that the Report of 1834 was a wrong prescription based upon a faulty diagnosis, and that its "continued endorsement . . . has seriously distorted the history of the British Industrial Revolution"[31]. It carried the day, however, with social consequences that were rendered endurable among the framework knitters of Nottingham and district only by massive private charity in defiance of the New Poor Law. The coming of the hosiery factory and the release of urban land for building that had been held too long in the dead hand of burgess rights unleashed the pent-up energies of the locality, and the social conflicts that had been exacerbated to breaking point by the workhouse test were slowly appeased in the growing warmth of Victorian prosperity. In the light of regional history, there is nothing to reverse the trend of current opinion that if the benefits of the Industrial Revolution to the labouring classes were unduly delayed, the explanation is to be found less in the nature of the economic process itself than in the exigencies of twenty years of war and the blunders of devoted but doctrinaire public servants. The latter, able, energetic and perhaps too single minded, were encouraged in their self-deception by local experiments that, as far as those of Nottinghamshire were concerned, gave rise to optimistic reports that were founded on theoretical preconceptions rather than on a true assessment of the facts, with results on subsequent social policy that are only now coming to light. Regional historians of the period have no more urgent task than to follow up these initiatives, and to place the responsibility for some of the most painful aspects of the distress of the time where it most properly belongs.

That this book should serve as an introduction to a discussion of the first transition to industrialism is an indication of the advance that the study of economic history has made since it was written. Such an intention was latent in the original design, but the necessary equipment, both of method and matter to accomplish it, was lacking. It took the form instead of a study of social institutions and processes rather than an analysis of economic forces, but in so doing it provided an emphasis on the social pre-requisites of a particular phase of economic change, an emphasis to which attention is perhaps all the more due now that economic and demographic enquiry has begun to elucidate the mechanism by which the change took place. This provides the main excuse for its reappearance after more than thirty years.

J. D. Chambers

Nottingham, August 1964.

NOTES

1. A. Cossons, *The Turnpike Roads of Nottinghamshire* (Historical Association Pamphlet, 1934); H. S. Twells, "The Beginning of a Turnpike Trust", *Derbyshire Archaeological Society Journal* (subsequently referred to as D.A.S.J.) (1946); A. C. Wood, "The History of Trade and Transport in the River Trent", *Thoroton Society Transactions,* LIV (1950).

2. F. A. Wells, *The British Hosiery Industry* (1935); D. E. Varley, *A History of the Midland Counties Lace Manufacturers' Association* (Long Eaton 1959); N. Cuthbert, *The Lace Makers' Society* (Nottingham 1960). See also S. D. Chapman, *Life and Work of William Felkin* (M.A. thesis, 1960, Nottingham University) and, with C. A. Aspin, *James Hargreaves and the Spinning Jenny* (1964).

3. R. A. Fitton and A. W. Wadsworth, *The Strutts and the Arkwrights* (1958); Turpin Bannister, "The First Iron Framed Buildings", *The Architectural Review*, April 1950; H. R. Johnson and A. W. Skempton, "William Strutt's Fireproof and Iron Framed Buildings 1792–1812", *Transactions of the Newcomen Society* (1956) and M. H. Mackenzie, "Calver Mill and its Owners", *The Derbyshire Archaeological Journal*, vol. LXXXIII, 1960. See also S. D. Chapman, "The Pioneers of Worsted Spinning by Power", *Business History Review* VII, 1964–5, and forthcoming article, "The Transition to Factory Spinning in the Midlands Cotton Spinning Industry", to appear in *The Economic History Review*, 1965–6 and S. Pigott, Hollins, *A Study of Industry, 1784–1949* (Nottingham, 1949).

4. R. S. Smith, *The Willoughbys of Wollaton, 1500–1643, with special reference to Early Mining in Nottinghamshire* (Ph.D. thesis, 1964, Nottingham University) and "England's first Rails: A Reconsideration" in *Renaissance and Modern Studies,* Vol. IV; G. G. Hopkinson, *Development of the Lead Mining and of the Coal and Iron Industries of North Derbyshire and South Yorkshire 1700–1850* (Ph.D. thesis, 1958, Sheffield University) and "Leadmining in Eighteenth Century Ashover", *D.A.S.J.,* VI–VII (1952); W. H. Walton, "The Early Use of Coke in Derby", *D.A.S.J.* (1953) LIV; R. A. Pelham, "The Willoughby Ironworks", *University of Birmingham Historical Journal,* IV, No. 1, 1953; S. C. H. Whitelock, *Two Hundred and Fifty Years in Coal: The History of Barber and Walker and Co. Ltd.;* Nellie Kirkham, "Old Drowned Work in Derbyshire", *D.A.S.J.* (1950); A. Raistrick and E. Allen, "The South Yorkshire Iron Masters 1690–1750", *Economic History Review* (1939); H. Green, "Notts.-Derbyshire Coalfield", *D.A.S.J.,* LVI (1935).

5. G. E. Mingay, "The Agircultural Depression 1730–50", *Economic History Review* (1956).

6. J. D. Chambers, *Modern Nottingham in the Making* (Nottingham, 1950), "Enclosure and Labour Supply", *Economic History Review,* 1953, *The Vale of Trent 1670–1800* (Economic History Review Supplement, 1957), "Population Change in a Provincial Town Nottingham 1700–1800" in *Studies in the Industrial Revolution,* ed. L. S. Pressnell (1960).

7. W. G. Hoskins, Essays in Leicestershire History (1950) and "The Leicestershire Farmer in the Seventeenth Century", *Agricultural History*

(U.S.A.), Jan. 1951; Joan Thirsk, *English Peasant Farmers: The Agrarian History of Lincolnshire from Tudor to Recent Times* (1957).

8. J. D. Marshall, "The Nottinghamshire Reformers and their Contributions to the New Poor Law", *Economic History Review* (3), 1961. See also his "Nottinghamshire Labourers in the Early Nineteenth Century", *Transactions of the Thoroton Society*, 1960.

9. See below ch. X conclusion.

10. See Maurice Beresford, "Habitation and Improvement: The Debate on Enclosure by Agreement" in *Essays in Economic and Social History of Tudor and Stuart England*, ed. F. J. Fisher (1961).

11. See examples cited in *Vale of Trent*, pp. 6–7.

12. J. D. Chambers, *Laxton: A Guide* (1964).

13. See R. S. Smith, *The Willoughbys of Wollaton*, op. cit., pp. 102, 295, where he says: "The state of agricultural incomes in the Trent Valley was probably the final determinant of the demand for coal".

14. See *Vale of Trent*, p. 13, note 8, and other examples of industrial location under the influence of population cited in Thirsk, "Industries in the Countryside", in *Essays in Economic and Social History of Tudor and Stuart England*, op. cit.

15. W. H. Chaloner, *People and Industries* (1963), p. 8.

16. The fluctuations of village populations are being investigated. There seems no doubt that the period 1690–1720 was one of substantial growth, possibly at a rate comparable to that between 1730–60. The rate undoubtedly accelerated in the last quarter of the century especially in industrial villages. This, in conjunction with the growth of Nottingham by natural increase from about 1750, marks a new era in demographic history.

17. *Vale of Trent*, pp. 8–9.

18. From information kindly supplied by Rev. C. Bolam, the present minister at High Pavement Chapel.

19. The whole of this is based on the work of Mr. S. D. Chapman. See Note 2 above.

20. According to Henson, a quantity of Indian spun yarn had been put out by a London hosiery merchant to a number of workmen, but they refused to work it on account of its "stubborness", when compared with silk. It was sent to Nottingham, where a workman of the name of Draper, who lived in Bellar-Gate, undertook to make it into stockings, from a twenty-gauge silk frame. So fine was the material, that he doubled four threads for the leg, and five threads for the heels and completed the first pair of cotton stockings ever made in England in the year 1730. G. Henson, *History of the Framework Knitters* (1831), p. 163.

21. A. H. John, "Aspects of English Economic Growth in the first half of the Eighteenth Century", *Economica*, May 1961, and "The Course of Agricultural Change 1660–1760", in *Studies in the Industrial Revolution*, ed. L. S. Pressnell.

22. Phyllis Deane and A. W. Cole, *British Economic Growth 1688–1959* (1962), Ch. II. See also "The Take-Off in Britain" by Phyllis Deane and H. J. Habakkuk in "*The Economics of Take-Off into Sustained Growth*", ed. W. W. Rostow (1963).

23. A. W. Coats, "Changing Attitudes to Labour in Mid-Eighteenth Century England", *Economic History Review*, Aug. 1958, and "Economic Thought and Poor Law Policy", *ibid*, Aug. 1960.

24. See Fitton and Wadsworth, *op. cit.*, and Chapman, *op. cit.*

25. See *Vale of Trent*, p. 61, and W. H. Chaloner, "Mrs. Trollope and the Early Factory System", *Victorian Studies*, Dec. 1960.

26. For examples of radical manufacturers see Chapman, *op. cit.*, and A. V. Mitchell, *Radicalism and Political Repression in the North of England* (M.A. thesis, 1958, University of Manchester) on the Painite sympathies of William Strutt.

27. See D. C. Barnett, "Ideas of Social Welfare 1780–1834" (M.A. thesis, 1961, University of Nottingham).

28. "Let us make relief in cases where there are a number of children a matter of right and an honour, instead of a ground for opprobrium and contempt. . . . by giving effect to the operation of friendly societies, individuals would be rescued from becoming a burthen upon the public, and, if necessary, be enabled to subsist upon a fund which their own industry contributed to raise. These great points of granting relief according to the number of children, preventing removals at the caprice of the parish officer, and making them subscribe to friendly societies, would tend, in a very great degree, to remove every complaint. . . . ". Debates on Whitbread's Minimum Wage Bill, 1795–6. Bland, Brown & Tawney, *Select Documents*, pp. 562–3.

29. Except for the expenditure of limited sums "For carrying out Public Works and . . . Employment of the Poor" under the Act of 1817. See M. W. Flinn, "The Poor Employment Act of 1817", *Economic History Review*, Aug. 1961. Dr. Flinn notes, however, that after 1834 "No longer was public money being used for the creation of employment, but, ironically, it was now to be employed for the incarceration of those for whom employment could not be found. In the seven years after 1834, well over half the money available for loans under the 1817 Acts was used for workhouse construction". *Ibid.*, p. 90, n. 1.

30. Marshall, *op. cit.*, p. 388, n. 6.

31. M. Blaug, "The Myth of the Old Poor Law and the Making of the New", *Journal of Economic History*, June 1963, p. 152, and *The Poor Law Report Re-examined*, ibid., June 1964. He writes of the Old Poor Law as follows: "It contributed, so to speak, a welfare state in miniature, combining elements of wage escalation, family allowances, unemployment, compensation, and public works . . . Far from having an inhibiting effect, it probably contributed to economic expansion". For the disastrous effect of the New Poor Law in Nottingham during the years of trade depression, see W. Rowarth, *Observations on the Administration of the Poor Law in Nottingham* (1840).

PREFACE TO THE FIRST EDITION

THE general purpose and the method of this book differ somewhat from those of most other books of its kind. It attempts to show the movement of local history during the period preceding the Industrial Revolution on the background of national history, and local material that cannot be related to the facts of national history either as an example of, or as an addition to, existing knowledge has been generally excluded.

The study of local history has lately made rapid progress among all classes of students, from the village school to the university, partly because it is interesting in itself, but to an increasing degree, because it brings the student into touch with particular aspects of general history. With the inner eye of local knowledge he can read between the lines of the text-book and see what is really happening; instead of being merely an exercise to be mastered, history becomes an experience to be shared. This is especially the case with social and economic history, the raw material of which exists in such abundance everywhere, and it is hoped that teachers of this branch of the subject will find here some help in bridging the gap between the village or county and the national life. It may be, also, that the specialist student of economic history will find something of interest in a study that enables generally accepted views to be seen in their application to a particular case.

A word may be said on the arrangement of the book. It is mainly concerned with the facts of economic history—the changes in industry and agriculture, the level of wages and prices, the operation of the Poor Laws—but these are placed in the institutional and also the cultural setting which the time and place provided. This setting is treated in the opening chapters which deal with the rise of the gentry, the distribution of political power in relation to property, and the machinery of local government, and in the final chapter on the changes in social life and in the organisation and character of popular education. It was hoped, by this means, to give a more complete and therefore more accurate picture than if the facts of economic history were presented, according to prevailing custom, in isolation from the political and cultural manifestations of the time. Some justification for this treatment is found in the statement made by Mr. G. D. H. Cole in his admirable Introduction to Defoe's *Tour*. Speaking of the economic history text-books on this period, he says,

> "But the picture of economic and social England in the Augustan Age is left woefully incomplete and more than a little misleading even in the best of the text-books. In all of them, there is too much about Mercantilism and the 'Domestic System', and too little about the social and economic structure of the British community in the dawning time of the modern age";

and it is hoped that the present attempt to combine the two, and thereby show the essential harmony that existed between the squirearchy and the rising industrial interests, may do something to fill in the picture.

Finally, it should be said, this work makes no claim to be a contribution to antiquarian lore; it is essentially an attempt to use local history in the service of general history and it is addressed to those students and teachers who regard local history in the light of a means, not an end. To them I would say, as Thoroton inimitably said when he addressed his *History of Nottinghamshire* to Sir William Dugdale:

> "Yet I made hard Shift to be as little justly to blame . . . as possibly I could, so that I hope you will not disown me; and if you do not, I shall be less solicitous what others think, for I allow no Man for a Judge who hath not done something of this Nature himself."

It remains for me to express my thanks for the generous help I have received from so many quarters. The work was originally begun as a thesis for the Ph.D. degree of London at the suggestion of Prof. L. V. D. Owen, M.A., Head of the Department of History, University College, Nottingham, and my sincere thanks are due to him for his interest and help in its progress throughout. I was enabled to devote a period of full-time study to the subject by the grant of a History Research Scholarship by the University College, Nottingham, and the publication of the work has been made possible by the aid of the Publication Fund of the University of London. The cost of the maps and sketches has been met by a grant from the Research Committee of University College, Nottingham. My thanks are also due to the Editor of *Economica* for permission to quote from an article on "The Worshipful Company of Framework Knitters" which appeared there in 1929.

It is not possible to acknowledge adequately the help I have received in the actual writing of the book; some of my obligations appear in the text, but I cannot omit to mention the debt I owe to my friends and colleagues of the Department of Adult Education, and of the Department of History, and to Professor H. H. Swinnerton and Professor R. Hewitt, all of whom have helped me by reading parts of the book, by giving me information, or in other ways. I have been especially fortunate in securing the help of a number of local students whose skill has supplemented mine where it was weakest, in the making of maps. Mr. Herbert Green, B.A., of Cottesmore Road School, has drawn the map and diagram on pages 88 and 142, and has also helped me in the verification of references; Mr. A. Cossons, Head Master at Beeston, has drawn the map on page 78, Miss Grace Shepherd the one on page 154.

I am particularly grateful for the help of Mr. W. E. Tate, Headmaster of the Council School, Sutton Bonington, who has drawn the map showing enclosures in relation to types of soil on page 144, and also compiled the schedule of enclosure data for every village in the county given in Appendix II. This is a most useful addition to the book, and has been of great help in writing the chapters on Agriculture. Finally, I have to thank Mrs. J. L. Hammond for lending me her very valuable note-books containing extracts from the Home Office Papers, and perhaps more for her kindly encouragement in a difficult task.

Two omissions of importance have been found necessary in the final preparation; the chapter on Transport Changes has been omitted owing to lack of space, and it is hoped, will appear elsewhere. The original Bibliography has been rendered superfluous and obsolete by the preparation of a complete bibliography of printed historical sources for the county which has been undertaken by a number of students of Local History under the general oversight of Prof. L. V. D. Owen. This will appear separately, and does away with the need of a Bibliography here.

CONTENTS

PART II

THE RISE OF MODERN INDUSTRY AND AGRICULTURE

PART III

SOCIAL CONDITIONS UNDER THE SQUIREARCHY

PART I

THE GROWTH AND ORGANISATION OF THE SQUIREARCHY

CHAPTER I

THE AGRARIAN BACKGROUND

Dr. Thoroton, in explaining the reasons for embarking on his great history of Nottinghamshire, says:

> "The Art of Physic, which I have professed (with competent success) in this county, not being able for very long Time to continue the People living in it, I have charitably attempted to practise upon the Dead, intending thereby to keep all which is or can be left of them, to wit, the Shadow of their Names (better than precious ointment for the Body), to preserve their Memory as long as may be in the world."

But it is by no means all the Dead who are to receive these kindly attentions; only the owners of landed property, "the Nobility and Gentry of our County," as he himself says.

This exclusive attention to the owners of landed property is of importance in the present enquiry. Dr. Thoroton wrote in 1677, on the eve of the eighteenth century; he is the point of departure from which this book sets out to explore the later period, and his view that local history was the history of the "landed interest" must be carefully considered before undertaking a study of the period that followed.

If Thoroton had written between 1625 and 1635 instead of between 1665 and 1675 he would have written differently; he could scarcely have omitted to mention, for instance, the part played in local affairs by the Crown and the Church. And had he written a century before that he would have found two additional factors which had either totally disappeared in his time or had suffered political and economic eclipse. These were, first, the forty religious institutions which had landed property up to the middle of the sixteenth century, and secondly, the army of semi-proprietors grouped under the general title of copyholders in whose position a vital change was at that time taking place. It is owing to the elimination of these factors—the monasteries, the copyholders, the Crown and the Church—as rivals to the gentry that Thoroton is able to place them on the pedestal of unchallenged local supremacy, and unless something is known of the way in which this elimination took place it is impossible to obtain a true grasp of the local situation in the eighteenth century, which is the object of this study.

In regard to the first of these, the Dissolution of the Monasteries, a very brief treatment of the way in which the chief monastic estates were distributed will be sufficient to show the powerful impetus which this event gave to forces already at work making for the triumph of the large rural capitalist.[1] The Earl of Shrewsbury was granted the Lordships, granges and manors in twenty-five villages and towns in Nottinghamshire, including, of course, the Rufford Abbey Estates, besides many others in different counties.[2]

[1] The capital value of the monasteries (on the basis of their annual net income of £136,361) is estimated at about £20,000,000 in modern money. Cf. Tawney, *Religion and Rise of Capitalism*, p. 310. Considering the size of the population, not more than five million, the subsequent mania of land speculation can easily be understood. The same writer states that the best book on this subject is Liljehren, *The Fall of the Monasteries and the Social Changes in England leading to the Great Rebellion* (1924), but this book does not appear to be obtainable in England. The subject has been briefly treated by F. H. Herbert, *The Dissolution of the Monasteries* (dealing with Staffordshire only), but the author refers to the "appalling complexity of the task" and states that any enquiry into the original grants of the lands of religious houses would throw little light on the permanent results of the transfer of monastic property—cf. p. 6. For further treatment of the economic aspects of the Dissolution of the Monasteries see Marti, *Economic Causes of the Reformation* (1930).

[2] Throsby's Thoroton, Vol. III, p. 338. It should be remembered that this specially lavish grant was the reward for prompt service in connection with the rebellion of Robert Aske. On the whole, the sales of monastic lands greatly preponderated over the gifts. See Fisher, *Political History of England*, 1485–1547, p. 483, and Appendix II, p. 499, in which the distribution of monastic lands is summarised. See also *The Religious Institutions of Old Nottingham*, by W. Stevenson and A. Stapleton (1895), p. 6.

The Stanhopes obtained lands formerly belonging to Shelford Priory in twenty villages and towns.[1] The Whalleys, by reason of Sir Richard Whalley's connection with Protector Somerset,[2] were "easily let into purchase Abbey lands of which he had a convenient share of this and other counties", which enabled him to find good matches for most of his twenty-five children; the Newstead property was made over to the Byrons;[3] the Felley Priory lands passed to the Bolles family which also had some of the Worksop Priory lands in Osberton;[4] Beauvale Priory came into the Morrison family and hence to the Earl of Essex,[5] while Thurgarton was awarded to Wm. Cooper, a servant of the King, and a son-in-law of John Toll of London.[6] Other well-known families who obtained land, usually by purchase, from the same source were the Clintons, the Cliftons, the Strelleys, the Willoughbys, the Musters, the Pierreponts, the Millingtons, the Markhams, the Morrisons, the Nevilles, the Husseys, the Hackers, the Swifts.

Dr. Thoroton, who was separated from these events by little more than a century during which a social and political revolution had taken place, was fully aware of their importance, and was not afraid to express his disapproval with considerable force:

> "The plow upheld all," he writes in his introduction, "till that stupendious Act, which swept away the Monasteries, whose Lands and Tythes being presently after made the Possessions and Inheritances of Private Men, gave more frequent Encouragement and Opportunities to such Men—further to improve and augment their own Revenues by greater Loss to the Common-wealth, viz., by enclosing and converting Arable to Pasture, which as certainly diminishes the Yearly Fruits, as it doth the People."

The part played by industrial and mercantile capital at this time is also important. For instance, Wallingwells Priory passed to Richard Pype, Leatherseller, and

[1] Thoroton, *op. cit.*, I, p. 289.
[2] *Ibid.*, I, p. 250.
[3] *Ibid.*, II, p. 283.
[4] *Ibid.*, II, p. 274, and III, p. 402.
[5] *Ibid.*, II, p. 245.
[6] *Ibid.*, III, p. 59.

Francis Bowyer, Grocer, of London.[1] The site and surrounding property of Welbeck were first sold to Richard Whalley of Screveton, who later resold a large part of it to Edward Osborn, "citizen and cloath worker" of London,[2] who sold it again, after which it passed to Sir Charles Cavendish, and so to the Duke of Newcastle. The manor of Lenton was granted by Charles I to four citizens of London, a sadler, a dyer, a skinner and a scrivener, who sold it to Alderman Gregory, a local butcher and grazier;[3] Blyth Priory lands in Elton were bought by Sir John Lion, citizen and alderman of London,[4] and Mr. Grice, a London tailor, obtained ecclesiastical land in Hawksworth.[5] Perhaps the best example of the transition from merchant to country gentleman is that of Sir Wm. Hollis. Originally, it is said, a successful baker of London,[6] Lord Mayor of the City, and master of an income of £10,000 a year, he bought lands at Haughton from the Stanhopes, in addition to land in other parts of the country, and erected the well-known Hall at Haughton where the head of the family resided and played the part of local potentate with great éclat for many years. The "good Sir William", who came to the property in 1542, was among the leading magistrates of the county, was twice High Sheriff, and like the popular squire he was, kept open house for twelve days at Christmas and brought a following of fifty servants in blue coats and badges to the Coronation of Edward VI. His son paid £10,000 for the title of Baron of Haughton in 1615, and offered £10,000 for the post of Secretary, but was outbid and obtained the title of Earl of Clare for the bagatelle of £5,000.[7]

The purchase of land by urban speculators did not always have this happy result. More frequently the

[1] Thoroton, *op. cit.*, II, p. 206. [2] *Ibid.*, III, p. 381.

[3] *Ibid.*, p. 41, and Godfrey, *Parish and Priory of Lenton*, p. 32.

[4] *Ibid.*, I, p. 214. [5] *Ibid.*, I, p. 203.

[6] Firth, *Highways and Byways of Notts.*, p. 281. For account of Holles Family, see *Thor. Soc. Trans.*, 1922, pp. 47 *et seq.*

[7] Brown, *Lives of Nottinghamshire Worthies*, p. 178.

land passed into the hands of absentees, which tended to make the burden of local government lie more heavily on those who resided in the county and performed the functions attaching to their positions. It was complained, for instance, in 1625 that the number of resident gentry had been greatly diminished since several of them had been bought out by citizens, and many manors to the value, it was said, of between £5,000 and £6,000 a year had passed into the hands of "foreigners" such as the Earl of Devonshire or Mr. Soames, Alderman of London.[1]

The purchase of landed estates by city men no doubt often resulted simply in the transference of rural property and rural function to new and perhaps better hands; but the more frequent result was a succession of rapid sales with the consequences of increased rents and fines, the hastening of enclosure and possibly eviction of tenants. A few examples may be cited from Thoroton to indicate the processes at work. The village of Elton from Domesday to the Dissolution had belonged to the Priory of Blyth; it then came into the possession of someone by the name of York, who sold it to Sir John Lion, Citizen and Alderman of London, who left it to his nephew, who sold it to a man named More, whose stepson in Thoroton's time "obtained the utmost profit the Lordship was any way able to yield him by means of the extremest rack rents now paid".[2]

Another example is "Staunton with Orston", formerly belonging to the Priory of Haverholme, in Lincolnshire, of which Thoroton tersely says:

"Sir Thomas Tresham, Knight and Geo. Tresham, Gent. 5.E.6. passed this manor to Thomas Gravesend and Bartholomew Garewey of London, Gent. who Feb. 30 6.E.6. conveyed it to

[1] *Victoria County History of Nottinghamshire*, II, p. 287, henceforward referred to as *V.C.H.*, Notts.

[2] Throsby's Thoroton, I, p. 215. There appear to have been farms in the village, besides the Hall farm, at a rent of £3 6*s.* 8*d.* per oxgang besides 8*s.* apiece rent-corn, and every three oxgangs paid a load of coal at Grantham worth 16*s.* and a capon 12*d.*; the oxgang varied according to the type of soil, the equivalent given by Thoroton being from 12 to 18 or more acres, p. xv.

Jereme Brand, who married Brigit daughter of Anthony Staunton Esq. and by her had Robt. Brand, who sold it about the 28. Eliz. to his cousin Wm. Staunton Esq.—for £1200 whom it made in turn Lord of the whole Town, which enabled his Posterity the better to inclose and sell."[1]

Some idea of the relative importance of these changes is given when it is realised that the average value of the estate of the ordinary tenant-in-chief in the county (not including the very largest such as the Archbishop of York) was only £20 per annum for the period 1470–1540.[2] Estimates made at the end of the century placed the annual value of three of the biggest estates in the county, all of which had been augmented to a greater or less extent by the monastic windfall, at the following figures:

Willoughby lands, £600 a year.
Earl of Shrewsbury, £1,500 a year.
Lord Scroop at nearly £400 a year.[3]

Even allowing for the increase in rents which had taken place in the century the figures indicate the change that had taken place in the relative position of the local ruling class.[4]

It would be a mistake to imagine that the changes we have described invariably resulted in the advantage of the old established gentry. In some counties at least, many families failed or refused to enrich themselves out of the ecclesiastical spoils, and like the class

[1] Throsby's Thoroton I, p. 304. This appears to refer to the Manor of Staunton Haverholme.

[2] *V.C.H.*, Notts., II, p. 281, quoting Phillimore, *Inquisitions Post Mortem of Notts.*

[3] *Ibid.*, p. 286, quoting *S.P. Dom.*, Eliz., CCLXV, 81; CCLXXXVIII, 34; CCLXI, 85.

[4] The financial supremacy of the local gentry and nobility was of course only at the beginning of its career. A century later the union of the local houses of Clare and Cavendish is said to have given the heir, the Duke of Newcastle, an estate of £40,000 per annum. (White's *Directory of Notts.*, 1832, p. 433.) On the other hand, David Hume, the philosopher, boasted of an independent fortune of £1,000: and by 1769 considered himself really opulent "for I possessed a fortune of £1,000 per annum". (*Essays*, World's Classics, pp. 609 *et seq.*)

of small occupiers, actually declined and in some cases disappeared under the new regime. In Lincolnshire, for instance, where many of the gentry were staunch in their loyalty to the old religion, even to the point of treason against the terrible majesty of Henry VIII, hardly a family of old standing survived the middle of the seventeenth century, unless enriched by trade or marriage, while a number are said to have disappeared or become extinct through their inability to adapt themselves to the new order.[1] This does not seem to have been the case with the gentry of Nottinghamshire; few, if any, failed to take advantage of the times; and the earth that was slipping from the hands of monk and peasant was shared, not unequally, among the scions of the old baronial houses and the new men from the towns.

A specially good example of the commercialism which reigned among the rulers of the countryside is afforded by the history of the Willoughbys of Wollaton. This family was of mercantile origin but had long shed its medieval association with wool as well as its plebian name of Bugge, and had become one of the leading families of the county. It may be said, therefore, to stand midway between the older and the newer aristocracy, and to have some of the characteristics of both. Fortunately, the mass of correspondence left by this family has been preserved and edited, and its domestic history laid bare. We have here a picture, not of a turbulent knight, browbeating juries, or quarrelling with his neighbours, or a boisterous squire drinking himself under the table after a day with the hounds, but a harassed business man, engrossed in accounts, and a testy parent worried by a family of headstrong daughters. At one time he is wrangling over the transport and sale of coal from the Wollaton mines,

[1] See *V.C.H.*, Lincs., pp. 324–6; *Lincs. and Notts. Arch. Soc. Papers*, 1850–60, pp. 335 *et seq.*, and cf. Prothero, *English Farming Past and Present*, p. 85, in which he states that "in the two centuries that followed the dissolution of the monasteries few of the gentry retained their estates intact unless they were enriched by marriage, trade or the practice of law. The lawyers generally belonged to the rising middle families."

propounding a scheme for sending coal via Hull to London, considering proposals for improved pumping machinery, listening to his agent's complaints of stagnation of trade, while debts mount up, "besides usurie, which eateth to the very boone"; at another receiving complaints from his wife of the conduct of his youngest daughter who insists on marrying a Cavendish of Hardwick; makes so light of her modesty that she has him constantly about the house, goes off on foot with him into the forest for a whole day, after the horse, which was to take them for a drive, had run away, being tired of waiting for "your dater's trimming".

"If you can come," writes the distracted mother, "make an end of it, which being done one the soden you may saufe cost which otherwise she means to put on you, for she talkes of many nue gownes which she intends to have of riche stuffe", and in preparation for his journey she sends him a basket with two rounds of brawn in it and three tongues, and thinks she had better brew three hogsheads of beer against his homecoming.[1]

It is true, the Willoughbys stood above their contemporaries in the range and scope of their business enterprise, but they did not stand alone, as the enclosure history of the county abundantly shows. Again, the achievement by which they are best known, the somewhat florid mansion which they erected at ruinous cost in Wollaton Park, is an outstanding example of the active interest which the newly enriched gentry took in æsthetic as well as in the moneymaking arts.

But the energy of the Willoughbys extended to another and far more exacting field. The sixteenth century is the period of experiments in navigation comparable in daring to the aerial feats of to-day; bands of pioneers in pigmy boats tried again and again to break through the iron circle of the Arctic Seas into the Eldorado of the East; and of all these attempts, none was more praiseworthy in its courage nor more

[1] Hist. MSS. Commission, *Middleton Papers*, pp. 171, 2, 3; 180, 1, 3.

practicable in its design than that of Sir Hugh Willoughby, the Captain General of Chancellor's famous expedition to the White Sea in 1553. The vessels were separated in a storm; Chancellor returned and wintered at home; Willoughby in his boat the Bona Esperanza of 120 tons went on and two years later was found, with all hands frozen to death, off the icy coast of Nova Zembla.[1]

From such examples as these, we may safely say that the gentry adorned as well as dominated the local society. But there is another side to the picture. If they represent their age in its great qualities of enterprise, energy and daring, and also in its literary and æsthetic triumphs, the characteristic by which they were best known to their contemporaries was their unscrupulous avarice. In this they were only following the example of the Crown itself; and there is evidence that they were not wholly immune from conscientious scruple in doing so. For instance, in February, 1545–6, after the orgy of the monastic dissolution, the Chantries Commissioners consisting of Sir J. Markham, Wm. Cowper, Nicholas Powell, Esq., and John Wyseman, Gentleman, who were acting for Derbyshire as well as Nottinghamshire, were surprisingly loath to make the clean sweep of the Chantries which was expected of them. "Although they were well aware of the intention of the Crown", says Dr. Cox, "they had the courage in several instances to exceed their instructions and with laudable honesty to make plain the good service that was being done". And again, the Commissioners of 1547 [2] like their predecessors "were bold enough to set out the great need of these foundations".[3]

Again, the rack renting, increase of fines, consolidation of farms, with which the new landlords were charged

[1] See Williamson, *Hist. of Brit. Expansion*, Vol. I, p. 88; Hakluyt (Everyman ed.), Vol. I, p. 251; Pollard, *Political Hist. of England*, 1547–1603, p. 304.

[2] Sir Gervase Clifton, Sir J. Hersey, Sir Anthony Nevil and Wm. Holles. For best account of Notts. Chantries, see *Chantry Certificate Rolls of Notts.* edited with introduction by A. Hamilton Thomson, *Thor. Soc. Trans.* (published separately without date).

[3] *V.C.H.*, Notts., II, p. 63.

were due to more than mere lust of gain. Prices rose rapidly after 1550, while rent and fines could, in many cases, be increased only when leases or copyholds fell in. Until that happened the occupier was reaping an unearned increment which the landlord, as Mr. Lipson says, was unable to intercept. When his turn came, it is not surprising that it frequently took a form which could have only one result: the complete surrender of the lease or copyhold into the lord's hands. As a contemporary explained, a landlord found it "a great abatement of a man's countenance" when he had to live on fixed rents in an age of soaring prices, "and therefore gentlemen doe so much studie the Increase of theire landes, enhauncing of their rentes and so take farmes and pastures into theire owne hands".[1]

Whether these tendencies be imputed to avarice or economic necessity, the effect was the same; there was a general increase in rents; small farms were frequently turned into large, copyholders into leaseholders, and tenants at will; large scale capitalist farming had taken a great stride forward while the peasant on his family holding had fallen back.

Other influences were making for the same result. Owing to the debasement of the coinage, followed by the influx of wealth from the new world, prices were rising far faster than wages. The large-scale farmer employing a number of hands obtained another form of unearned increment which the small farmer employing only his own family was denied.[2] And as grain-growing had been rendered relatively less profitable owing to greatly increased output per acre following

[1] *The Commonweal of the Realm of England* quoted by Tawney, *op. cit.*, p. 199. For an excellent summary of the rent-raising question, see Lipson, *Econ. Hist. of England*, Vol. I, pp. 144–9; and for its effect on the copyholder, see Tawney, p. 309. It is interesting to note as an example of the importance of the unfixed fines that the rents on the Southwell leases remained the same from the time of Henry VIII to 1831, while the fine on renewal had been raised in one case to £500. James, *Southwell Schools*, p. xix.

[2] It has been estimated recently that the lag of wages behind prices between 1500 and 1600 was sufficient to quadruple profits. See Hamilton, "American Treasure and Rise of Modern Capitalism," *Economica*, 1929, p. 356.

upon improved cultivation, there was a natural tendency to enclose and convert arable farms to pasture with evil effects upon the small grain-growing farmer of the open village. All these tendencies strengthened the movement for large scale pasture farming, for the taking over of leases and copyholds by the landlord, the absorption of small farms by large ones resulting in the relative decline of the small grain-growing yeoman farmer, who, less than half a century before, was regarded as the rock upon which the commonwealth was built.

The change in the position of the peasant was not only sudden, but also unexpected. Up to the beginning of the century the auguries had been in his favour. It is true the large grazier had already made himself felt; demesnes had been leased out and intakes on the outskirts of the manor had been taken over by large farmers; small farms had been swallowed up, and even villages decayed before the great changes which we have described. But the class of copyholders, the rank and file of the farming population, was not threatened, as long as the low prices of the fifteenth century were maintained. Indeed, the household economy of the small peasant enjoyed an advantage, since its outgoings in wages were relatively less than those of the bigger farmers. Many copyholders thrived, and put field to field and even farm to farm, as farmers with a family of industrious sons and daughters are doing to this day, while among the freeholders there was even the practice of family settlements, "so that every Jake would be a gentylman and every gentylman a knight or a lord".[1] It should be remembered that copyhold tenure was easily alienated as the freehold was known to be in the hands of the lord and therefore there was no need for expensive investigation into title deeds but a comparatively simple process of transference in the Court of the Manor.[2] Also the subdivision of the great estates was facilitated about the same time, partly by

[1] Starkey's *Dialogue*, 1538, quoted Tawney, *Agrarian Problem*, p. 39.
[2] Tawney, *op. cit.*, p. 86 and note.

the political policy of Henry VII which was a direct affront to the great baronial houses with their retinues, and also to the legal facilities devised at this time for overcoming obstacles to free alienation of entailed estates.[1]

But the peasantry were not destined to enjoy this position for long. The Dissolution of the Monasteries and the revolution in prices, in alliance with the incipient commercialism already at work, placed the smaller farmer in great danger, unless he had complete and undisputed security of tenure or could obtain the protection of the courts. An interesting example has been preserved by Thoroton in which the copyholders of a manor, the manor of Arnold, made assurance doubly sure by buying out the manorial rights for themselves. Apparently they acted in co-operation as a body in order to protect their common rights.

The manor, says Thoroton, had been conveyed to the Crown in the time of Edward VI. The tenants consisted mainly of "Copyholders of Inheritance: they in King James's time purchased the Mannor for the preservation of the Customs and Commons, the Township being within the Forest of *Shirewood*".

But the copyholders of Arnold had the good fortune to be copyholders of inheritance and also to have been tenants of the King; they were not afraid of eviction, only of an invasion of their rights of common, hence co-operative action on the basis of legal security was made possible. In the great majority of villages the copyholders were not so fortunate; they had no legal protection against the increase of rents or fines since they did not hold by inheritance from father to son but by periodic arrangement with the Lord of the Manor. In such cases the tenants of the manor had, in the long run, to bow to the will of the lord, who naturally wanted to take advantage of the rising prices and the increasing value of his land. He might do this by

[1] See Johnson, *Disappearance of Small Landowner*, pp. 9–13. For the best survey of the whole subject of the legal position of the copyholder, see Tawney, *op. cit.*, 287–310, and Lipson, *Econ. Hist. of England*, Vol. I, pp. 135–40.

substituting tenants at will whose rents could be adjusted to the market value of their holding for copyholders or long lease holders whose rents and fines had remained unchanged for long periods, or he might lease his demesne to a single large farmer, or even a tradesman with a butcher's or a tanner's business in the neighbouring town; or he might turn it into a park, which had the double advantage of giving to its owners the hall-mark of social prestige and to the owner's steward an opportunity of keeping it nipped bare like a lawn by the harmless and necessary sheep. There were many who would have joined in the pious thanksgiving of the merchant Stapler of Holme near Newark who built a house and wrote in one of the windows:

> I thanke God, and ever shall,
> It was the Sheepe hath paid for all.[1]

The Enclosure Inquisition of 1517, which we shall deal with more fully later on, showed that a greater proportion of enclosure for the purpose of "sport" had taken place in Nottinghamshire than in any of the other counties examined; but such sport as took place in the parks at Wiverton, Wollaton and elsewhere was not incompatible with profit from sheep rearing. After all, the "bloody minded baron", to use Mr. Tawney's phrase, had been muzzled by Henry VII, and if he turned to hunting and capitalist farming it was a change that brought advantage to the public weal as well as tragedy to the villages which he encompassed with his park palings.

A specially good example of the social dislocation which so often followed from agrarian enterprise is afforded by the case of Wollaton Park and the village of Sutton Passeys upon which it was built. We have alluded above to the magnificent hall, built of Ancaster stone in exchange for Wollaton coal, which the Willoughbys completed at ruinous cost in the year 1588; its architectural merits may be a matter of doubt, but

[1] Throsby's Thoroton, III, p. 157.

the park in which it stands is as beautiful as velvet turf and majestic trees can make it. This park had been enclosed many years before in the reign of Henry VII at the expense of four cottages decayed, four ploughs put down and eighteen persons displaced. At the same time, the demesnes of the adjacent villages of Wollaton and Sutton Passeys were let out to a tanner of Nottingham. In 1667, when Thoroton wrote his history, he was unable to find any trace of the latter village, the site of which, he thinks, was entirely occupied by Wollaton Park, and the editor of the *Middleton Papers* describes it as a vanished village, mainly within the present Wollaton Park. Since the village was in existence in 1558, and is entered on a subsidy roll for that year, it is reasonable to suppose that its disappearance is connected with the Hall that was built thirty years later.[1]

Thus the Willoughbys can be made to represent the shadows as well as the high lights of Tudor enterprise. In neither case were they typical of the new gentry as a whole; they represented existing tendencies in their extreme form. The rest of the gentry were somewhere between; only a handful of them made parks of the villages which their houses overlooked; a larger number enclosed their villages and converted a considerable acreage to pasture, as we shall show later, but the majority seem to have been content with the extinction of copyhold tenure and its substitution by a form of land holding which would enable the landlord to take advantage of the rise in prices. It is of considerable interest to note that the survival of copyhold and similar tenure, as far as we have been able to ascertain up to the present, is almost entirely confined to manors held, at the time of the changes we have described, either by the Crown or the Church. Thus, out of thirty-five villages in which copyhold is known to have survived

[1] See Hist. MSS. Commission, *Middleton Papers,* pp. 55 note, and 397. Throsby's Thoroton, Vol. II, p. 208, and Godfrey, *Hist. of Lenton Priory,* p. 99 n. For enclosure of Wollaton Park, see *Domesday of Inclosures,* Thoroton Soc. Record Series, I, p. 69.

until modern times four were in the fee of the Bishop of Lincoln on the Manor of Newark, ten in the Liberty of Southwell and Scrooby, six (including long leasehold) under the Prebendaries or the Chapter of Southwell, thirteen on the royal manors of Tickhill and Mansfield or the Duchy of Lancaster, and two were doubtful.

It is scarcely necessary to say that the survival of copyhold does not necessarily imply the survival of the small occupier. In several cases, especially the villages formerly belonging to the Crown, the copyhold estate was occupied in modern times by one or two large farmers, while Clipstone was described in 1832 as "one of the poorest and most decayed villages in Bassetlaw".[1] It is, however, a matter of some significance that the proportion of survivals of copyhold on the estates of Church and Crown should be so overwhelmingly large; unless further research reverses these findings, it would appear that copyhold tenure had a far smaller chance of survival on the estates of lay lords, who preferred to substitute for it a form of tenure more capable of adaptation to the new era of commercial agriculture.

An example of the way in which this might be done has been given by Mr. Tawney in the case of North Wheatley, and as it throws a vivid light on the undercurrents of seventeenth-century village politics we shall deal with it in some detail. The two hundred tenants of North Wheatley[2] were tenants "of inheritance to them and theirs for ever" and paid for every oxgang of land 16*s.* 8*d.* rent and upon every alienation 12*d.* for every oxgang. This looks like a case of copyhold by inheritance and fixed rents and fines, subject to the

[1] White's *Directory*, 1832, p. 417.

[2] *V.C.H.*, Notts., II, p. 288, erroneously gives the number as 800. The whole document is printed in Tawney, *Agrarian Problem*, p. 414. Bland Brown and Tawney, *Documents of Econ. Hist.*, pp. 258–60. A later writer thinks that the "two hundred tenants" was probably a conventional figure as there were only eleven names on the Subsidy Roll in 1628. Cf. article by S. A. Peyton, "Tudor Subsidy Rolls," *Hist. Rev.*, Vol. XXX, p. 249. It may be noted that the extortions practised by the Commonwealth government against the copyhold tenants of sequestered estates were more flagrant than those of private landlords. Cf. James, *Soc. Policy during Puritan Rev.*, p. 85.

protection of the courts. But about the 4th James by an order of the manorial court (the court of the Duchy of Lancaster) their fine for alienation was raised to 2*s.* 6*d.* for every acre, "which amounteth nowe to 45*s.* an Oxgang"; and their rent for the herbage and pannage of the Common had been raised from 6*s.* 8*d.* to £16 16*s.* 2*d.* per annum. This, as Mr. Tawney says, is rack renting with a vengeance. But the interest of the North Wheatley case does not end here. If it illustrates the rack renting of Crown Tenants, who, Mr. Tawney thinks, were possibly more favourably situated than those of ordinary manors,[1] it also shows very clearly what was likely to happen on those manors—the great majority —which were in the hands of enterprising agents or lessees holding from absentee lords. For instance, we find that the lawyer who had been employed to renew the leases to the demesne had taken it out at the old rent, but in his own name, and had villainously raised the rent on the tenants by £56 a year. But there was worse to follow; his impecunious majesty had been pleased to sell the manor to the City of London, and the City had sold it to two gentlemen, of the name of Cartwright and Brudnell, and the tenants were afraid they were likely to be "utterlie undon in case Mr. Cartwright and Mr. Brudnell should (as they saie they will) take awaie from yor Tennants the said demeanes and woods after the expiracon of their leases"; finally they had lost the possession of the documents which witnessed to their inheritances, and to the fines upon their copyholds, demesnes and leases. These—the Court Rolls and records of the Manor—had formerly been kept

> "under severall Locks and Keys, whereof yor Ma^{ts} Stewards have kepte one key and yor Maties Tennant . . . have kept an other keye. But nowe they are att the pleasure of the Stewards and Officers transported from place to place, and the nowe purchasers doe demand the Custody of them, wch may be most preiudiciall to yor Ma^{te} poore Tennants".

[1] See Tawney, *op. cit.*, p. 298.

What was the fate of the two hundred tenants of the Manor of North Wheatley? Mr. Tawney does not tell us. The King referred the complaint to the Commissioners for the sale of Crown Lands, and no more is heard of it. Two hundred years later, however, the village is described as being "mostly held on copyhold tenure, paying a fine on the death or change of tenant, equal to one and a half year's rent".[1] It is interesting to note that by 1630, when the above petition was presented, it was recognised that a reasonable fine "should not exceed one and a half year's rent".[2] It would appear, therefore, that the tenants of North Wheatley were among the fortunate minority which succeeded in obtaining the protection of the courts; but it should be remembered they had borne their rack renting for twenty years before they were driven by further intolerable oppressions, to make known their grievances.

If such was the struggle of North Wheatley to retain its customary rights, the position of less fortunate villages can well be imagined. Copyholders with unfixed fines—that is, we are told, the copyholders of two manors out of every three[3]—leaseholders, tenants at will, had no protection against increased rents or fines; and since the market conditions of the sixteenth and seventeenth centuries favoured the larger unit of production—especially in the parts suitable for pasture—and since the appetite for rents is not easily surfeited, large numbers of the smaller tenants must inevitably have been swept away. Thoroton reminds us that "engrossing of farms was the Depopulation first complained of" and points to Elton where there were not half so many farms as in Old Time. Moreover, Elton remained open, which shows that the area of enclosure is itself no true criterion of the extent and intensity of the agrarian revolution. We shall say more of the distribution of enclosure at a later stage; we are concerned here only with the social

[1] White, *op. cit.*, p. 359. [2] Tawney, *op. cit.*, p. 296 n.
[3] Lipson, *Econ. Hist. of England*, Vol. I, p. 148.

revolution with which it is so intimately concerned. In the social scale the gentry were now, beyond all question, at the top; the largest section of the peasantry were small tenant farmers, paying from £40 to £100 a year in rent without rights of proprietorship or even security of tenure, many of whom, it was said, lived more penurious lives than their own labourers. There was, of course, a strong body of freeholders reinforced by the remnant of the copyholders, especially strong in the grain-growing divisions of North and South Clay, where the peasant proprietors were frequently in the ascendant and villages were large—sometimes larger than in the nineteenth century, as the Subsidy Rolls prove. The Poll Book of 1722 shows that the strength of the freeholders throughout the county, though probably diminished in comparison with what it had been in the seventeenth century, was still formidable; about 1300 resident freeholders appear to have recorded their vote at that election. What proportion of the total number this represents we cannot say; the indications are that the proportion is a high one; but it excludes, of course, the copyholders and leaseholders. Besides voting, the freeholders sat on juries, especially the Grand Jury, and assisted the Justices in the legal and administrative business of the courts; they were the only "popular" element in county government, and, as we show later, a diminishing one. Their influence upon local politics was however small, and tended to grow smaller, and important as they were in the aggregate, there can be no doubt that in a county such as Nottinghamshire was at the end of the seventeenth century, real power lay in the hands of the landed gentry; the laws which they made at Westminster they administered in Quarter Sessions, and if Thoroton is to be believed, they consulted their own interests both in the making and the breaking of them. He cites the case of enclosures, which, he says, will never cease until

"the Lords, and such Gentlemen as are usually members of the House of Commons, who have been the chief, and almost only

Authors of, and Gainers by this false-named Improvement . . ., think fit to make a self-denying Act in this Particular, [which] would be as vain to think of, as that any Law which hinders the Profit of a powerful Man should be effectually executed".[1]

It is not surprising that, in Thoroton's mind, local history should be identified with the history of the landed families, and that they alone were deemed worthy of having all that was left of them, to wit, the shadow of their names, preserved as long as may be in the world.

[1] Throsby's Thoroton, p. xvii.

CHAPTER II

THE COUNTY IN TRANSITION

THE first thing that strikes a student regarding the early history of the Nottinghamshire gentry is their unruliness. In an age when England was trembling on the verge of civil war and violence of every kind was practised as a normal method of politics, it is perhaps too much to expect a newly enriched aristocracy, rulers of a thinly populated shire, of which probably a quarter was still occupied by forest and scrub, to observe an entirely peaceful demeanour, unmarked by local jealousies or family feuds.

On the other hand, the disorders among the local aristocracy, which continued practically to the end of Elizabeth's reign, show the danger which her strong government had successfully negotiated. Sir John Stanhope, for instance, heir to the Shelford Priory Estates, had many quarrels with Sir Charles Cavendish of Welbeck Abbey, which culminated in an exciting little battle in Sherwood Forest. Sir Charles, with two pages and a housekeeper, was attacked near his house by Sir John and twenty horsemen. A pistol shot brought Sir Charles and his horse to the ground, but in spite of this he and his two men and boy unhorsed six and killed two on the spot, a third fell down in the forest and was thought to be dead, and a fourth was unlikely to live. Some unarmed workmen came up and Sir John fled with his party.[1] The Queen called them both to account and ordered them to give the sheriff sureties for their good behaviour, having heard, possibly, of a rather similar victory over great odds on the

[1] Brown, *Lives of Nottinghamshire Worthies*, p. 163.

highway near Gadshill. Another sanguinary feud was that of Sir John Holles of the Worksop Priory Estate and the Earl of Shrewsbury of Rufford, championed by Gervase Markham. Holles wrote to Markham in the following strain, ". . . I affirm that you lie and lie like a villain, which I shall be ready to make good upon yourself or upon any gentleman my equal." On returning from the peaceful ceremony of christening his son Denzil Holles, at Haughton, he accidentally met Markham, upbraided him, drew his sword and ran him through up to the hilt and out towards the small of the back. Markham's patron, the Earl of Shrewsbury, immediately raised 120 servants and tenants to apprehend Holles, who called upon his kinsman Lord Sheffield to come to Haughton with sixty men out of Lincolnshire and prepare for a siege. The stage was set for battle, but the curtain was rung down when it was found that Markham's life was not in danger, only his "gallantry".[1] The day of the overmighty subject with his band of retainers seems to have returned, and a considerable portion of the armed forces of the county was made up of the personal following of the landed gentry, Sir John Byron supplying twenty men to the musters of 1542, another gentleman fourteen, and various others bands of six or seven,[2] while Sir John Stanhope is said to have brought all his tenants armed to the election of 1592.

The incidents we have recorded all belong to the half-century following the attack on the Church, an event which snapped old ties and submerged accustomed standards and threw the country into the maelstrom of domestic and foreign complications from which she was lucky to emerge without disaster. The period was exceptional and the restiveness of the local gentry was merely a symptom of the fever that raged in the body politic.

Two powerful antidotes to these irresponsible tendencies were at work. The first was moral, and there-

[1] *Ibid.*, pp. 176, 177. [2] *V.C.H.*, Notts., II, p. 287.

fore impossible to assess with accuracy; the second was political with concrete results that can be more easily measured. The first sprang from the Reformation, which besides letting loose the arrogance and acquisitiveness of the commercial classes gave rise also to a spirit of intense moral earnestness. The modern discrimination between political, religious and economic questions had not fully developed; the logic of the Christian society was taken seriously by the leaders of thought, and public questions, which a hundred years later were solved by the simple process of reckoning up profit and loss, were treated as matters of conscience and passionate ethical debate. It would be unsafe to ignore this side of sixteenth-century life in our treatment of the new governing aristocracy, or to imagine that local magistrates were never carried away by the moral cross-currents of their time. Not only did they have to endure the thunders of Latimer, they also heard themselves prayed for in a prayer composed by Edward VI himself:

> ". . . We heartily pray Thee, to send thy holy Spirit into the hearts of them that possess the grounds, pastures, and dwelling places of the earth, that they, remembering themselves to be thy tenants, may not rack and stretch out the rents of their houses and lands, nor yet take unreasonable fines and incomes after the manner of covetous worldlings, but so let them out to other that the inhabitants thereof may both be able to pay the rents, and also honestly to live, to nourish their families, and to relieve the poor."

Perhaps it takes more than language such as this to prevent a landlord from laying field to field, but if he still sups with the Devil on the morsel of enclosures, he will fain lengthen the spoon by administering the laws more justly.

At any rate it is not difficult to set examples of public-spirited service and religious devotion alongside those of lawlessness and arrogance which we cited above. The very family of Stanhope, whose notorious escapade we have already mentioned, can be utilised to point the opposite moral. Greatly enriched by the property of Shelford Priory, the family served the State in numerous capacities and proved their abilities in many fields. The head of the house, Sir Michael, was executed in 1552 for his association with Protector Somerset, but his wife successfully brought up nine of their twelve children, one of whom sat in the King's Council of the North, two others were gentlemen in waiting on Queen Elizabeth, another was doctor of Civil Law, another inherited the family property at Shelford; four daughters were married, while Lady Ann herself continued to keep "a worshipful house, relieved the poor daily, gave good countenance and comfort to the Preachers of God's word" [1] and handed on a tradition of loyalty which was only quenched in the sack of Shelford House and the slaughter of its garrison in the Civil War. "Sir", said Col. Stanhope, when General Poyntz summoned him to surrender, "I keepe this garrison for the King, and in defence of it I will live and die," and since his body was found after the siege naked, on a dunghill, covered with wounds, he may be said to have fulfilled his pledge.[2]

Other examples of public-spirited service in the seventeenth century are not difficult to find; no one would impute base motives to the Nottinghamshire Roundheads, Hutchinson and Ireton, whose single-minded devotion to their cause is above suspicion. No one can deny equal honour to the Duke of Newcastle who ruined and exiled himself on the opposite side; and some light upon the springs of his action may be found in the character of his wife whose devotion to him was at least as remarkable as his to the King. An authoress of many books, and a dabbler in science, "that princely woman, the thrice noble Duchess of Newcastle", boasted

[1] Throsby's Thoroton, I, p. 290. The prayer is given in Tawney and Power, *Tudor Econ. Docts.*, III, 62.

[2] Firth, *Highways and Byways of Notts.*, pp. 106–10. The aspersion of Lady Hutchinson that Stanhope "came but meanly off after his brave adoes but sat in his chamber and came not forth that day" appears to be the outcome of spite. She also glossed over the slaughter of the garrison.

of an education in which dancing, fiddling, singing, prating of several languages came second to the inculcation of modest and civil, honourable and honest principles.[1] She condemned the frivolous tendencies of her time, especially the writing of romantic tales, which should produce nothing but "foolish amorosities and desperate follies"; as for her books, they were intended "to beget chaste thoughts, nourish a love of Virtue, kindle humane Pity, warm Charity, increase Civility, strengthen fainting Patience, encourage noble Industry, crown Merit, instruct Life and recreate Time".[2] What more could even a Puritan wish for?

The example of a less-exalted, but perhaps more typical local personage is given in the funeral sermon upon Lady Frances Clifton, who died in 1627; she fed and clothed the poor, she gave help to the injured or the diseased, "was any sicke or sore this house was an Apothecaries Shop open to all Commers without money or exchange, and yet all this without the least cackling of merit, her left hand scarce knowing what her right hand did". "Who knoweth not," asks the preacher, as though he had read Wycliffe only yesterday, "that great births have the strongest ties to chayne them to their duties by which their ancestor rose or flourished." [3]

But although the gentry were not lacking in a sense of moral obligation and public service, the force which really controlled them was political. The Tudor monarchy allowed the gentry a large measure of liberty and perhaps a little licence; but it got the work of the country done by them, and was able to hand over to the Stuart despotism the handsome legacy of a local government that was at once efficient and unpaid. A brief treatment of this phase of local administration in which the squirearchy were apprenticed to their business, is necessary for an understanding of what is to follow.

[1] *Life*, p. 158, ed. Firth., 2nd Edition.
[2] *Ibid.*, p. xxv.
[3] W. Fuller's sermon dedicated to Gervase Clifton, 1627.

The Gentry as Public Servants

It would take too long to enumerate all the activities of the gentry as guardians of the county in the name of the State. Besides the routine duties connected with the holding of Quarter Sessions, duties which year by year were growing as the social administration of the newly unified State was thrust upon them in statute after statute, they had to represent the Government in times of emergency, and above all, in times of economic stress. The methods of controlling the available corn supply may be seen from the regulations drawn up at different times, and finally consolidated in the Book of Orders of 1587. The counties were to be divided up into small sections for their more efficient oversight; juries of local farmers were to be empanelled, and enquiries into existing corn supplies carried out; the names of persons having corn in granaries or in the fields; of bakers, brewers, corn dealers, maltsters, and those who had corn over and above their family needs—all these were to be noted and their movements watched, and if necessary, their stock to be sold to "poor artificers and labourers" or supplied to nearby markets. Moreover, Justices were to attend markets and "see that the poor were provided with as much favour in the price as by earnest persuasion can be obtained"; and inspectors were to be appointed to see that the bakers should "deal fairly with the poor".[1]

In years of shortage such as 1576, 1586–7, 1619–23, 1630–3, the Justices are seen making this system work; they fix prices of corn, check the activity of brewers, buy corn for distribution at low rates to the poor, ensure a supply of seed corn, criticise the restraints placed by the Government itself upon the free sale of corn which they say is a burden upon the small husbandman, who has to take such prices as the townsman may offer him.[2]

[1] See Gras, *Evolution of Eng. Corn Market*, 236–41, and *Tudor Economic Documents* by Tawney and Power, Vol. I., 141–167.

[2] See *V.C.H.*, Notts., II, pp. 289 *et seq.*

But the work of regulating the corn supply was only a part of the duties which at this time were being thrust upon the gentry. Far more important as an illustration of the gentry in the rôle of public servants was their administration of the Poor Law of 1601. The great system of national poor relief which this Act embodied depended for its success upon one condition: the just and efficient administration of the law by the local magistrates and parish officers; and that condition could only be fulfilled if the degree of driving force from the centre was sufficient to overcome the dead weight of inertia embodied in an unpaid and inexpert local administration. The only government to achieve this level of energy was the government of Charles I, which imparted to the Elizabethan system a momentum that enabled it to function without structural alteration until the dawning of the industrial age. The best example of its activity is seen in the following extract from the Magistrates' Report to the Privy Council of their work for the year 1636–7:

Laneham—6 poor people in receipt of weekly relief;
a stock of hemp valued 16*s.* for setting the poor on work;
no "wanderers" have come within the boundaries
4 poor children to be placed out apprentices.

Eakring— 6 impotent and aged in receipt of relief;
a stock of material worth 20*s.*
one vagrant punished.
4 poor children placed out as apprentices.

Stokeham—"they have in that Towne noe poore people but such as are able to maintain themselves".
Wanderers none.

and so on, through nineteen other villages of this division.[1] When it is realised that besides providing the personnel for this tedious and detailed administration, the gentry were also used for assessing and collecting the heavy and unparliamentary taxation of Charles's

[1] Quoted in full in Leonard, *Eng. Poor Relief*, p. 361.

autocratic government, and were harried, along with their neighbours, by distraints of knighthood, forced loans and benevolences, and were goaded by Archbishop Laud to close with their own hand the source which was most likely to feed their pockets—the enclosure of arable for pasture—it is not surprising that Charles waved his banner in vain from Standard Hill. They joined him eventually, but not without hesitations and apostasies, and out of the sixty notables of the county who took part, fourteen were on the side of Parliament.[1]

The Restoration found the gentry in the happy position of being free both from the interference of the Stuart despotism with its machinery of political, economic and moral coercion; and also from the hateful domination of the sectaries, against whom the war had really been fought. They celebrated their victory over the latter by persecuting Dissenters, especially Quakers, while the fall of the Stuart despotism enabled them to push on with their agrarian reconstruction, free at last from sentimental and governmental restrictions. Through their control of Parliament they placed what ought to have been an insurmountable barrier between themselves and the normal risks of enterprise by obtaining a monopoly of the home market for their grain and cattle and a bounty on the export of corn [2] which shielded them from the effects of over-production. They were now the masters of the State, and if they tended to identify the State's interests with their own they were doing only what might be expected of a class which combined in its own hands the aggregate of national wealth with the possession of supreme political power.

[1] See list in *Memorials of Old Notts.*, edited by E. L. Guilford, p. 171. Prof. Trevelyan says, "When the long Parliament met there was no Cavalier party, and even after one had been formed at the outbreak of the war, it did not contain all the nobility or much more than half the gentry of England."—*Eng. under the Stuarts*, p. 160.

[2] 12 Chas. II, 4; 22 Chas. II, 13; 1 Wm. & Mary, 12. Cf. Cunningham, *Eng. Ind. and Commerce*, Vol. II, pp. 540–1. See also p. 197 below.

The County and Parliament

Under these conditions it is important to consider the ways and means adopted by the landed interest to obtain the consent of the people of the country to their long, and in many respects glorious, tenure of power. To what extent, we may ask, did the people of Nottinghamshire participate in the political life of the nation?

In the first place it should be noticed that the franchise of Nottingham and Newark, the two chief urban centres of the county, was wide enough to include the great majority of the adult males; Nottingham, at least, may be said to have enjoyed something approaching adult male suffrage; in the county where the franchise remained in the hands of the freeholders, the yeomanry were still strong, especially in the North. Moreover, the county boasted of one great landowner who was able, owing to his wealth, and willing, owing to his principles, to take the lead in combating injustice from whatever source it might come. We refer to Sir George Savile, a Nottinghamshire landowner, but a knight of the shire for Yorkshire, the greatest of the Independent Country Gentlemen, the "Bayard of politics", "whose name contemporary satirists employed as a synonym for probity".[1] But in spite of the wide franchise of Nottingham and Newark, the survival of the yeomanry, and the reflected glory of Sir George Savile, it is impossible to make a case for popular control of politics in the Nottinghamshire of the eighteenth century.

The most independent body of voters were the freeholders, classified according to their wealth into two parts, the greater and the lesser freeholders. The power of the latter may be inferred from the fact that in 1662 an Act was passed prohibiting all freeholders of less than £100 a year from shooting game even on their own ground, and in the reign of Anne, those with

[1] See Namier, *Structure of English Politics at the Accession of Geo. III*, p. 9; Hammond, *Village Labourer*, pp. 54–5; Trevelyan, *Early Life of Chas. James Fox*, p. 247.

less than £600 a year were excluded from sitting in the House of Commons.[1] The greater freeholders no doubt remained independent and influential, but the lesser freeholders, like the smaller tenants, were being squeezed out by their larger neighbours, as we show elsewhere, and were scarcely in a position to afford independent views. In any case, the opportunity for expressing them was very limited since no election was contested in the county from 1722 till the beginning of the nineteenth century.[2]

In the boroughs, it is true, there is an appearance of political vitality. But though Newark had several hundred voters at the end of the century—householders paying scot and lot—the houses which gave them their vote were in the possession of the Duke of Newcastle "which gives him an influence in the elections that the whole weight of the independent part of the people cannot resist with success".[3]

As for East Retford, it is sufficient to note that the Corporation claimed and exercised the right of creating voters to suit itself although such a right had "no other sanction than that of a bylaw made by (itself), which has several times been determined by the Court of King's Bench to have no validity". In spite of King's Bench the Corporation created twenty-two electors in order to keep one of the seats safe for the nominee of the Duke of Newcastle.[4]

In Nottingham there was more freedom of choice, and considerable excitement at election times, but until the famous elections of 1776 and 1778, when the Framework Knitters actually secured representatives pledged to advance a bill on their behalf in the House of Commons, there appears to have been no real political issue at stake outside the manœuvring of aristocratic factions. Indeed, until the emergence about 1780

[1] Stats. of Realm, 22–23 Ch. II, XXV; 4 Wm. & Mary, XXIII; 9 Anne, V. See also Trevelyan, *Eng. under Stuarts*, pp. 472–3; and *Blenheim*, Ch. I.

[2] Blackner, *Hist. of Nottm.*, p. 303.

[3] Oldfield, *Hist. of the Original Constitution of Parliament*, 1797, p. 327; Cornelius Brown, *Hist. of Newark*.

[4] Oldfield, *op. cit.*, pp. 384–6.

of deep-seated economic problems which caused the voting mass of the borough to look for help to the legislature, local parliamentary politics were something in the nature of a public entertainment, all the more agreeable in that the onlookers were remunerated, less lavishly perhaps, but more certainly than the performers themselves.

The chief performer was the Duke of Newcastle, who, according to the most recent student of the subject, was usually able to secure, sometimes at prodigious expense, the return of his own candidate in four out of the eight seats available, e.g. one county member and one member for each of the boroughs of Nottingham, Newark, and Retford.[1] The onlookers were the burgesses of the boroughs mentioned, who were almost sure of getting something, if it was only free beer for the lesser sort and a banquet for the select. Of course they got more if there was a really fierce fight. In the famous election of 1754, when the control of local politics by the Duke of Newcastle was rudely challenged by Mr. Plumptre, whose own father had represented the borough for thirty-two years, the utmost efforts on both sides were put forth to the great good fortune of the local burgesses (about eighteen hundred in number). On the one side was the Duke himself, Recorder of the Borough and large landowner, his nominee Lord Howe of Langar, supported by Abel Smith the Banker and his two sons. On the other side was Mr. Plumptre the apostate, who after a life time of Whiggery had suddenly embraced Toryism on being asked to stand down for his second cousin, Lord Howe; he was supported by the Earl of Middleton, John White, M.P. for Retford, and John Thornhaugh, Knight of the Shire, who forgot their political indebtedness to the Duke and secured their tenants for

[1] Namier, *Structure of Politics at the Accession of Geo. III*, p. 9— the total number of seats controlled by the Duke of Newcastle after forty years of electioneering, and the loss of a large part of his fortune, is here stated to be no more than twelve.

the Whig renegade. The town played its part by threatening to stone the interloper, Lord Howe; he answered the challenge by gallantly "walking the town" accompanied by the most prominent members of the Corporation, and by Abel Smith and his two sons.[1] According to the local annalist, Bailey, the candidate even went so far as to entertain a number of the Burgesses "for months" before the election at his seat at Langar Hall (their families receiving a golden half-guinea every week), where he regaled them for some days before the election with such profusion that some of them died as a consequence.[2] Lord Middleton struck a shrewd blow at the very heart of the opposition by means of his banking account. He had a large sum of money "lying dead" in the hands of the Smith family, he threatened not only to withdraw it, but to persuade all his friends to do the like unless the Smiths would consent to give up the cause of the Whig candidate.[3]

The cause of the Duke of Newcastle was clearly precarious; the occasion called for all his skill; his stewards in Nottingham set to work to secure his dependants, ways and means of influencing other voters were examined; his estate agents in other parts of the county were informed of the Nottingham voters in their "collections", the Excisemen were worked with due discretion and the poor burgesses "with whom money and the best bidder is become the byword received petty bribes, etc., etc."[4] And the Duke was rewarded by seeing his candidate returned with a substantial majority. The result of the poll was: Howe, 980 votes (901 single), Sir Willoughby Aston (Tory), 924, and Plumptre, 915.

[1] See Namier, *op. cit.*, p. 116, for a full description of the election.

[2] Bailey, *Annals of Notts.*, p. 1222.

[3] The attack was repulsed, not, however, without loss. See Namier, *op. cit.*, and note.

[4] Namier, *op. cit.* See also *Alphabetical List of Burgesses and Freeholders* (Nottingham, 1754) with MS. comments such as: "Cheatham Joseph, F. W. K., wished his right hand might rot off if he voted for Howe only. 'Tis said he had 30 Gs. Harrison Thomas, Inn holder, refused a licence. Pearson John, F. W. K., turned out of his house." See also p. 48 note 1 below.

The election of 1754 shows how completely passive was the political life of the town at this time. Although it concerned an important borough in which most of the adult males had votes, the election was fought out with tremendous enthusiasm and at great cost, entirely by county magnates, and the only question at issue was whether the Duke of Newcastle should get his nominee in or not. It should be noted, however, that one of the principals had as his second, the great banking family of Smith; and though they were browbeaten by a powerful lord, they persevered and were rewarded in the next generation by having a Smith elevated to the peerage, the first man of definitely commercial origin whom George III could be persuaded to ennoble.[1]

The real issues in local politics, it seems clear, were not political, but personal. Within the oligarchy of ruling families there were conflicts and divisions, and the function of the parliamentary election was to decide which of the aristocratic factions should be given the duty and privilege of ruling the State and enjoying the perquisites. To the modern observer there were many questions which might also have been considered, such as enclosures, common rights, poor relief, settlement, wages, prices, housing conditions, prisons, workhouses, but until 1778 no election was ever fought upon any of them; as far as is known they were never even mentioned. The reason seems to be that those who had the vote had no grievance upon these matters, and those who had a grievance had no vote. But within the hierarchy of property owners which, in the eighteenth century, constituted the political nation, there was a process of differentiation at work; some went up and joined the lords, like Smith the Banker; others went down and joined the poor, like the apprenticed framework knitter, but though he was poor he was still a burgess and had the vote, hence the election of 1778, when the stockingers (in close alliance, it may be noted,

[1] Namier, *op. cit.* See also Halévy, *A History of the English People in* 1815, p. 300 n.

with the Smiths) fight an election on the question of wages, get their man in, and through him introduce a bill to regulate the wages in the stocking industry. Times are clearly changing, the landed interest is being challenged from two sides, the side of the new commerce and finance in the persons of the Smith family —and the Arkwrights, Boultons, Wilkinsons, and of others who were building the new England—and also, but prematurely, from the side of the new proletariat.

This last episode, the challenge of the new proletariat, with its combination pitted against an association of masters, with its futile appeal to Parliament, followed by strikes and riots and ending with a bargain between masters and men, epitomises with remarkable fidelity the latent stages of the new industrial society. It enables us, with more than usual success "to catch the Manners, living as they rise"—the manners of the new industrialised world—and is worth treating in some detail as a fitting conclusion to our description of an age that was drawing to a close.

The Framework Knitters' Election and the Strike of 1779

The events of 1776–9 were the culmination of a crucial phase in the development of the Framework Knitting industry. Besides the growth of capitalist organisation, which we shall describe elsewhere, the period was marked by rapid technical advance. Experiments in cotton spinning, ending with the migration of Hargreaves and Arkwright to Nottingham, the invention of the eyelet-hole machine, on which elaborately fashioned gloves and waistcoat pieces could be made, and of the Derby Rib machine, which profoundly altered the style of ordinary hose, stand out from a multiplicity of smaller technical innovations.

Henson, in a long chapter [1] devoted to this subject,

[1] Henson, *History of Framework Knitters,* pp. 256–355 (henceforward referred to simply as Henson). Felkin, *History of Machine Wrought Hosiery and Lace,* pp. 84–142 (henceforward referred to simply as Felkin).

speaks of a "fever" for mechanical experimenting and invention; half-starved stockingers spent their hours of unemployment in devising new methods of ornamentation and their last coin in buying tools and materials. The culminating point of this period of activity was reached when Point Net Lace, a web of hexagonal mesh, was made on the stocking frame about 1776–7.

The result of the increased scope given to the stocking machine at this time was of little advantage to the stockingers. Fashions fluctuated so rapidly that the new inventions sometimes became obsolete before they had repaid their cost to the inventor, and periods of high prosperity in newly adopted branches of the trade alternated with deep depression. The coarser branches of manufacture suffered in their turn from this instability; wages tended to go down on account of the competition of the more popular novelties, while the cost of living steadily rose. These influences were reinforced by the war with the American Colonies and their European allies. The cumulative effect was that the Stockingers of the Midlands and London combined to form an effective organisation and petitioned Parliament as one body.

According to Henson, associations began to be formed in the chief stocking-making districts about the year 1776.[1] In the summer of 1777 negotiations took place between the committees appointed in London and Nottingham to arrive at some course of action. The London stockingers were anxious to aim at an advance of prices; those of Nottingham were satisfied to maintain them at the existing rate.[2] However, by 1778, differences had been composed and a joint appeal of the three Midland Counties and London was made to Parliament for a bill to regulate wages upon an agreed basis. List of prices for all kinds of work, eyelet-holes, tucked, turned and plain work, were sent in by workmen from all parts to enable the Committee to draw up an authoritative bill of rates.[3] Subscriptions were collected from

[1] Henson, p. 383. [2] Letter to *Nottingham Journal*, March 28, 1778.
[3] *Nottingham Journal*, Jan. 3, 1778.

the trade itself, and from the gentlemen and tradesmen of the town,[1] who, as long as the proceedings were untainted by violence or destruction of property, were whole-heartedly in support of the operatives.

The preparations of the journeymen were not allowed to go unchallenged by the hosiers, who formed a counter association, appointed Samuel Turner, a local lawyer, as their secretary, and organised a strong opposition when the matter was brought up in Parliament. A petition, presented in February, 1778, by Mr. D. Parker Coke, a member for Derby,[2] elicited a reply from the "Manufacturing Hosiers of Nottingham Town and County" in a petition which declared the fixing of a definite basis of wages by law would imperil the prosperity of all. A bill was at length introduced but was lost by a majority of 52 to 27.[3]

The resolution of the stockingers was not in any way shaken by this setback. After an abortive attempt to revive the moribund Framework Knitters' Company[4] they turned once more to Parliament as their last resort. The men held a meeting on the race-course on August 4, 1778, and decided to petition Parliament again. To defray the expenses incidental to such procedure a toll of 3*s*. 1*d*. was to be raised from each frame, to be paid to a central committee through village committees appointed for this purpose.[5] Further, owing to the fact that many members of the Association were burgesses of Nottingham and therefore had the vote, it was possible to obtain the election to Parliament of two sympathetic members, one Abel Smith, the Banker's son, "a brother framework knitter", as he is styled in the *Journal*,[6] standing definitely as the representative

[1] *Ibid.*

[2] *H.C.J.*, Vol. 36, p. 635.

[3] *Ibid.*, p. 728.

[4] *Ibid.*, p. 742.

[5] See letter to Associated F.W. Knitters of the Town and County of Nottingham in *Nottingham Journal*, Aug. 15, 1778.

[6] *Nottingham Journal*, Oct. 3, 1778. Abel Smith was the son of Abel Smith the banker of Nottingham. The description of him given by Pilkington, the Clerk, indicates that Abel had become free of the Company by paying his fee.

of the Association, and Charles Medows, who also promised "to exert his uttermost influence on behalf of poor manufacturers".

The election was fought with a dignity that was rare for that period and was not without a touch of effective pageantry. A fine procession was organised at which the flag of the Association was carried alongside the Union Jack, followed by the officials of the Framework Knitters' Company, the Committee of the Association, the body of Framework Knitters two by two, a band of clarinets and French horns, and finally the candidate Abel Smith, the whole election being characterised, according to the local Press, without "the least confusion, disorder or irregularity happening".[1]

The composition of the General Committee was representative of all sections of the opposition and included delegates of the more reasonable hosiers, who were willing to have wages fixed. There had always been a number of sympathisers for the operatives among the hosiers.[2] These, constituting, we may say, the extreme right of the Committee, were supported by a representative of the tradesmen, who was made chairman, and one of the master-stockingers; then came representatives of the Knitters' Association, of the stockingers in the county, and of the industry from London, Derby and Leicester. The Midlands Stockingers' Association, as it was called, looks an impressive body, and its committee, according to Henson, was made up of men of splendid talent.[3]

An opportunity to demonstrate its power was given to the Association on the death of its Parliamentary representative, Abel Smith. At the nomination of his brother, Mr. Robert Smith, who was selected to represent the cause of the stockingers, the Town Hall was more crowded than at any time since 1754.[4]

Preparations were now complete. A new petition

[1] Sutton, *Date Book of Nottingham*, p. 116, quoting *Nottingham Journal*.
[2] See letter of "Amicus" in *Nottingham Journal*, Aug. 29, 1778.
[3] Henson, p. 394.
[4] *Nottingham Journal*, Feb. 6, 1779.

was submitted and in the debate that later ensued, was supported by moderate and persuasive speeches from the representatives of the trade.[1] Evidence given before the Committee was printed and circulated by the Association among a limited number of subscribers,[2] a copy of which is in the possession of the Municipal Library at Derby. This document, together with the report given in the *Journals of the House of Commons*, is sufficient testimony to the justice of the stockingers' cause. The investigation brought to light, in the words of a modern writer, "a degree of sweating scarcely paralleled by the worst modern instances".[3]

There was, however, no attempt on the part of the stockingers to impeach the hosiers as a body; the blame was mainly laid upon the high price of provisions which justly called for an increase of wages. In addition, they asked for some consideration in the matter of frame rent. They also drew up and presented a list of prices, but this, according to Henson, would have proved unworkable as the great variety of work which the frame was then capable of, made strict classification impossible. The general aim of the stockingers was to accomplish such an improvement as would place them on a level with their brethren in Ireland.[4] This modest aim had considerable chances of success. To the intense delight of the stockingers, their Bill passed its first reading with but one dissentient vote.[5] A prosperous issue was confidently anticipated for the "Glorious Cause",[6] and appeals for subscriptions received an enthusiastic response. The tradesmen of the town were again

[1] *Nottingham Journal*, 1779, May 8 and May 29.

[2] Henson, p. 395. Henson states that no copy has survived. This is true of the schedule of prices but not of the minutes of evidence.

[3] Webb, *Trade Unionism*, p. 45.

[4] Speech of Robert Smith reported in *Nottingham Journal*, May 8, 1779. According to the evidence of one witness, a list of prices had been issued by the Lord Mayor of Dublin in 1749, and proved of great advantage to framework knitters in Ireland. When he was working in Dublin, twenty years earlier, he paid 2*s*. a week frame rent and could earn 15*s*. to 16*s*. a week (Irish currency). *H.C.J.*, Vol. 37, p. 372.

[5] *Nottingham Journal*, May 8, 1779.

[6] *Ibid.*, May 15, 1779.

eager in their support of the stockingers; butchers solicited from customers, landlords from guests; people collected in every lane and highway.[1] The vocational distinctions between the various sections of the working and trading classes were forgotten, and all united against a common oppression.

The second reading of the Bill took place on May 29. The speech of Mr. Robert Smith, as reported in the *Nottingham Journal*, was in the same subdued key as were all the utterances of those who represented the cause of the journeymen. The measure, he said, was intended merely to prevent unfair competition between opulent masters and poor manufacturers. The Framework Knitters, he assured the House, had formed no combination; they came submissively to the Legislature with a humble plea for protection.[2] His persuasive eloquence availed only to win a majority of one vote for the Bill. Its fate was all but sealed. Need, a powerful hosier and joint owner of Arkwright's cotton mill, is said to have determined the issue by seeking the support of the venal Cornish members. At the third reading on June 8, a Cornish member moved that the Bill should be read that day two months, and the motion was carried by 57 to 18. In the words of Wilkes, "the Cornish and Devon miners had sunk a new pit for the agents of the Bill".[3] The *Nottingham Journal* announced that the Bill was lost "to the great joy of many master-stockingers and to the inexpressible affliction of hundreds of poor stockingers who crowded the lobby in expectation of hearing that the Bill for their relief had passed".[4]

The Ten Days' Strike of 1779

The fury of the Nottingham stockingers knew no bounds. The news came on June 10. Almost immediately the market-place filled. The windows of an

[1] Henson, p. 397. [2] *Nottingham Journal*, May 29, 1779.
[3] Quoted by Henson, p. 401.
[4] *Nottingham Journal*, June 12, 1779, *q.v.* for description of riots.

obnoxious hosier on Parliament Street were smashed; every window shutter and tile of the house of Need, cotton manufacturer as well as hosier and chief opponent of the stockingers, was smashed. The rioting continued next day with a systematic harrying of the principal hosiers in the town. The Riot Act was read. The crowd submissively dispersed, only to gather again at Need and Arkwright's mill, where the windows were smashed. The soldiers on duty at the Castle were constantly called out to quell the mob, and were as constantly confronted by a preternatural calm, which was followed by further outrage on their departure. The County stockingers on the third day began to pour in. Two rioters were captured. The only alternative to bloodshed was complete pacification. This was attempted and temporarily achieved through the mediation of one of the Committee of the stockingers, who assured the multitude that there would be a meeting of the hosiers and the stockingers' committee on the following day at which the grievances of the journeymen would be fully dealt with. In order to placate the mob still further, the two prisoners were released and peace reigned for a brief space.

The meeting took place at the Feather's Inn on Monday, June 17. The conference lasted five hours and ended in deadlock between the men's representatives and the hosiers, though the accounts given by the two parties differ considerably. The hosiers declared their proposals were accepted by the men's Committee, but rejected by the men themselves;[1] the Committee, on the other hand, declared that they never did agree, and that only one of their body (Jones the hosier) was willing to consider the terms.[2]

Further rioting was inevitable. The stockingers patrolled the streets, entered the houses, and declared they would break every frame that worked that day. At six in the evening, while a sham attack was made upon Need's factory, in order to distract the attention

[1] *Ibid.*, June 19, 1779.

[2] Henson, p. 406.

of the soldiery, a numerous body set off to Arnold, where he had his house and a large number of frames. Apparently the whole of these were systematically thrown out of the windows of the shops in which they stood before news reached Nottingham.[1] A posse of cavalry was sent to restore order, but the rioters had been warned by the watchmen posted at intervals along the route and had completely dispersed before the cavalry arrived.

Three hundred special constables, including most of the gentlemen and many of the tradesmen of the town, were sworn in by the civic authorities, and publicly instructed in their duties through the columns of the *Journal*.[2] The hosiers also deemed it expedient to make public demonstration of their solidarity, and on June 19 a manifesto denouncing the misdeeds of the stockingers was published, signed by sixty-five principal hosiers of the town.[3]

The rioters, far from being cowed, crowned their misdeeds with the burning and complete destruction of the house of Wilkinson, a master-stockinger, who had made himself unpopular by his evidence before the Committee.[4] This final outrage convinced the Mayor that it was time to take the enraged stockingers seriously, and on June 18 he issued a proclamation declaring that further disorders would meet with the utmost severity of the law.

The rioting now came to an end. It is probable the fury of the populace, rather overwhelmed with their own last act or terrorism, was beginning to evaporate. The declaration of the Mayor was followed by a soothing statement from the hosiers, who promised to give reasonable recompense for labour, and remove every oppression.

Peace was made more secure by the remarkable lenity of the magistrates who appear, as Henson says,

[1] Henson, p. 407.

[2] *Nottingham Journal*, June 19.

[3] *Ibid.*, June 19 and 26.

[4] He was the master of the "marvellous apprentice" who declared he could make 18 pairs of hose a week.—Henson.

to have viewed the actions of the mob as little more than the escapades of naughty children. Insignificant fines, and short terms of imprisonment, were distributed among the captured ringleaders, and a public apology in one case was considered sufficient punishment for the assault upon a magistrate. One man only was in danger of losing his life, Mephringham, the leader in the destruction of Wilkinson's house. He was captured at Lincoln and charged with the capital offence of house burning, but, according to Henson, the chief witness against him was abducted by the prisoner's friends until the trial was over, with the result that Mephringham escaped with a fine of 6*s*. 8*d*. and three weeks' imprisonment for frame-breaking.[1] The only people who gleaned little comfort from this happy sequel to ten days' serious rioting were the hosiers whose frames had been smashed and property destroyed to the extent of some thousands of pounds. An attempt was made by them to wreak vengeance upon the men's committee. Pilkington the clerk, and Wright were brought up as accessories before the fact of frame breaking but the Grand Jury refused to bring in a Bill. Herring, who had previously been apprehended and liberated, was betrayed to the Press Gang; he escaped and was betrayed again, and again made good his escape. The hosiers are then said to have entered into an agreement to forfeit £500 if any one of their number employed him or any master-stockinger from whom he might get work.[2]

The hosiers were now masters of the situation, but they appear to have met the men's representatives from time to time to discuss the question of wages; in 1787 a wages agreement was entered into between the parties that was adhered to without substantial modification for twenty years.[3]

The incident we have described clearly shows that the eighteenth century was drawing to a close; industrial issues had emerged which pushed the faction fights

[1] Henson, p. 415. [2] *Ibid.*
[3] Felkin, *Hosiery and Lace* p. 230.

of the aristocratic houses momentarily into the background; owing to the accident of a democratic franchise in an industrialised town the proletariat had possession of the vote; it availed them nothing, as we have seen, but it is interesting to speculate upon what might have been if the same political conditions, the enfranchisement of the town labourer, had obtained in other towns on the eve of the Industrial Revolution.

CHAPTER III

THE COUNTY UNDER THE SQUIREARCHY

THE period of the Restoration marks a new phase not only in the political, but in the administrative history of the County. From the rise of the Tudor centralisation, it had formed part, as we have seen, of a unitary state, deriving its vitality from the nerve centre in Whitehall. It was now left to live its own life, free not only from control of the centre, but even from guidance or supervision. Reluctantly at first, but compelled by the sheer pressure of everyday routine business, the gentry shouldered the burden of local government, and carried it, or perhaps stumbled along with it, for a century and more, as best they could.

Any attempt to describe this phase of the County history must of necessity rely mainly upon the records of Quarter Sessions. For some reason as yet unexplained, the records that were compiled without interruption up to the outbreak of the Civil War, and again during the Commonwealth, break off at the Restoration, and are either missing altogether or exist only in an incomplete form for the rest of the century.

Mr. Hampton Copnall, writing on this subject, says: "Up to this date (January, 1661), the records are well and carefully kept, but from this date to the end of the century they are imperfect"; while for the period January, 1661, to April, 1674, he could find no records at all.[1] The Borough Records were also very scanty at this time. The author of Volume V writes, "The minutes are singularly dry and meagre for the whole reign of Charles

[1] Hampton Copnall, *Nottinghamshire County Records of the Seventeenth Century*, p. 2.

II . . . so sparse are the entries and so commonplace . . . that one might be tempted to imagine that an almost universal lethargy had seized the Town Council." [1]

The reluctance of the local gentry to take up again the duties which by law and tradition devolved upon them is seen also in the difficulty which the Government of the Restoration had in persuading men to serve as magistrates. Lord Clarendon in 1665 complained that many persons named in the Commissions of the Peace had neglected to "take out a Dedimus", and therefore were unqualified to perform a single act of justice, and for a whole generation successive Judges in their charges at the Assizes continued to make the same complaint. Indeed, Mr. Webb estimates that not more than half the 2,500–3,000 Justices in the Commissions between 1650 and 1700 took the trouble to qualify for their functions, while the diarist, Evelyn, was vainly solicited by Chas. II himself to qualify.[2]

It would appear from this that the cessation of control from the centre was likely to be followed by decay in the counties, owing to the passive resistance of the gentry to the call of duty, unsupported by the spur of coercion. The opening of the eighteenth century, however, sees them regularly treading the dreary mill of their sessions, and copiously recording their actions in the Rolls and Minute Books which now line the shelves of the County Muniment Room in almost continuous series up to the present time.

It is interesting, but perhaps unprofitable, to speculate upon the reason for this change. Is it that the inertia of the post-war years had been shaken off and that the gentry had awakened once more to their public responsibilities? Or is it that the pressure of social needs was growing and that a closer application to their duties was forced upon them as the only alternative to administrative

[1] Borough Records, Vol. V, p. viii. A hiatus occurred in the records of Cambridgeshire from 1670–89. Cf. Hampson, *Settlement and Removal in Cambridgeshire*, p. 275, in *Camb. Historical Journal*, 1928.

[2] Cf. Webb, *Parish and County*, p. 321.

collapse? There is no doubt that the chief social problem, the problem of pauperism, was causing universal concern, amounting almost at times to panic, while the extraordinary legislation relating to it, far from introducing improvements in the existing machinery, merely added a further burden in the shape of the Settlement regulations. New devices for employing the poor, independent of the existing framework of poor-relief, were being tried in several parts of the country, but elsewhere, including Nottinghamshire, the Elizabethan mechanism of County and Parish had to suffice. From now onwards, the Justices and parish officers were caught up in the net of Settlement, and it was drawn round them by the ineluctable pressure of the poor rate. Everybody was interested in settlement because everybody was interested in poor rates; hence, the Justices of the Peace who, in the great majority of cases, had the last word in the question of a person's settlement, and therefore of his poor relief, were the focus not only of those who received, but those who paid for the poor relief. The elaboration of a national system of settlement, like the national system of apprenticeship of Elizabeth, greatly increased the pressure upon the local government, and unless the magistrate was immune not only from public spirit, but from the prevailing preoccupation in regard to the poor rates, he could not escape having to bear his share of the burden.

It might be thought that, having once undertaken these unpaid and onerous duties, the Justices would have set about the task of recouping themselves for the tedious and sordid toil that had been pressed upon them. Such was the case in some parts; the scandalous traffickings of London Justices were a byword, and Edmund Burke did not exaggerate when he described the majority of them as infamous, ignorant, and "the scum of the earth".[1]

But the infamy of London was not confined to its Justices; it penetrated elsewhere, and it may be that the quality of London justice was comparable to the quality

[1] *Ibid.*, p. 325.

of London morals in general. The country districts were in a happier case; there is no evidence, in Nottinghamshire at least, that the County magistrates seriously abused their powers, or that those of the borough were guilty of anything worse than political partisanship in the granting of licences of ale-houses.[1] But though the justice administered in the local courts was probably not corrupt, it was certainly crude and brutal. In a society that supported an army of vagabonds and the merest travesty of a police force, opportunities for evildoing were necessarily plentiful, and the only means of checking it known to the eighteenth century was by weighting the law with terrible punishments. Life and property must be protected, especially property which was far more vulnerable than life.

In the main, there were three social categories in the eighteenth century: the people of quality, the tradesmen, and the poor. While the first two were divided from one another by recognised social distinctions, the third was divided from both by a social gulf. Poverty was a social form of original sin; the possession of wealth a form of salvation, the hall-mark of the elect. A breach of the law by the poor, therefore, was an aggravation of their already unsatisfactory moral state, and the punishment took cognisance of more than a mere legal offence. This explains why it was possible for a couple of typical magistrates, sitting in Quarter Sessions, in the parlour of an inn, enveloped in the somnolent atmosphere of beer fumes and smoke, to inflict the penalty of a "severe whipping" or even to send men and women into the semi-slavery of West Indian plantations for the trumpery offence of stealing a beer mug, or spade, or a pair of iron horse gears, or seven yards of linen.[2]

The following extract from the Borough Records shows the streak of ferocity which came to the top when

[1] In 1755 it was stated that twenty licences had been suspended for political motives. King's Bench, Vol. 96, p. 858. This is probably an echo of the election of 1754.

[2] See Hampton Copnall, *Notes of Proceedings at General Quarter Sessions*, 1736–7.

the local magistrates had to punish an offence that incurred public expense as well as moral opprobrium:

"It is ordered by the Court that Susanna Tate Ruth Blackston and Mary Beresford who have lately been delivered of Bastard Children now chargeable to the parish of St. Mary in this Town shall on Wednesday next be tyed in the Ducking Stool at St. Mary's Workhouse after they shall have been whipped at the house of correction and drawn from thence along Stoney Street the High Pavement Bridlesmith Gate and round the Malt Cross and then to the workhouse again." [1]

It would be a great mistake, however, to think that the will of the local magistracy was imposed upon a resentful and oppressed population. In the first place, the organ of government through which it operated, the Court of Quarter Sessions, was associated in its work with certain quasi-democratic bodies such as the Gentlemen of the Grand Jury, or the "Grand Inquest" of the County, the "Primum Mobile of the Court" as it was called by a writer in 1725, and the Constable Juries of farmers and labourers drawn from the divisions into which the County was organised for judicial and administrative purposes. Both of these organs represented an area or a class of local opinion, and during the early part of the century at least, the chief public business of the County appears to have been transacted through them by judicial process of presentment in the full and open court of Quarter Sessions to which anyone in the County had the right of access.

Again, the dictatorship of property was tempered by certain characteristics which modern equalitarian society would find intolerable. For instance, the labouring poor could always protest, and sometimes did, by means of a riot; this, as Mr. Halévy reminds us, was among the tacitly acknowledged rights of all free-born Britons,[2] and distinguished them from the "slaves" of other countries. In London the right was vigorously exercised again and

[1] Borough Records, Vol. VI, p. 126; for another case of whipping three women, see p. 57.

[2] See Halévy, *History of the English People in* 1815, pp. 130 *et seq.*

again, and Parliament itself had sometimes to submit to it. In Nottinghamshire it was exercised very infrequently, not more than three or four times in the first sixty years of the eighteenth century. In 1757, an important meeting of magistrates, at which the majority of local notables were present, called for the purpose of raising recruits for the Seven Years' War, was violently broken up by the mob; in the other cases the objects of popular fury were millers and cheese merchants who were accused of creating a scarcity;[1] thus the rulers of the County were only once molested.

It would seem from this that protest against the will of the squirearchy was possible, but that it was never made; the principle upon which it rested—the principle of property—was accepted both by those who had it and by those who had it not; those who did not possess it had a profound respect for it, and were willing to give it authority over them. Moreover, the kingdom of the elect, the property owners, was a hierarchy, in which promotion was always possible to those who could secure a first instalment of the means of grace. And this, of course, was money. Not even beauty was a satisfactory substitute. "A gentleman marrying a beautiful young girl of little or no fortune is generally so much laughed at that no man would choose to have it made public beforehand."[2] To adapt a phrase of Professor Trevelyan, "English snobbery was at its beneficent task" of welding society together in the eighteenth as well as the thirteenth century, which helps to explain why a group of squires, without the intervention of the State, indeed, without an effective police force for their own protection, were able to rule a community which they themselves had partially despoiled in the course of their economic evolution.

The Machinery of Local Government

Quarter Sessions. The driving force in the public affairs of the County was the Court of Quarter Sessions,

[1] See Bailey, *Annals of Notts.*, 1231, Sutton *Date Book*, p. 41; *Cal. H.O. Papers*, Oct. 31, 1766, Nos. 301, 302.

[2] *Parl. Hist.*, XV, p. 60.

a judicial, administrative, and quasi-legislative body, "one of the most original and characteristic of all British institutions."[1] It met at the Shire Hall, Nottingham, four times a year, viz. at Easter, in July, at Michaelmas and in January, and, in each case, was adjourned first to Newark and then to East Retford. Besides these twelve regular sittings of the Court, additional adjournments were often held in other towns and villages in the County: Blyth, Mansfield, and on rare occasions, in such small places as Barnby Moor and Harworth.[2]

During the first half of the eighteenth century, there would probably be on an average thirteen or fourteen sessions of the Court per year.

The meeting of the Justices does not appear to have been the great event sometimes imagined. Often enough the Court consisted of no more than two Justices, and the same amount and kind of business was recorded as when the Bench numbered half a dozen. Sometimes it happened that no Justices appeared at all, in which case the clerk duly recorded that the Court was not held "for want of Justices".[3] The more usual number was three or four, but on special occasions the judicial might of the County would be made to turn out in imposing force. For instance, in 1732 an adjournment was held at Mansfield at which no less than eleven Justices appeared, among whom were the High Sheriff and such notables as Viscounts Howe and Galway. The reason for this sudden access of zeal on the part of individuals who were rarely known to take part in the administrative business of the County was the necessity of discussing the £2,000 fine levied upon the County by Sir Littleton Powys

[1] Halévy, *op. cit.*, p. 34. For best account of procedure of Court of Quarter Sessions, its characteristic confusion of powers and development of quasi-legislative authority, see Webb, *Parish and County*, Ch. IV and V.

[2] MS. Minute Book, Feb. 15, 1732. For a good account of the Shire Hall, see article by H. Hampton Copnall in *Thor. Soc. Trans.*, 1915.

[3] This appears to have occurred especially at Newark adjournments, see MS. Minute Book, Jan. 11, 1743; April 3, Oct. 2, 1758; Jan. 8, April 23, Oct. 1, 1759, etc.

of the King's Bench for the repairing of the County Hall.[1]

Attendance at all the sessions and adjournments of the court could not be expected of Justices who lived scattered among the six divisions of the County; and in view of the execrable condition of the roads of that time, it is not surprising to find them restricting their attendance mainly to the sessions which were held in the particular part of the County in which they themselves lived. The result was that the administration of the County affairs tended to become split up among three co-ordinate groups of Justices, each responsible for its own district, though of course the arrangement was not rigidly adhered to.

The only official place of meeting was the Shire Hall, "alias the King's Hall", on High Pavement, Nottingham, but excepted from the boundaries of the borough by the Charter of Henry VI. The adjourned sittings of the Court in other parts of the County were sometimes held in private houses but more frequently in the parlours of the best inn of the town—"at the Sign of the Deer" or "at the Sign of the Angel", "where all matters were agitated amidst the smoking of pipes and the cluttering of pots and the ordure of a narrow room infested with drinking and a throng".[2]

The Monthly Meeting.

The Justices of each division were also expected to meet once a month in order to settle the current administration of the division and prepare the ground for Quarter Sessions. What the exact functions of the Justices in their monthly meetings were is not quite clear, but in the seventeenth century they were found summoning

[1] MS. Minute Book, Vol. 24, Aug. 27, 1731. For another Sessions attended by Viscount Galway, see MS. Minute Book, July 15, 1748, East Retford. The cattle plague was raging at this time and constant adjournments are recorded for granting or withholding certificates to remove cattle from infected areas. This probably accounts for his appearance on the Bench.

[2] Quoted by S. and B. Webb, *Parish and County*, p. 424. For a quarrel between J.P.s of North and South of County, see Copnall, *op. cit.*, p. 14.

offenders to be brought before them and binding them over to good behaviour or causing them to appear at Quarter Sessions; they were informed of murders, felonies and outrages in their district; made orders in bastardy which were afterwards confirmed at Quarter Sessions; called not only the village constable before them but also the churchwarden and overseers apparently to enquire into the working of the statutes which they had to administer concerning rogues and vagabonds, setting the poor on work, and binding children apprentices.[1]

It is obvious that the monthly meetings formed a very important part of the administrative routine; but as no minutes of their proceedings have survived, it is impossible to give anything like a complete picture of their function or procedure.

The records left by the Petty Constables, who had to attend the meetings with their lists of freeholders and their Quarter Dues, do something to throw a little light upon this side of the Justices' activities, though in general they avoid specific mention of the term "monthly meeting". The constables of Bleasby, however, are a little more communicative, and from the regularity with which they include entries upon this topic, it seems safe to say that the meetings were held not once a month but about three or four times a year—regularly in April, September and October or December, sometimes in January and less frequently in July.[2] The monthly meeting had probably merged into a form of Petty Sessions.

The Single Justice.

Besides their work at Quarter Sessions and Monthly Meetings, they had a certain judicial and administrative authority sitting individually in their own houses. They

[1] Hampton Copnall, *Notts. County Records of Seventeenth Century*, p. 12.

[2] MS. Town Book Bleasby, especially 1772–9 and following years 1749, 1760, 1771. The last meeting of the year was generally called a "private sessions". Meetings were usually held in the largest town in the division, e.g. Bingham, Southwell, East Retford, but also smaller places like Blyth and Screveton.

kept an eye on the administration of poor relief, generally with the effect of mitigating the harshness of parish officers, examined the mothers of bastards and the source of origin of doubtful strangers; took "a view of highways" and presented offending parishes, restrained morals by fining for the offence of swearing (at a shilling a time) or profaning the Sabbath, or tippling in ale-houses, etc. They also tried to hold even the scales of justice in the contentions of quarrelsome villagers, as the following example shows: John Trinbury, in justification of his assault upon the Rector of Elton, complained that at the funeral of Ellen Ragsdale three or four years earlier, the said Rector was so drunk that he could not say the usual prayers for the dead, but fell asleep at the reading desk and had to be disturbed by the Parish Clerk—"and then he went to the grave with the corps and bid them put her in saying God help thee poor Nell without any other prayers or ceremony and afterwards was led home by the clerk". On the following day the Rector answered in a similar sworn statement that he was abused by the said John Trinbury in a very scandalous manner, being called a knave, a rascal and a "paultry scrub" and having his clothes pulled off his back by the said John and his wife and daughter.[1]

Of these activities of the Single Justice by far the most important was the administration of the Poor Laws, and this will be considered in some detail in a later chapter.

The executive functions of local government were mainly in the hands of the High Constables, the Treasurers and the Sheriff with his army of bailiffs. As nothing of importance has been revealed by the records touching the work of the last, except occasional com-

[1] MS. Session Rolls, Oct. 25, 1709. The Rector had already been presented on a charge of blasphemy for having given utterance to the following cogent question: Was God Almighty a drone? If not, what was he doing before he made the Earth? (Rolls Notts. Sessions, Dec., 1708). In regard to the habit of swearing, it may be remembered Squire Western permitted this indulgence to no one in the parish except himself.

plaints against the Sheriff's servants, it will not be treated further. One or two features of the offices of the High Constable and Treasurer will be briefly touched upon.

The High Constable.

In the seventeenth century one High or Chief Constable was appointed in each of the five smaller Hundreds—Rushcliffe, Broxtowe, Bingham, Thurgarton and Newark, and three in the very large Hundred of Bassetlawe, which was divided into three parts, North and South Clay and Hatfield.[1]

Towards the middle of the eighteenth century, however, the area over which the High Constable had authority was reduced by about half, each officer being responsible for one of the two divisions into which the five smaller Hundreds were divided. The High Constables were appointed by Quarter Sessions usually from the ranks of the yeoman farmers or lesser gentry,[2] and generally held their office for life.[3]

As in other parts of the country, the High Constables of Nottinghamshire found themselves gradually being deprived of certain independent functions which had invested them with quasi-magisterial powers, while at the same time their burden of administrative routine continued to grow more heavy. This is part of a tendency towards an oligarchical concentration of powers into the hands of the Justices which marks the history of the squirearchy in the eighteenth century; and the authority of the High Constables was its first victim. In 1683 they were forbidden to hold Private Sessions for hiring servants without the presence of two J.P.s, and in 1737 their power of calling meetings of Petty Constables for administrative purposes was severely curtailed, except when there happened to be no Monthly Meeting of Justices. Shortly afterwards, two High Constables were

[1] See Copnall, *op. cit.*, pp. 16–17. [2] *Ibid.*

[3] For appointment of Constables on decease of predecessor see MS. Minute Book, April 6, 1741; Jan. 13, 1741, etc., etc. For case of Chief Constable requesting to be relieved of his office on account of his great age, see *ibid.*, July 10, 1699.

actually presented for calling unnecessary meetings,[1] in spite of the notorious neglect of duty on the part of Petty Constables, particularly in regard to their attendance at Constable Juries[2] and Monthly Meetings and their failure to make presentments[3] and to send in lists of freeholders for service on juries. It would appear that the Justices regarded the decay of the Jury of Presentment without misgiving, the reason being probably that it left more scope for the method of presentment by the Single Justice and advanced the authority of the Justices' Bench.

In addition to his work as intermediary between Petty Constable and Quarter Sessions in judicial matters, the High Constable was entrusted with the duty of presenting and, on account of the non-existence of a county surveyor, of repairing decayed bridges in his division, he had to enforce the use of prescribed weights and measures, and make search from time to time for anyone using unlawful measures, he had to pay the expenses incurred by Petty Constables in the transporting of vagrants, and most important of all, he had to collect the County Rate, or as it was called in this county, the Quarter Dues, from the Petty Constables and hand them over to the Treasurer at Quarter Sessions.

The assessing and collecting of the County Rate was regularised by the Act of 1739[4] which empowered the Justices to make a general assessment for all county purposes upon each town and parish, the prescribed sum to be taken from the money raised by the Poor Rate. The parish accounts illustrate the procedure for the raising of county revenue more clearly. For instance, the Quarter Due of Bleasby appears to have been fixed at 6*s.* 7*d.* but varied in number collected from eighteen

[1] See Copnall, *Notts. County Records of Seventeenth Century,* p. 66; *Notes from Notts. Quarter Sessions,* 1736–7, p. 7; MS. Minute Book, Oct. 1, 1739.

[2] The penalty for this offence appears to have been 2*s.* 6*d.* per man. See MS. Minute Book, July 12, 1756.

[3] See *ibid.,* Oct. 2, 1738. In this case, the whole constable jury of Broxtowe were presented for this offence and fined sixpence each.

[4] 12 Geo. II, 29.

in 1753 to eight in 1759.[1] The collection seems to have taken place immediately before the Meeting of Quarter Sessions so that the Chief Constable could appear with the required quota and hand it over to the Treasurer; thus twelve were collected in January, ten in April, four in October, etc.[2]

The responsible and tedious duties of the High Constable were remunerated by a system of allowances which was regulated in 1739, according to the following scale:[3]

For every acquittance of Quarter Dues, 4*d.*
For every notice of Justices' Meetings, 3*d.*
Every freehold bill 6*d.*, and every assize bill 6*d.* and no more.

Many other troublesome and onerous tasks fell to the lot of the High Constable upon which the schedule is silent. It may be noted that the records have so far revealed no instance of a High Constable being dismissed from his office for corrupt practices or neglect.

The Treasurers.

For financial purposes the County was divided into two parts, over each of which a Treasurer was appointed. The north part consisted of the broad Hundred of Bassetlawe, the south part of Bingham, Newark, Thurgarton, Rushcliffe, and Broxtowe Hundreds. The south part, being considerably the more wealthy and populous of the two, contributed two-thirds to the county revenue, and the north part one-third. The Leen Bridge, for instance, was upheld at the expense of the whole County "in such proportion as other matters are contributed to, i.e. South Division to pay two-thirds, and North Division one-third".[4]

The office of Treasurer dated from the beginning of the seventeenth century, and was generally held by a substantial farmer, or a gentleman, often one of the Justices themselves.[5] For a short time in the middle of

[1] MS. Town Book Bleasby, 1753 and 1759. [2] *Ibid.*, 1765.
[3] MS. Minute Book, Jan. 14, 1739.
[4] *Ibid.*, Aug., 1732, Shire Hall Sessions.
[5] Copnall, *Notts. County Records of Seventeenth Century*, pp. 12–14.

the century the officers were amalgamated and the high salary of £27 per annum was paid to the single treasurer of the County.[1]

The chief objects of expenditure were the gaols, the bridges, the payment of salaries to gaolers and keepers of Houses of Correction,[2] the transport and maintenance of vagrants,[3] pensions to maimed soldiers, the provision of bread for prisoners in gaol, paying the Sheriff for the conveyance of prisoners, and providing compensation for the victims of highway robbery. The following interesting extract illustrates the last object of expenditure:

> It is therefore ordered by this court that the Treasurer of the hundred of Bassetlawe (where the robbery took place) doth on or before the 20th May next pay to the said Robert Williamson the said sum of £18 7*s.* which he was robbed of . . . . . out of the supply of two quarter dues now granted and ordered to be levied on the said Hundred for that purpose.[4]

Besides having to keep account of these transactions he not infrequently had to perform direct administrative duties which to modern ideas of division of labour were hardly compatible with the functions of the County Book-keeper. The Treasurer for the South Divisions had to view and repair the House of Correction, to provide cushions and carpets "for the use of the County", to employ one or more skilled workmen to view the County Buildings and make an estimate in writing of the charge of repairing and fitting them and to contract with them for the work to be done.[5] In keeping with the eighteenth-century custom, the remuneration of the Treasurers was scandalously low; the Treasurer for the south part appears to have received £18 per annum, his colleague for the north had the magnificent sum of £9

[1] MS. Minute Book, April 18 and 21, 1748.

[2] The prisons were theoretically self-supporting, but Caleb Parr, the Keeper of the County Gaol, complained that the fees from prisoners were very small and very seldom to be got, and so he was awarded a salary of £20 a year (Jan. 14, 1739). [3] *Op. cit.*, Oct. 4, 1725.

[4] Copnall, *Notes from Notts. Quarter Sessions*, 1736–7, p. 14.

[5] *Ibid.*, p. 11, etc.

per annum. It is an amazing feature of eighteenth-century life that the current administration of a large and populous county could be carried on with such insignificant cost, without giving rise to serious charges of corruption or negligence.

County and Parish.

To omit from a survey of the system of local government of the eighteenth century a consideration of the part played by the parish is impossible, but lack of space forbids more than a brief treatment. The records of the following villages have been examined: Bleasby, East Bridgford, Laxton, Sutton Bonington, Kingston-on-Soar, and the urban parish of St. Peter's, Nottingham; and although this does not exhaust the list of parishes of which documents are extant, they may be used as a basis for tentative reconstruction of that active organ of local administration and social life, the eighteenth-century parish, before it was finally "strangled" in the early nineteenth century.[1]

Of the six parishes examined, one appears to have been in the hands of a small group of leading farmers, and to have corresponded to the type generally known as the "close vestry". It is worthy of note that this parish, Kingston-on-Soar, had been enclosed at an early date and had suffered the usual effects of depopulation following upon conversion to pasture.[2] In the same district is Sutton Bonington, unenclosed until 1775–7, and showing unmistakable signs of corporate village action in which a considerable number of the inhabitants concur. The most democratic parish of all is certainly the urban parish, St. Peter's, which altered its boundaries, defied the Corporation, appointed a paid overseer, refused to accept the magistrates' nomination to one of the offices, called together its members by toll of church bell, and generally behaved like a vigorous, perhaps tumultuous, democracy, efficient as far as one can judge, and without recorded corruption. A type of parish government in-

[1] See Webb, *op. cit.*, pp. 146–72. [2] See p. 187.

termediate between the close oligarchy of Kingston and the more democratic bodies of Sutton Bonington and St. Peter's is illustrated by East Bridgford, Bleasby and Laxton. In this group, parish affairs appear to be in the hands of eight or ten persons, four or five of whom, in different selections, are responsible for signing the parish accounts year by year. At East Bridgford the Vicar's name is regularly found at the head of the signatures, the only case, with the exception of St. Peter's, in which there is evidence of the incumbent having taken any share in the administrative affairs of the parish.

There is little evidence of democratic control of parish affairs by the vestry in the records of these villages, but that is no real indication that reference to public opinion was never made. For example, the Bleasby documents contain no instance of a special meeting of the vestry to support the parish officers in some particular course of action as is the case in Sutton Bonington and St. Peter's, but there is evidence of the annual assembly of the Town Meeting. The nature of the business transacted at the Town Meeting is never disclosed; the only reason for its being recorded at all seems to be that it provided the constable with an excuse for charging a fee of one and sixpence for calling it.[1] Similar meetings in other parishes may have gone unrecorded because the officers did not make a charge for calling them. Thus lack of record of public meetings should not be taken as proof that they were never called, or that the parish as a whole had ceased to exercise any control over its communal affairs. This is further illustrated by the following case in which an overseer was brought by the inhabitants before a Justice of the Peace to answer for the malversation of parish funds. This occurred in the parish of Laxton where no direct record of popular control has been found. The decision of the Justice is entered in the parish book in the following terms:

[1] MS. Town Book Bleasby, 1748–79. Town meetings are very regular after 1776.

"Whereas complaint was made to me one of his Majesty's Justices of the Peace . . . by several inhabitants of the Parish of Laxton against the accounts of Thomas Skinner and Gervase Cullen in ye last 3 preceeding pages of this book particularly against the two last articles of forty shillings and 3 pounds pretended or said to be paid to John Hunter and Mr. J. Keyworth and whereas it appears to me upon a full hearing of ye said Inhabitants Skinner and Cullen that the said sums are not justly charged, the same being pd. by them upon their own acts only and not upon act of the Inhabitants or by or with their consent or privity. I do therefore disallow of the sd. two articles and adjudge that they are Debtors to the sd. Inhabitants upon the balance of the said accounts the sum of four pounds six shillings and fourpence farthing and do order them to pay the same to the present overseers of the poor.

E. A. W. BECHER."[1]

The above extract is the more interesting in the fact that four months earlier these same accounts had been allowed and passed by the ruling group, of whom no less than ten had appended their signatures.[2] This seems a clear case of the authority of the vestry exposing the doubtful practices of the parish officers and overriding the oligarchy who had connived at them.

The tendency of the parish to self-government was assisted by the apathy of the Justices, who, in the matter of filling parish offices, appear to have been satisfied with a mere ratification of the choice of the vestry. In the parish of St. Peter's, the churchwardens, sidesmen, "collectors of the poor," overseers and surveyors were appointed at the same public meeting as though the source of authority for all these offices resided equally in the vestry, and in one case, the recommendation of the Justices to the office of Overseer of the parish was actually turned down.[3] In East Bridgford even

[1] MS. Town Book Laxton, June 7, 1729. [2] *Op. cit.*, Feb. 8, 1728–9.

[3] April 15, 1754. These were the days in which the election of a Churchwarden might give rise to faction fights and pamphleteering as was the case at Newark in 1751 when the Vicar employed a great mob and an orchestra of French horns to intimidate the opponents of his own candidate. See *An impartial relation of some late Parish transactions at Newark*, 1751 (Bod. Lib., Gough Collection Notts. (II), 3).

the constable was nominated in the vestry meeting with the other parish officers; in Bleasby the Justices permitted the offices of Constable and Overseer to be filled by the same person, who also made himself responsible for the work of the surveyor; in Laxton and Sutton Bonington parish offices went by rotation among a group of inhabitants, in Kingston by the caprice of the oligarchy.

The corporate life of the vestry was further encouraged by the frequency with which it met to pass the accounts of the parish officers and the increasing responsibility which this entailed; the Poor Law officers usually presented theirs in May or June; the Constable and Surveyor of the Highway and occasionally the Field Master in October or December. As each of the overseers and churchwardens generally had separate accounts, there would, in a well-regulated parish where the full complement of officers was appointed, be at least six detailed accounts to check and audit regularly year by year. After 1760 when Poor Law accounts swell to three or four times their former bulk, this work would require close attention. The mere act of meeting together several times in the year to pass accounts and to fill vacant offices would tend to crystallise those who were interested in parish affairs into the character of a ruling group, and this was probably assisted by the realisation on the part of the retiring officer of the social possibilities which the event conferred. Thus William Bady of Sutton Bonington spent his balance of 1*s*. 10*d*. due to the town in settling the accounts of his office of Constable,[1] the officers of Laxton spent two shillings of the town's money in passing their accounts,[2] while it was agreed that the Overseers of St. Peter's were never more to include items for eating and drinking at any parish meeting in their accounts.[3]

Besides revealing the character of parish government as a whole, the records have brought out certain in-

[1] MS. Constables' Accounts Sutton Bonington, April 23, 1723.
[2] MS. Constables' Accounts Laxton, 1725.
[3] MS. Vestry Minutes St. Peter's, Nov. 21, 1786.

cidental features of considerable interest which may be briefly enumerated here. It was not unknown for women to fill and perform the offices of Overseer of the Poor and Surveyor of the Highway. Four cases of women overseers have been found,[1] two at Laxton and two at Sutton Bonington.[2] No difference is to be observed in the accounts of women officers; they take the same journeys, issue the usual doles of money and material and hand round the same gifts of shoes, hats, shifts and "britches". Three cases have been found of women performing the office of Surveyor of the Highway. The Town Book of Sutton Bonington, for instance, contains the following entry under the date December, 1752:

"Ann Winfield gave up her accompts as Surveyor of the Highways

Recd. by levy	5.	6.	11.
Made of the Town Bull . .	1.	14.	3½
	7.	1.	2½
Laid out	6.	8.	0.
Remains due to ye Towne . .		13.	2½

Allowed by us: JOHN OSBORNE, HART BUCK, THOS. WINFIELD."[3]

In each case, the holder of the office is a widow, a fact that suggests that the woman was unable or unwilling to find a substitute for her deceased husband when his turn to take office came round and so had to perform the duties herself.

The parish officers, of course, received no direct remuneration for their services, although from the frequent items for "my charges", it would seem that their expenses at least were refunded by the parish. One

[1] MS. Accounts of Overseer of Poor, Laxton, 1804 and 1806.

[2] MS. Town Book Sutton Bonington, 1753 and 1756.

[3] See also Accounts of Overseers of Highways, Laxton, 1804 and 1831, where Widow Ann Swinburn holds a similar office, but is not burdened with the care of the Town Bull.

case, however, has been found of the appointment of a salaried Overseer of the Poor; it occurs in the urban parish of St. Peter's, and was made in the following circumstantial manner:[1]

"Mem^d itt is agreed that the sd. George Pindar (just appointed Overseer) shall take care in a particular manner to save the Parish what money he can in Managing the Office of an Overseer and shall Act in the nature of a Parish Husband and shall assist in collecting the Assessment and Paying the poor wh. is the reason why no Collectors are chose this yeare and the sd. Parish does hereby agree to Allow the sd. George Pindar the sume of four pounds this next yeare for his pains."

In 1727 his salary was raised to £5 and one shilling for every certificate of settlement. He disappears after 1731 but between 1741–5 one of the Overseers is regularly paid a small salary on account of the extra trouble of the Workhouse, and in 1771 it was agreed that the Overseer, Mr. J. Ward, should receive ten guineas in addition to his ordinary allowance of fifteen shillings. Evidently the payment of one of the Overseers was fairly regularly undertaken by the Vestry of St. Peter's in the eighteenth century. It is hardly conceivable that St. Peter's, which was not the largest or most populous parish in the town, was unique in this respect, but the records of its neighbours do not exist to throw light upon the question. The duties of this over-worked officer in the country districts certainly went unremunerated, and when his multifarious and often disagreeable duties are considered—the collection of the poor rates, granting and refusing demands for relief, initiating the removal of newcomers who were liable to become chargeable, taking up the mothers of bastards before the Justices, arranging for the apprenticeship of children, making grants of money, food and clothing to the Workhouse, distributing coal and other forms of relief to the poor, having their cottages thatched, their shoes repaired, their clothes mended, buying tow

[1] MS. Vestry Minutes St. Peter's, 1718.

for their spinning and selling the product, giving relief to those who came in with Justices' "passes", helping the Constable in time of cattle plague, every item of which had to be entered up in the Vestry Book and submitted to the scrutiny of neighbours as well as magistrates —it is not surprising that his office was unpopular and too frequently filled by "obscure people, lacking in consideration for the feelings of the poor".[1]

Similar charges have been made against the Parish Constable,[2] and, considering the very large number of blank presentment papers [3] returned to the Quarter Sessions with the words "Omnia bene" or "we have nothing to present" scrawled across them, it would appear as though the villages were singularly free from crime or that the Constable took his police duties very lightly. As in the case of the Overseer, the Constables' neglect may be explained by the fact that the office was filled by the small farmers and "husbandmen" of the village, with other calls upon their time and energy besides those of their over-burdened office. Their expenses, of course, were covered by the parish and included in the "disbursements" as follows: [4]

For going to Nottingham—my charges .	2.	3*d.*
My charges at the sessions . . .	1.	10*d.*
" " " " size bill meeting . .	1.	6*d.*
" " " " land tax " . .	3.	0*d.*

Sometimes, however, the Constable received a special guerdon for the performance of duties demanding extraordinary courage, as when a sum of thirty-five shillings was paid to seven constables "who at the hazard of their lives guarded a Man to Prison for insulting the Mayor".[5]

[1] See the very noteworthy report of Committee on Parish Apprentices, 1767, where evidence of neglect is given from 1715. *H.C.J.*, Vol. 31, p. 248.

[2] For his reluctance to send a vagrant to be whipped, see Burn, *Hist. of Poor Law* (1764), p. 164.

[3] Sent in by the constable juries which sat for each division. One blank would therefore represent the work of probably a dozen constables.

[4] MS. Town Book Bleasby, 1751.

[5] Borough Records, Vol. VI, p. 258.

To cover the expenses of the Constable's office—the writing of notices and summonses, powder and shot for bird scaring, wages of the herdsman, etc., a levy, usually of 4*d*. or 6*d*. in the pound, was raised from the inhabitants of the parish.[1]

The police arrangements of the borough were, of course, different from those for rural parishes, and were undertaken, not by individual parishes, but by the Corporation. A list of 1754 shows that a force of no less than twenty-nine constables,[2] equipped with gilded staves bearing ferrules and spikes,[3] was employed by the Corporation. They were to present no person out of envy or ill-will, nor leave any unpresented for favour or affection,[4] and they were required to be sufficiently nimble and active to chase small boys from the Church Yard in time of Divine Service.[5]

Besides constables, the Corporation employed four blue-coated watchmen to guard the city's slumbers. They also were armed with staves and carried a hand-bell with which to raise the alarm in times of emergency.[6] The efficiency of this force was called in question in 1746 when it was complained that the Town was in great need of a good night watch against thieves and housebreakers, to supply which the Justices ordered the Constables to summon fourteen different householders each night who were to find fourteen able and sufficient men to watch the streets of the city, and so on every night until all householders had performed this duty, when a further order would be made touching the premises.[7]

The establishment of a force of Constables, however inefficient, under the authority of the Corporation, would at least obviate the confusion of function between the different officers which is so conspicuous a feature in the government of rural parishes. For instance, in

[1] See Constables' Accounts of Laxton where rate is usually given, and MS. Session Rolls, Jan. 29, 1718, for a new assessment at Beeston where the rate was 4d. in the pound rent.

[2] Borough Records, Vol. VI, p. 259.

[3] *Ibid.*, p. 176.

[4] *Ibid.*, p. 260.

[5] *Ibid.*, p. 266.

[6] *Ibid.*, pp. 77–9.

[7] *Ibid.*, p. 215.

Bleasby the Constable united the office of Overseer with his own, and included in his list of charges such items as "paid for ingin the Town geat" and "paid to cure the lass of Itch"; at East Bridgford, where the offices were divided, the Constable included items like the following among his accounts:[1]

Paid to the poor prisoners . . .	1. 0.
Paid on account of ye Base Child's Sickness and Buriall . . .	11. 9.

And the confusion was repeated in the orders of the Justices which, even in poor law matters, were addressed to the Constable as well as to the Overseers and Churchwardens. On the other hand, when the cattle plague was raging in the north of the County in 1758–9, it was to the overseers of the poor that the magistrates addressed themselves in their attempt to check the movement of cattle from parish to parish.[2] To the Justices the terms Overseer and Constable were roughly synonymous; it was left to those officers to sift their respective functions as best they could.

The Field Master.

In the Parish Books of Sutton Bonington and Laxton, side by side with the accounts of the statutory parish officers, there occur the accounts of an archaic village officer called the Field Master—an interesting link with manorial origins—whose duty it was to let the common grass of the town, and probably to supervise and pay the wages of the herdsmen and "field tenters" and pindars.[3] The Field Master's accounts were submitted to the scrutiny of the vestry and entered into the Parish Book side by side with those of the other parish officers. The accounts of the Field Tenter at Sutton Bonington for the year 1769 were entered as follows:

[1] MS. Constables' Accounts E. Bridgford, 1746.
[2] MS. Session Rolls, Sept. 17, 1758.
[3] In Bleasby and East Bridgford and sometimes in Laxton (i.e. 1786) this was done by the Constable.

Disburst.	18. 0. 10½
Recd. by Levy	17. 17. 9¾
Due to him	3. 0¾

Further, the policy of the village touching the question of letting the Town Grass was sometimes entered in the Vestry Minute Book, or as it was more frequently called, the Town Book.[1] The following is taken from the Town Book of Sutton Bonington under the date 1757:

"Agreed by those whose names are undersigned being Inhabitants in Sutton Bonington End to Lett every Horse Common in the said end att the rate of ten shillings a year and any person that hath any Commons unstockt to Receive ten shillings for every such unstockt Common the money arising from the Lett commons to be paid each year at Lammas to the Field Master.

And that the Cowe Commons shall be lett at the Rate of fifteen shillings a Common and for every unstockt common to be allowed ten shillings."

The Turn of the Century

Such was the structure of the County under the squirearchy; a group of humdrum, but dutiful magistrates at the top, with a handful of overworked and underpaid amateur officials below them, and at the bottom, the parish with its own vigorous corporate life revolving round the village "ruling group". Possibly we are understating the degree of energy which this system possessed. One magistrate at least brought an infectious enthusiasm to his work that could hardly be described as humdrum. We refer to Sir Thomas Parkyns, who, besides building a school, a hospital for four widows, a vicarage, a roof for the chancel of the Parish Church, and a monstrous house for himself; besides compiling a Latin Grammar which was to supersede all others, and scattering Latin inscriptions everywhere; besides writing a book on wrestling and practising the art himself and encouraging others to do the same by having a number of young men

[1] i.e. at Bleasby, East Bridgford and Sutton Bonington. The books of Laxton and Kingston have lost their title with their covers.

(beef-eaters all of them, for he could scarce tolerate a "sheep biter" or anyone else with a sign of a pap bottle about him) in the house to wrestle on the hearthrug in his drawing-room; besides these things he was an energetic magistrate, both in Quarter Sessions and in his own locality, and in 1721 produced a most interesting pamphlet on the subject of servants, who he declared had become the masters while the masters had vilely and contemptibly become their slaves. And in order to correct this unfortunate reversal of nature, he drew up a list of wages for nearly every industry in the County, and the Court of Quarter Sessions paid it the honour of including a portion of it in the Assessment of wages of 1723.

Perhaps Sir Thomas Parkyns represents the squirearchy at its best, and if it was, to modern standards, a poor best, it was good enough to keep the County quiet, reasonably secure in its life and property, and as far as we know, contented, for the better part of a century. There were, of course, occasional highway robberies, and in the borough, complaints of house-breaking and theft,[1] but there was none of that systematic lawlessness which made everyday life in London streets a perpetual adventure.[2] Towards the end of our period a change comes over the scene. Industrialism was spreading, not only into the framework knitting villages which had long been familiar with the harsh rhythm of the stocking frame, but also in the heart of the County, along the quiet banks of the Leen, the Meden and the Dover Beck, which from 1770 rapidly became dotted with the new cotton and worsted factories.[3] There was also a rising volume of complaint from underpaid workers faced with an increase of prices; harvests were less abundant after 1765 and population was growing; the grotesque system of Settlement was having its effect on the morals of the working population, and crime, vice, and drunkenness were everywhere on the increase.

[1] Borough Records, Vol. VI, p. 215.

[2] See Webb, *Statutory Authorities*, p. 408.

[3] See Lowe, *Agric. Survey*, pp. 70–1.

In 1787, owing to the activity of a group of Evangelical reformers led by Wilberforce, a society for the Reformation of the Manners among the Lower Orders was organised and proceeded to initiate a powerful campaign to awaken the magistrates to their moral as well as administrative responsibilities. In county after county the Justices' Bench was moved, not only to enforce the law with more vigour, but also to supply the deficiencies of the existing law by legislative and therefore extra-legal decisions of its own. At the behest of the newly awakened conscience of the Justices' Bench, the lawful but excessive pleasure seeking of the poor as well as the unlawful action of the criminal was made to come under the ban. The sale of drink, the number of public-houses, the times at which they might be open, were in many counties subjected to extra-legal regulation by the magistrates. In Nottingham a campaign developed towards the same end. It took the form of a complaint in the local press regarding the notorious increase of crime, the cause of which, it was asserted, was to be found in the leniency with which the owners of public-houses were treated by the magistrates. "Eleven felonies of the blackest sort" had been designed or executed in Nottingham, the reason being, according to the writer, that certain alehouses were allowed to harbour rascals. Quarter Sessions had ordered them to be suppressed, but nothing had been done. "Gentlemen are desired to be free in their censures whenever they find cause." [1] Whether this outburst had any definite effect we cannot say; at least in 1787 a decision was taken in the direction advocated. The Justices of the County declared their intention of refusing, when they sat in Brewster Sessions, to grant a spirit licence to any person who did not sell wine, chocolate, coffee, tea, ale, beer, or other liquors,[2] which clearly represents an attempt to

[1] *Nottingham Journal*, Jan. 16, 1779.

[2] Webb, *County and Parish*, p. 543, quoting *Nottingham Journal*, July 21, 1787. See also MS. Minute Book, July 9, 1787 (Liberty of Southwell and Scrooby).

prevent the exclusive sale of spirits in the demoralising atmosphere of the "gin palace".[1]

The action of the Justices was reinforced by voluntary self-protective measures on the part of the middle class of town and county. In 1788, a rotatory system of night watching was introduced in Nottingham by which the citizens undertook to guard each other's slumbers in turn, or by deputy.[2] About the same time an association was organised in the County for the purpose of detecting crime, and bringing it to the notice of the magistrates, who, it was said, welcomed any assistance to stem the rising tide of lawlessness. The following quotation from a speech by the President of "The Nottingham Association for the prosecution of felons and swindlers" will explain its objects and methods:

> "My principal aim has been to render it (i.e. the Society) a *Terror to evil doers*, a scourge to the lawless depredator . . . to be the means of checking the growing propensities of the fraudulent and designing in order to protect the property of the neighbourhood in general, and that of our own members in particular . . . and the concurrence of the Magistracy with our united exertions, (has been shown) by granting allowances in aid of the expenses attending such convictions; and in some instances, even where conviction was not obtained, the efforts were judged so laudable as to procure unsolicited remuneration. . . . It would redound much to the general good of the Association were every Member to be secretly watchful over the conduct of such as are in the least suspected (in their neighbourhood), especially such as have been in their employment, and who know the different apartments and recesses in their Dwellings or other buildings, and to be circumspectly vigilant in pursuing (the least trace of guilt) through the most intricate mazes and windings. . . ."[3]

The zeal of the members was stimulated by means of a system of rewards, graduated according to the type of

[1] For similar policy pursued in London, see George, *London Life in Eighteenth Century*, p. 36. At the same time there was an agitation led by Gilbert Wakefield for the building of a new town gaol. See *Memoirs* by Gilbert Wakefield, I, p. 300.

[2] Blackner, *Hist. of Nottm.*, p. 281.

[3] Articles of the New Nottinghamshire Association for the prosecution of felons and swindlers instituted in the year 1789—published 1814, Nottingham Ref. Library.

crime for which conviction was secured: in the case of murder or arson, ten guineas; horse stealing and forgery, five guineas; swindling, four guineas, etc.

At the time the above speech was made (1814) this Society had been in existence thirty years, and according to the statement of its president, had diffused itself through all sections of society over a great part of England and Ireland. Societies were also formed for more charitable purposes; for distributing funds to deserving families, for providing fuel and clothes in winter-time, or free medical attention, and above all, for providing education for the poor. The existing system of government had failed, wholly or in part, to supply these needs and new voluntary organisations rapidly emerged to fill the many gaps which it left. They went further; not only did they supplement the government of the squirearchy; they began to supersede it. The work of "enlightening the streets" of Nottingham was taken over by a body of Commissioners under a special Act obtained in 1761, and so relieved the Corporation of a duty that was soon to become onerous. Unions of parishes under "Incorporated Guardians of the Poor" began to reappear in the latter half of the century and take over the duties of County and Parish in regard to the poor law, in spite of the failure that had attended similar experiments at the end of the seventeenth century. Again, owing to the collapse of the system of parochial road repair, a new authority, or rather a host of new authorities, the Turnpike Trustees, sprang up to take its place. These were followed by the development of a similar organisation of canal transport, the Cromford, Nottingham, and Grantham Canal Acts being obtained in rapid succession towards the close of the century.[1] By this time the County was linked up with the chief industrial districts of the country; the tempo of its economic life had been speeded

[1] 29, 32 & 33 Geo. III—see collection of Local Acts in Nottingham Ref. Library. The Act of 1761 for "Enlightening the Streets, Lanes, and Passages of Nottingham" appointed a body of Trustees which was empowered to raise a rate of not more than £230 per annum for the purpose of providing lamps and paying lamplighters, etc.

up and a new race of masters—the Smiths, the Arkwrights, the Strutts and the Morleys—were sharing the power of the squirearchy, and also their responsibilities. But though the squirearchy was assisted, or even superseded, by the emergence of new voluntary organisations, the Magistrates' Bench was more than ever the supreme authority in the County. Its authority was enhanced by the respect in which it was held by the Government, which accepted its guidance in social policy. The most outstanding case of this was, of course, the inauguration of the Justices' Poor Law by the magistrates of Berkshire, who laid down on their own authority a scale of relief for underpaid labourers which became the basis of national policy towards the poor. Quarter Sessions were now, more clearly than ever before, a quasi-legislative body, a creator as well as an administrator of the law. Moreover, whatever democratic characteristics the system had formerly possessed were being imperceptibly shorn away; the Grand Jury, composed of substantial men of the County with administrative as well as judicial duties, was, by the end of the century, practically excluded from all share in local government; the High Constables had similarly lost all traces of independent authority; the constable juries of the divisions of the County seem to have fallen into decay, and their function of making presentments had been taken over by the Single Justice acting on his own authority. The Justices were thus a local oligarchy, free not only from the supervisory authority of the central government but from the checks which the juries and High Constables had formerly been able to exercise. They worked to an increasing extent through a staff of paid servants, and withdrew from the publicity of the open court into the privacy of magistrates' meetings. Thus decisions upon county policy—particularly in regard to poor law expenditure and the licensing of public-houses—decisions of great importance to the bulk of the county inhabitants—were taken in private and promulgated with the force of law.

To what extent this authority was used for evil and

oppression is beyond the scope of this book; the records of the last years of the eighteenth century and the first thirty years of the nineteenth century, which alone can answer the question, have not been examined, but there is no doubt that an intense reaction against the overwhelming authority of the Justices' Bench was felt throughout the country towards the end of this period. The explanation is not to be found in the selfishness or corruption of the Justices in regard to the policy pursued in county affairs. In their expenditure upon poor relief, upon new gaols and county halls, one of which was built in Nottingham in 1773 and is still in use, upon workhouses and bridges, and in their somewhat pedantic control of liquor licensing, they were certainly not pursuing their own material ends; indeed, in so far as these activities increased (as they did) the amount of county rates, the magistrates were laying burdens upon themselves; but in the administration of one department of their authority they were undeniably guilty of a gross, indeed, tyrannical abuse of power. We refer to their administration of the Game Laws.

"It is characteristic of the country gentlemen," write Mr. and Mrs. Webb,[1] "that it was not to the love of money that their judicial impartiality and intellectual integrity succumbed, but to their overmastering desire to maintain their field sports and protect the amenity of their country seats. . . . In the hands of the country gentleman of the eighteenth century and still more of the beginning of the nineteenth century, the Game Laws became, it is clear, an instrument of terrible severity,"

and they go on to quote the furious words of Brougham:

"There is not a worse constituted tribunal on the face of the earth . . . than that at which summary convictions on the Game Laws take place. I mean . . . a brace of sporting magistrates. I am far from saying that . . . they are actuated by corrupt motives, but they are undoubtedly instigated by their abhorrence of that *caput lupinum*, that *hostis humani generis* . . . that *feræ naturæ*—a poacher."

[1] Webb, *Parish and County*, pp. 597 *et seq*.

And it was largely owing to the universal indignation which the Game Laws aroused that the squirearchy were so ruthlessly stripped of their powers in the period of reform from 1828–35; they continued as a bench of magistrates because no other feasible alternative presented itself; but they were no longer the unchallenged autocrats of the countryside.

PART II

THE RISE OF MODERN INDUSTRY AND AGRICULTURE

CHAPTER IV

DISTRIBUTION OF INDUSTRY AND POPULATION

THE surface configuration of Nottinghamshire, at the first glance, contains few striking features. Closer observation will show, however, that the County forms part of a definite geographical district, lying within well-marked natural boundaries. On the west are the hills of Derbyshire; on the east are the Lincolnshire Cliff and the Belvoir Ridge (a spur of the Leicestershire Wolds), and the south is closed in by the old granite rocks of Charnwood. The shallow saucer of Nottinghamshire which lies between is crossed through the east centre by the Trent, which, at its entry into the County at Thrumpton, forms a natural gateway between the highlands of the adjoining counties of Leicester and Derby. Near the same place it receives two important tributaries, the Derwent from Derbyshire and the Soar from Leicestershire, along the valleys of which modern railway lines run to converge at the pivot of Trent Junction, just over the border. The accompanying map illustrates the geographical unity of the county more clearly.

The parallel system of hills on the east and the west, with the broad Trent Valley between, caused the main lines of communication to take a north and south direction. Of these there were two, one on the east from Nottingham via Bingham to Newark, East Retford and Bawtry, the other on the west through the villages of Basford, Bulwell, Linby to Mansfield, Worksop and the North. The former and more important route pivoted upon the half-way town of Newark, which, from the point of view of communications, was in a fortunate position. Situated at the junction of two important roads and commanding the only bridge over the Trent east of the Pennines which gave on to an unobstructed road to the north, it was regarded as the most convenient gateway between North and South. In 1609 it was described as a great thoroughfare and a post town, "and the Kinges subjects" it was said "do usually travel from the north parts unto the south parts through the said town and likewyse back again",[1] and as late as 1795, when modern industry in the form of cotton factories and breweries was making its appearance in the town, the majority of the population were said to be tradesmen and inn-keepers.[2]

East Retford, the next town on the route and third borough in the County, was more notorious for its political corruption than notable for its economic importance. It was situated on the River Idle and drove a considerable river trade in lead from Derbyshire, timber from Sherwood Forest and wheat from surrounding claylands, all of which were generally transhipped at East Stockwith or Gainsborough for Hull or Nottingham. The cutting of the Chesterfield-Stockwith canal in 1775, which killed the trade of Bawtry, hitherto an inland port of considerable renown, stimulated that of East Retford,[3] which now had a direct line of communication between the agricultural east and the manufacturing west.

The corresponding road system that threaded the western side of the county passed from Nottingham via the Forest towns of Basford, Bulwell, Papplewick and Linby to Mansfield, and thence to Worksop, Bawtry and the North. Of these towns, Mansfield and Worksop were the most important calling places, and were described by Leland as pretty market towns.[4] Both were

[1] Cornelius Brown, *Hist. of Newark*, Vol. I, p. 179, quoting Exchequer depositions. [2] *Ibid.* [3] Throsby's edition of Thoroton, III, p. 280.

[4] Leland's *Itinerary* (Hearne's edition), Vol. I, pp. 84 and 85. Throsby is at fault when he quotes Leland as describing Mansfield as a "pore street", Throsby's edition of Thoroton, II, p. 312.

centres of thriving agricultural populations, made up largely of yeoman farmers, enjoying the blessings of an expanding market and a steady price for their product. It is worth noting, too, that Mansfield, from the time of Elizabeth, boasted of a Free Classical Grammar School, endowed by local landed proprietors, but the rise of manufactures in the eighteenth century, we are told, caused a relapse of classical learning and led to its displacement by an education more suitable to the needs of a rising industrial centre.[1]

By 1795 the town boasted of several cotton and woollen spinning factories, a vigorous trade in wall and building stone, and a large stocking manufacture.[2]

The economic development of Nottinghamshire before the growth of textiles and mining depended mainly on its favourable geographical situation as a convenient corridor between the North and South, and on its production of grain, sheep and cattle, and of timber from the Forest. Its relative position in the counties may be shown by the following list of seventeenth-century assessments:

Date of Assessment.	Position of County of Nottingham out of 40 English Counties.
1636	21st
1641	29th
Mar. 25. 1649	29th
Dec. 25. 1649	28th
1660	28th
1672	28th
1693	24th
	Position of Borough of Nottingham out of 18 towns assessed.
1641	15th
	Out of 13 towns assessed.
1649	11th

[1] See Ch. IX.

[2] Throsby's Thoroton, II, p. 314. There were 700 hand-frames in Mansfield in 1800. Horner Groves, *Hist. of Mansfield*, p. 366.

In each case, the county of Rutland, one-sixth of the area of Nottinghamshire, paid a higher assessment. The reason for the comparatively low position of Nottinghamshire in the scale of counties is found in the following terse summary of its resources by Sir George Savile, one of the biggest (and best) of its landowners. "The idea I gave Lord Rockingham of this county" he writes in 1769 "was four Dukes, two Lords and three rabbit warrens, which, I believe, takes in half the county in point of space." [1]

Population.

In proportion to area the population was small. The most densely populated parts were the Vale of Belvoir, where the villages clustered thickly together, and the valleys of the Trent and Soar; at the other extreme were the Wolds, the marshy "Car land" in the north, and the Forest district where villages were generally small and widely separated. According to the Hearth Tax returns of 1690 the total number of houses in the County was 17,818,[2] which may be said, roughly, to represent a population of from 90 to 95,000, or not much more than three times what it had been in Domesday.[3] A century later, in 1793, a careful census of the County was taken by private persons, according to which the population was 115,598.[4]

These figures, of course, include the population of the Borough of Nottingham, which Macaulay states was about 8,000 in 1685.[5] This estimate, however, seems to be excessive, as the number of householders paying hearth tax in 1674 was only 967, which (if every householder was included) would give a population of

[1] The list of assessments is given in Thorold Rogers, *Hist. of Agric. and Prices*, Vol. V, pp. 118–20. For Sir Geo. Savile's remark, see Hist. MSS., Comm. 26, Papers of Savile Foljambe, p. 147.

[2] Chalmers' estimate, quoted by Cunningham, *Ind. and Comm. Modern*, p. 700.

[3] A conservative estimate of the population in Notts. in Domesday is 28,300. I owe this to the kindness of Miss H. M. Keating, who is investigating local population changes. [4] Lowe, *Agric. Survey of Notts.* (1798), p. 177.

[5] Macaulay, *Hist. of England*, Vol. I, p. 265.

between 5–6,000.[1] Sixty years later when Deering wrote, after the town had become one of the chief centres of the rising industry of framework knitting, the population was stated to be 9,890, a figure which is increased by later estimates to 10,720.[2] Forty years later, in 1779, another census of the town was taken and the figure arrived at was 17,711, a significant rise in so short a period.[3] The distribution among the parishes was as follows:

Parish of	No. of Houses. Inhabited.	Empty.	Families.	Souls.
St. Mary's .	2,314	57	2,584	12,637
St. Peter's .	446	10	497	2,445
St. Nicholas .	431	9	475	2,502
	3,191	76	3,556	
Brewhouse Yard (extra parochial)				127
				17,711

The relative increase from 1674 may be given as follows:

Year.	Population.	Rate of Increase per Annum.
1674	5–6,000	—
1739	10,720	80
1779	17,711	174·8
1793	25,000 [4]	520·6
1801	28,861 [5]	482·6

The reason for the large increase from 1674 must be attributed partly to the migration of rural workers to find employment in the framework knitting industry, and partly to the excess of births over deaths. The first of these causes is seen at work in the parallel list of industries given by Deering for the years 1641 and 1739.[6] They show a considerable decline in several trades — tanners, ironmongers, linen-weavers, were

[1] Quoted by Potter Briscoe, *Chapters in Notts. History*, p. 54.
[2] Deering, *Hist. of Nottm.*, p. 13, and Lowe, *Agric. Survey of Notts.* (1798), p. 186.
[3] Lowe, *op. cit.*, p. 184.
[4] *Ibid.*, p. 175.
[5] *V.C.H.*, II, p. 317.
[6] Deering, *op. cit.*, pp. 94–5.

greatly reduced in numbers—but the tailors had increased from 28 to 52, bakers from 22 to 40, and inn-keepers from 14 to 41. By far the greatest increase, however, had taken place in the framework knitting industry. In 1641 the town boasted of only two master framework knitters; in 1739 there were fifty employing no less than 1,200 frames.

It is probable that the same effect was experienced in the villages where framework knitting took root. The only published material for a study of the movement of population in the villages is the marriage registers, a source that can give no more than a rough estimate. Several marriage registers have been examined in this connection with interesting results. The number of marriages contracted in the framework knitting villages,[1] in every case examined, shows a marked tendency to increase in the period 1740–60, and the increase is continued into the nineteenth century.

The increase among the industrialised villages may be contrasted with the static condition of the purely agricultural villages, the registers of which give no indication of a definite movement in any direction.[2] In the case of the mining villages like Nuttall, Trowell, Teversall, the evidence of increase, though certainly visible, is much less marked than where the framework knitting industry was followed.

If the history of the stocking-making villages were pursued into the nineteenth century it would show that they continued to expand by fairly regular increases at each census during the first fifty years of the nineteenth century. After that a marked decline took place, so that in some cases the population at the end of the century was little more than half what it had been in 1850. While the stocking industry retained its domestic characteristic of home production it provided the main source

[1] The marriage registers of the following villages have been examined for the period 1700–1800: Woodborough, Oxton, Calverton, Lambley, Gedling, Cotgrave, Basford, Beeston.—*Marriage Registers of Notts.*, Phillimore and Blagg.

[2] See register for Colston Bassett, Kelham, Plumtree, Maplebeck.

of livelihood for thousands of village folk; but upon the gradual introduction of the power-driven factory about 1850 in the town and its environs, the village industry began to decay and the population to dwindle.[1]

The second cause is the excess of births over burials. This may be shown as follows:

	Baptisms per thousand.	Burials per thousand.
1732–9	35·9	31·1
1772–8	?	32·4
1789–93	36·8	28·8

From the beginning of the eighteenth century Nottingham had the reputation of a clean and healthy town. Deering in 1739 wrote: "Agues are rare, few men Hypochondriacal, few women afflicted with Hysterical Disorders, nor do we meet with many Rainbow Complexions. . . ." About 6 per cent. of the population reached the age of seventy, but among the infant population the mortality was extremely high: nearly 40 per cent. of those who were born died in infancy. This may be further illustrated by the following quotations from the christenings of High Pavement Chapel: [2]

Esther, the fourteenth child and the sixth now living.
Samuel, the fourteenth child and the sixth now living.
Samuel, the nineteenth child and second now living.

For a time, the rate of infant mortality actually went up, as we show above, and the following illuminating explanation is given: "Where poor people are forced

[1] See *V.C.H.*, II, pp. 311 *et seq.*, for rise and fall of population in Bingham, East Bridgford, Cotgrave, Calverton, Oxton, Woodborough, Lambley, Epperstone, etc. In some villages, i.e. Ruddington, Arnold, etc., power-driven factories were established on the spot and population continued to grow. For the best treatment of population at this time, see Griffiths, *Population Problems at the Time of Malthus*, and also *Econ. Journal*, Hist. Section, 1929, p. 429.

[2] Warren, "Early Records of a Presbyterian Congregation", in *Transactions of the Unitarian Historical Society*, Vol. I, April, 1917 (Nottingham Ref. Library). Many similar examples, it is said, could be given. Deering gives the following figures for the period 1732–9: Births, 2,694; died in infancy, 1,072. It should be noted, the year 1736 is omitted, when small-pox caused the deaths to exceed births by more than 380; pp. 78–82.

to neglect their offspring to procure a subsistence, it is no wonder if half of those who are born die young."[1] Towards the end of the century, however, several causes operated to reduce this wastage of life. Certain improvements in diet such as a constant, in fact excessive, supply of fresh meat, a development of market gardening and the sale of green vegetables, the substitution of tea for beer, which was making marked progress even among the working population, as Deering shows, no doubt helped to improve the health at least of the adult population; in 1781 these influences were re-inforced by the foundation of the General Hospital, which, besides saving lives, was a permanent laboratory for the study of diseases. Doctors and nurses were at last able to learn their business under conditions which made scientific observation possible; in 1790 they opened a special fever ward and by the beginning of the nineteenth century vaccination for small-pox was being administered without charge. It is scarcely surprising therefore that, towards the end of the century, the rate of mortality should show a tendency to decline, e.g. from 32·4 to 28·8 per thousand of the population.

Another factor in the growth of population was a slight increase in the birth-rate. This may be partly due to the decay of the Apprenticeship regulations. While men were compelled to serve a seven years' apprenticeship before being able to earn a journeyman's wage, or permitted to marry, the age of marriage was postponed longer than it would otherwise have been. With the rise of capitalist industry and the widespread collapse of the apprenticeship system in the eighteenth century, youths in their teens could earn as much as grown men, and the bar to early marriage was removed. Indeed, early marriage and a large family were encouraged by the economic condition of an industry like framework knitting in which much of the work was done in the homes of the workmen and shared by members of his family. Stockingers were notorious for their early

[1] Lowe, *op. cit.*, p. 186.

marriages and large families. At the same time, owing to the policy of paying rent out of poor-rates, there was a plentiful supply of houses—a gilt-edged security to landlords—and another bar to early marriages was removed.

Industries.

Until the economic changes of the nineteenth century took place, Nottinghamshire was essentially an agricultural county. The extensive clay lands north and south of the Trent were especially suitable for corn-growing, while the valleys of the Trent, Soar, Smite and Devon provided very rich pasture land. In spite of these advantages, food scarcity was far from being unknown. The *State Papers* for the sixteenth and seventeenth centuries contain many reports from the County Justices complaining of the shortage of corn, and giving their attempts to share up the existing supplies as equitably as possible,[1] and even in the eighteenth century occasional food riots, caused more by increase of price than actual shortage, were not unknown.[2] These outbursts would have occurred more frequently had it not been for the ease with which supplies of provisions could be brought into the town by means of the river Trent. Deering, in his list of imports by the river, includes "grocer's goods",[3] and notices frequently appear in the local press announcing the arrival of vessels at Gainsborough laden with foodstuffs for Nottingham.[4]

The import of foodstuffs was made easier by the existence of abundant coal supplies in the immediate neighbourhood of the town, which were exchanged for the agricultural produce of neighbouring counties, a circumstance for which the Justices in periods of food shortage had reason to be thankful.[5]

[1] *S.P. Dom.*, 1587, Vol. CXCVIII, Feb. 22, No. 57; 1631, June 13, Vol. CXCIII, No. 79; 1631, April 2, Vol. CLXXXIX, No. 12, etc.

[2] Bailey, *Annals of Notts.*, p. 1,231; *Cal. H.O. Papers,* Oct. 31, 1766, Nos. 301, 302.

[3] Deering, *op. cit.*, p. 91.

[4] Ayscough's *Nottingham Courant,* 1758–62, and Cresswell's *Nottingham Journal,* 1762–83, *Leicester and Nottingham Journal,* 1758–83.

[5] *S.P. Dom.*, Jas. I, CXIII, No. 22.

Coal.

Very little is known of the coal industry of Nottinghamshire. Its antiquity is shown by the fact that coal was mined at Cossall on the Manor of William de Mortein as early as the reign of Edward I.[1] So scanty, however, is the information regarding the growth of the industry that Galloway, the historian of coal-mining, asserts that the Nottinghamshire Coalfield was scarcely heard of at all in the seventeenth century.[2] Yet to the seventeenth-century inhabitant of Nottingham a constant supply of coal for daily use seems to have been one of the accepted amenities of his life. So plentiful was the supply that he "who at night when he goes to bed has not a handful of fuel, may the next morning in the shortest day of winter, have coals brought to his door to dress his dinner with".[3]

This particular good fortune arose from the proximity of the Wollaton pits which, from the sixteenth century, supplied the town with fuel.[4] The Wollaton pits were situated at the southern extremity of a line of surface mines on the edge of the limestone ridge that stretched along the western boundary of the County from Shireoaks in the north to the Leen at Nottingham. Until the middle of the nineteenth century this low escarpment formed the eastern boundary of the Midlands Coalfield. It was thought that the coal seams either did not continue under the limestone, or that the general eastwards dip of the strata would involve boring to too great a depth.[5] The miners of the eighteenth century never ventured eastwards of a line from Teversall southward to the Leen, through the villages of Brookhill, Eastwood, Bilborough and Wollaton.[6] According to the survey of 1774

[1] Caley MSS., Nottingham Ref. Library, quoting Escheats, 12 Edward I, p. 26.

[2] Galloway, *Annals of Coal Mining*, p. 188. Cf. also *Coal Industry of the Eighteenth Century*, by Ashton and Sykes (1929).

[3] Anonymous Historian of Nottingham, 1641, printed in *Thor. Soc. Trans.* (1898), Vol. II, p. 27.

[4] Hist. MSS. Com. 42, *Middleton Papers*, p. 172, etc.

[5] *Concealed Coalfield of Yorks and Notts.*, by Walcot Gibson, p. 1.

[6] Lowe, *Agricultural Survey*, p. 5.

Nottinghamshire possessed fourteen pits, three at Wollaton, three north of Bilborough, three south of Nuttall, two between Eastwood and Langley Mill, and three at Teversall.[1]

The further development of the mining industry in this county was very slow. For the first forty years of the nineteenth century the horse-gin was still the main source of winding power; the men themselves were often lowered into the pits by means of chains round their thighs, and the method of working seems to have been based upon a private agreement between contractors who got the coal and the owner or lessee whose business was confined to selling.[2] So little is known of the history of Nottinghamshire coal-mining before 1840 that no further account of its development is possible and any further references that may be made to it here will be confined to the wages of the workmen and the price of the commodity.[3]

Framework Knitting.

The most interesting, and it may be said, the most important feature of the economic history of this county has still to be mentioned—namely, the Framework Knitting industry. The romantic story of its inception, and the heroic struggles of the Calverton clergyman, spurred on by the coyness of his sweetheart and the caprice of the Queen, need not be told again, but it may at least be said that no other great industrial invention has sprung so completely equipped from the brain of a man, without (as far as is known) the prompting of

[1] Chapman's *Survey of Notts.*, 1774.—Coal was also mined at Selston from the time of Edward IV (Caley MSS., No. 67).

[2] The contractors were known locally as the butty, who was in charge of the underground working, and the stever, who saw to the sorting and stacking of the coal at the pit-head. "Stever" is not to be found in the *New Oxford Dictionary*, but occurs as "stover" in the *Middleton Papers*, p. 169. The above account is based upon the written statement of a Nottinghamshire miner and upon family tradition, the present writer's ancestors having worked mines in the way described above.

[3] For later history of mining in Notts., see *Rambles round Nottm.*, 1856, Nottingham Ref. Library.

economic demand, or the suggestion derived from earlier experiments. It was the spontaneous production of a great mechanical genius, incarcerated in a country parsonage, and born in an age when the fruits of mechanical invention were distributed, not according to principles of justice, but according to principles of State. Queen Elizabeth, fearful of its effects upon the hand-knitters, frowned upon the stocking frame.[1] William Lee took it to France and died there, it is said, of a broken heart. By sheer good fortune the seed which he had sown remained embedded in English soil, and at first by slow stages and then by rapid strides, developed into the hosiery industry of to-day, with its ramifications in every part of the world. An attempt will be made in later chapters to trace in some detail the economic organisation of the industry from its beginning in 1589, but it is sufficient here to indicate its development in the different localities where it took root as far as available statistics will permit.

The first seventy years of the history of framework knitting was a period of comparatively slow progress. The machine as perfected by Lee was able to produce work as fine in quality as that of the most skilful hand-knitter and at ten times the speed, yet in 1664, after seventy years of life, the industry could muster no more than 650 frames.[2]

This slow progress may possibly be accounted for by the opposition of the hand-knitters. Elizabeth was no doubt actuated by solicitude for the hand-knitters when she refused to grant Lee a reward for his invention,[3] and it is known that the first frame-worker to establish himself in Leicester encountered great prejudice against woven stockings and had to work in secrecy and at night.[4] It is also worthy of note that the petition sent to Cromwell in 1655 for the incorporation of the industry included

[1] There seems no reason to discount Henson's account of the treatment of Lee by Elizabeth or to doubt that he failed to obtain a patent.

[2] Henson, p. 60. [3] *Ibid.*, p. 45.

[4] Gardiner, *Music and Friends*, p. 811; and Thomson, *Hist. of Leicester* (1849), Vol. I, p. 436.

strong assurances that no harm was to be apprehended by the hand-knitters by the introduction of the frame. "The common tedious way of knitting," the petitioners say,[1] "multiplies needy people here rather because the people of other nations outwork those of this therein rather than by any hindrance they receive from the best artisans of this manufactory." The "best artisans" they point out, "bend their endeavour all they can to the foreign vent, as well as leaving the home sale in great part to the common knitters"; and what harm was done to the hand-knitters was the work, they maintain, of those who had intruded themselves into the industry without serving a proper apprenticeship and who refused to submit to the control of the majority of frame-workers who had already formed themselves into a self-styled Company. They go on to claim that the industry "is fit to be owned as a native establishment and as the nonpareil of handicrafts", and loftily deride those who urge "the same exploded clamours against the use of engines in trading which the file and hammer workers of a single pin did heretofore".

In spite of these elaborate apologies, the stocking frame could not fail to have a disastrous effect upon the hand-knitting industry when it is realised that the maximum production of the hand-knitter was a hundred loops a minute, while in the same time Lee's perfected frame could knit from 1,000 to 1,500.[2] Nevertheless, it would be a mistake to think that the hand-knitting industry was necessarily doomed to rapid extinction. As Miss Pinchbeck has shown, it survived under miserably sweated conditions in many parts of the British Isles until the end of the eighteenth century, and in parts of Scotland until the twentieth.[3] Its effect upon the chief

[1] Petition to Cromwell, 1655, given in Deering, *op. cit.*, pp. 303–7, and referred to *S.P. Dom.*, 1655, Dec. 27, Vol. CII, No. 72.

[2] J. H. Quilter in *Hosiery Trade Journal*, Feb., 1902.

[3] Apparently the hand-knitters of Cumberland and Westmoreland were not affected until the second half of the eighteenth century. For the best treatment of this question see Pinchbeck, *Women in Industrial Revolution*, pp. 226 *et seq.*

centres of industry was, however, disastrous, as the following extract from Defoe shows:

"The city of Norwich and parts adjacent were for some ages employed in manufacturing stuffs and stockings. The latter trade which was once considerable is in a manner wholly transported to London by the vast quantity of hose wove by the frame, which is a trade within this 20 years almost wholly new, . . . and whereas the hose trade from Norfolk once returned at least 5,000 shillings a week and as some say twice that sum 'tis not now worth naming." [1]

Besides having to face the opposition of the hand-knitters, the first framework knitters had to struggle hard to keep the industry from being transplanted abroad. By a series of accidents, the attempts of foreigners to capture the industry failed, and it remained to the end of the century essentially an English handicraft.

Through all its early vicissitudes the industry never completely deserted the county of its origin, Nottinghamshire, where there were over 100 frames at work in 1660.[2] By far the most important centre of manufacture, however, was London, which, at this time, boasted of 400 frames, mainly in the districts of St. Luke's, Norton Folgate and Shoreditch.[3] To these must be added a considerable number that found their way abroad in spite of all efforts of the Framework Knitters' Company and of the Government.[4] In 1696 a final effort was made to put a stop to the exportation of stocking frames by the Act 7 and 8, William III, 20, which imposed the heavy fine of £40 as well as the forfeit of the machines upon anyone found exporting frames or any part of a frame.

[1] Defoe, *Giving Alms no Charity*, 1704, p. 19.

[2] Report of Commission into Condition of Framework Knitters, 1845, p. 15, based apparently upon Henson, p. 60. Henson gives no authority for his statistics here or elsewhere, but as no other evidence exists for the statistical history of the industry before Deering, his figures have been accepted as they stand.

[3] Henson, p. 60.

[4] See *S.P. Dom.*, March, 1660, Vol. CCXX, No. 53; August, 1678, pp. 373, 375, 396, 399; and *Britannia Languens*, p. 409 (*Early English Tracts of Commerce*, MacCulloch), where it is stated that the silk and woollen stocking industry was much decayed owing to foreign competition.

From the Restoration to the end of the century was a period of rapid expansion if the figures given by Henson are reliable. By 1695, the number of frames in London was said to have increased to 1,500; many had been taken to Ireland and about 400 had been exported.[1] The main stimulus of this rapid growth was the vigorous export trade, and even France, our chief commercial and political rival, imported about 8,000 dozen hose from the Port of London per annum until the outbreak of war in 1692.[2] The loss of trade with France on account of the long war was made up by the increase of trade with Portugal, which, in the first years of the eighteenth century, imported each year nearly 20,000 dozen hose.[3]

The commercial *rapprochement* with France at the end of the war in 1713 was loudly condemned by the English wool merchants, who feared that the profitable trade with Portugal would be thereby endangered. Among the numerous petitions sent up to the House of Commons from all parts of the country, one purported to come from the "Merchants, principal Traders, Masters, and great numbers of Workmen belonging to the trade and Manufacture of Framework Knitting in behalf of themselves and several thousands in the Town of Nottingham and places adjacent".[4] The petition set forth that to discourage the trade with Portugal would prove of evil consequence to the Stocking Industry, the decay of which would tend to the utter ruin of thousands of families who would become burdensome to the parishes they lived in. From this it would appear that the industry had reached considerable proportions in the Midlands at this time. It may be noted further that among the large number of petitions presented on this subject none came from the framework knitters of London

[1] Henson, p. 87.

[2] *House of Commons Journals*, Vol. 18, pp. 394 and 398.

[3] *Ibid.*, Vol. 17, p. 397—amounts of export of hose to Germany, Spain, Lisbon, Constantinople, etc., are given in the *Nottingham Mercury*, 1715–20.

[4] *H.C.J.*, Vol. 17, p. 408.

or from the Company, who seemed content to let their brethren of the Midlands take the lead. This fact, taken in conjunction with Henson's account of the migration of stockingers from London to Nottinghamshire about the same time,[1] suggests that the centre of gravity was gradually moving to the Midlands. The following figures are given for the year 1727,[2] and illustrate this movement more clearly:

In the South.		In the Midlands.	
London . . .	2,500	Leicester . . .	500
Surrey (500–700) *av.* .	600	Nottingham . .	400
Towcester (Northants)	150	Scattered in the villages of Notts., Leicester, and Derby . .	3,750
Odiham (Hants) / Reading (Berkshire) .	100		
	3,350		4,650
Total (roughly) . . .	8,000		

The expansion of the trade in the Midlands continued still more rapidly after this date, mainly on account of the migration of stocking frames from London. In the period 1732–50 it is said that 800 frames were taken from London to Nottinghamshire alone.[3] In reference to this notable movement, Deering, the local historian, writes:[4]

"The hosiers of London finding they could be fitted from the Country with as good work at a cheaper rate than the London Framework knitters could afford, the Bulk of the Trade has since shifted from thence and the chief dependence they had left was upon fashion work and this also by degrees left off; what now remains in London hardly deserves the name of trade."

He goes on to show the great extent of the trade in Nottingham, where, he said, were 1,200 frames, and

[1] See Ch. V.

[2] Henson, p. 106. In the same year was passed the Act 12 Geo. I, 34, which extended the penalty of death to frame-breakers. The reason for the inclusion of framework knitters in this clause is unknown, as there is no evidence of unrest among the journeymen at the time, but see p. 122, note 1.

[3] *H.C.J.*, Vol. 26, p. 780.

[4] Deering, *Hist. of Nottm.*, 1739, p. 100.

scattered among the neighbouring villages were a further 1,800, a total of 3,000 for the County.[1] "Upon these 3,000," he writes, "depends the living of the masters, 3,000 workmen, a considerable number of winders, sizers, seamers, woolcombers, framesmiths, setters up, sinker makers, stocking needle makers, joiners and turners—upwards of 4,000 in all."

The advantages which the Midlands could offer—cheap labour, low house rents and food prices, and freedom from interference by the Company—proved irresistible. By 1782 the preponderance of the Midlands over all other framework knitting areas was overwhelming, as may be shown in the following list:[2]

Nottinghamshire, Leicestershire, Derbyshire	17,350
Dublin	700
Cork	300
London	500
Tewkesbury	650
Northants	300
Scotland	200
Total	20,000

The seat of the industry was thus definitely established in the Midlands within an area roughly bounded by Chesterfield in the north, Market Harborough in the south, Newark in the east, and by Ashby-de-la-Zouch in the west.

In 1730, a new phase of the stocking industry opened with the introduction of cotton hose, and from this time a keen interest was taken among Nottingham stockingers

[1] *Op. cit.*, p. 101. Note.—The *Victoria County History*, Vol. II, p. 297, erroneously gives the number of frames for the whole county as 1,500. This would be true of the number for the town alone about the middle of the century (see Felkin, *Hosiery and Lace*, p. 71). Both the *V.C.H.* and the local historian, Blackner, also state that there were only fifty framework knitters in Nottingham owing to a misinterpretation of Deering, who is referring to master stockingers only. See *ibid.*, p. 37.

[2] Felkin, *op. cit.*, p. 117.

in the question of cotton spinning. The women of Tewkesbury, where a cotton hosiery industry had been carried on for many years, were specially adept in this art, while the workers of India were able, according to Henson, to make the finest cotton hose by hand at the low price of sixpence per pair, the corresponding price in England being 2*s*. 3*d*.[1] The chief reason for the inability of the Nottinghamshire operatives to compete with this double rivalry was that the spinners of the district were quite unable to produce a cotton yarn equal in fineness and durability to that either of the women of Tewkesbury or of India.[2] For this reason, says Henson, the operatives bent all their energies towards devising a mechanical mode of spinning which would supply them with yarn of the desired quality at an economic price. A great fillip was given to this campaign of invention when, according to Henson, Paul removed to Nottingham in 1739[3] with his unsuccessful spinning machine, from which time Nottingham is said to have been in the throes of a fever of mechanical enterprise that was only allayed thirty years after when Arkwright set up his mill in Hockley.

"It would be tedious," says Henson, "to narrate the various abortive attempts which were made in Nottingham to spin cotton partly by hand and partly by machinery from 1740–1767; suffice it to say that though Jones and Foster and several others made some progress and improvements of Paul's method yet it was still very inferior to West of England spun cotton." And "the repeated failures of Nottingham mechanics caused the mechanical spinning of cotton to be regarded nearly in the same light as projects for discovering perpetual motion",[4]

[1] Henson, p. 364. For best account of this competition and "Tewkesbury Act" which followed, see Wadsworth and Mann, *Cotton Trade and Industrial Lancashire*, 1931, p. 484 and note. [2] *Ibid*., p. 359.

[3] *Ibid*., p. 364. There is no corroborative evidence for Henson's statement that Paul visited Nottingham in 1739. He was at Birmingham in 1738 and at Northampton in 1743 and in view of the interest of Nottingham hosiers, would probably pay a visit to the town. See Baines, *Cotton Industry*, p. 124; Robt. Cole, *Origin of Spinning by Rollers*. See also Jenks, *Migration of British Capital*, p. 13, for part played by Smiths the Bankers.

[4] Henson, p. 365.

a condition of expectancy which no doubt had something to do with the notable migrations of Hargreaves and Arkwright to Nottingham and the success they achieved there. Hargreaves found a patron in one Thomas James, by whose help he was enabled to build a small factory in Mill Street, but the yarn which he produced, though superior to anything spun in the neighbourhood, was described as a poor article, full of tender places, bumps and burs and was with difficulty made into stockings. Arkwright, of course, obtained the financial assistance of Need, the hosier, and his partner Strutt,[1] who enabled him to build a factory in Hockley, and supported him through the early period of experiment and failure, during which the imperfections of the roller system were corrected, until his final triumph in 1775. It would seem, therefore, that the cotton stocking industry of Nottingham played a very material part in the establishment of the cotton spinning industry at the end of the eighteenth century, although the inner history of this phase of the cotton industry has not yet been laid bare.

The next crisis which the industry had to surmount was the dislocation of trade caused by the American War of Independence. The hosiers, it would seem, were filled with apprehension for their trade, and petitioned in favour of an accommodation with the colonists.[2] Their allegations of impending ruin, however, were characterised by the Mayor and Aldermen as highly exaggerated and as representing calamities "which were never yet nor in the remotest probability ever will be felt by the inhabitants of this Town".[3] Indeed, in the darkest period of the war, when the political power of England seemed to be on the point of collapse, Nottingham appears to have been enjoying a period of commercial prosperity. A visitor in June, 1780, reported to the Government that all the trading towns in the

[1] *Ibid.*, p. 368.

[2] According to a counter-petition of Mayor and Aldermen, *H.C.J.*, Feb. 22, 1775.

[3] *Ibid.*

neighbourhood of Nottingham had more orders than they could possibly execute and were in a state of the most perfect tranquillity.[1]

The most notable event in the history of Framework Knitting during the period of the American War was the Strike of 1779. As will be shown later, it was rather the incidence of high food prices and low wages than of unemployment and bad trade that brought about the appeal to Parliament and the subsequent rioting and frame smashing. After this event the Stocking Industry enjoyed a period of twenty years' comparative peace and tranquillity, largely owing to the establishment of agreed wage lists through the co-operation of stockinger and hosier.[2] At the end of the century, however, the method of making stockings in sections and sewing them up by hand was introduced, and the market for the ordinary wrought, i.e. narrowed hose, was undermined.[3] The price agreements between hosier and stockinger began to be disregarded about 1805,[4] and the trade, through the prevalence of cheap inferior work, fluctuating wages and high price of food, rapidly drifted into Luddism.[5] The effect of the lack of an assured standard of wages such as had been arrived at by negotiation between masters and men between 1787 and 1805 is shown in the remark made by one of the Pentrich Luddites of 1817 on the eve of his execution: "If the employer would but fix a price upon the work so that the workman might know what he has to receive, Luddism would have ceased long ago." [6]

The framework knitting districts of England—the

[1] Hist. MSS. Com. 35, Marquis of Lothian, p. 369.

[2] Felkin, *Hosiery and Lace*, p. 230.

[3] Report of Committee of 1812 on condition of Framework Knitters, Appendix, p. 25.

[4] *Ibid.*, p. 26.

[5] It should hardly be necessary to say that Luddism in Notts. had no connection with the introduction of steam power, but the well-known play "The Machine Wreckers" has revived this delusion and makes a disclaimer necessary.

[6] "Some particulars concerning behaviour and execution of Brandreth and other Luddites, with an account of Oliver's Tour, including letters they wrote and speech of Lord Middleton," pamphlet, 1817, in Nottingham Ref. Library.

counties of Nottingham, Derby and Leicester—now became the scene of an ever-deepening tragedy, devoid even of the relief of violent revolt. Recurrent unemployment and starvation wages whittled away still further by the deductions of middle men, combined to reduce the stockinger to a condition of destitution scarcely equalled in any other industry.[1] Yet the industry continued to grow. In 1780, it has been stated, there were 20,000 frames in the industry. Between 1780 and 1845 the number of frames was more than doubled—in 1812 it was estimated by Blackner at 29,588;[2] during the following twenty years of periodic bad trade and ever dwindling wages the number rose to 33,000, distributed among 13,000 men, 10,000 women and 10,000 youths,[3] and in 1844 the number had reached the total of 48,482.[4]

The growth of the industry may be tabulated as follows:

Date.	No. of Frames in the Country.	No. of Frames in the Midlands.	No. of Frames in Notts.
1660	660	—	100
1714	8,000	—	400
1739	—	—	3,000
1780	20,000	17,000	—
1812	29,000	25,168	9,285
1833	33,000	28,500	10,500
1844	48,482	44,040	16,482

From what has been given, it will be seen that the economic development of Nottinghamshire is based upon three main industries: agriculture, mining, and framework knitting. The minor industries, brewing, brickmaking, tanning, pottery, will not be dealt with here as nothing beyond the barest fragments is known about them, and their influence upon later development has

[1] For conditions in Leicester, where the net wage of many adult stockingers for a week's work was 4*s.* 6*d.*, see *Life of Thomas Cooper*, 1879, pp. 137–42.

[2] Blackner, *Hist. of Nottm.*, 1815, p. 243.

[3] Report of Select Committee on Exportation of Machinery, 1841, Q. 1999, 2000, 2001.

[4] Report of Commissioners to enquire into Condition of Framework Knitters, 1845. Appendix, Notts., p. 13.

been negligible. Material is available for the further study of only two of the major industries—framework knitting and agriculture—and an attempt will now be made to trace the details of their economic structure to the period at which they adopted the essential characteristics of modern industry.

CHAPTER V

ORGANISATION OF THE FRAMEWORK KNITTING INDUSTRY

Early Importance of Capital.

THE Framework Knitting industry was probably unique among domestic handicrafts in the amount of initial capital which was required for setting up the machine. It should be remembered that Lee's frame was, for those days, an exceedingly delicate piece of mechanism; in the opinion of the petitioners of 1655 [1] it was the most complicated machine for the manufacture of articles of apparel that was to be found in the world at that time. Lee himself is said to have spent seven years in making his first silk stocking frame, "the most wonderful act of a single genius", says Henson, "ever displayed, even in this mechanical age"; and the making of the two thousand and more separate pieces of steel and lead, each requiring the greatest accuracy of workmanship, was no light task for the native engineering skill at a time when specialisation in frame making was unknown. A tribute to the worth of English mechanics is to be found in the fact that no matter where the frame was taken during the seventeenth century, to Venice, to Rouen, to Amsterdam, the industry withered on account of the lack of skilful workmen to keep the machines in repair.[2] The stocking frame, thoroughly English in idea and construction, helps to set off the many debts contracted by seventeenth-century industry to foreign mechanical skill.[3]

[1] Petition to Cromwell referred to *Cal. S.P. Dom.*, Aug. 1, 1655, Vol. C, 1, and quoted by Deering, *Hist. of Nottm.*, p. 307.

[2] See Petition, *op. cit.*

[3] See Smiles, *Lives of Engineers* (1874), Vol. I., pp. iv *et seq.*

Specialisation in the making of frames can be traced back as far as the middle of the seventeenth century when the work was undertaken by the framesmith, mentioned in the petition quoted above. Eventually, his function became specialised into that of making the heavier steel parts of the frame; the more delicate work of making the sinkers[1] was undertaken by the sinker-maker, the needles by the needle-maker, and the different parts were assembled by the setter up.[2]

The value of the completed machine in the seventeenth century before these functions had become specialised was naturally very high, and we hear of an Italian merchant buying a number of frames for export abroad, from which he naturally expected a profit, for £80 each.[3] It was admitted at the time that this was a high price; and it is probable that the average price was lower. In 1718 a framesmith of Selston had two frames, one of which, "with some spare iron", was valued at no more than £8, the other at £7 10*s*.[4] Besides finding a very heavy initial capital, the framework knitter, in the early days of the industry, had to meet very considerable working expenses, as the stocking frame, up to 1660, according to Blackner, was a double-handed machine, the stockinger having to employ a labourer to complete the motions of knitting.[5]

This tendency for the industry to fall from its very inception into the hands of the small capitalist was encouraged by a spirit of independent enterprise on the part of many of the stockingers themselves. It is true the framework knitters of London formed themselves, before the middle of the seventeenth century, into a self-styled Company, and attempted to control the industry on the traditional lines. But the petition which sought

[1] "Sinkers," see Appendix No. 1.

[2] This term is first used by Deering in 1739 when there were eight setters up. There were also at this time in Nottingham fourteen framesmiths, five sinker-makers and twelve needle-makers.

[3] *S.P. Dom.*, 1658–9, Vol. CLXXXIV, 34, No. 1.

[4] MS. Notts. Sessions Rolls, Aug. 26, 1719.

[5] Blackner, *Hist. of Nottm.*, p. 214, also Appendix to Report of 1812, p. 25.

to have the Company's position regularised by the Protector's seal is full of complaints regarding what was, to the petitioners, the piratical activities of many of their own number. Men would be found who would teach anyone the art of knitting for a substantial fee; others would take their frames and workmen abroad; and some there were, even at that early date, who did not shrink from bringing the name of Framework Knitting into disrepute by turning out bad work in order to capture the market.

From all that has been said, it is clear that from the beginning capital played an important part in the Framework Knitting industry, and that the emergence of the capitalist hosier, owner of frames, and "putter out" of work on a large scale could not long be delayed.

By the middle of the seventeenth century considerable specialisation had been reached in the different processes of manufacture. The petitioners of 1655, in an effort to impress the Government with the importance of their calling, point out that the profits of the industry are "diffused among merchants, owners of ships, houses, dyers, winders, throwsters, sizers, seamsters, trimmers, wire drawers, needle makers, smiths, joyners, turners, with many other assistants", and they themselves, they modestly conclude, are merely the "prime wheel", and gather only thereby an ordinary ability to make the rest move. They insist that their trade is chiefly done with foreigners, and the home market is mainly left to the hand-knitters.

> "Not only is it (the Framework Knitting industry) able to serve your Highnesses dominions with the commodities it mercantably workes," they point out, "but also the neighbouring countries round about where it has gained so good repute that the vent thereof is now more foreign than domestick and has drawn covetous eyes upon it to undermine it here and to transport it beyond the seas." [1]

It will be seen from what we have said that the rise of a capitalist organisation, with the ownership, machinery

[1] Deering, *op. cit.*, p. 303.

and material vested in the entrepreneur might be anticipated at an early date in the history of the Framework Knitting industry. A combination of economic and technical factors in favour of the large producer precipitated this event at the end of the seventeenth century, and from that time, the industry rapidly assumed all the usual characteristics of capitalist organisation, except that of the factory system of production. The phases of this movement are best seen in the history of the Chartered Company set up to regulate the industry in 1662, and in the brief efflorescence of Trade Unionism which followed the collapse of the Company's powers in the middle of the eighteenth century.

From Chartered Company to Trade Union

We do not propose to give here an account of the rise of the Company, details of which can be found elsewhere.[1] We wish only to allude to the influence of the Company upon the growth of the industry in the Midlands, and the light that the Company throws upon the development of its organisation. In the first place, the Company's powers of regulation were not limited to London, but extended throughout the whole of England and Wales, and any framework knitter who was not a member was liable to prosecution. The powers of the Company were vested in its "Court of Assistants", appointed by name for life, with power to choose a master and two wardens from their own number and to fill up vacancies in their own ranks by election. The industry in the country districts was to be regulated by deputies appointed by the Court of Assistants who were empowered "to rule and govern all Persons exercising the Trade of Framework Knitting, in the same way as the Master, Wardens and Assistants may do", and a court sat in Nottingham from time to time for this purpose.

The nature of the regulations will be seen from the following summary of the Company's by-laws:

[1] See article on "The Worshipful Company of Framework Knitters" (1657–1779) in *Economica,* November, 1929 (No. 27), by J. D. Chambers.

The entrance fee to the journeyman who had completed his training was 15*s*.; in addition to that, payment had to be made upon taking apprentices. The master of apprentices was called a "work-house keeper", and before he could aspire to this status he had to submit a proof-piece of workmanship, usually a pair of fine silk stockings, to the examination of the Wardens of the Company.[1] Upon the acceptance of this he had to pay 13*s*. When he took an apprentice he had to present himself and his apprentice before the officers of the Company within a certain time; or pay a fine; moreover, a member could only take a second apprentice after seven years' membership and a third after he had become a member of the Court of Assistants or Livery, or had filled one of the offices of the Company. The binding of the apprentice cost the master 9*s*.; if he were dismissed without reference to the Company the master was fined 3*s*. 6*d*. Further, if the master refused to serve after having been appointed to one of the Company's offices he might be fined again, up to the amount of £10. Besides enriching the coffers of the Company, these clauses must necessarily have operated against the journeymen who desired to become masters, and the masters who wished to take apprentices. Whatever the attitude of the London workmen may have been, those of the Midlands were not long in making their complaints heard.

In January of 1693 a petition of framework knitters in and about Nottingham was presented, setting forth that

"the Master and Wardens, etc., of their Company, living constantly in London, have by their many by-laws imposed severe penalties upon the petitioners, compelling them to come to London for their Freedoms, choosing petitioners for their stewards when they pleased, which office is only expensive; and laying great fines for refusal to serve therein, so that by their by-laws they raise about £200 per annum amongst the petitioners, who have

[1] This practice was commuted for a payment of 10*s*. before the end of the century.

no manner of benefit thereby, and praying relief in the Premises; and the moneys so raised may be applied to set the poor of their Trade in the Country, who are very numerous, to work." [1]

Nothing further is heard of this dispute, but it is interesting evidence of the rise of a country manufacture, a potential, if not actual, competitor with the London centre, and definitely opposed to the form of control exercised by the oligarchy of London masters. At this time the trading masters of London had many advantages, owing to the fact that the industry was mainly concerned with the export and luxury trade in fancy silk goods—gloves, waistcoat pieces, fine silk hose—which necessitated close contact with the market; but as the hand-knitting industry gradually succumbed to the machine, the emphasis of production was laid more and more on the cheaper lines of woollen and worsted in order to meet the growing demands of the industrial population. For this purpose the Midlands were to prove themselves far better situated than London, owing, not only to the proverbially low rents, prices, and wages of the country-side, but also to their proximity to the supply of wool. The attraction of the country had not yet led to a definite shifting of industrial capital, such as occurred a few years later, and the fact that the Company could enforce its authority over the country stockinger, even to the point of making him come to London to take out his freedom, or to bind an apprentice, or to serve as steward, must have been a strong deterrent to such a tendency. Indeed, the stockinger of London, if he happened to be a member of another London Company, need not take out his freedom with the Framework Knitting Company at all,[2] a further argument for remaining in the City. It cannot be doubted that the aim of the Company from its inception had been to discourage the growth of a country manufacture and maintain, as far as possible, a monopoly of the trade for the London masters.

A further stage in the struggle between the urban and

[1] *H.C.J.*, Vol. 11, Jan. 9, 1693.

[2] See Unwin, *Industrial Organisation*, p. 105.

country manufacturer is reached in the dispute of 1699, in which the restrictions placed by the Company on its growing rival in the Midlands are again the object of controversy. In this case the protest raised was the result of the joint action of the three framework knitting counties of the Midlands—Nottingham, Derby, and Leicester. On January 19, 1699,[1] a petition was presented in the House of Commons purporting to come from framework knitters of those three counties, complaining that the Master and Wardens, who resided in London, were making by-laws and orders contrary to the law, that were very vexatious to country stockingers. "For instance," the petition continues, "they compel every apprentice when out of his time to go to London, though above a hundred miles from thence, to take out his Freedom; and many other exactions are imposed on the petitioners to the great decay of the trade."

The severe criticisms made against the Company attracted the attention of the House, and a committee was appointed to investigate the case. In the evidence submitted and given in the *Commons' Journals*, interesting light is thrown upon the Company's objects and methods.

One of the worst abuses with which the Company was charged was its insistence upon calling men up to London to take up their freedoms. James Shaw complained that he had been put to such heavy expense by the journey to London and the payment of entrance fees that he had to work half a year to restore his position. Benjamin Green knew a man who was ruined on this account, and was never able to return to the country again;[2] and when it is realised that the man would have to pay 15*s.* for admission, and £1 2*s.* 6*d.* for the binding of each apprentice, in addition to the expense of the journey, such a calamity is by no means incredible.

A further source of complaint was the payment of

[1] *H.C.J.*, Vol. 13, 1699, Jan. 19. This joint action of 1699 is an interesting forerunner of the well-known association of the Midland counties in 1776, one of the most notable combinations of the eighteenth century, but in the first case it was the work of small masters, in the second of journeymen.

[2] *Ibid.*, Vol. 13, p. 316.

quarterage. One witness, Gregory Willmott, declared there were 2,000 country stockingers paying 6*d.* per quarter, for which they obtained no appreciable advantage, and for which it was said no account was ever rendered.

A third subject for complaint was the practice of arbitrarily choosing stewards and compelling them to provide a feast for the officials of the Company. If they refused to accede to this well-established custom they were fined from £6 to £10, in accordance with the by-laws of the Charter. The witness, Benjamin Green, having been chosen steward, was summoned to make a feast; on his refusal an action was brought against him in London, which involved him in a charge of £50. A collection had to be made to raise the fine of one man to prevent him from going to prison. In spite of the fact alleged by one of the witnesses, that "the by-law had been overruled in several arguments in Common Pleas", the Company still continued to choose stewards and insist upon their annual feast.[1]

A case was brought before the Court of King's Bench upon this point, and apparently about this period, and a definite decision against the by-laws was given. It was urged that the feast was only for merry-making, and not for serious consultations on the affairs of the Company; therefore, declared the Judges,

"the by-law is unreasonable to compel a man to make a dinner for the luxury of others without any benefit to himself or the rest of the Company. And . . . members of a Corporation are not bound to perform by-laws unless they are reasonable, and the reasonableness of them is examinable by the Judges. Then this by-law to make a dinner cannot be good in this case of a new Corporation".[2]

Stewards continued to be chosen and dinners to be compulsorily given in spite of old Father Antic, the law. By a fortunate lapse of the clerk, a bill of fare was casually

[1] *H.C.J.*, Vol. 13, p. 316. This iniquitous practice continued throughout the eighteenth century; see M.S. Court Book, 1745, pp. 12, 15, 145, 150, for cases of stewards preferring to pay a fine of £6.

[2] King's Bench, Vol. XCI, p. 972.

entered into the minute book of the Company in June, 1766, and runs as follows: "Two hams, one to a dish; one dozen of chickens, two to a dish, half boiled and half roasted; two dishes of beans and two of peas, and three gooseberry pies, with bread, beer, fruit, greens, and wine, as usual. All the above particulars to be very good." It is pleasant to know that a ray of sunshine was not wanting to cheer the Company's declining years.

The defence of the Company against these charges was anything but convincing. The monetary exactions upon their members were fully admitted. The sum of £1 2*s.* 6*d.* demanded for the binding of an apprentice was said to be accounted for as follows: 3*s.* 6*d.* for the Clerk for enrolling; 1*s.* to the Beadle; 1*s.* 6*d.* to the Company; 6*d.* for parchment; 2*s.* King's duty; 2*s.* 6*d.* in accordance with the Orphans' Act, and—a significant item—10*s.* to the Company in lieu of a proof piece.

The admittance fee of 15*s.* upon new members went wholly into the strong box of the Company, with the exception of 2*s.* for the King's duty. Of the remaining 13*s.*, the sum of 10*s.* was taken "in lieu of a silver spoon", 2*s.* to the Clerk, and 1*s.* to the Beadle.[1]

With regard to the charge of compelling men to come to London to take out their freedoms, they made the significant answer that only such as were apprentices to freemen of London were compelled to make the journey, and that the rule did not apply to ordinary members of the Company. May we conclude from this that the migration of London masters to the Midlands had already commenced, and that the compulsory journey to London imposed upon their workmen as well as themselves was merely a part of the Company's campaign of harassing the new country manufacturers, who had the knowledge and experience of the London market combined with the economic advantage of the countryside? If so, then there is some explanation of the statement put forward by the Company that the fines were very moderate and

[1] *H.C.J.*, Vol. 13, p. 316. The Company took 1*s.* 6*d.* for which no account was given above, the amounts totalling only £1 1*s.*

that they were only exercising a right in electing two persons from the country to be stewards to provide a feast on Michaelmas Day for the officials of the Company on pain of forfeiting £10.

But the Company was fighting a losing battle. The forces of legalised privilege were opposed to the pressure of economic change. This sprang from the widening market for cheaper goods, and it was embodied in the rising industrial capitalist anxious to take advantage of the new conditions, but nothing was done by Parliament to weaken the shackles of the Company upon him; no more was heard of the enquiry quoted above, and the new master was left to work out his industrial destiny in his own way.

The close of the seventeenth century was a period of rapid growth of the framework knitting industry, as well as of conflict. Between 1660 and 1727 the number of frames in England is said to have grown from 600 to 8,000, and a vigorous export trade, especially with Portugal, had developed.[1] In addition to the export trade, the machine industry was beginning to supply the home market, owing to the decline of the handicraft industry of knitting. The development of the coarser branches of the trade made possible by the gradual substitution of the machine product for that of the hand-knitters, opened up enormous possibilities. Here was a steady, ever-expanding market, unaffected by violent fluctuations of fashion, and calling for less skill on the part of the operative. Moreover, the stocking frame itself had been improved, with the result, we are told, that one man could now perform all the operations of knitting which had formerly been impossible, owing to a defect in the machine. If this is true, it helps to explain the rapid conquest of the hand-knitting market which the machine made at this time.[2] It also helped

[1] See above, p. 93, note 3.

[2] Blackner states that until the Restoration a labourer was required to enable the frame worker to complete the motions of knitting. Henson gives a somewhat different explanation but agrees that a simplification of the machine took place. See Blackner, *Hist. of Nottm.*, p. 214, and Appendix to Report of 1812, p. 25.

to make possible the employment of cheap, unskilled, unapprenticed labour and brought about a crisis in the history of the industry which is of great importance in the economic development of the Midlands.

The War of the Spanish Succession, says Henson, had reacted adversely upon the stocking industry, and there was much unemployment among the London journeymen. Their troubles were aggravated by the practice that had become widespread among the more enterprising hosiers, of employing a large number of apprentices. The journeymen, driven to desperation by the flagrant breach of the by-laws, took the obvious step of approaching the Company, which had been expressly formed for the purpose of maintaining the old restrictions regarding apprentices. The case of the journeymen, sympathetically considered at first, was finally laid before the whole body of the Court of Assistants and Livery. These two bodies, owing to the high fees necessary for membership, must have been composed of the most wealthy hosiers and masters in the industry, in addition to those non-framework knitters who had chosen to join the Company for reasons of their own. The result of the appeal was that a majority of the adjudicating body favoured the cause of the infringers of the Charter, and it was found impossible to take action against them. The journeymen then took the law into their own hands and resorted to the means that have always presented themselves to oppressed framework knitters; they smashed their opponents' frames, threw them out of the window into the street, and beat their apprentices. These disorders continued without any interference for three nights, at the end of which the infringing masters capitulated and promised to abide by 5th Elizabeth.[1]

From the history of the Framework Knitters' Company up to this point, the advantages derived from incorporation by this new and thriving industry stand out fairly

[1] Henson thinks this occurrence took place in 1710, but admits uncertainty on the point, p. 96. It is accepted without question by George, *London Life in Eighteenth Century*, p. 237.

K

clearly. From the beginning the Company set itself the task of preventing the exportation of machinery abroad,[1] in which they appear to have had considerable success. In 1696 the Company obtained the insertion of an important clause into a finance Bill, by which the exportation of frames, or any part of a frame, should be punished by a fine of £40 and forfeiture of the machinery,[2] and so vigorously was the Act administered by the Company, through its powers of search, that the French, Spaniards, Flemings, and Italians continued for a hundred years to build their frames on the model of those made in the seventeenth century, all later improvements, such as the sley, casterback, and hanging bit, etc., being unknown to them until the opening of the nineteenth century.[3] In pursuit of this particular form of protection all sections of the Company would, no doubt, be of one mind, as a national monopoly of the industry would benefit workman as well as employer; and in the Company's attempt to stifle the growth of a country manufacture which might compete in the London market, the interests of men and masters were both served. But a split within the Company itself was inevitable owing to the development of capitalist organisation based upon the employment of cheap labour and concentrating on the coarser branches of production.

The action of 1710, in which the governing body refused to put the apprenticeship regulations into force at all, except after compulsion by the journeymen, throws a vivid light on the character of the Company at this time. It evidently consisted of two types of masters. Those who considered the journeymen's case sympathetically, were presumably in favour of maintaining accustomed standards of work by the old method of apprenticeship, which suggests that they were still engaged on the "fancy" goods, such as waistcoat pieces, fine silk hose,

[1] *S.P. Dom.*, March, 1660, Vol. CCXX, No. 53; August, 1678, Vol. CDVI, No. 38; *S.P. Dom.*, Entry Book 334, p. 537, and *H.C.J.*, Vol. 11, Dec. 11, 1693.

[2] 7 & 8 Wm. III, 20, Section viii.

[3] Henson, p. 88.

and so on, for which the London trade had always been famous. On the other hand, there were those—the majority—whose interests were best served by employing cheap unskilled labour, the manufacturers, we may presume, of the coarser woollen and worsted products which required less skill in the making. After the crisis of 1710 a number of them took the important and unusual step of transporting their machinery to a part of the country where they would be able to employ cheap labour without the interference of the journeymen with their apprenticeship restrictions. From this time the Company changed its character. Instead of being a monopolistic organisation of London masters, dictating to the country districts, it becomes a struggling organisation of the remnant of the London trade, and since it must find support somewhere in order to harass the new giant in the country, it makes an alliance with the journeymen there, who look to it for protection against the menace of cheap labour. The inner history of this transformation cannot be written, as no documentary material exists upon it, but outward and visible signs are not wanting to suggest an inward and spiritual change. It is at this time that the industry begins to grow most rapidly at Nottingham and the Midland centres; according to Henson, the number of frames in the Midlands in 1727 was greater than in the south; [1] a witness reported to a committee of the House of Commons that 800 frames were taken from London to Nottingham between 1732 and 1750; [2] the local historian, Deering, writing in 1739, says: "The hosiers of London, finding they could be fitted from the country with as good work at a cheaper rate than the London framework knitters could afford, the bulk of the trade has since shifted from thence—and what now remains in London hardly deserves the name of Trade".[3] It would seem from this that the attractions of the countryside in the shape of low wages, rents and prices, reinforced by the

[1] *Ibid.*, p. 106.
[2] *H.C.J.*, Vol. 26, p. 780.
[3] Deering, *op. cit.*, p. 100.

agitations of the London journeymen, had resulted in the rapid shifting of the centre of gravity from London to the Midlands. More than this, the nature of the trade had undergone an important change. Instead of concentrating on the more expensive lines of production, such as fancy silk hose, gloves, waistcoat pieces, which during the Restoration period had formed the staple output of the industry, the bulk of the trade was concerned with the cheaper branches of woollen and worsted hose, which at this time were taking the place of the hand-knitted article. We hear of worsted hose being introduced into Scotland in 1682 by the New Mills Silk Manufacturing Company, but apparently without success.[1] Again, the author of *Britannia Languens* includes the *woollen* stocking industry among those which were suffering from foreign competition.[2] By 1704, as we have said, the hand-knitting industry of Norfolk is stated to have been reduced almost to nothing, while the manufacture of worsted hose on the frame had become definitely established at Leicester.[3]

For the cheaper branches of production the market was comparatively steady, and at this time capable of great expansion, hence the special advantages of the London silk trade—its close contact with the fashionable world, both at home and abroad—waned as the new trade waxed. Further, there was a plentiful supply of good wool dressers from both Nottinghamshire and Leicestershire, and of silk from Sir Thomas Lomb's mill at Derby, which rapidly became the leading centre for silk hose. Finally, with the development of cotton hosiery, first mentioned in 1695 by John Cary of Bristol,[4] and introduced into Nottingham, according to Henson, in 1730, a new branch of cheap hosiery was opened up.

[1] Warner, *Silk Industry of the United Kingdom*, p. 357.

[2] *Britannia Languens*, p. 409.

[3] The production of cheap hand-knitted stockings was forcibly advocated as early as 1674. See interesting petition of wool combers quoted by Thomson, *Hist. of Leicester*, Vol. I, p. 431.

[4] *Essay of Trade*, quoted by J. P. Thomas, *Mercantilism and East Ind. Trade*, p. 128.

Whatever the reason for the change in the character of the industry, there is no doubt that the Framework Knitters' Company suffered a serious shock. The masters remaining in London, found themselves face to face with powerful competitors in the country whom they tried to coerce into joining the Company by invoking against them the apprenticeship regulations. One master is said to have had twenty-nine apprentices; another no less than forty. Trials at law took place, but victory invariably lay with the infringing masters, owing apparently to the discovery of technical flaws in the regulations; and the Company had to admit that its powers were restricted to the control of its own members. New by-laws were obtained and a fresh attack was threatened upon non-members, who, of course, constituted the great bulk of the trade. But the forces of "free trade" in industry were too strong; they included not only the masters but the gentry, who joined with them in protesting against the Company's interference; and also the unapprenticed workmen, some of whom, particularly at Southwell, took an active part against the Company. The main support of the Company in the Midlands was now drawn from the apprenticed journeymen, who could see the danger of the increasing employment of cheap unskilled labour. In 1752 a campaign of enrolment was opened. The *Nottingham Journal* announced that a Court of Deputies would sit at the Crown Inn, Nottingham, to receive admissions at the rate of 5*s.* per man, but no quarterage would be asked of journeymen, "many of whom (though not old) are scarce able to get Bread. . . . Then let us immediately agree to be of one mind for the general good and heartily join with one voice to proclaim the Court our protection! And no more Colts!" As though in answer to this appeal petitions were sent to the House of Commons by hosiers, gentlemen and framework knitters of Nottingham, Mansfield, Leicester and Godalming, praying for relief from the interference of the Company; a committee

[1] See p. 122 below.

of enquiry was appointed and the powers of the Company were declared to be vexatious and injurious to the trade. Thus ended the last serious attempt to enforce the apprenticeship regulations in the stocking industry.[1]

It may be noted here that the same degree of freedom had been obtained by this time in other trades. In the seventeenth century the Justices had administered the Apprenticeship Act of Elizabeth with considerable vigour; the records show that a large number of indictments were made for breaches of the regulations in almost every trade practised in the County, and cases came from small villages as well as larger centres.[2]

Examples of prosecution for the breach of the apprenticeship regulations occur occasionally in the eighteenth century, but in 1737 the Act had become a dead letter, as the following case shows:

"22nd April, 1737. John Whitelamb of South Leverton being indicted for exercising trade of shoe maker contrary to the 5th Elizabeth, not having served an apprenticeship to it, moved to have it quashed, the offence being said to be done in a country village, alledging that the Statute does not extend to trades carried on in such places. Respited until next Sessions."

At a subsequent Sessions, on October 7, 1737, the indictment was quashed, "the offence being said to be done in a country village".[3]

Even after the events we have recounted, and the decay of compulsory regulation of industry in town and country, attempts were made by the framework knitters to re-establish the Company, and on one or two occasions to re-impose the restrictions of apprenticeship. Numbers of stockingers joined the Company in the period 1776–9 when an appeal was being made by the men to Parliament for the purpose of regulating wages, but the actual influence of the Company upon the course of events seems

[1] *H.C.J.*, Vol. 26, p. 794; Henson, p. 99; Felkin, *Hosiery and Lace*, p. 75; Chambers, *Worshipful Company of Framework Knitters* in *Economica*, Nov., 1929, in which evidence is drawn from the Company's Letter Books.

[2] Hampton Copnall, *Notts. County Records, Seventeenth Century*, p. 127.

[3] Hampton Copnall, *Notes of Proceedings at Quarter Sessions*, 1736–7.

to have been nil. Its place as a form of protection for the men had been taken by the Stockingers' Association of the Midlands which carried through the negotiations with the masters, obtained the return of sympathetic members to Parliament, and on the failure of the projected scheme of Parliamentary regulation of wages, it conducted the case of the men during the serious strike that followed.[1] Thus the freedom of the employers to buy labour in the cheapest market was answered by the combination of the operatives in defence of an agreed standard.

It does not appear that the men's organisations were impeded in their activities by the Combination Acts, to which a very stringent addition had been made in 1777 (17 Geo. III, 55) on the very eve of the frameworkers' agitation. Moreover, by the Act 12 Geo. I, 34, the destruction of a stocking frame was punishable by death and an attack upon a master's home by transportation. In spite of this, hundreds of frames were destroyed, several houses attacked and one totally demolished in the rioting of 1779, but the penalties inflicted for these crimes took the form of small fines or short terms of imprisonment. The officers of the Associated Stockingers were prosecuted and the Society's box and papers were seized, but the charge against them seems to have been one of fomenting riots, or being concerned in frame-breaking, not of organising a combination; and, far from being cowed, the men's leaders actually called a meeting in the Papist Holes in the Park and obtained a resolution to contest the legality of the proceedings taken against them.[2]

Fresh offices were opened and subscriptions invited for a new campaign; the hosiers answered by issuing a flamboyant declaration against the introduction of all

[1] See Ch. II above.

[2] *Nottingham Journal*, Aug. 28, 1779. Apparently the Act 12 Geo. I, making it a capital offence to destroy frames, was a dead letter. It was superseded by the Act 28 Geo. III, 55, which made frame-breaking a minor felony punishable by fourteen years' transportation. This also was wholly ineffective, and the death penalty was restored by the famous Act of 1812. See Cobbett's *Parliamentary Debates*, Vol. XXI, pp. 810 *et seq.*

pernicious restraints on the workman or employer, whether attempted by Charter or Act of Parliament;[1] neither side seems to have anticipated action under the Combination Laws, while the attitude of the Judges, the magistrates and the Grand Juries before whom the offending stockingers had been brought was characterised by a leniency that is truly remarkable. The squirearchy was not yet prepared to play the tyrant at the behest of offended industrialism, and the hosiers had to content themselves by betraying one of the most intrepid of the men's leaders to the Press Gang, and on his escaping they are said to have entered into a bond not to employ him, after which he took ship to America.

Both sides were willing to negotiate, and in 1787 an agreement was arrived at that lasted without much modification for twenty years. Even after the Combination Acts of 1799 and 1800, which, according to Blackner, had the effect of breaking up the funds of two branches of the men's organisation, meetings continued to take place, and it was agreed to increase frame rents as an alternative to lowering wages.[2]

The promise of peaceful collaboration between employers and trade union was not to be fulfilled; for this the reason seems to be not in the Combination Acts, but in the dislocation of the Continental market caused by the French War, the consequent slump in production, and also in the production of a cheap form of hosiery known as "cut-ups"—made in sections and sewn together by hand—which made their appearance about 1795 and rapidly undermined the position of the ordinary "wrought" wear. But another, and more deep-seated, reason was to be found in the structure of the industry itself; effective organisation, especially in a declining

[1] *Nottingham Journal*, Sept. 18; Oct. 2, 1779.

[2] Blackner, *op. cit.*, p. 235, and Report of Committee on Framework Knitters' Petition, 1812, p. 17. For the best account of the subsequent period, see Hammond, *Skilled Labourer*, pp. 221 *et seq.* The mildness of the authorities in Nottinghamshire to the strikes of 1779 may be compared with that of the Master Weavers of Manchester towards Weavers' combinations of 1781. See Wadsworth and Mann, *Cotton Trade and Industrial Lancashire*, p. 371.

market, was impossible in an industry that was scattered throughout the towns and countryside of three counties; in the middle of the nineteenth century there were still 4,621 workshops in Nottinghamshire for 15,000 frames, an average of $3\frac{1}{4}$ per shop.[1]

This so-called "Domestic System" of production, "Domestic" only in the sense that a part of the workmen were employed at home instead of in a factory, was so characteristic of the industry and has left so many features of interest both in the town and the countryside, and perhaps in the character of the population to-day, that a description of its rise and organisation must be attempted.

The Rise of the Domestic System in Framework Knitting

We have alluded at the beginning of this chapter to the importance of capital in the development of framework knitting; the cost of the frame, the expensive nature of the material, silk, upon which it worked; the fact that until the period of the Restoration the frame was by no means technically perfect and was expensive to work, the rapid changes of fashion in the shape and colour of knitted goods; all these factors tended to produce the characteristic figure who was to dominate but, unfortunately, not to absorb the industry until the time of the factory system, namely, the capitalist hosier, whose influence was felt in ever widening circles in the attics and workshops of town and country. Whether he descended from a master framework knitter, who prospered and extended his range of operations further and further afield, or from the dealers in knitted goods—the hosiers of old—we cannot say; probably from both. At least he is referred to under both titles, though the title of hosier eventually became predominant. His function in the eighteenth century appears to be clear. He is, in the first place, the owner of a large number of frames,

[1] Report of 1845. Appendix, Notts., Statistical Table of Frames in Notts., pp. 10–11.

perhaps a hundred or more; some of them would probably work under his own supervision in his own shop, while others would be let out for hire to his workmen in their own homes. Besides his own workmen, other stockingers, private owners of frames, had become dependent on him for material and were his paid workmen in all but name. His double function may be summed up as follows: as an agent of production he gave out raw material to men who paid a rent for the use of his frames either in his shop or their own houses; he also gave out work to private owners of frames, many of whom were master stockingers employing journeymen; as an agent of distribution he sold the finished article, possibly in a shop of his own, or to wholesale dealers.

It is difficult to trace the steps by which the hosier reached his full economic stature, but there seems no doubt that the period of the Restoration gave the first marked impulse to his progress. By the end of the seventeenth century it is said, "the trade was carried on by two sorts of employers: one was hosiers who made their own goods and kept retail shops; and the other made their goods and sold them either to their connections by taking orders or to the retail hosiers".[1] Probably it is from the former class, the hosiers who produced as well as distributed, that the later hosier descended.

The evolution of the capitalist hosier outlined above was especially rapid in the Midlands where the trade was scattered among a large number of small villages at considerable distances from the centres of distribution. Obviously the conditions encouraged—indeed, necessitated—the rise of an entrepreneur class who would be able to bring the scattered producers into closer touch with the consumers' demands.

According to the Borough Records, there were hosiers with a stall in the market in 1647,[2] but whether they were hosiers in the sense of the word used above we cannot say; possibly they were merely dealers in hand-

[1] Henson, p. 96. [2] Borough Records, Vol. V, p. 250.

knitted goods. It is easy to suppose, however, they would soon be brought into touch with the products of the frame; and it would not be long before the dealer in the town with the advantage of capital, market facilities and native enterprise, asserted his leadership over the craftsmen in the country by putting out work to them and eventually hiring their frames. Be that as it may, there is no doubt that the hosier class in Nottingham grew in number and prosperity, as the following extracts from the Borough Records testify: in 1704 one hosier was included among the list of burgesses; in 1718 the list contained two hosiers, and in 1721 another hosier became a burgess; from 1731 onwards scarcely a year passed without at least one hosier being numbered among the new burgesses, while in 1742 there were actually six, of whom four, being qualified neither by birth nor servitude, had to buy the privilege at a cost of £15 each.[1] Between 1758 and 1760 when the printed record ceases, the number of hosier-burgesses amounted to thirteen. As an example of the rapid rise of the hosiers at this time, it is only necessary to point to the career of Mr. Samuel Fellows,[2] who, having been robbed of his patrimony by unscrupulous relatives, was apprenticed to a framework knitter in 1706, became a hosier, took a substantial house in High Pavement, and from Overseer of the Poor of St. Mary's in 1726, rose by the usual gradations of Sheriff and Alderman to Mayor in 1755. The greatest tribute to the wealth he accumulated and his most lasting memorial has been the Hart and Fellowes Bank of which his grandson was one of the founders in 1808.

An interesting sidelight on the structure of the industry is given in 1727, when the manufacturers of Nottingham united with the magistrates of the town and county to send a letter to the Company stating that "Putters-out" were seriously inconvenienced

[1] For a list of burgesses, see Borough Records, Vol. VI, pp. 310–56.

[2] *County Pedigrees*, Phillimore, p. 56, and article in *Nottinghamshire Guardian*, Sept. 1, 1923, entitled "Old Nottingham Family's Unique Record".

by the embezzlement of material by their workmen, and asking for the co-operation of the Company in obtaining a clause for its prevention in the Bill on Woollen Manufacture pending before the House. The letter was signed by the Mayor and four Aldermen and thirty-seven others, including Sir Thomas Parkyns, the wrestling magistrate of Bunny, and the equally prominent manufacturer, Samuel Fellowes, the employer, according to Henson, of forty apprentices.[1] Further light is thrown upon the state of the industry by Deering, who, writing in 1739, states that there were fifty "manufacturers" in Nottingham at that time, all trading direct with London and others who traded with Leicester.[2] He goes on to say that they were "putters-out" of work, which makes it clear they were employers or hosiers, though this term is not actually used.

During the greater part of the eighteenth century, at least, the stockingers appear to have brought their work at intervals of a week or a fortnight in person to the hosier's warehouse, generally an attic or some other part of his dwelling-house, where it was weighed and examined.[3] An allowance of $\frac{1}{4}$ oz. to every pound of yarn weighed out was made on account of wastage due to winding.[4] With that deduction, the stockinger was expected to return the same weight of manufactured goods as of raw material supplied by the hosier. The latter kept the work in its rough state until he re-

[1] MS. Company Letter Book, April, 1727, p. 129. Does this letter explain the inclusion of framework knitting in the Act of 1727 which made the breaking of frames a capital offence? Does it also explain why the penalty of death for frame-breaking was never imposed in the eighteenth century? The Nottinghamshire hosiers appear to have been interested only in the part of the Act dealing with embezzlement of material; but they were given the whole Act, including the penalty of death for frame-breaking. The collaboration of the hosiers and the gentry is significant. See also p. 94, note 2.

[2] Deering, *op. cit.*, p. 101. The term "hosier" is used in the sense of "capitalist manufacturer" throughout the enquiry of 1753. See *H.C.J.*, Vol. 26, p. 781, etc.

[3] *H.C.J.*, Vol. 36, p. 740. The *Nottingham Journal* contains many advertisements for the sale of dwelling-houses having rooms suitable for a hosier's warehouse—see almost any issue of about 1760.

[4] *Stocking Makers' Monitor*, 1817 (Nottingham Ref. Library), p. 35.

ceived orders from his customers, who were generally shopkeepers, pedlars, or merchants for export abroad, when the goods were dyed to suit their taste.[1] By the middle of the eighteenth century, the hosier had almost completed his development. The struggle with the Company in 1753 not only reveals the wealth of individual hosiers, three of whom possessed over a hundred frames each,[2] but shows the strength of the whole class which could persuade a House of Commons not yet converted to *laisser faire* to reduce to a nullity the Company's restrictions and to give a public blessing to free competition.

A further step still required to be taken before the hosier reached his full economic stature. This was the establishment of warehouses in London for the sale of goods produced in the Midlands. From the evidence afforded by the local press,[3] it would seem that agents experienced in the London trade were appointed by Nottingham manufacturers to keep them informed of the changes of fashion and the state of the market in London, the foremost centre of consumption. This naturally led to the establishment in London of warehouses working in conjunction with the hosiers in Nottingham. The classic example is that of the firm of I. & R. Morley, originally yeoman farmers of Sneinton, who took up the business of hosier and prospered so well that towards the close of the eighteenth century they established a warehouse in London. The exact date of the foundation cannot be ascertained, but the warehouse was certainly in full swing by 1797.[4] It consisted of a house situated in Russia Row, Cheapside, of which the basement was used for storing the goods

[1] Macpherson, *Annals of Commerce,* 1805, Appendix No. 4.

[2] *H.C.J.*, Vol. 26, p. 786.

[3] *Nottingham Journal,* Jan. 31, 1778. The following advertisement occurs: "Young man of experience of London trade and has sold to most of capital houses in town would engage with any hosier either to sell on commission in London, or to assist in the country."

[4] *A Hundred Years of Progress,* by F. M. Thomas, p. 2. Note.—The Manager of the Cheapside warehouse is of opinion that the foundation was considerably earlier.

sent from Nottingham and the upper rooms for the dwelling-house of the manager, Mr. John Morley.

The experiment of the Morley brothers appears to have been a great success from the beginning. Early in the nineteenth century it was found necessary to take more commodious premises for the London business, which migrated to a house in Lad Lane; this in its turn was superseded in 1850 by a new warehouse on the same site, known at the present day as 18 Wood Street, Cheapside, "on so magnificent a scale that to many it seemed incredible that premises so vast should ever be needed".

During this period the Nottingham branch had similarly prospered. A warehouse was set up at an unknown date in Greyhound Yard,[1] where the work of giving out material, taking in the finished product, packing it and sending it to London was performed without interruption all through the turmoils of the Luddite riots. During the period 1840–60, when the conditions in many branches of the industry were at their lowest ebb, the Morley firm is said to have advanced by leaps and bounds, owing to the business acumen of the philanthropist, Mr. Samuel Morley. The work of production was still performed in the cottages of the work people, the Morley firm not being very favourably disposed towards the factory system. It should be remembered that the best wrought work, in which the firm specialised, could only be produced on the narrow hand frame until Cotton perfected his invention in 1861. The firm then began seriously to contemplate the change and in 1866 the first factory was built in Manvers Street, Nottingham.

The achievements of the Morley firm should not be allowed to dwarf those of other less familiar manufacturers. As early as 1812 a Mr. Hayne of Nottingham possessed frames to the value of £24,000;[2] Messrs.

[1] *A Hundred Years of Progress,* by F. M. Thomas, p. 17.

[2] First Report of Committee on Framework Knitters' Petition, 1812. Appendix V, p. 16.

Brettle & Company of Belper employed 2,000 frames on cotton hosiery alone, spread about the neighbouring villages for twenty miles round in shops containing from two to ten frames.[1] Messrs. Ward & Company, also of Belper, employed no less than 4,000 frames scattered throughout the three counties of Nottingham, Derby and Leicester. Besides the actual operatives, this large quantity of machinery provided employment for 2,000 seamers, 800 winders, 100 framesmiths, needle-makers and sinker-makers, 100 dyers and bleachers, 300 embroiderers or cheveners, and 200 menders, trimmers and makers up.[2] Such were the vast ramifications of the Framework Knitting industry under the so-called Domestic System of production.

The Putting-out System: the Work of the Middleman

The growth of the capitalist structure of the industry based upon the scattered workshop involved, as we have seen, the development of the "Putting-out" system. This in its turn gave rise to a partial integration of function, which, while it served the ends of the larger capitalists, permitted, indeed, encouraged the rise of a host of petty entrepreneurs, working partly as the agents of the large firm, and partly in competition with it. This will be seen the more clearly by examining the functions of the "Middleman", the intermediate agent between employer and workman, the pivot upon which this ramshackle and persistent organisation worked.

At what period the hosiers dissociated themselves from the work of production and left it in the hands of the middleman it is difficult to determine. Henson states that early in the eighteenth century hosiers of London let out their frames to master stockingers, to whom they delegated the whole work of production while they confined themselves to the work of selling. Many

[1] Report of Commissioners appointed to enquire into condition of Framework Knitters, 1845, Notts., Q. 4905, 4906.

[2] *Ibid.*, Q. 4490, 4491.

hosiers, he remarked, knew no more of the trade than the buying and selling prices.[1]

We know, also, that by the middle of the eighteenth century there were three hosiers of Nottingham each of whom employed over a hundred frames, "and many other dealers in the aforesaid manufacture employing many manufacturers in different parts of the country".[2] In these cases, where hosiers were obviously engaged on a large scale, the work of producing and selling must have become largely differentiated, the specialised function of two distinct agents. By the time of the enquiries of 1778 the master stockinger seems to have been little more than the agent of the hosier, with the duty of subletting the frames, taking out and bringing in the work and supervising the actual work of production.

The master stockinger had by this time lost his essential characteristic of complete independence; the frames he employed were usually the property of one or more hosiers; the work he produced was partly, if not wholly, the property of the hosier. Obviously the character of the master stockinger's function had undergone a change of such a kind as to make this title no longer appropriate. An acknowledgment of the change is seen in the fact that by 1779 the operatives were sometimes in the habit of making a definite allowance from their wages to the master for taking in their work and bringing out fresh material,[3] which indicates that he played the part of an intermediary between the hosier and the operative.

[1] Henson, p. 186. For case of a London hosier still employing men under his own direct supervision in 1779, see *H.C.J.*, Vol. 36, p. 741.

[2] *Ibid.*, Vol. 26, p. 781.

[3] *Ibid.*, Vol. 37, p. 371; Vol. 36, p. 740. One interesting deviation from this development is that at Tewkesbury, where it is said a hosier sold the raw material outright to the stockinger and bought back the manufactured article. "The men are compelled", stated the witness, "to buy the cotton wool from the masters and sell it to the spinners and then purchase the thread from the spinners." The men were charged 2*s.* 4*d.* a pound for cotton, which, it was asserted, did not cost the masters 18*d.* The men who bought the cotton wool were in this case merely journeymen working the frames of the hosiers.

This is, of course, a period of great expansion in the industry, when one modification after another was being made upon the hand frame, and fashion was fluctuating with bewildering rapidity.[1] These conditions would lend added importance to the position of the middleman, who would relieve the hosier of the work of direct supervision and allow him to pay unfettered attention to the work of distribution.

By 1810 the middleman had become thoroughly established in the industry, even to the point of paying the operatives in bread and beer instead of money.[2] By this time the middlemen were in a strategic position of great strength, and in consequence were able to exploit, in different degrees, both the hosier and the operative. But, while the latter was almost helpless, the hosier could always give out his work to another middleman or even, by direct contract, to the stockingers themselves. The men of Carlton, for instance, continued to hold their frames direct from the hosier, and to bring in their work personally to the warehouse.[3] It was agreed by all that the workmen fared much better under the system of direct relationship with the hosier as they were thus free from the exactions of the middleman; but it could not be adopted to any great extent, it was said, because of the untrustworthiness of many of the journeymen who needed the personal control of the middleman as an inducement to honesty and good workmanship. In another place it was pointed out that by employing the middleman the hosier had to do with one man instead of twenty and was able to get his work done more quickly and cheaply.[4]

Again, the rapid rise of the middleman at the end of

[1] Henson devotes a long chapter to this hectic period of which the outcome was the point-net lace machine.

[2] See especially the evidence of Edward Allen of Sutton-in-Ashfield where the village dentist, grave-digger and shoe-maker were paid in goods given to the stockingers in lieu of wages. Select Committee on Framework Knitters' Petition, 1812, pp. 30–3.

[3] 1845 Report, Appendix, Notts., Q. 1444–6.

[4] *Ibid.*, Q. 1078, 4831, 516, 517, etc.

the eighteenth century can also be attributed to the influence of the stockingers themselves. They had before complained of having to lose half a day in taking their work into the warehouse. In the case of thousands of stockingers scattered over a wide countryside, the journey to the town with their produce would result in the loss of a whole day and put them to considerable expense and trouble. The convenience of putting their work into the hands of a trustworthy middleman and taking the raw material from him on his return was obvious, but they failed to realise that by doing so they had made themselves dependent upon him for employment. Unfortunately for the stockinger these two effects of the system were practically inseparable.

The anomalous position of the middleman is well seen in the way by which he was remunerated for the work he performed. The hosier appears to have regarded him in the light of a contractor who made what profit he could out of the transaction of letting out frames and material to the operatives. This is proved by the fact that it was the exception and not the rule for the hosier to make any definite allowance to the middleman. The larger firms did make an allowance, it is true,[1] but the smaller hosiers exercised no control but left him free to make what bargain he liked with the workmen; the price he paid to the workmen, it was said, had nothing to do with the price paid by the hosiers at the warehouse.[2]

The operatives, on the other hand, frequently regarded themselves as the paid workmen of the hosier, who employed the middleman to let out frames, put out and take in work for which certain recognised deductions were made from the workman's wages. For instance, in the glove branch the middleman was allowed 8*d.* a dozen for taking in, winding, "getting up" and returning the work to the warehouse.[3] But he gained a profit to which, according to the workmen, he was not entitled by letting

[1] 1845 Report, Appendix, Notts., Q. 74. [2] *Ibid.*, Q. 540 and 1951.
[3] *Ibid.*, Q. 338.

out the work at a lower rate than what he himself was receiving from the hosier. This was a source of very great discontent to the operatives, who regarded it as a piece of trickery on the part of the middlemen.[1] In the towns, where the hosier could exercise a closer supervision over the middlemen and where the workmen themselves could more easily discover the warehouse price, this practice was not so common as in the country districts. Here, the "bag hosier"—a middleman who was also a petty manufacturer—ruled supreme, and was known to have dismissed men who ventured to make enquiries as to what the real price of their labours should be.[2] A few of the larger hosiers, however, took upon themselves the responsibility of paying the middleman; they set a definite price at which work was to be let out to the workmen and did not allow it to be infringed with impunity.[3] An allowance was then made to the middleman according to the amount of work he brought in. Besides these sources of remuneration, there was the profit derived from frame rent, and in some cases, from the supervision of the by-processes of the industry, such as winding and seaming, formerly done by the stockinger's own family.

It has been pointed out above that the middleman hired frames from the hosier in addition to those which he himself possessed. He sublet the frames at an increased rent; sometimes the rent would be doubled; generally the increase was not more than 50 per cent. A very considerable income was drawn from this source by the larger middlemen, some of whom employed as many as 160 frames.[4] It must not be thought that this large number was held from one hosier alone; hosiers would seldom let out more than sixty frames to one man;[5] many middlemen had only three or four; the average seems to have been about ten or fifteen. But there was nothing to prevent the middleman from taking

[1] *Ibid.*, Q. 150, 177–80, etc., etc.
[2] *Ibid.*, Q. 1953, 2642.
[3] *Ibid.*, Q. 177 and 583.
[4] *Ibid.*, Q. 1874.
[5] *Ibid.*, Q. 907.

frames from more than one hosier except the opposition of the hosiers themselves. As a result of this large accumulation of frames in the hands of the middlemen, there arose the vicious practice of "stinting". In times of bad trade, and they were frequent, the middleman would be unable to keep the whole of his frames fully occupied, but he generally had to pay rent to the hosier even when they were idle, and in consequence demanded it from the workmen. In order to give colour to his demand for rent the middleman would spread out what little work he had over a large number of frames, so as to keep them at least partially occupied. The more unscrupulous middlemen were charged with deliberately taking more frames than they could possibly keep in full employment in order to get the rent by means of the system of stinting. When it is remembered that good second-hand frames were plentiful and could be bought for anything between £6 and £10, and that the cost of upkeep was reckoned at £1 per year divided equally between owner and operative, it will be seen that the customary rent—1*s.* to 2*s.*—represented an extortionate rate of interest on capital expenditure. An example of the profits enjoyed by the middlemen from frame rents is given by a writer in 1817. "A bag master has twenty or thirty frames of his own besides taking out work for thirty or forty more. He gets 1*s.* 9*d.* for each of his own and a shilling neat profit for each of the others"—an income of £4 to £5 a week from frame rent alone, by which means he might, if he wished, set up as a manufacturer in competition with the old-established houses. It is not surprising to hear it said that many hosiers rose in a few years from a condition of obscurity to a state of affluence and splendour—"and having quit this mortal life, they left behind them some thirty, some forty and some a hundred thousand pounds".[1]

[1] *Stocking Makers' Monitor*, 1817, pp. 51 *et seq.* An interesting attempt was made by the Midland stockingers led by Nottingham to organise a market for their own produce independently of the hosiers, and the scheme is explained in the *Monitor*. See copies in Nottingham Ref. Library.

In the towns, the middlemen frequently took control of the by-processes of the industry, such as winding and seaming, which in the country districts were usually undertaken by the stockinger's family. Sometimes middlemen had seaming shops on their own premises where they employed women and girls in embryo factories, just as they employed the stockingers themselves. In some cases, the middlemen let out the seaming to individual women who employed girls of about nine years of age to do the work. They appear to have acted merely as overseers, as agents of the middleman, if the evidence of one of them, Mary Hatfield, may be regarded as typical. She employed a number of girls at her own house on seaming gloves, and paid them the same price as she received from the middleman, but she deducted 6*d*. a week from the wages of each one for the privilege of standing in her house and for the use of candles and fuel.[1]

Finally, it was the duty of the middleman to collect the finished products from the workmen in the frames under his charge and from any other stockinger to whom he may have let out material, and return it to the warehouse. If the hosier were only in a small way he would examine the work carefully himself, otherwise this work was delegated to a "taker-in"; any faulty or dirty articles would either be rejected or deductions would be made to compensate the hosier for the loss incurred. The middleman would transmit the loss to the stockinger responsible for it, suitable deductions being made from his wages. Complaints were often raised that the most frivolous objections were made in times of bad trade by the hosier or the middleman in order to put the burden of unsaleable goods upon the workman.

The importance of the middleman's functions led to specialisation among the middlemen themselves. Thus some took out silk goods only; others concentrated on gloves, pantaloons, drawers, or different branches of hose-weaving such as white cotton tops and half-hose.[2]

[1] *Op. cit.*, Q. 650. [2] *Ibid.*, Q. 5350, etc.

The Commission of 1845 examined twenty-seven middlemen or "undertakers" from Nottinghamshire and Derbyshire, all of whom were engaged upon one or at most two specialised branches of production. The hosiers of Belper, however, went a stage further and employed managers of departments to superintend the production of special "lines". For instance, Mr. John Hancock was manager of the silk department for Messrs. Brettle & Company of Belper; Mr. Thomas M. Cullum was manager of the cotton department of Messrs. Ward's house, also at Belper.

The Coming of the Factory

The economic structure of the Framework Knitting industry has now been sketched and it has been shown to take the form of an adaptation of the old domestic system to meet the needs of the new industrial society. The question now occurs: why was this antiquated form of organisation permitted to exist so long? The introduction of the factory system had been a subject of speculation all through the terrible years following the Napoleonic Wars, but nothing had been done. The masters advanced various reasons against the factory; they pretended to fear that the gathering of a large number of men within the walls of a factory would be subversive of law and order and destroy efficiency of production. The industry had been able to supply the needs of the market and to provide an adequate return for capital invested in it, and therefore there was no direct incentive to utilise new systems of production that would involve great expense on the part of the manufacturers; while the operatives feared that the introduction of power machinery would increase their miseries by overstocking the market still further.

Finally, it was urged in defence of the domestic system that the stocking frame could not be adapted to steam-power. This was only partially true. Brunel had invented a circular frame in 1816, which in Felkin's phrase was destined "to become one of the cheapest and most effective looms the world has ever seen",[1] but this destiny was unaccountably delayed for a further period of nearly forty years.

Perhaps another reason for this delay may be put forward. It should be remembered that the introduction of the factory system would in all probability result in the abolition of frame rent. The justification of frame rent put forward by its defenders was that as long as the machinery was placed in the hands of workmen and kept in their own houses, the owners must insure themselves against loss by means of frame rent; with the machinery locked up in a factory under the eye of the owner this insurance would no longer be necessary. But frame rent was more than an insurance; it was an additional source of income enjoyed not merely by the owners, but by middlemen who contracted with the owners and sublet the frames to the operatives; rent was often paid whether the frame was being used or not, in time of sickness and unemployment and sometimes even when the frame belonged to the operative himself. Extraordinary as this may appear, the evidence on the point is quite clear.[2]

A man who refused to pay frame rent owing to the fact that he worked his own frame, as William Hutton found as early as 1740, had the utmost difficulty in obtaining employment; and even if he bought material and made it up himself, Hutton says he had to sell his goods at a loss.[3] He could obtain equality of treatment only by paying the same frame rent as those who hired frames from the employers, unless he chose (as sometimes happened) to take out work at rates considerably below those generally prevailing. Frame rent was thus partly a commission paid to the employer for finding the operative work. The adoption of the factory system would abolish the excuse for it and a valuable source of income would be destroyed. To what extent this con-

[1] Felkin, *Hosiery and Lace*, p. 496.
[2] See p. 297, and Report of 1845, Appendix, Notts., Q. 4989, 560, 2363.
[3] *Life of Wm. Hutton*, p. 63.

sideration weighed with the larger manufacturers we cannot say; their profit from frame rent, apart altogether from the profits of manufacture, were generally said to be between 5 per cent. and 7½ per cent.; but a host of smaller mouths had to be fed—middlemen, bag hosiers, speculators in frames, stockingers who had bought frames and hired them out to learners—all of whom would swell the chorus against a change that would reduce their earnings. Perhaps this helps to explain why a machine like Brunel's circular frame, invented in 1816, was permitted to lie idle more than thirty years.

In 1840 a machine on the same principle was shown at an exhibition of arts and manufactures held in Nottingham, but it received unfavourable notice because the manufacturers disliked the idea of making hosiery in the shape of a bag; they resolutely set their faces against "roundabouts".[1] An improvement upon Brunel's patent was effected by a Belgian, Peter Claussen, in 1845, and although the hosiers reluctantly admitted its immense powers of production, they refused to take it up.[2] It was feared both by masters and men that the introduction of circular machinery suitable for the production of shirts, pantaloons, etc., would so greatly increase the output of these cheaper commodities that the finer and more costly wrought hosiery would be driven out of the market. So far no successful attempt had been made to apply steam-power to the narrow stocking frame producing the better qualities of hose, with their varieties of colour, shape and ornamentation, although according to Felkin a "power stocking frame" had been invented at Loughborough as early as 1828. Rotary frames producing ten articles at once were in existence in 1845,[3] but no attempt seems to have been made to apply power to them. It seems plain that the manufacturers lacked the inclination rather than the means to introduce the factory system into industry.

The time was coming, however, when the factory

[1] *Hosiery Trade Journal*, Nov., 1904.

[2] Felkin, *op. cit.*, p. 498.

[3] 1845 Report, Notts., Q. 456.

system could be advocated even by the hosiers. Profits were steadily falling; in 1833 it was reported that the profits of the hosiers had decreased in an equal if not a greater ratio than wages,[1] and the succeeding period was one of ever increasing depression. At the same time the significant fact was revealed that the number of houses had decreased, a sign that the smaller hosiers were dropping out of the race, unable to face the terrible competition.[2] Again, it was well known that steam-power had been adopted with great success in Germany, and the competition of the steam-driven circulars of Chemnitz was having a serious effect upon our American trade.[3] The cumulative effect of these influences was to overcome the popular objection to circular frames which from 1845 began to come into general use. A factory was built by a Mr. Collins of Leicester in 1845 in which circular frames were for the first time driven by steam;[4] in 1854 it was reported that steam-power factories were increasing in number in Leicester; by the new method one man could produce eighty dozen a week and the wide hand framework was said to be completely undermined by the new machinery.[5]

The circular frame, however, was only suitable for shirts, pantaloons, drawers and inferior stockings made in sections and sewn together by hand. The finer hose, with its variety of pattern, colour and shape, was still made on the old hand-frame, and it was thought that no substitute for the hand-frame could be devised for this sort of work. The problem, however, was solved by William Cotton of Loughborough, who patented his straight-bar knitting machine in 1851 [6] and so removed the last technical obstacle to the adoption of the power-

[1] Factories Enquiry Commission, 1833, Vol. XX, C. 1, p. 185.

[2] *Ibid.*

[3] Report of Select Committee appointed to consider Stoppage of Wages in Hosiery Manufacture, 1854–5, Vol. XIV, Q. 3265.

[4] Leicester Public Library, Pamphlets, Vol. VI, "Leicester Stockingers."

[5] Committee on Stoppage of Wages in Hosiery Manufacture, 1854–5, Vol. XIV; Minutes of Evidence, Q. 81, 3225, 3260.

[6] *Hosiery Trade Journal*, Dec., 1902; and Committee on Stoppage of Wages, 1854, Minutes of Evidence, Q. 3668.

driven factory. The hand-frame, however, was by no means ousted; but in 1874 frame rents were abolished and the last fortress of the domestic industry surrendered. Even after this event, the hand-frame continued to be worked in many villages of Nottinghamshire for the production of particularly delicate articles, but the great majority of them have within the last few years been taken into the factories, so that the "domestic" industry of framework knitting may now be said to be extinct.

CHAPTER VI

AGRICULTURE—THE PROGRESS OF ENCLOSURE

THE history of Nottinghamshire agriculture during the period of our survey is perhaps the most important of all the topics treated. The changes through which it went were of a revolutionary kind and included in their range nearly the whole area of the County and in their effects the great majority of its inhabitants. In order to understand them fully it is necessary first to consider briefly the main characteristics of the agricultural system which previously obtained.

Nottinghamshire, we need hardly say, was part of the country in which the Teutonic system of agriculture was least affected by survivals of earlier methods, and the open arable fields and common rights characteristic of that system prevailed throughout the greater part of the County. But certain parts of the County, e.g. the extreme west, owing to the nature of the soil and the difficulty of settlement, were very sparsely populated, and some, e.g. in the Forest District, not populated at all until modern times; in the former the agricultural system (even if it was coeval with that prevailing in the rest of the County) seems to have been modified by the physical features of the district; in the latter, where it was introduced by later settlers—by monks, for instance, and more modern pioneers—it was probably different in character from the first.

Much more research is necessary before these modifications of, and divergences from, the Midland System can be indicated with certainty; but there is no doubt that they existed. Enclosures were being made—on what scale it is impossible to say—by the monastic houses at least from the fourteenth century; the sparsely scattered villages of the Forest District made use of the enclosures from the waste for the purposes of temporary arable cultivation as a regular feature of their system of agriculture in the seventeenth century, and probably much earlier. Further to the west, in the limestone and shale district on the Derbyshire border, the regularity of the Midland Field System seems to have been broken up at an early date. At least, there is remarkably little evidence, either in the form of Parliamentary enactment or any other, regarding the enclosure of the open field in this part of the County, which suggests that it took place piecemeal over a long period, without the kind of disturbance which it created in the more densely settled parts of the County cultivated on the Midland System. It is a fact of some significance that practically all the Enclosure Acts for the western district affected the waste only and not the arable, the latter being enclosed by other means at unknown periods. The following is a complete list of Enclosure Acts for the district:

Acts enclosing Waste in the Lime and Coal District[1]

		Acres according to the Act.
1775.	Brinsley	1,388 (mostly waste)
1791.	Eastwood . . .	299
1794.	Sutton in Ashfield Hucknall-under-Huthwaite	2,000 (actual amount enclosed was 3,092 acres according to award)
1795.	Kirkby in Ashfield . .	1,400 (actual amount enclosed was 2,023 acres according to award)
1774.	Greasley. . . .	350
1796.	Gateford and Shireoaks .	— (acreage not stated)
1808.	Annesley . . .	582 (award figure)
1808.	Skegby	— (acreage not stated)
1808.	Bilborough . . .	400
1803.	Worksop . . .	— (acreage not stated)
1865.	Selston	704 (award figure)

[1] See Appendix II.

In other parts, as may be seen from the map,[1] Parliamentary enclosure was mainly concerned with open arable fields, and so persistent was this system of agriculture that in several villages open fields continued to exist until the middle of the nineteenth century, and may be seen under the old rotation of winter corn, spring crop and fallow in Laxton to-day. It can hardly be doubted, from what we have said, that the open field village developed differently in different parts of the County according to the exigencies of the agricultural situation, or the date and manner of the original settlement.

This difference between the agriculture of the wilder and less fertile parts of the County and the rest, even if it is only a matter of the degree to which the "Midland System" was able to develop, is very important in considering the later rural history of the County. In the former district, the central problem of agriculture, except in a few spots of great fertility, was how to subdue Nature and wrest a livelihood from her; in the latter, the question was how to coax a fuller livelihood by improved technique, or changes in rotation or type of crop, from a rich soil that had been cultivated according to a traditional system for centuries. In the first case the difficulty was a physical one; a "hungry" soil, that absorbs the labours of men and the rains of heaven with equal avidity, and the same result, or (in the neighbourhood of the coal measures) a sticky blue clay soil, which, by those who have had experience of it, is commonly thought to have the Devil in it.[2] In the other part of the County the obstacle to agricultural development was a social obstacle, the force of village custom embodied in the complex form of the Midland Field System. How could this system, built up for purposes of subsistence agriculture, adapt itself to the changes of the later Middle

[1] See p. 143.

[2] The writer was born and bred in this part and has no reason to think well of its agricultural qualities however beautiful it may be in the wooded districts. See also "Features of Notts. Agriculture", by H. G. Robinson, *Journal of Roy. Agric. Soc.*, 1927.

Ages? A money economy had developed; a national market had grown up; unaccustomed demands were being made; above all, the demand for wool; and then came the revolution in prices, the monastic revolution, and the rise of rents of the sixteenth century. These questions, no doubt, affected all parts of the County; but in the western half an answer was to be found in the abundance of virgin soil (unattractive though much of it was), that remained to be cleared and cultivated; the village as a group could add to its open fields by temporary enclosure for arable purposes from the waste, and at the same time increase its pasture by "rough grazing" the exhausted arable fields.[1] Again, individuals could strike out on their own; squatters settled on the expanse of waste, with or without the permission of the lord of the manor; their chief enemy was not the lord of the manor, but the sandy soil which made it impossible in many parts to secure a supply of water. Agrarian enterprise in the Forest Area was only in its infancy when the monasteries were dissolved and their effects fell into the hands of the new landlords. In the seventeenth century, when the Crown could no longer sustain its ancient rights, the local lords began to extend their claims, real and imaginary, to the soil of the Forest and its environs, and once in actual possession they cleared, enclosed, ploughed and planted it in wholesale fashion. The duke differed from the squatter only in the scale, not in the nature of his operations, and by the exertions of both a very large area of waste land was eventually brought into cultivation or plantation, from which we have the forest as well as the farms of to-day.

In the rest of the County agricultural development took a different course. Here the problem was how to adapt an ancient and complex system to the changing demands of the time. How, for instance, was the open

[1] See map of Forest Village opposite p. 155 showing enclosures in form of brecks and growth of large enclosed properties. For best treatment of whole question of field system, see H. L. Gray, *English Field Systems*, Harvard Historical Studies, Vol. XXII.

field village to take advantage of the high price of wool when the best land was divided into a multitude of tiny strips held in intermixed ownership, its meadow parcelled out among the tenants of the village and its pasture cumbered with a network of inviolable common rights? Above all, how could it meet the greatly increased demands of the landlord after the price revolution of the sixteenth century except by a reorganisation which would give more scope to individual capital and enterprise? The conditions of the time demanded a relaxation of the restraints which the old field system imposed, and the only way to achieve it was by a progressive reduction of corporate control and common usage of the land, ending, eventually, in enclosure.

This does not mean, as is sometimes assumed, that agricultural improvement could take place only through wholesale enclosure; there were transitional phases, such as the substitution of four for three fields, or three for two; the consolidation of strips into larger holdings (an example of which may be seen in the reorganisation of Laxton in 1908), the engrossing of open field farms into fewer hands, the taking in of small enclosures by the larger freeholders, and so on; but in the end wholesale enclosure triumphed, as was to be expected under the social and political circumstances of the time, and it is to the history of enclosure, in the sense of a slow adaptation of agrarian means to economic ends, that we must turn in order to understand the history of local agriculture during the period of our survey.

Enclosure of Common and Common Field

It is not easy to discover a satisfactory way of approach to this subject, but since we are concerned as much with the method as the matter of local history study, the attempt must be made.[1] We have suggested above that

[1] For very interesting treatment of enclosure on lines somewhat similar to those followed here, see Gray, *op. cit.*, Ch. IV. For a general survey of the problem, see Slater, "Enclosure of Common Fields Considered Geographically", *Geog. Journal*, Jan., 1907.

modifications of the usual Midland Field System occurred in the County, in spite of the Teutonic character of the settlement. The reason, therefore, must be looked for not in any racial difference between east and west, but, as we have already indicated, in the difference of the soil upon which the Teutonic invaders settled. This may be seen more clearly in the accompanying sketch of a cross section of the County.

The line of enquiry indicated above may be pursued further. If it helps to explain modifications in field systems it will also throw light upon the progress of agricultural innovations in the open field village itself. Where the situation of the village lent itself to changes in agricultural practice—to the production of wool or beef instead of corn, for instance—there, it is reasonable to expect, more rapid progress towards enclosure would be made than elsewhere. We may, therefore, expect to find some correspondence between types of soil and the progress of enclosure, or to express it in another way, a similar response of townships similarly situated to the common stimulus of the market.

But though townships might be similarly situated in regard to the quality of the soil, they might be very differently situated in regard to the tenure upon which the soil was held, and this was likely to have a great effect upon the use to which they put it. For instance, a township that was divided among numerous owners—freeholders, copyholders of inheritance, long leaseholders, some large, and some very small—would have many conflicting interests to overcome before enclosure could take place; while one that was in the hands of a single owner and occupied mainly by tenants-at-will, or short leaseholders and so on, would be free from obstacles of this kind, and its technique could be modified without the necessity of considering the interests of those who might suffer by such a change.

Both these conditions, the agricultural situation and the type of tenure will be considered in the present chapter, and the progress of enclosure will, as far as

SKETCH OF SECTION ACROSS NOTTINGHAMSHIRE

Noted for prevalence of waste and lack of permanent pasture — hence Field Systems unstable

Noted for fertility of soil, and suitability both for arable and permanent pasture—hence Field Systems more or less stable

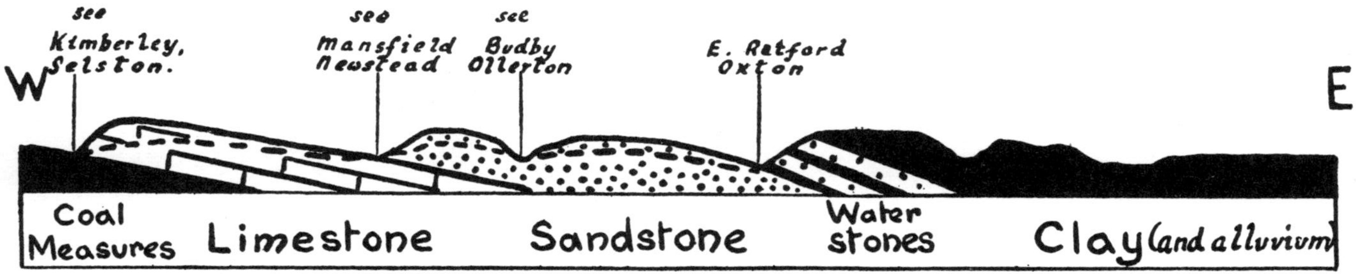

Water Table indicated by broken line

In the Limestone, Coal, and Sandstone Districts the surface soil is dry and unproductive except where the Water Table comes to the surface and forms springs

possible, be shown in relation to them. But it is clearly impossible to consider their influence in every one of the large number of townships under review; all that can be done is to suggest what appear to be the main principles of local enclosure history and illustrate them as far as available evidence permits. Owing to the valuable help of Mr. W. E. Tate of Sutton Bonington, this survey of enclosure history is more complete than at first appeared possible, and his schedule of Nottinghamshire enclosures given in the Appendix, together with the map for which he is largely responsible, have been of the greatest assistance in the work of this chapter.

Something should be said of the sources used for a treatment of the agricultural characteristics of the County, a subject upon which the historian can speak only with hesitation. The first source is Lowe's *Agricultural Survey*, which, after comparison with modern geological surveys, has been made the basis of the map given; besides this, there are the writings of Young and Marshall for the agricultural practice of the County, and the papers on Nottinghamshire Agriculture published in the Journals of the Royal Agricultural Society for 1844 and 1888, and again in 1927, and finally, the excellent handbook on the geography of the County by Dr. Swinnerton. From a study of these sources we have distinguished three main agricultural divisions, in each of which a special characteristic predominates.

The first division we have called the Pasture District, because owing to the nature of its soil and situation it can be utilised for pasture with greater profit than any other part of the County. It consists of three main sections, the first of which is made up of the riverside townships of the Trent and the Soar, situated on alluvium, interspersed here and there with patches of marl, and especially productive of good cattle pasture and rich meadow land. It is marked on the map as "Trent Bank" and according to Lowe, whose boundaries have generally been followed, should include most of the district known as The Trent Hills. Since a large part of this consists of deep red marl clay, suitable for grain growing, we have excluded four villages, situated wholly on the marl, from the Trent Bank and included them in the arable area. The second division of the Pasture District is the Wolds, a high, bleak, sparsely populated district of very stiff clay—mainly boulder clay—difficult to work for arable purposes, but suitable for permanent pasture and sheep rearing. Thirdly, there is the district described by Lowe as the Vale of Belvoir in which the prevailing soil is a stiff, rich clay, mixed in places with marl and alluvium from the rivers Smite and Devon. It stretches from the Trent Hills to the eastern boundary of the County, and although arable farming is possible in all districts, it makes specially good "fattening" pasture, both for sheep and cattle. These three areas constitute the Pasture District.

The second main agricultural division is the Arable District, mainly given over to grain production. It consists of two compact masses of marl clays, the first running from the outskirts of Nottingham almost to Misterton, and the second comprises part of the district known as the Trent Hills, stretching from East Bridgford to Radcliffe. The soil generally is of a deep clay with an admixture of sand and is not difficult to drain, owing either to its height, as in the case of the Trent Hills, or to the existence of numerous streams running across the clay.

Thirdly, there is the largest of all the agricultural divisions, comprising the Marshes of the Car in the north, the sandy forest area, the coal and limestone district on the Derbyshire border and a small sandy tongue of land on the extreme east looking into Lincolnshire. The soil characteristics of these areas differ considerably; alluvium of the marshes, the sand of the Forest district, the limestone and shale of the western district and the gravel of the tongue of land east of the Trent; but different as they are in regard to their formation they have one characteristic in common which influenced their enclosure history, namely abundance of commonable waste. It is difficult to find a name for this composite area with its single common feature, and the title we have given it, the "Natural Waste" area, stands for lack of a better.

The General Progress of Enclosure

Before going on to discuss the relationship of enclosure history to the factors we have mentioned above, it is advisable to give a general view of the progress of the movement in order to see it as a continuous and slowly accelerating process from medieval to modern times.

Thoroton gives the first example of a disputed enclosure in the sixteenth year of Edward I, when sixteen tenants of Epperstone threw down the ditch set up by a local baron round a wood in which they claimed rights of common.[1] Another case occurred in the following year in which men of Misterton succeeded in preventing the enclosure of their common by the lord of the town, "though some lawyers did not like the verdict",[2] and a case of enclosure of arable brought against the Abbot of Welbeck, who appears to have been in the right, occurred in the following reign.[3]

The beginning of enclosure in earnest occurred in the reign of Henry VII, when Gabriel Armstrong, the Lord of Thorpe in the Glebe, in the extreme south of the County, was found by the Commissioners of Henry VIII, in 1517, to have enclosed ninety acres of arable for conversion to pasture, with the result, says Thoroton, that the lordship was eventually populated in his time by a single shepherd.[4] The results of this enquiry in regard to Nottinghamshire is here summarised as a brief indication of the extent and character of the enclosure of that time.

[1] Throsby's Thoroton, III, p. 36.
[2] *Ibid.*, p. 328.
[3] *Ibid.*, p. 343.
[4] *Ibid.*, I, p. 75.

DOMESDAY OF ENCLOSURE, 1517 [1]

	Area.	Total Area Enclosed.	Enclosed but remaining Arable.	Conversion and Enclosure for Pasture.	Percentage of Area of Hundred Enclosed.	No. of Ploughs Put Down.	No. of Houses Decayed.	Displacement of Population.
Thurgarton . .	71,750	159	3	156	·02	—	2	6
Rushcliffe . . .	41,570	399	13	386	·09	2	4	12
Southwell, Scrooby and Beckingham Liberties	46,200	262¼	—	262¼	·05	—	—	—
Bassetlaw . .	184,530	621	19	602	·03	3	5	18
Broxtowe . . .	81,470	287	35	252	·03	4	4	18
Newark . . .	39,830	44	—	44	·01	—	—	—
Nottingham Town .	2,610	—	—	—	—	—	23	89[2]
Bingham . . .	55,760	723½	28	695¼	1·2	10	13	62
Totals . . .	523,720	2,495¾	98	2,397½	—	19	51 [3]	205

Of the total area converted and enclosed for pasture, no less than 744 acres were enclosed for sport, a higher proportion than in any other Midland county.

Nothing is known of the further progress of enclosure in the sixteenth century until the reign of Elizabeth, when, according to Thoroton, villages in the Vale of Belvoir and the Valley of the Trent were enclosed for the purpose of conversion to pasture.[4]

The Star Chamber Proceedings and the Registers of

[1] Leadham, Thoroton Soc. Records Series, Vol. II, p. 70. The figures quoted above do not agree with those given by Professor Gay in his articles in the *Roy. Hist. Soc. Trans.*, Vol. XVIII, p. 233, and *Quarterly Journal of Economics*, Vol. XVII, p. 580, and the area of the county given is less by about 13,000 acres than the modern area. See Swinnerton, *Nottinghamshire*, p. 6.

[2] The presentment of twenty-three decayed houses in Nottingham is peculiar to the returns so far published. It is probably part of the widespread decline of towns in the sixteenth century which called forth the Act 27 Hen. VIII, 1, for the "reedyfyeng of dyvers Townes in the Realm" among which Nottingham was included.

[3] The fifty-one decayed houses comprise forty-seven messuages (i.e. houses with land) and four cottages (without land), see Leadham, *op. cit.*, p. 4.

[4] Throsby's Thoroton, I, pp. 232, 304, and Wake, *Hist. of Collingham*, p. 117.

the Privy Council [1] are said to contain evidence of the continuance of the enclosure agitation in the seventeenth century, and the returns of 1631 show that small enclosures were taking place in many parts of the County, especially in Thurgarton and Bassetlaw, while the Justices actually asserted, according to the writer in the *Victoria County History*, that "there be few habitations among us that live in the Champaign", an untruth gross and palpable, actuated, possibly, by the desire to plead poverty in order to avoid taxation.[2] Within the two years 1629–31, a total area of 1,135 acres is said to have been enclosed in different parts of the County,[3] and in 1637 £2,010 was paid by Nottinghamshire landowners in fines for enclosure leading to depopulation, and in the following year a further £78 was paid.[4]

The Quarter Sessions Records of the County also contain evidence of enclosure in the form of indictments for converting arable into pasture contrary to the Act 5 Eliz., 2, and for enclosing the King's Highway with a hedge,[5] and by the middle of the century the Dutch engineer, Vermuyden, had succeeded in enclosing a considerable portion of the drowned lands in the north of the County.[6]

From the Restoration the movement seems to have continued somewhat more rapidly. Thoroton notes several villages that had been enclosed "since the late troubles", and as will be shown in more detail later, the Forest District at this time was being subjected more and more to the attrition of enclosure by the large proprietors. The following entry from the *Rector's Book of Clayworth* for the year 1676 shows that enclosure was also taking place in the villages of the Clay District. "It was agreed among such as had grounds still un-

[1] Gay, *Roy. Hist. Soc. Trans.*, Vol. XVIII, p. 222; Gonner, *Com. Land and Inclosure*, p. 262.

[2] *V.C.H.*, II, p. 290, quoting *S.P. Dom.*, Chas. I, Vol. CXCIII, No. 79.

[3] E. M. Leonard, *Roy. Hist. Soc. Trans.*, Vol. XIX, p. 133.

[4] Gonner, *Eng. Hist. Review*, Vol. XXIII, p. 487.

[5] Hampton Copnall, *Notts. County Records of Seventeenth Century*, p. 62.

[6] See page 158, note 3.

enclosed ith ley-field, to let them altogether for a yearly rent",[1] while Ogilby's survey of the County about the same date shows that more than half of the roads over which he travelled were enclosed.[2] No further record of enclosure has been found until the epoch of parliamentary enclosure, which began in earnest in this County in 1759. The progress of this phase of the movement may be shown as follows:[3]

	Common and Common Field.		Waste only.
Up to and including			
1760 . . .	13,010	acres	—
1761–70 . .	21,722	,,	—
1771–80 . .	32,080	,,	2,908
1781–90 . .	12,651	,,	—
1791–1800 . .	34,392	,,	2,948
1801–10 . .	12,180	,,	4,808
1811–20 . .	2,500	,,	1,122
1821–30 . .	2,200	,,	—
1831–40 . .	—	,,	35
1841–50 . .	—	,,	—
1851–60 . .	3,269	,,	—
Total . .	134,004	,,	11,821

Total area enclosed by Act between 1759 and 1860 = 145,825 acres = 27·2% area of County.

The above list represents only the amount of enclosure by Acts in which the acreage is stated ; there was in

[1] *Rector's Book of Clayworth*, p. 20, and for enclosed pasture see p. 63.

[2] Gonner, *Eng. Hist. Review*, Vol. XXIII, p. 492. It should not be assumed, however, that the roads marked as enclosed necessarily passed through enclosed villages. Such places as Bunny, Wysall, Mansfield, for instance, were not enclosed until the eighteenth century, although the roads through them, according to Ogilby, were enclosed in the seventeenth century.

[3] Taken from Slater, *English Peasantry and Enclosures*, Appendix, with the addition of the following Acts included in local collection but omitted by Slater: Orston and Thoroton 2,200 acres (1793); East Bridgford (1796) 1,300 acres; Grasthorpe (1799) 350 acres; Sutton-on-Trent (1803) 1,800 acres of open field and 540 of waste. Even these figures require revision owing to frequent discrepancies between figures given in Acts and those of the Awards. See below, Appendix II.

addition an indefinite area enclosed by a number of Acts in which the acreage is not stated. The difference which this makes to the percentage of county area would appear, according to a table compiled by Professor Gonner, to amount almost to 30,000 acres, which brings the acreage enclosed by Act of Parliament to 170,000 acres or 32 per cent. of the County area, a figure at which Dr. Slater has also arrived.[1]

Estimates of acreage are not easy to compile, as the greater part of the County was enclosed without parliamentary sanction, for which little or no record has been left; but an estimate of the position at the end of the eighteenth century may be attempted, subject to correction after more detailed investigation:

	Acres.	Percentage of County Area.
Old enclosures (before 1700):		
Common and common field	55,000	10·3
Waste (permanently enclosed) . . .	10,000	1·9
(This estimate does not include much temporary enclosure from the Forest district.)		
Enclosed by Act of Parliament, 1700–1800:		
Common and common field	133,000	24·8
Enclosed without Parliamentary Sanction, 1700–1800	220,000	41·1
Open in 1800:		
Common field and common	50,000	9·4
Waste land and Forest in 1800:		
(Estimate—a surprisingly high one—sent to Board of Agriculture 1794) . . .	68,000	12·5
Total	536,000	100·0

[1] Gonner, *Com. Land and Inclosure*, p. 280. One point is very obscure; for the decade 1761–70 Gonner appears to state that no enclosure of common took place in the County, but the following Acts for that period definitely mention common or waste; Lowdham (1765); Epperstone (1768); Carlton on Trent (1765); Balderton (1766); Normanton on Soar (1770). No explanation of the method adopted in the calculation is given. The estimate of waste land is given in General View of Waste Lands in Kingdom of Great Britain in Tracts concerning Board of Agriculture, 1794.

Progress of Enclosure and Type of Soil

We can now go on to consider the history of enclosure in the different agricultural areas into which we have divided the County, and compare the progress made. From the outset, however, it will be found that one district—the "Natural Waste" district—was so different in its characteristics that comparison is almost impossible. So abundant was the waste in the greater part of this area, that the new land could be broken up and the old land allowed to relapse into rough pasture in a way that was quite impossible elsewhere. The permanent arable fields, meadow and common, which characterised the rest of the County, were less prominent here, their place being taken, to some extent at least, by temporary enclosures from the Forest, thus the enclosure history of this area must be treated separately. Comparison, however, is possible between the Pasture and the Arable districts, both of which had been settled and cultivated from very ancient times.

The relative progress made by enclosure in these two divisions may be seen at a glance by the following table:

Township in which Common and Common Field was Enclosed before 1700.		Total No. of Townships in Division.	Approx. Area of Division.	Approx. Area Enclosed.	Percentage of District Enclosed.	Av. Area of Township.	Av. Area of Enclosed Township.
Certain.	Probable.						
Pasture District							
23	11	119	178,000	45,000	25·3	1,496	1,324
Arable District							
4	3	81	138,000	6,000	4·1	1,702	857

It will be seen that enclosure had affected the pasture district to a very considerable extent—almost a quarter of its area and more than a quarter of its townships—before 1700, the area in the arable district being inconsiderable. There may have been more enclosure than is represented above, as only those townships which appear to have been wholly or mainly enclosed have been included, so that the petty enclosure which was taking place in both districts has been omitted. Moreover, a number of doubtful cases such as Shelford, Kelham, Willoughby on Trent, all in the pasture district, have been omitted, so that the estimate probably errs on the conservative side.

Another point of interest is that the size of the enclosed townships was considerably below the average for the districts taken, especially in the Arable district. It would appear, therefore, that in both districts the small township was more liable to enclosure than the large, but that the most important factor of all was the suitability of the soil for pasture purposes.

To what extent the townships enclosed at this time were actually converted from arable to pasture farming it is impossible to say; but it may be noted that depopulation is expressly stated by Thoroton and other writers to have taken place as a consequence of these enclosures in eleven townships, all of which were in the Pasture district. Two villages in the Arable are also seen to have suffered a decline in population from this cause, though no definite complaint was made. The villages are Grove (1,300 acres) where a large park was made and only twenty houses remained in the eighteenth century, and Saxondale (684 acres) where Thoroton speaks of "the few inhabitants now left".[1] Another township in the Clays, Bevercotes (734 acres), probably enclosed about the same time, consisted at the end of the eighteenth century of only five or six houses. Other examples of enclosed townships from which no complaints are heard but which are shown to be very small at the end of the eighteenth century, are:

Thrumpton	979	acres,	apparently 3 occupiers in 1790
Thorpe by Newark	713	,,	9 houses in 1790
Edwalton	831	,,	13 poor houses in 1790
Attenborough / Toton	1,322	,,	15 houses in 1790 / inconsiderable in 1790
Radcliffe on Soar	1,122	,,	3 farms—greatly improved by a "reputable grazier"

[1] Throsby's Thoroton, III, p. 264, and I, p. 286.

Although the evidence is far from complete, there seems to be no doubt that the townships enclosed before 1700 frequently dwindled in size, while farms grew larger, a circumstance that is more compatible with conversion to pasture on a considerable scale than with continued arable farming. This conclusion is confirmed by the attitude of Thoroton; his view of enclosure was simple; according to him,

"enclosing and converting Arable to Pasture . . . as certainly diminishes the Yearly Fruits, as it doth the People, for we may observe that a Lordship in Tillage, every Year affords more than double the Profits which it can in Pasture, and yet the latter Way the landlord may perhaps have double the Rent he had before; the Reason whereof is that in *Pasture* he hath the whole Profit, there being required neither Men nor Charge worth speaking of; whereas in *Tillage* the People and their Families necessarily employed upon it . . . must be maintained, and their Public Duties discharged, before the Landlord's Rent can be raised or ascertained. But this *Improvement* of Rent certainly causes the Decay of Tillage. . . ." [1]

It should not be thought, however, that pasture farming necessarily meant sheep farming. In the Wolds and parts of the Vale of Belvoir, this may have been the case, but side by side with the growth of sheep farming there was a decided development in cattle grazing. For instance, 400 acres were enclosed in Elizabeth's reign at Langford, and let to the butchers of Newark, apparently for the purpose of a cattle pasture, since the sheep walk was "very casual and no great account made of it".[2] Again, the demesnes at Wollaton and Sutton Passeys (a decayed village) were leased to a tanner of Nottingham, which probably indicates cattle pasture, and Thoroton gives an interesting note on Alderman William Gregory, who bought the Manor of Lenton, and "by grazing raised very considerable estate from the lowest beginning", upon the proceeds of which he built one of the best seats in the town.[3] He is everywhere described

[1] Throsby's Thoroton, I, p. xvi.

[2] Wake, *Hist. of Collingham*, pp. 117 and 118.

[3] Throsby's Thoroton, II, pp. 41–2.

as a "Gentleman" except in the parish registers of St. Mary's where he is set down as a butcher.[1] Finally, there is the testimony of the local historian, Deering (1739), who says:

"In 1641 there were no less than 61 butchers in the town with a population of only 4,000; and although the number of butchers has not greatly increased during the succeeding centuries in spite of a doubling of the population, they still supply meat for five times the number of people." [2]

It would be mistaken, therefore, to associate all early enclosure for pasture with sheep farming, and especially in the riverside townships of the Trent and the Soar and parts of the Vale of Belvoir which are specially suitable for cattle rearing and dairying.

If the enquiry be now continued into the eighteenth century, it will be found that enclosure made very rapid progress in both districts, completely outstripping all previous movement, so that by the end of the century the position was roughly as follows:[3]

	Percentage of Area.			
	Enclosed before 1700.	Between 1700–1800.	Open in 1800.	Unknown.
Arable District . . .	4·1	59	30	6·9
Pasture District. . .	25·3	59·7	13·5	1·5

From the above it will be seen that the arable area was not seriously affected by enclosure until the eighteenth century, but even then it scarcely kept pace with the progress made in the pasture districts, and in 1800 nearly a third of the area still remained open.

Its relatively slower progress is not difficult to explain. In the first place the disadvantages of growing grain in

[1] Godfrey, *Hist. of Parish and Priory of Lenton,* Pedigree of Gregory of Nottingham, Note 2.

[2] Deering, *Hist. of Nottm.,* pp. 94 and 96.

[3] A misleading statement occurs in *V.C.H.,* II, p. 377, to the effect that several villages still remained open in the South-Eastern or Clay District in 1844. It should be remembered there were three distinct Clay Districts and the villages alluded to were not in the south-east of the County, but in the Clay District north of the Trent. Similarly, Gonner is entirely at fault in stating that the Vale of Belvoir was mainly open at the end of the eighteenth century (*Com. Land and Inclosure,* p. 262). Lowe gives only two places as being open—Cropwell Bishop and Elton (p. 155, edition 1798).

the open field were not sufficient to overcome the great difficulties and expense of enclosure; it may be noted that excellent grain crops are grown in the open fields of Laxton to-day. Open field agriculture was by no means wholly incapable of improvement without enclosure; it could be made more efficient by consolidation of strips, and enclosure of stocking closes and meadow land. There is evidence that petty enclosure of this kind was taking place in the arable district throughout the sixteenth and seventeenth centuries. Towards the end of the eighteenth century a number of villages undertook more drastic reorganisation in the form of an increase in the rotation of crops and in the number of arable fields, and in this condition remained open until the middle of the nineteenth century. We shall return to this question again; we mention it here as part of the process of improvement which the open-field corn-growing village undertook as an alternative to wholesale enclosure, and thereby postponed that revolutionary change until the price of grain was such as to repay the great cost and trouble which it involved. In a number of cases it was postponed until the middle of the nineteenth century.

We will now consider the third agricultural district—the Natural Waste District—and see how the progress of enclosure was affected by the existence of improvable waste upon a scale which is found in few other counties.

Enclosure from the Natural Waste of Forest, Moor and Fen

The most extensive area of waste was found in the part shown on the map as the Forest district, which, if the fenland of the Car is included, stretched for a distance of thirty miles north and south and ten miles at its widest place east and west. The Forest district should not be confounded with the Ancient Forest of Sherwood, which included such villages as Carlton, Gedling, Lambley, Oxton, Calverton, that belonged more properly to the Clay district, and excluded much open moorland in the neighbourhood of Worksop. The boundaries of the Forest district have been drawn on the map with an eye to soil distinctions alone, and without reference to the area over which the Crown claimed the ancient rights of vert and venison.

Besides the Forest district there were the drowned lands of Hatfield Chase, of which about 6,000 acres were situated in the extreme north of the County in the district called the Car, the Limestone and Coal district, a large part of which was rough moorland and woodland, and the low-lying and sandy tract called by Lowe the Tongue of land East of the Trent.

Much of this extensive district was mere heath and shrub and must constantly have been subjected to the encroachment of petty enclosure.[1] The wooded districts offered greater resistance, but the stubbing up of trees was, of course, no great difficulty in those days.[2] A survey of 1609 gives the following figures:[3]

	Acres.	Roods.	Perches.
Enclosures (temporary?) .	44,839	1	4
Woods . . .	9,486	—	23
Waste	35,080	2	6
Clipstone Park . .	1,583	1	25
Bestwood Park . .	3,672	—	—
Bulwell Park . .	326	3	2
Nottingham . . .	120	3	9
	95,117	3	36

It is difficult to think that the figure given for the enclosed area represents permanent enclosure; it almost certainly included a large area of temporary enclosure known as "Brecks" or "Breaks" taken in by the forest villages. A map of a forest village has been shown opposite in order to illustrate the method adopted by the villages to

[1] Much of the land between Worksop and Retford was already enclosed in Leland's time—Leland's *Itinerary*—edited by Hearne, Vol. V, pp. 85–6, edition of 1710.

[2] See *Rector's Book of Clayworth*, p. 135.

[3] Quoted in the Fourteenth Report of Commissioners to enquire into State of Woods, Forests, etc., 1792. The large amount of enclosure probably included Forest breaks or "brecks", i.e. temporary enclosure.

utilise the surrounding wastes, and is further explained by Lowe, the county surveyor, who wrote of it as follows:[1]

"there was always about each forest village a small quantity of inclosed land in tillage or pasture, the rest lay open, common to the sheep and cattle of the inhabitants and the king's deer. It has been besides an immemorial custom for the inhabitants of townships to take up breaks, or temporary inclosures of more or less extent, perhaps from 40 to 250 acres and keep them in tillage for five or six years. For this the permission of the Lord of the Manor is necessary and two verderers must inspect, who report to the Lord Chief Justice in Eyre that it is not to the prejudice of King or subject. They are to see that the fences are not such as to exclude the deer".

It is probable, too, that the religious houses of the district—Welbeck, Rufford, Newstead, Worksop, Blyth—all of which produced wool for the Flemish and Italian markets—had taken in considerable areas, since, as we have seen, the Abbot of Welbeck was able to enclose twenty-four acres of arable outside the gate of his monastery in spite of the protest of the King's tenants of Carberton, who claimed rights of common on it.[2] The silent nibbling of the Forest by the monastic sheep and oxen was succeeded by the bustling enterprise of their lay successors. Sir Wm. Savile, for instance, obtained permission to plough up and sow as much of his soil in Sherwood Forest as he liked in order to destroy coneys and their burrows.[3] Sir John Byron tried to take in Bulwell Moor in 1601 but was prevented by the copyholders and the tenants of the Manor, who petitioned the Privy Council and were maintained in their rights.[4]

[1] Lowe, *Agric. Survey of Notts.*, 1798, p. 21—see also report cited above for a similar explanation, where the temporary enclosures taken in by the Forest villages are called Brecks, p. 14. For laws relating to newly planted timber, see Garnier, *Hist. of English Landed Interest*, Vol. II, pp. 42 *et seq*.

[2] Throsby's Thoroton, III, p. 343. The Flemish and Italian merchants kept lists of monastic houses that could be relied on for wool, and the following Notts. monasteries are included: Rufford, Welbeck, Mattersey, Blyth, Worksop, Shelford, Lenton, Newstead. See Cunningham, *Eng. Ind. and Commerce*, Vol. I, Appendix D.

[3] *Cal. S.P. Dom.*, Feb. 27, 1636–7, Vol. CCCXLVIII, No. 50.

[4] *Ibid.*, 1601, Vol. CCLXXIX, No. 112.

John Trueman, Verderer of Sherwood, petitioned in 1663 for a commission to enquire into contracts for the enclosure and ploughing up "of thousands of acres" in the Forest by agents of local proprietors,[1] and a letter of the Duchess of Newcastle in 1711 shows that the cutting down of timber and the enclosing of land was taking place on a considerable scale on the Newcastle estates.[2]

The change that was gradually overtaking the ancient Forest of Sherwood at this time is feelingly described by a contemporary, the anonymous historian of Nottingham, who wrote in 1641:

> "I have myself seen in that lordly Lindhurst and other parts of this Forest numberless numbers of goodly oak without Bush or Twig saving the Top Bush, such for tall and streight as a man would concieve the Cedars of Lebanon . . . to be, where now there is nothing to be seen but Oves and Boves et prora campi grazing upon a Carpet Green, not so much as a Bush for a Nightingale to rest in. . . .
>
> "Infandum jubet hoc spolium renovare dolorem. . . .
>
> "Yet there are some reliques of the Ancient Beautie of this Forrest in the parts of Belhaigh and Birkland, though these be shrewdly gelded and pruned, which woods . . . consist only of fair and stately Oaks." [3]

One outstanding example of this early forest enclosure is that of Bestwood Park, "a mighty great park" in Leland's time,[4] but described by Thoroton as "parcelled up into little closes on one side and much of it ploughed, so that there is scarce wood or venison which is also likely to be the fate of the whole Forest of Sherwood".[5] Lowe, writing more than a century later, notes that it was divided into eight farms.

[1] *Ibid.*, 1663, Petitions, Vol. LXXXIX, No. 63.

[2] Hist. MSS. Com., *Portland Papers*, Vol. II, p. 233, the letter protests against the Duke of Leeds being made Justice in Eyre; he was a personal enemy and could put a stop to her enclosures.

[3] MS. copy in Nottingham Ref. Library. The destruction of timber went on rapidly during the Civil War, and it is stated that not a tree was left standing in Clipstone Park. See article in *Journal of Ecology*, Vol. XV, No. 1, February, 1927, p. 140.

[4] Leland's *Itinerary*—Hearne's edition, 1710, Vol. I, p. 85.

[5] Throsby's Thoroton, II, p. 279.

The Car.

To the north-east of the old Forest area was an extensive tract of boggy land in the north of the County, known as the Car, that was partially drained and to some extent enclosed in the seventeenth century.

In 1630 Sir Cornelius Vermuyden was commissioned by Charles I to drain the drowned lands known as Hatfield Chase, of which an area of about 6,000 acres, known as the Car, was situated in this part of the County. The project met with the fiercest opposition from the inhabitants, who damaged his works, beat his workmen, and assailed the Privy Council with loud complaints.[1] In spite of these obstacles Vermuyden continued his efforts to reclaim the land, and recompensed himself by enclosing on a considerable scale. In 1634 it was complained that he had enclosed a thousand acres near Misterton for his own use and excluded the petitioners from rights of common.[2] The land still remained, however, in a boggy state, and in many parts it was impossible to use horses for ploughing, the operation being performed by manual labour. How much was brought into cultivation, or enclosed by Vermuyden, it is impossible to say; it is certain, however, that at the end of the eighteenth century further drainage work was undertaken and a large tract of extraordinary fertility was added to the cultivated area of the County.[3]

It will be seen, therefore, that enclosure of waste from the Forest and marsh area was going on steadily

[1] *Cal. S.P. Dom.*, 1630, Vol. CLXVIII, No. 3; Vol. CLXXIV, No. 16; 1632, Sept. 15, Vol. CCXXIII, Nos. 30, 31; 1633, Sept. 24, Vol. CCXLVI, No. 65; 1633, Nov., Vol. CCL, No. 55, etc.

[2] *Ibid.*, 1634, Vol. CCLXXIX, No. 102. See also accounts of riots and destruction of 8,000 acres of corn, etc.—1653, Vol. XXXVII, No. 11; 1653, Vol. XXXIX, 95, No. 24.

[3] *Journal of Roy. Agric. Soc.*, First Series, Vol. VI, p. 41. Vermuyden claimed that he had drained 60,000 acres in the three counties of Notts., Yorks, and Lincs. (*S.P. Dom.*, 1653, Vol. XXXVII, No. 11) and Council of State settled 7,400 acres on participants in the scheme as compensation for damage by rioters (*S.P. Dom.*, 1653, Vol. XXXIX, 95, No. 24), but much of it was only partially drained.

long before the era of Parliamentary enclosure. One exception to this general tendency is the Tongue of land east of the Trent, which appears to have been unaffected by the movement. It was a poor district of low-lying gravel, and the waste was incapable of improvement except after the expenditure of capital on a scale which only an improving landlord of the eighteenth century could attempt. The enclosures made elsewhere would add considerably to the cultivated area of the County, since the soil was too light to be used for permanent pasture. Apparently the land taken from the waste of the Forest and its borders was brought into temporary cultivation and allowed to lapse into pasture for sheep and brought back again into cultivation after it had recovered, permanent pasture being very limited in extent. It is interesting to note that the famous agricultural "improver", Gervase Markham, born of an old Nottinghamshire family at Cottam, recommended a form of "convertible" husbandry that could easily be adopted to the "brecks" of the Forest villages; it consisted of a sequence of crops occupying ten or twelve years, whereof three to four years were spent in "lying at rest for grass". Whether this course was adopted by the Forest villages it is impossible to say; the extent of waste land was so great that they could allow more than three years of grass for the recuperation of the arable.[1]

In the eighteenth century the progress was much more rapid, and owing to the developments in technique, and probably, also, to the improvement of the soil, after the partial cultivation we have described, large areas were brought into permanent cultivation, or enclosed for plantation.

[1] See Ashley, *Bread of our Forefathers*, pp. 32–3. For cases of enclosure for permanent pasture, see Haughton, Annesley, Ranby, Serlby, Kimberley, and the monastic sites of Newstead, Felley and Welbeck. In most of these cases the area was small and the date of enclosure uncertain. The account of Markham given in *D.N.B.* gives his birthplace as Cotham. Apart from this, the article is extremely good and much superior to account given in Cornelius Brown's *Worthies and Celebrities of Notts.*

Enclosure in the Natural Waste District in the Eighteenth Century

The waste of the Forest area was partly enclosed by Act, but more largely by private agreement of the proprietors. It is impossible to give the exact acreage of the former since the area is not always stated, but at least 4,000 acres were enclosed by Act in the eighteenth century and a further nine to ten thousand acres in the nineteenth century. But the most rapid progress was made by private enclosures, of which Lowe, at the end of the eighteenth century, gives an account. For instance, Leland's "mighty great park" of Bestwood, an area of 3,700 acres, was divided into eight farms, and was only one among a number of tracts taken into cultivation from the Forest. Another example of change from park into farm land occurred in Clumber Park, which, at the end of the eighteenth century, contained 2,000 acres in regular and excellent course of tillage, "besides pasture for three or four thousand sheep", and in Newstead Park, from which three farms were taken in 1794.[1] In addition to these, enclosure from the waste was taking place on a considerable scale by private individuals in many different parts of the forest. An interesting list of private enclosure is given by Lowe, which shows that a total area of 10,366 acres, of which only 600 were for the purpose of plantation, had been enclosed in the latter part of the eighteenth century by eight individuals in twelve different parts of the Forest and borders. Finally, there was the unrecorded absorption of waste in the form of brecks by the Forest villages, each of which, according to Lowe, took on an average a hundred and fifty acres for purposes of temporary cultivation.[2]

[1] Lowe, *op. cit.*, pp. 22, 23, 150.

[2] A convenient average of the figures given by Lowe, p. 21. This figure is by no means excessive. A breck of 200 acres is mentioned by Cox, *V.C.H.*, I, p. 376, and the map of Carberton, p. 155, shows a considerable area lying in brecks. The making of brecks was subject to the jurisdiction of the Sherwood Forest Court which also concerned itself with the protection of the commoners in the forest. Rights of common, such as gathering windfall wood,

Besides these inroads made upon the Forest, there were the plots of squatters and cottagers living on the outskirts of the centres of population, especially round about Mansfield, and producing potatoes and vegetables for the local markets. They paid a trifling sum to the lord of the manor, it is said, but were limited, in the early nineteenth century, to the enclosure of no more than one acre of ground.[1]

In the Lime and Coal district similar absorption was taking place. And in addition nearly 7,000 acres were enclosed by Act of Parliament. There was also in the east of the County the great work of improvement carried out by Mr. George Neville, of Thorney, who reclaimed much of the sandy waste east of the Trent by drainage and enclosure, and brought 700 acres of the best of the moorland into cultivation, and planted another 200 acres with trees.

Enclosure for Plantation

Besides the area brought into cultivation from the waste of the Forest, a smaller, but still considerable area was enclosed and planted with trees so that the glory of the old Royal Forest has been to some extent restored. The period of plantation began at the close of a campaign of indiscriminate destruction carried out by the Restoration Government, and associated with the admiralship of the Duke of York. Extravagant grants of timber had previously been made by the Commonwealth Government; a certain Mr. Clark, for instance, was given the right of felling the incredible number of 28,000

pasture of animals, housebote, haybote, were extensive, and the inhabitant of the Forest district felt himself a privileged person in comparison with the less fortunate inhabitant of the purlieus, i.e. who lives *en pur lieu,* in the void and open space around. The court also undertook to preserve the privilege of water, a very important matter in the sandy soil of Sherwood. Wells and sykes (surface water) were open at all times of the year to all animals but goats, which were prohibited as they were offensive to the deer. The old forest area covered about one-fifth of the County, but was rapidly encroached upon, especially from the East and North, after the close of the Middle Ages. Cf. *V.C.H., loc. cit.*

[1] White's *Directory of Notts.*, 1832, p. 523.

trees for his own use by the Committee for the sale of Traitors' Estates.[1] But a period of systematic destruction opened with the Restoration. In 1664 the wharf at Bawtry was clogged with timber; in 1670 it was said that the forest still contained 4,500 loads of serviceable timber, sufficient for the frames of four third-rate ships,[2] and large quantities were sent from West Stockwith and Hull to Deptford, but in the same year it was reported that "not any more timber is left in the woods".[3] The result of this rapid clearance of timber was seen in the many complaints of the destructiveness of the deer which were now deprived of shelter. They roamed in the cornfields, woods, and meadows, many miles from the Forest, "to the insupportable injury of the land holders". Many were killed by enraged tenants, and serious loss was feared by the verderers unless something was done. The deer, it was complained, were unable to find shelter since the wood in the middle of the forest was wellnigh destroyed. As they multiplied at their usual rate, they were unable to get food in hard weather and wandered into people's barns and fields and ate their cabbages and carrots; while the standing corn was saved only by employing watchmen at night to drive them away.[4] About this time, however, plantation was taking place on a big scale and the deer became confined to the enclosed parks. By the end of the century, the herds of deer that once roamed free in the open Forest of Sherwood were entirely extirpated,[5] their place being taken by private herds confined within the pales of ducal parks.

One of the first parks for purposes of sport in the Forest area was made in 1661, when Sir Patrick Chaworth

[1] *Cal. S.P. Dom.*, 1655, Vol. XCVI, No. 52.

[2] *Ibid.*, 1664, Vol. XCIV, No. 70, and Jan. 6, 1670, Vol. CCLXXXII, No. 9.

[3] *op. cit.*, 1670, Vol. CCLXXXIV, No. 154. For account of destruction of Forests from Reformation to 1771, see Garnier, *Eng. Landed Interests*, Vol. II, pp. 42–67.

[4] *H.C.J.*, Vol. 16, p. 118, Feb. 21, 1708; and *V.C.H.*, I, pp. 376–7; and Hist. MSS. Com., *Portland Papers*, Vol. V, p. 375, *Foljambe Papers*; 15th *Report*, Appendix, Part V, p. 142.

[5] Lowe, *op. cit.*, p. 97.

was given the right to enclose 1,200 acres in the Manor of Annesley.[1] Similarly, the Duke of Newcastle made a very good bargain with the Crown for enclosing and planting 4,000 acres of Clumber Park in 1708.[2] Although this part of the Forest had been dismantled of almost all its wood before the Duke of Newcastle took it over, by 1778 it had been replanted by him in a manner "that reflects honour upon his taste and will in time restore it to more than its pristine beauty".[3] Lowe, writing of Clumber Park in 1798, describes it as a new creation; thirty years earlier it was a black heath full of rabbits, having a narrow river running through with a small boggy close or two . . . "but now, besides expensive plantations, above 2,000 acres are brought into regular and excellent course of tillage, maintaining at the same time three or four thousand sheep".[4]

The widespread movement for plantation is thus summed up by Defoe's editor in 1778:

"the spirit of plantation has nowhere exerted itself with more vigour and effort than in this county. The Dukes of Norfolk, Kingston, Newcastle and Portland have made prodigious plantations. Lord Byron, Sir Charles Sedley, and many others have given a new shade to their respective estates, but Sir George Saville has planted a whole country: so the Shirewood forest may once again be cloathed in all the dignity of wood".[5]

The rapidity with which plantations were made increased as the century wore on. Lowe gives a list of twenty-three parks of the total area of 7,197 acres in the district of the Forest and its borders, of which the majority had been planted after 1760. By the end of the century very little waste of any value either for agriculture or plantations was left in the Forest area. The two open districts of considerable extent that remained lay between

[1] *Cal. S.P. Dom.*, 1661, July 10, Vol. XXXIX, No. 37.

[2] Add. MSS. 33060, 3 *et seq.* The park was to remain the property of the Queen, during which time the Duke was to have a pension of £1,000 a year. After her death the park was to be "resumed" by the Duke.

[3] Defoe, *Tour through Britain*, Vol. III, p. 64 (1778).

[4] Lowe, *op. cit.*, p. 22.

[5] Defoe, *op. cit.*, p. 64 (1778).

Rufford and Mansfield, and between Blidworth and Newstead. They were described as poor barren land suitable for little else than rabbit warrens.[1]

The greatly increased value and beauty of the Forest after plantation were bought to some extent at the expense of the inhabitants. In a bill of charges purporting to show the cost and trouble of maintaining the King's deer in plantations there occurs the following significant item: [2]

To enclose 2,000 acres which I now let at £300 per annum with a strong pale .	£6,000
Land witheld from enclosure and cultivation	£10,000

Again, in 1722 the Duke of Kingston prayed leave to enclose certain barren closes amounting to 1,217 acres that lay in the rangership of Sherwood Forest in order to enlarge his park of Thoresby.[3] In both these cases rights of common would be lost by the neighbouring villages, and in the first case there might have been some displacement of population. Similar infringements of popular rights, but perhaps on a smaller scale, would necessarily take place wherever large areas of the royal forest, which had always been subject to certain rights of common, were enclosed and planted.

The greatest sufferer by the plantations was the Crown. There is no need here to enter into the dubious methods by which the old Royal Forest was wrested from the possession of the Crown and passed into the hands of the local landowners, nor the abuses that were practised at the expense of the Crown in regard to the sale of fallen timber.[4] By the end of the century the Crown had no other property in the forest than the Hays of Birkland

[1] Lowe, *op. cit.*, p. 96.

[2] Add. MSS. 33060, 72, date 1715.

[3] *Treasury Papers*, 1722, Vol. CCXL, No. 86.

[4] See Fourteenth Report of Commissioners appointed to enquire into state of Woods and Forests, etc., 1792, and for a long account of forest abuses and methods by which the Duke of Newcastle obtained possession of Lindhurst and Norman's Woods, see petition of John Trueman, Verderer of Forest of Sherwood, praying for a special commission to stay the felling of timber and enclosing plains in the forest, etc. *S.P. Dom.*, 1663, Vol. LXXXIX, No. 63.

and Bilhagh, but even here the soil was claimed by the Duke of Portland as part of the Manor of Edwinstowe.

We have now accounted for nearly 30,000 acres of land brought into cultivation from the waste by enclosure and another eight or nine thousand enclosed for plantation. So rapid had been the progress that it was possible for Lowe to state at the end of the eighteenth century that there was little waste land of value remaining in the County; the only districts of importance being two sandy tracts we have mentioned. There was, however, a considerable amount of open field still unenclosed as we show in the next section.

Summary

We may now summarise the conclusions to be drawn from this side of our enquiry as follows: Where the nature of the soil lent itself to pasture, enclosure made progress from an early date and involved the conversion of arable to pasture for cattle as well as for sheep. The process continued steadily throughout the whole period and was almost completed by 1800. Where the soil was primarily suited to grain-growing, little enclosure took place except in a few villages of small size until the eighteenth century, but although it made rapid strides it was still far behind the Pasture district in 1800, almost one-third still remaining open at that time. In the parts of the County where waste predominated there was steady enclosure of waste for temporary conversion to arable from very early to modern times; towards the end of the seventeenth century there was a movement in the direction of enclosure for sport and in the eighteenth century for plantation and permanent arable, so that by 1800 the Forest area in particular had undergone a revolutionary change. A good deal of open field remained to be enclosed in the nineteenth century, but comparatively little of the original waste tracts remained except two sandy areas of doubtful value.

Influence of Tenure upon the Progress of Enclosure

We have seen that the enclosure of common field and common progressed at different rates in the three divisions into which we have divided the County; but it would be a mistake to think that economic considerations alone accounted for the difference. A very important contributory factor was the nature of the tenure; a township wholly occupied by tenants-at-will or short leaseholders, under a single landlord may be expected to have a different enclosure history from another township, even where the soil and situation are the same, in which property is divided among a large number of freeholders and copyholders of inheritance. In order to indicate the nature of this difference we will take first of all the townships which are known or believed to have been enclosed before 1700 in the Pasture and Arable divisions and examine, as far as we can, the nature of the tenure upon which they were held:

Townships Enclosed Before 1700 in Pasture District

Name.	Area. (Acres.)	Distribution of Property at time of Enclosure according to Indications given by Thoroton.
Hawton	2,168	One chief owner.
Cotham	1,350	" " "
Shelton	845	" " "
Car Colston	1,642	Several substantial freeholders persuaded to enclose by the largest landowner, Richard Whalley.
Flawborough	976	One chief owner.
Wiverton	1,023	" " "
Colston Bassett	2,447	Two chief owners.
Thorpe-in-the-Glebe	863	One chief owner.
Thrumpton	979	" " "
Barnston, Langar	3,868	" " "
Tythby	583	" " "
Edwalton	831	Apparently two chief owners.
Attenborough, Toton	1,332	" " " "
Wollaton, Sutton Passeys	2,064	" " " "

TOWNSHIPS ENCLOSED BEFORE 1700 IN PASTURE DISTRICT—(*continued*)

Name.	Area. (Acres.)	Distribution of Property at time of Enclosure according to Indications given by Thoroton.
Normanton-on-Wolds	803	Apparently two chief owners.
Ratcliffe-on-Soar	1,222	Two chief owners.
Kingston	1,312	One chief owner.
Stanton-on-Wolds	1,406	" " "
Meering	483	" " "
Thorpe by Newark	640	Apparently two chief owners.
Probably enclosed:		
Owthorpe	1,639	One chief owner.
S. Collingham	3,017	Apparently divided.
Langford	2,179	A number of substantial proprietors.
Barnby-in-Willows	1,845	Ownership undetermined.
Stanford-on-Soar	1,500	One chief owner.
Holme Pierrepont, Adbolton	2,198	One owner.
West Bridgford	1,115	" "
Gamston	442	" "
South Muskham	2,730	Divided property.
Colwick	1,271	One owner.
Total acreage	44,773	

No. of townships in which property was concentrated in the hands of a few owners	28
No. of townships in which property was divided amongst a number of owners	3
No. of townships unclassified	1
Total	32

TOWNSHIPS ENCLOSED BEFORE 1700 IN ARABLE DISTRICT

Name.	Area. (Acres.)	Distribution of Property at the time of Enclosure according to Indications given by Thoroton.
Kneeton	962	Three owners.
Saxondale	684	One owner.
Grove	1,324	" "
Cottam	599	Divided property.
Probably enclosed:		
Bevercotes	734	One chief owner.
Halloughton	988	One leaseholder.
S. Wheatley	645	One chief owner.
Total	5,936	

It would appear from the evidence we have given that townships enclosed before 1700 were in nearly all cases entirely or very largely owned by a single proprietor at the time of the enclosure. In such townships enclosure could be carried through without interference or obstacle, and therefore was undertaken at an early date wherever economic conditions were favourable. Further proof of this proposition can be given by demonstrating its converse, namely, that townships, even in the Pasture district in which land was divided among numerous freeholders, were among the last to be enclosed. The following table will illustrate this; it includes all the towns in the Pasture district which (as far as can at present be ascertained) were divided among numerous owners at the time of their enclosure according to indications given by the Poll Book of 1722 and by John Throsby in his peregrinations of 1790.

Name.	Freeholders who Voted in 1722. Resident.	Non-resident.	Throsby 1790.	Enclosure.
Aslockton . .	8	1	Divided property	20 Geo. III (with Scarrington).
Balderton . .	16	2	„ „	6 Geo. III.
Beeston . .	13	7	„ „	46 Geo. III.
Bramcote . .	5	1	In several hands	11 Geo. III (with Stapleford).
Bingham . .	16	3	Sixteen substantial freeholders mentioned by name	Enclosed without Parliamentary sanction "upwards of 100 years" according to Throsby but later than 1778 according to Lowe. Earl of Chesterfield was Lord of Manor and very influential here.
E. Bridgford .	18	1	A number of freeholders	36 Geo. III.

Name.	Freeholders who Voted in 1722. Resident.	Non-resident.	Throsby 1790.	Enclosure.
*Chilwell . .	9	0	Divided	Probably enclosed without Parliamentary sanction in eighteenth century.
Coddington .	12	3	In several hands	33 Geo. II.
Cropwell Bishop.	11	0	Several reputable freeholders	42 Geo. III.
Cropwell Butler	8	3	Omitted by Throsby	27 Geo. III.
N. Collingham .	11	2	In several hands	30 Geo. III.
Hickling . .	35	1	One chief owner and others	15 Geo. III.
Keyworth . .	10	2	Divided among several freeholders	38 Geo. III.
Sutton Bonington	23	1	Several small freeholders mentioned in enclosure award	14 & 15 Geo. III.
Stapleford . .	21	1	Several freeholders	11 Geo. III.
Willoughby-on-Wolds	20	3	,, ,,	33 Geo. III.

* Townships marked thus were probably enclosed very early in the eighteenth century or even before 1700.

With the possible exception of Bingham and Chilwell, all the townships given were enclosed late in the eighteenth century or early in the nineteenth century, which shows that the subdivision of property among numerous hands tended to delay the progress of enclosure in comparison with that made by townships in which the large proprietor was supreme.

It is also worthy of note that all the townships but two were enclosed by the same method, namely, by Act of Parliament. It would appear then that enclosure by Act can generally be associated with a considerable division of ownership of the property enclosed. What was the position of the townships which were enclosed without parliamentary sanction? We have shown that in the case of the great majority of "early enclosed" townships, property had become concentrated in the hands of a few owners at the time of the enclosure. Was this also the case with townships enclosed by "private agreement" in the eighteenth century? The following list of all the townships so enclosed in the Pasture and Arable districts, together with the distribution of property as far as that can be ascertained, will show that this generally was the case.

ARABLE DISTRICT

TOWNSHIPS MAINLY ENCLOSED WITHOUT PARLIAMENTARY SANCTION BETWEEN 1700 AND 1800, AND THE DISTRIBUTION OF THE PROPERTY

Name.	Area of Township.	Freeholders who Polled in 1722. Resident.	Non-resident.	Approximate No. of Owners in 1790.
Darlton	1,506	0	1	One proprietor who was selling portions to different people.
Fledborough	1,448	1	1	One principal owner.
Gonalston	1,342	0	3	One owner.
Hoveringham	900	5	2	Lately purchased by one owner.
Hockerton	1,386	1	3	" "
Kirklington	1,977	0	2	" "
Boughton	1,347	0	1	One principal owner.
Maplebeck	1,196	0	4	One large owner and few freeholders.
Marnham	2,305	2	6	One owner.
Saundby	1,412	1	1	" "
Thurgarton	2,572	0	11	One large leaseholder.
West Burton	954	0	4	One principal owner.
Wiseton	1,045	(?)	(?)	One owner.
Winkburn	2,371	1	0	Apparently one chief owner.

PASTURE DISTRICT

Name.	Area of Township.	Freeholders who Polled in 1722. Resident.	Non-resident.	Approximate No. of Owners in 1790.
Averham .	. 2,120	1	0	One owner.
Bingham .	. 3,069	16	3	Sixteen owners mentioned, several non-resident.
Bradmore	. 1,254	0	1	One owner.
*Chilwell.	. 1,421	9	0	Divided property.
*Kelham .	. 2,072	2	5	One owner.
Kilvington	. 491	2	0	One resident proprietor, four non-resident mentioned.
Kinoulton	. . 3,077	1	3	One chief owner.
Newton .	. 3,128 (with Shelford*)	0	1	" " "
West Leake	. 1,603	1	1	Two principal owners.
Rolleston .	. 1,627	(?)	(?)	One owner.
*Shelford.	. 3,128 (with Newton)	1	2	" "
South Scarle	. 1,093	3	1	(?)
Stragglethorpe	. 3,704 (with Cotgrave)	(?)	(?)	One principal owner.
Staythorpe	. 651	(?)	(?)	One owner.

No. of townships in which property was concentrated in few hands	24
No. of townships in which property was divided among a number .	3
No. of townships unclassified	1
Total	28

* Townships marked thus were probably enclosed very early in the eighteenth century or even before 1700.

SUMMARY

From what we have said two important considerations emerge: first, that throughout the whole enclosure movement the lead was taken by the large proprietor: the townships in which he was supreme were ahead of those in which property was divided among a number of owners. Secondly, not only were they ahead in point of time, but they adopted a different method; the latter, as will appear from the list given on pages 168–9, generally had to apply for an Act of Parliament in order to overcome the opposition to enclosure; the former did not require to do this. But the importance of our enquiry does not rest here; it also helps to explain the decline in the numbers of the freeholders. In the "old enclosed" townships they had largely disappeared, as Thoroton shows, before enclosure took place. The same appears to be true of the townships wholly enclosed without parliamentary sanction in the eighteenth century. In the list given above it will be noticed that the evidence given by Throsby in 1790 in regard to the number of owners corresponds very closely to the number of resident freeholders who voted in 1722, in spite of the fact that enclosure had most probably in all cases taken place in the interval. Evidently, the freeholders had disappeared *before*, not after, enclosure as is so often assumed. Possibly they had been bought out before enclosure in order to facilitate its progress; the same thing has been done in Laxton in our time for the same purpose. Mr. Davies, in his important study on the "Small Landowner",[1] states that occupying owners had almost ceased to exist in parishes enclosed by other than parliamentary means previous to 1780; the explanation seems to be that they had gradually been bought out by the large proprietor, a process which, as we have seen, was very actively at work in the Pasture district from the sixteenth century onwards, and became equally active in all areas in the eighteenth century. Their disappearance, then, in these parishes was probably not a consequence of enclosure, but an antecedent condition to its successful operation by the larger proprietors.

[1] Davies, "The Small Landowner, 1786–1832, in the Light of Land Tax Assessments"—*Econ. Hist. Rev.*, Jan., 1927, Vol. I, No. 1, p. 111.

CHAPTER VII

AGRICULTURE—THE AFTER-EFFECTS OF ENCLOSURE

We have treated enclosure as the method by which agricultural organisation and technique were adapted to the changing needs of the community during a period of accelerating economic growth, and have seen that the lead in this important movement was everywhere and at all times taken by the larger proprietors. The economic gain was beyond calculation; land that could produce only indifferent crops of corn was turned over to pasture; land that produced good corn was made to produce even better pasture or more corn; thousands of acres of forest and moor were brought into cultivation and plantation; money and skill were lavished upon the fens.

Economic gain on this scale was necessarily bought at the expense of considerable social dislocation; and owing to the character of the political society within which these changes took place, the social effects received less attention than they deserved. Under the aristocratic regime of that time, depending for its monopoly of political power mainly upon the possession of landed wealth, the history of enclosure could not have been other than it was; the gain was great, but the social effects were in proportion to it, and at least as permanent, and it is important to consider them if the full character of the movement is to be understood.

I.—The Destruction of the Open Field Village

One of the consequences of the process we have described was the destruction of an interesting social organisation as well as an archaic system of agriculture. It should be remembered, the open fields with their scattered properties and rights of common involved a good deal of corporate action as well as litigious dispute. It was no easy matter, in a populous village, where property rights were divided among numerous owners, to regulate rights of common, as the history of Laxton shows; and not a little statesmanship was required to carry through any kind of village reorganisation without recourse to the law courts. It is, of course, well known that, in the sixteenth and seventeenth centuries, the tenants of the village not infrequently protected their rights by joint petitions to the Privy Council, followed sometimes by actions at law. In one case, as we showed earlier,[1] the community actually bought the manor right out in order to protect its rights of common. The open village, of course, had its corporate organisation coming down from the manor, and the part played by the manorial court in expressing the will of the community may be seen to-day in Laxton, where the Court Leet not merely exists, but is regarded as indispensable.[2]

In the eighteenth century, the open village made a more vigorous struggle for its survival in Nottinghamshire than might be supposed from the contempt in which that system has been generally held. It is usually assumed, for instance, that the Act of 1773 which was passed to enable the tenants of an open field village to effect improvements in their methods more easily, was a dead letter. Dr. Slater was able to find only one instance of its operation in the country, and is inclined, therefore, to think no advantage was taken of it; but there is evidence in Nottinghamshire that it played a more important part than is here attributed to it. The best example of its influence is that of Oxton, which increased

[1] See Ch. I, p. 14.

[2] See "Open Fields of Laxton," by J. D. Chambers, *Thor. Soc. Trans.* (1928). For adverse criticism of social and economic aspects of open field cultivation, see very interesting pamphlet "Vindication of Regulated Inclosure of Commons, etc." by Joseph Lee (1656) quoted by Nichols, *Hist. and Antiquities of Leicestershire*, Vol. IV, Pt. I, p. 95.

its rotations under the provisions of the Act, by the addition of a clover crop in the open field and added a fourth field to the arable area. It remained open until 1852.[1] A number of villages in the north of the County also appear to have made use of it. According to the Directory of 1844 much of the Clays was still "in large common fields, most of which were cultivated under the Act of 1773".[2] It would appear therefore, that the open field village, especially in the parts most suitable for grain-growing, was capable of improvement in other ways than by enclosure, and that the Act of 1773 was instrumental in delaying this transformation in a number of cases. It is interesting to speculate what might have happened if instead of encouraging enclosure, the State had made a serious attempt to adapt the existing system to the new conditions; as we have shown, the attempt would not have been foredoomed to failure, at least in the grain-growing districts, and its success might have done something to preserve that social basis of co-operation arising out of a more distributed tenure of land, which, according to the Tribunal Report of 1924, distinguishes the agriculture of foreign countries from that at home.[3]

II.—Rent

If Thoroton is to be believed there was one cause only of enclosure, and that was the desire on the part of the landlord for increased rents. A landlord, he says, would get nearly twice as much after he had enclosed and converted a lordship than before, owing to the fact that less labour was employed relatively to the value of the product. He shows further that enclosure was

[1] Lowe, *op. cit.*, p. 37. The Act mentioned is 13 Geo. III, 81, and it permitted changes to be made in the cropping and rotation of the open field by means of a majority of three-fourths of the occupiers, and consent of the owner and tithe owner. Unanimous consent had formerly been required; see Slater, *Enclosures and Eng. Peasantry*, Ch. IX.

[2] White's *Directory of Notts.*, 1844, p. 38.

[3] See Agricultural Investigation Tribunal—Final Report, 1924, pp. 65 and 134.

frequently the prelude to a series of rapid sales, of which the following is a good example:

"This lordship, (Kneeton) was enclosed in my time by Geo. Lassells Esq. and shortly after sold to the Lady Dormer, from whom it passed to Sir Henry More and so to the Marquis of Dorchester, who about the year 1665 sold it to Sir Frances Molyneux, Bart., who hath repaired and well built the seat and makes it his habitation."

Apparently the population was considerably diminished by the time Thoroton wrote. Another interesting case is that of Car Colston enclosed 38 Elizabeth by Richard Whalley, of Screveton, owner of the Manor,

"who prevailed upon the rest of the owners, neither very few nor inconsiderable, to enclose the fields; after which I do not find that either he or they or any of them ever found any great improvement in their fortunes, though the rents were much increased, nor have their posterity much to brag about, most of them having resigned their shares to new purchasers".[1]

In such cases enclosure may well have been an incentive to speculation, which would be likely to raise the rent still further. Such abuse of enclosure appears to have been not uncommon in the eighteenth century. Thus the enclosed farms of Newark Charities were rack-rented so that they fell vacant and became ruinous; when the lease came to an end nothing was given as compensation for improvement. One tenant, it is said, erected at his own charge two stables, a dovecote, a corn chamber and a wall to the yard, but when the lease fell in and the farm put up to auction in the Parish Church, he was outbid by 20*s.* and so lost his farm and money spent on improvements.[2]

A Notts. farmer, surveyor and enclosure commissioner of great experience has an interesting note on the question of rack-renting in the County. He says:

[1] Throsby's Thoroton, I, pp. 302 and 206.

[2] An impartial relation of some Parish Transactions at Newark 1751, Gough Collection, Bodleian Library.

"I am sorry to say some landowners are so jealous of any profit accruing to the tenant that they are constantly enquiring into his profit: and without considering his losses, expenses, etc., etc., by advancing his rent on the least suspicions of advantage, he is driven to the waste and destruction of his farm for his own present support."

Another observer, a few years later, wrote:

"Rents have been in many instances raised in a most extraordinary proportion, even on the leasehold lands. . . . We have heard of some instances particularly on the banks of the Trent, where they have been raised in a proportion of three to one! And that under circumstances which left the farmer no choice between acceptance and dismission." [1]

The other side of the rent-raising question is well put by Arthur Young, who shows that in some cases at least the raising of rent was a necessary incentive to improvement. Speaking of land, the rent of which had been raised from 2*s.* 6*d.* to 12*s.* an acre, he said:

"When landlords valued it so much the tenants did the same and found it was impossible for them to live without going quickly to work with improvements; land at 1*s.* 6*d.* an acre is not valued by a tenant; a few straggling sheep will pay the rent, but raise it to 10*s.* such sloven's conduct will not do; the soil must be applied to some other use or the farmer will starve."

Some landlords actually refused to raise rents out of fear of losing their popularity. They were afraid, he says, of having "hats off and God bless your honour" but twice instead of thrice, and on rent day they liked to have a bow six inches lower than common with a long scrape; and what crowns all is to have half a dozen tenants meeting at a hedge ale house, and nothing disrespectful to their landlord passing. "This is popularity . . . and we are not to wonder that landlords find it more captivating than 5*s.* per acre per annum." [2]

[1] Lowe, *op. cit.*, p. 160; *Beauties of England and Wales* (1813), Vol. XII, p. 38.

[2] Young, *Eastern Tour*, Vol. I, pp. 219, 161. The usual rent for enclosed land in Notts. in second half of eighteenth century was 16*s.* to £1 per acre; old enclosure 12*s.* 6*d.*; see also Young, *op. cit.*, p. 135; Marshall, *Rural Econ. of Midland Counties*, Vol. I, pp. 16–17.

III.—Forced Sale

Enclosure of course involved a heavy outlay of capital upon the owner, and the smaller the property the heavier its relative incidence was likely to be. The Enclosure Act usually included a clause in regard to the raising of loans at moderate interest on the enclosed properties; but many owners preferred to sell a part or the whole of the property in order to meet or avoid the cost of making fences, drains, roads, gateways, within the time laid down by the Commissioners. The following example will illustrate the difficulty which the small owner had to face in this respect. A certain charity at Edwinstowe at the enclosure in 1818 had an allotment of 132 acres; of this the Trustees sold forty acres for the sum of £375 "which they expended in enclosing and fencing the remainder, except £97 14*s*. 6*d*. which is now in the Retford Savings Bank".[1] In this case, nearly £280 was spent in enclosing and fencing a property of 92 acres; if this amount includes the payment of lawyers' and surveyors' fees in connection with the enclosure as well as fencing and draining, the figure is by no means excessive.[2] It certainly illustrates the difficulties of the small owner in meeting the expenses of enclosure.

[1] White's *Directory of Notts.*, 1832, p. 416.

[2] See Hammond, *Village Labourer*, p. 98, for examples of enclosure costs. Curtler states on the authority of the Board of Agriculture that the average acreage involved in each Act was 1,162 and the average cost was estimated as follows:

	£	s.	d.
Obtaining the Act	497	0	0
Survey and Valuation	259	0	0
Commissioners' fees	344	0	0
Fences, etc.	550	7	6
	£1,650	7	6

See Curtler, *Enclosures and Redistribution of our Land*, p. 165. The following particulars of expenses of Nottinghamshire enclosures given in the awards have been kindly supplied by Mr. W. E. Tate: Hawksworth (1760), 640 acres, £566. Woodborough (1795), 514 acres, £3,630 (of which £1,961 went in permanent improvements). Tuxford (1799), 1,649 acres, £5,172 (of which £3,132 went in permanent improvements). Willoughby on the Wolds (1799), 1,695 acres, £3,169.

IV.—Differentiation of Crop according to Type of Soil and its Effect on Employment of Labour

We have shown elsewhere that a considerable area was enclosed and apparently converted to pasture in the early period of enclosure. The effect of such a change upon the employment of labour was disastrous, and there is no doubt that many families were displaced. At the same time there was constant extension of cultivation in the Forest area at the expense of the waste, but whether this absorbed any of the superfluous labour of the south-east it is impossible to say; there is no doubt, however, that vagabondage increased and that the town of Nottingham had constantly to take drastic steps to keep out families of wanderers, as we show more fully in a later section of this chapter.

The economic gain arising from the differentiation of crop according to the type of soil which enclosure made possible was thus bought at the cost of creating considerable unemployment for which there was no adequate provision. Moreover, such alternative occupation as existed was made difficult of access owing to the apprenticeship regulations and the poor law system based upon the parish.

In the eighteenth century the process of differentiation went on much more rapidly everywhere, and it was not left wholly to the occupier's choice of direction. The landlord also had a share in it. Blackner, writing at the beginning of the nineteenth century, declares that the landowners uniformly enjoined their tenants not to plough more than half and in many cases not more than one-third of their land, and points to the number of enclosures for pasture that had taken place within the previous twenty years as a confirmation of his statement.[1] According to Marshall, the chief authority for the agriculture of the Midland Counties, a clause was generally included in the terms of agreement between landlord and tenant settling the penalty for ploughing

[1] Blackner, *Utility of Commerce Defended*, 1805, p. 12.

up more than a stipulated amount of land.[1] In many cases economic reasons operated in the same direction, especially along the river valleys where dairy farming and fat cattle rearing took on an added importance with the growth of the urban centres. At Barton, Thrumpton, Attenborough, Wilford, Clifton, Chilwell, dairy farming increased rapidly,[2] and Throsby during his tour of the County at the end of the century, notes the large and open meadows bordering the Trent, of very rich land called "marches". "These grounds", he says, "are divided by land marks and are wholly mown every succeeding year without any manure used. The remaining part of the year they are stocked with milking cows and other cattle."

Further south, in the part of the County included by Marshall in his survey, there had been, from an early period, a good deal of sheep pasture, especially on the higher ground of the Wolds, but the land appears to have been unsuitable for fattening sheep, and so for this purpose the lambs were driven in the autumn into Worcestershire and the lower lands of Shropshire, and a supply of ewes brought back from the Worcestershire fairs for breeding—"a remarkable specimen", as Marshall says, "of the intercourse of districts".[3]

But arable farming was also increasing, especially in the Forest area where, as we have shown above, thousands of acres of sandy waste, unsuitable for permanent pasture, were brought into regular cultivation. The bulk of this was laid out in large well-planned farms, and cultivated, in some parts, according to the Norfolk four-course rotation, consisting of Turnips, Barley or Oats, Grass seeds or clover, Wheat. This tendency probably explains the following figures compiled by Gonner:[4]

[1] Marshall, *Rural Econ. of Midland Counties*, Vol. I, p. 22.

[2] Lowe, *op. cit.*, p. 29.

[3] Throsby, *op. cit.*, III, p. 246, cf. also Lowe, *op. cit.*, p. 21, and Marshall, *op. cit.*, p. 334. See also p. 290 for his eulogy of the "Trent water cows which come nearer my idea of what a cow ought to be than any other breed of the long horned variety".

[4] Gonner, *op. cit.*, p. 401.

Notts.	No. of Returns.	Places showing Increase.	Places showing Decrease.
Barley . . .	50	33	9
Oats . . .	46	34	5

It can hardly be doubted that in spite of the statements quoted above from Blackner and Marshall, the total quantity of land under arable was increased rather than decreased by enclosure, owing to the amount of light land brought in from the waste, combined with the development of dairy farming and fat stock rearing; this indicates a large net increase in total agricultural production. Moreover, the quality of sheep and cattle was rapidly improving and more attention was being paid to their well-being. A superior long-horned breed of cattle was introduced into the pasture land of the Soar Valley, and even in the Clay district, where dairy farming held a secondary place, efforts were being made to replace the inferior "woodland beasts" with a Yorkshire short-horn variety.[1] Similarly, experiments were being carried out on all sides in the production of new breeds of sheep, the new Leicestershire variety being the most popular among the "improving farmers". Combined with the extension of arable farming in the Forest area these innovations must have made heavy demands upon the supply of labour, but whether the demand was sufficient to absorb the redundant labour of the open field village is somewhat doubtful. Moreover, it would be a great mistake to think that enclosure was necessarily followed by improvements in every case. A later investigator came to the conclusion that really intelligent enterprise in the eighteenth century was "confined to the practices of the few and formed little or no part of those of" the bulk of Nottinghamshire farmers; [2] and Arthur Young noted that farmers in the Forest district often made no better use of their enclosures than to keep a few sheep on them or

[1] Lowe, *op. cit.*, pp. 123–4.
[2] *Journal of Roy. Agric. Society*, First Series, Vol. VI, p. 17. For severe criticism of agriculture of Vale of Belvoir, see Hist. MSS. Co., *Portland Papers*, Vol. VI, p. 83.

take successive crops of corn until they were exhausted and then leave them to turf themselves down.[1] Such agriculture as this, following upon enclosure, could not possibly employ the former population of commoners, squatters, and other semi-independent members of the open village community as well as the regular labourers. In such cases local unemployment must have resulted.

V.—Loss of Common Rights

It may be, as a seventeenth-century writer said, that "Ever since old Tusser's time it has been observed that where there has been most common, there is least good building and most poor",[2] but the sudden disappearance of the common unaccompanied by an adequate substitute that could be turned to immediate use,[3] was felt not merely by the squatter on the waste, but the day labourers, handicraftsmen and the very small farmers and cottagers who looked to the common to eke out their livelihood. Their position is thus summed up by an eighteenth-century pamphleteer:

"There are some in almost every parish who have houses and little parcels of land in the field with a right of common for a cow or three or four sheep, by the assistance of which the profits of a little trade or their daily labour they procure a very competent living."[4] Compensation for the loss of common rights was granted,

[1] Young, *Eastern Tour,* Vol. I, p. 427. In the south part of the County landlords prevented this by drawing up leases in which specific improvements were demanded as a condition for entry of a tenant. Marshall, *Rural Econ. of Midland Counties,* Vol. I, p. 20.

[2] MacCulloch, *Collection of Early Eng. Tracts on Commerce,* containing England's Great Happiness (1677), p. 265.

[3] For constructive proposals put forward by Board of Agriculture in 1796, on this point, but turned down by Parliament, see Hammond, *op. cit.*, p. 75, quoting *Annals of Agric.*, Vol. XXVI, p. 85.

[4] *Enquiry into reasons for and against enclosure of open fields,* 1767, p. 22. Slater thinks there were scarcely any labourers in the open field village without either land or common, *Enclosures and Eng. Peasantry,* p. 130. It may be noted that common right cottagers of Laxton, and small farmers, have until the present put forward the view quoted above against enclosure, but now that the common is made useless by the fact that motorists are allowed to leave gates on the swing they are apathetic about it.

of course, for those who could establish an unassailable legal claim to their possession. The Enclosure Acts for several villages in the north and west of the County, for instance, where common was abundant and the small owner still survived in strength, contained definite provision for allotment to be made out of the "residue" of the waste to owners of "ancient messuages, cottages, tofts, or toftsteads" having right of common. At Clarborough and Welham, for instance, one third of the free common or waste was to be divided equally among owners of tofts who also had land in the open fields, etc., with right of common, according to the proportion of their land in the open field.[1] In some cases the precise acreage of the allotment is stipulated—two acres for every ancient toft, or messuage, etc., at Beckingham (1776); at Blidworth the compensation was higher—one acre for every two hundred enclosed and for every Cow gate, half an acre.[2] As there were 3,000 acres of waste enclosed, this may be regarded as a substantial compensation for the loss of common rights. It is worth noting that the village consisted of one fairly large proprietor who had three farms, and a large number of others none of whom were worth more than £100 a year, and many were copyholders. The Manor belonged to the Archbishop of York, which, perhaps, helps to explain the survival of this really peasant village.

Compensation for the irregular use of the common by labourers and others was not given, except very occasionally, in the form of allotments for the poor. In any case, the occupant of a cottage with rights of common would have to stand by and see the common, which might easily be the most important part of his livelihood, exchanged for an allotment which the owner would probably sell rather than go to the expense of enclosing

[1] Enclosure Acts for Clarborough and Welham—for other cases, see Styrrup, Oldcoates and Harworth (1802), Ranskill and Scrooby (1802), South Leverton (1795), N. Leverton and Habblesthorpe (1795), Kirkby-in-Ashfield (1795).

[2] Blidworth, 1769. In most cases the Act authorises the commissioners to make allotment out of the "residue" of Common as compensation for loss of Common Rights according to their discretion.

it. It may be noted, however, that in the Clay district north of the Trent, labourers had frequently a few acres annexed to their cottages on which to keep one or two cows or pigs, and such landlords as Abel Smith, the Banker, allowed the cottagers on his estate the use of as much as eight or ten acres of arable land.[1] How far this was generally practised it is impossible to say, but it is certain that no such provision is to be found in the Enclosure Acts themselves.[2]

In illustration of the effects of loss of common rights it may be noted that the acute distress which the country framework knitters were suffering in the nineteenth century was attributed partly to this cause; many of them, according to Felkin, even lost their gardens, these having been absorbed by the neighbouring farms or parks;[3] ineffectual efforts were made to provide a substitute in the form of allotment gardens, but as these were often let out at exorbitant rents, the benefit derived from them was in many cases negligible. In reference to this question of the loss of common rights, the following extract from the pen of a Nottinghamshire farmer may be given to indicate the view which some contemporaries held of these social results of enclosure.

"If there be, in a highly refined and luxurious country like our own, one sight more painful than another, it is to see the honest labourer asking from door to door 'for leave to toil' that he may thereby get his bread, but asking in vain . . . because he who would willingly be employer is in as hard straits as he who craves to be employed. . . . This is no imaginary case, but an undeniable fact, the constant recurrence of which, under our own eyes, has induced us to allude to it. Can we wonder at men, born with the feelings of Englishmen, turning droopingly away, inwardly

[1] Hammond, *Village Labourer*, p. 156.

[2] One Act, that of Carlton in Lindrick (1767), includes a provision for allotting land on the waste for building cottages for the poor; where the poor expressly enjoyed land in the fields or common rights by charitable donation they were of course compensated in the award as for instance—6 acres at Sutton-cum-Lound and the rent (£24 per annum) used for the school; 24 acres at Hucknall Torkard, etc.

[3] See Commission of Enquiry into condition of Framework Knitters, 1845, Appendix, Notts., p. 16.

feeling that no man careth for them and that our very cattle are regarded more than they? . . . Let us, therefore, seek to show the poor and honest man that he is cared for and that his interests and happiness are identical with our own; and seek before it is too late to raise his broken spirits and dejected mien. As a means to so desirable an end, let him have something in which he is directly concerned; and nothing offers so rational an object of his care as his own small holding of land."

Forty-four years later it was estimated that the number of Nottinghamshire labourers who had a "run for a cow" was twenty-eight.[1]

The Decline of the Peasantry

The objective features of the agrarian revolution have now been set forth. It began with the slow integration of a capitalist structure in agriculture, among the peasants themselves as well as the larger graziers, following upon the emancipation movement of the later Middle Ages, and the growth of the wool trade. Already well under way, it received enormous acceleration from the economic and monetary crises of the sixteenth century. The ideals of the city were now definitely supreme in the country districts, and the pursuit of profit became the mainspring of rural life. During the Tudors and early Stuarts, a check to the free play of the "business instincts" was provided by the State, anxious to preserve the peasantry because of their military value, as well as their political power, and by the Church which placed the ideal of social justice before that of private profit. It is generally agreed that a brake was thereby placed upon the development of large-scale capitalist enterprise in agriculture, but at best it was no more than an ineffectual finger upon the spoke of the great wheel; the wheel moved, nevertheless, and as it moved, first one and then another obstacle was shaken off.

The first to go was the great bulk of the copyhold tenure, which was changed into leasehold and tenancy

[1] *Journal of Roy. Agric. Soc.*, First Series, Vol. VI, p. 38, and Second Series, Vol. XXIV, p. 512.

at will in order to obtain increased rents; and we have stated elsewhere that copyhold tenure is mentioned in only about thirty-five villages, and of these, all but one or two doubtful exceptions were, or had been, ancient demesne of the Crown or on the estate of the Church. We do not for a moment suggest that copyholders had elsewhere disappeared; but it is probably safe to conclude that they were elsewhere insignificant.

The decay of copyhold on such a scale must have had important social effects. It would mean, as we have said, increased rents in accordance with the increased price of commodities; for reasons that we have stated elsewhere [1] the large farmer was able to take advantage of the increased prices to a greater extent than the small farmer, and was consequently better able to meet the increased rents; hence there was a tendency to substitute the larger unit of holding for the smaller. This would necessarily mean the substitution of the existing body of copyholders by a smaller number of tenants and short-leaseholders, with the consequent displacement of a proportion of the population. These, presumably, would either become labourers or seek employment in the towns. When these changes were accompanied or followed by enclosure for purposes of converting arable to pasture, the effect on the rural population would be especially severe, as pasture farming called for large enclosed farms and employed little labour. Thus there were two conditions making for the decline of the peasantry: (1) the increase in the power of the landlord over the tenant, (2) the increase of pasture farming. When these two conditions combined, as, for instance, in the Pasture District of Nottinghamshire, where landlords had made themselves complete masters of many villages, the social effects of the agrarian revolution may be expected to show themselves more prominently than elsewhere, an expectation that is fully confirmed by contemporary observers as we show in our next section.

[1] See above, Ch. I.

Depopulation in the Pasture District

Most of the evidence cited on this subject is drawn from Thoroton, who, it should be remembered, was a Conservative and a Royalist, and a persecutor of Dissenters. It may be therefore that something should be deducted from what he says for his known prejudices; but there is corroborative evidence in several cases, and in many others he is speaking of townships within a few miles of his house in Thoroton village, and therefore directly under his observation as a Squire and a Magistrate.

The first examples he gives are those of Kingston and Thorpe, in the extreme south of the County. Of Kingston he writes, "The whole lordship hath long been enclosed and much depopulated", and of Thorpe,

> "Another lordship, Thorpe, which is scarcely discernible at all to-day, was entirely enclosed in Henry VII's time with hedges and ditches by one Gabriel Armstrong, which hath so ruined and depopulated the town that in my time there was not a house left inhabited of this notable lordship . . . but a shepherd only kept Ale to sell in the church."[1]

In 1759, according to Throsby, there were two houses and the remains of a church. It is important to note that this example of depopulation was not mentioned by the Commission of 1517, although the enclosure was then more than twenty years old.

About the same time there was the enclosure of Wollaton Park, which, according to the Commission of 1517, caused the displacement of eighteen persons and the decay of five cottages and ultimately brought about the complete disappearance of the former village, Sutton Passeys, "which", says Thoroton, "is now and long hath been totally decayed and only known by the name of Wollaton Park".[2] The Commission of 1517 reports the emparking of eighty acres of land at Holme Pierrepont which caused the displacement of thirty-six persons and

[1] Throsby's Thoroton, I, pp. 22 and 75.
[2] *Ibid.*, II, p. 208.

the ruin of eight cottages. Wiverton Park was enclosed at the expense of twenty-six persons displaced and five cottages ruined. At Lestrete and Grove (outside the Pasture district) parks were enclosed without any recorded inconvenience to the population, but it is worthy of note that of these two villages the first has disappeared and the site is not definitely known (possibly Steetly Chapel, all that remains of a decayed village two miles west of Worksop), and the second, a lordship of 1,300 acres, had only twenty houses and a population of about 110 during the eighteenth century.[1] Again at Morton, in the Forest district, the conversion of only forty acres of arable to pasture by a freeholder caused depopulation to the extent of eighteen persons and the decay of five houses.[2]

The next case of enclosure recorded is that of Langford, near Newark, where more than 400 acres, it is said on the evidence of the villagers, had been enclosed in Elizabeth's time by the Lord of the Manor, with the result that the village had been "dispeopled" and a dozen ploughs put down, the equivalent of fifty or sixty people. The object of the enclosure seems to have been the making of a cattle pasture, since a part of it was let to the butchers of Newark, while the sheep walk was "very casuall . . . and no great account to be made of it". It is stated by the historian of the district that traces of ruined cottages, hearth stones, fire grates, etc., had been turned up by the plough in the nineteenth century.[3] Thoroton does not mention the enclosure, but the village is described by Throsby at the end of the eighteenth century as "a few scattered dwellings".

Probably about the same time occurred the enclosure of Stanton on the Wolds, which was said by Thoroton to be depopulated in consequence. On the edge of the Wolds was Colston Bassett which had suffered in the same way.[4]

[1] Throsby's Thoroton, III, p. 264. [2] Leadam, *op. cit.*, p. 27.
[3] *Hist. of Collingham*, by F. G. Wake, pp. 84 and 117.
[4] *Ibid.*, I, p. 164.

About the time of the Civil War the enclosure movement began seriously to affect the district in which Thoroton himself lived, and the following cases of depopulation were noted by the historian:

(1) Langar and Barnston, where "Earl Howe hath made a park of the Closes . . . nigh his House, which is well stocked with deer, much better than the towns are with people, where so considerable parts of the Fields are inclosed; the too common fate of good land in this county";

(2) Elton, where "engrossing of farms was the depopulation first complained of . . . there being not so much above half so many farms as in old time altogether".[1] The township was merely reorganised and not enclosed and remained open until the nineteenth century.

(3) Flawborough, which "in time of late troubles was sold by the Duke of Newcastle to Sir John Crapley, whose sone hath been at great Charge and Loss to spoil a good Lordship for corn by enclosing and depopulating it as we think . . . Mr. Crapley is now (1675) rebuilding some good farmhouses but the lordship I doubt will not hastily recover its former state".

(4) Cotham, which "is now decayed, the houses pulled down and most of it enclosed being the inheritance of the Duke of Newcastle".

(5) Hawton, "a Lordship very much depopulated since the war and a great part of it enclosed since then too, which never fails to produce that effect".[2]

The majority of these villages lay at the junction of the clay with the alluvium of the rivers Devon and Smite, and provided rich pasture for both sheep and cattle. The enclosure of rich arable for the purpose of pasture was said to displace fifteen families per thousand

[1] *Ibid.*, p. 215.

[2] *Ibid.*, pp. 323, 344, 356. See also article, "Notes on Deserted Notts. Villages and Churches", by W. P. Phillimore, in *Old Nottinghamshire*, edited by Potter Briscoe (1884).

acres.[1] There is no need for astonishment, therefore, that complaints of depopulation arose from this district, and that Thoroton, a Conservative, a Royalist and an Anglican, with views of social well-being that dated from an earlier age, should express himself so forcibly:[2]

"This prevailing mischief in some parts of this Shire," he says, "hath taken away and destroyed more private families of good account than Time itself within the compass of my observations; yet some very few escaped where this devouring pestilence hath raged and amongst them (through God's great mercy) my own, which surely should not be envied being for the most part . . .

Prout negotiis
Ut prisca gens mortalium
Paterna rura robus exercens suis."

The displacement of population caused by enclosure in the south-east of the County helps to explain a sinister feature of town life which becomes prominent at this time, namely, the migration of labouring or labourless people to the town. The records of the Borough of Nottingham show clearly that the town was being invaded by migratory poor. In 1612 a complaint was made that the town was suffering from a "confluence of poor persons from forraine parts" and a fierce campaign was launched by the Borough Magistrates against building cottages, turning barns into habitations, etc.[3] In 1631 the Sheriff and Justices of Nottinghamshire, local landlords themselves, sent up to the Privy Council a letter regarding the local enclosures which leaves no doubt that serious depopulation had taken place with the most evil results to town and country:

"Where houses are pulled downe the People are forced to seeke new habitations. In other townes . . . (which) are (thereby) pestred

[1] Quoted by Slater, *Enclosures and Eng. Peasantry*, p. 96. The full table is as follows:

1,000 *acres of*	*Gives Employment before Enclosure.*	*Gives Employment after Enclosure.*
(1) Rich arable . . .	20 families.	5 families.
(2) Inferior arable . . .	20 "	16¼ "
(3) Stinted common and pasture .	½ family.	5 "
(4) Heaths and wastes . .	½ "	16¼ "

[2] Throsby's Thoroton, I, p. xvii.

[3] Nottingham Borough Records, Vol. IV, p. 305.

so as they are hardly able to live one by an other . . . and Causes Rogues and vagabonds to encrease. Moreover it doth appeare in those townes which are depopulated the People being expelled There are few or none Left to serve King when Souldjours are to appeare for his Ma^te^ service." [1]

On another occasion they complained that the prevalence of enclosure had actually reduced the County to desolation, but it is probable they were inspired more by the desire to escape taxation than to tell the truth.[2]

In order to prevent the ill effects of unchecked migration the Borough Magistrates ordered that no new tenements were to be erected without licence. And landlords were either to guarantee the maintenance of their existing tenants or cause them to "avoid" the town.[3] The punishments of people who persisted in harbouring inmates without observing the conditions laid down by the magistrates were frequent and continued into the eighteenth century. It cannot be doubted that enclosure was an important factor contributing to this movement of the labouring poor, and helped materially to recruit the army of vagrants that battened on the country in the seventeenth and eighteenth centuries.

A course of action which resulted in such serious social distress was bound to be viewed with alarm by a Government which depended for its defence and for a considerable portion of its income upon the very class which was being uprooted, while nothing could exceed the fury of denunciation with which it was assailed by prelates and pamphleteers and other keepers of the public conscience, outraged by this breach of accepted social justice.[4] Statutes were passed and commissions of

[1] *S.P. Dom.*, 1631, Vol. CLXXXV, No. 86, published by Miss Leonard in mistake for a Norfolk return—*Roy. Hist. Soc. Proceedings*, Vol. XIX, p. 144. Quoted by Tawney, *op. cit.*, pp. 418–19.

[2] *S.P. Dom.*, Vol. CXCIII, No. 79. Quoted *V.C.H.*, II, p. 290.

[3] Nottm. Borough Records, Vol. IV, pp. 364, 365, 381; Vol. V, pp. 103, 104, 106, 113, 154, 188, 192, 193, 327, 330, 336, 351; Vol. VI, p. 132.

[4] See list of authorities and quotations given by Lipson, *Econ. Hist.* (Medieval), pp. 141 *et seq.*, and especially sermons delivered by Latimer on March 8, 1549, and Jan. 28, 1548; prayer of Edward VI and speeches in Parliament summarised by Tawney, *Agrarian Problem*, p. 388.

enquiry appointed, and when the Crown was backed by the inflexible Archbishop Laud, who knew his mind and feared no man, the way was not easy for enclosing landlords and sheep farmers. They paid fines amounting to £2,010 for their enclosures in Nottinghamshire in 1637 and another £78 the following year,[1] and one of them wrote a letter explaining that he had complied with the orders of the Commissioners of Depopulation to throw open all his enclosures and apologising humbly for keeping hedges round three acres on the ground that they were necessary to mark the boundaries.[2]

It is a fact of some significance that the enclosure we have described was carried through silently and peacefully without riot or bloodshed, as far as is known. There is no record of a village Hampden bringing out his fellows "with bowes, pytchefforkes, clobbes, staves, swords and daggers drawn" as the village leaders of Chinley in Derbyshire did, "and ryotouslye dyd then and there assaulte and p'sue" the enclosing cormorants in the teeth of the Queen's officer who commanded them to keep the peace.[3] The explanation of this strange acquiescence on the part of the displaced population is given on pages 166–71, where it is shown that in nearly all cases, the property enclosed was in the hands of very few, and frequently of only one person. The occupants of the soil, therefore, were tenants, not proprietors and, of course, had no remedy against eviction; the freeholders had apparently been already bought out. As the Leicestershire pamphleteer already quoted pointed out: "when inclosure doth produce depopulation, it is only

[1] Gonner, in *Eng. Hist. Rev.*, Vol. XXIII, p. 487.

[2] *S.P. Dom.*, Chas. I, Vol. CCCCIV, No. 142, quoted Tawney, *op. cit.*, p. 391.

[3] Tawney, *Agrarian Problem*, p. 329. There is no evidence that the peasantry of Notts. took any part in the serious enclosure rioting in 1607 which affected the neighbouring counties, see Prof. E. F. Gay, "Revolt of Midlands and Inquisition of Depopulation in 1607," in *Roy. Hist. Soc. Trans.*, Vol. XVIII, pp. 212–222. See also Miss E. M. Leonard, *ibid.*, Vol. XIX, pp. 125 *et seq.* See also Nichols, *Hist. and Antiquities of Leicestershire*, Vol. IV, Pt. I, p. 83, for account of a violent riot in which forty to fifty "Diggers" were killed.

in such towns as are in the hands of one or few men, and not in such towns where there are several freeholders of small tenements."

The Arable and Waste Districts.

As we have shown elsewhere, there was comparatively little permanent enclosure of common field in these parts of the County before 1700, therefore the social effects were felt far less severely than in the Pasture district; but several villages appear to have suffered a diminution in their population as a consequence of enclosure; in particular, Grove, Saxondale, Morton, Haughton, Bevercotes, and probably Annesley, where houses were removed in order to bring the park up to the hall and gardens. These villages, like those in the Pasture district, were in the hands of large proprietors and the sufferers were tenants, who, of course, had no remedy, hence enclosures were carried through quietly.

Such was not the case, however, when the rights of freeholders or copyholders of inheritance were involved. For these there was not only the law of the land but the law of the fist, helped by "stave, pytchefforke, clobbe", and what not. As an example of this it is sufficient to allude to the treatment meted out to Vermuyden and his fellow-speculators when they tried to enclose some of the common, of which there was an abundance, as compensation for draining Hatfield Chase. The speculators first got the Crown on their side. Lord Willoughby made the stipulation that in return for "adventuring" the drainage of part of the great fen of Hatfield Chase, his father, the Earl, "should receive 30,000 acres, and his majesty a present of 3,000 acres, as a high acknowledgement of his gracious favour in the business".[1] The commoners of Misterton and Gringley, and other villages in the north of Nottinghamshire found themselves less generously treated, and petitioned that their meadows were spoilt and their common enclosed, and that they were "barred forth of North Carr and drowned

[1] *Lincs. and Notts. Archæological Papers*, 1850–60, pp. 332 *et. seq.*

forth of Thack Carr, and bereft of all means of livelihood".[1] No redress was obtained, and the commoners took the law into their own hands; they threw down the banks, broke up the sluices, and kept the districts in a state of riot and disorder up to the Civil War and after, and only the military despotism of the Commonwealth could restore it to a semblance of peace.

The explanation will be clear if the list of villages of which the open field as well as pasture was enclosed before 1700, given on pages 166–7, is compared with the following, in which the townships in the neighbourhood of the drainage schemes are given, with evidence regarding the nature of the tenure and enclosure history:

Name.	No. of Owners in 1612 given by Thoroton.	No. on Subsidy Rolls.		No. of Resident Freeholders who Voted in 1722.	Date and Method of Enclosure.
		1641.	1689.		
Finningley . . .	15 (with Auckley in Yorks)	—	40?	4	14 Geo. III
Misson	—	—	34	18	33 Geo. II
Misterton . . .	26 and above 40 others	105	110	56	11 Geo. III
West Stockwith .	8 and fifteen others	—	51	20	11 Geo. III
Walkeringham .	13	79	—	8	42 Geo. III
Everton. . . .	31 (with Scaftworth)	71	about 80 (with Harwell)	15	22 Geo. III (with Harwell)
Gringley-on-the-Hill	8	64	64	6	36 Geo. III

It will be noted that in these villages property was

[1] See *V.C.H.*, II, p. 288, quoting *Cal. S.P. Dom.*, 1633–4–5. See also *Cal. S.P. Dom.*, 1653, Vol. XXXIX, No. 24, August 31; 1656, Vol. CXXI, No. 57, April 15, etc., etc., and James, *Social Policy during the Puritan Revolution*, pp. 125–8, 185–6.

divided among numerous proprietors; in Misterton and West Stockwith (a small place of less than 700 acres) most householders must have been freeholders. This no doubt accounts for the great outcry that was raised when their common, drowned in some parts at the time of the spring tides twice every twenty-four hours,[1] was partially drained and enclosed by Vermuyden and his fellow speculators. Since the occupants were freeholders, or copyholders of inheritance, they could stand up for their rights, and successfully postpone, not only enclosure, but effective improvement for more than a century. Rioting and clamour on the part of the peasantry affected by enclosure should not always be taken as evidence of their eviction; such outbreaks may indeed be evidence of their immunity from eviction, which enables them to protect by force if necessary their threatened rights of common; while the silence with which it is carried through elsewhere may similarly indicate, not consent, but helplessness and despair.

We will now consider the question of the effects of the agrarian revolution upon the peasantry in the later phases of the movement.

Eighteenth-century Enclosure and the Peasantry

In some respects, this period of enclosure may be said to begin with the Commonwealth. Unlike the Stuart Monarchy and the Church, the Commonwealth was no enemy to enclosure; enclosure was a way to prosperity, and prosperity was not incompatible with the Puritan virtue of Godliness, and those who placed obstacles in the way of either might be treated as though they had offended both. An interesting example of this is given in the answer made by a clergyman of Leicestershire who, after very ably setting forth the advantages of enclosure, goes on to attack its opponents, consisting mainly of the "ruder sort of people" who "live upon the rapine and spoil of others":

[1] Swinnerton, *Geog. of Notts.* (Cambridge County Geographies), p. 34.

"The best things now-a-days", he says, à propos of the popular hatred of enclosure, "are worst spoken of by the multitude. There is a profane and levelling spirit now in the world, that cries out against government and speaks evil of dignities. What would they have? Forsooth, liberty of conscience. From what? From majesty and ministry. To what? To live as they list and sin cum privilegio. The golden reins of discipline please not; this yoke they cannot bear, but cast this off, and they may swear, lie, and rob and rifle and swill and swagger, riot and revel in a shameless excess and set sin on horseback to ride in triumph whither it listeth." [1]

Contempt of the multitude could hardly go further; "the paisent knaves" had lost their battle. As Mr. Feiling says, "The economic drift of this century was towards a sharper demarcation of classes and towards depriving the poor of such economic protection as the Tudor and early Stuart governments had managed to keep up for them." [2]

At the same time there was a development of agricultural technique; new methods were being advocated by a group of agricultural "improvers", of whom Nottinghamshire produced one of the most prolific. As early as 1629 the Nottingham landowner, Gervase Markham, began his series of books on the improvement of farming practice, and though a modern student has said that the seventeenth-century writers of agriculture scarcely obtained a hearing,[3] it is significant that Mark-

[1] Vindication of consideration concerning Common Fields and Inclosures, 1656, accompanied by a Vindication of Regulated Inclosures of Commons, by Joseph Lee, Minister of the Gospel; quoted by G. Nichols, *Hist. and Antiquities of Leicestershire,* Vol. IV, Pt. I, p. 99. See especially Tawney, *Religion and Rise of Capitalism,* pp. 253–73, and James, *Social Policy during Puritan Revolution,* Ch. III, for this subject. It should be noted that the Major-Generals appointed by the Commonwealth Government in 1655 made some attempt to check the evil effects of enclosure. Owing to the agitations in Leicestershire, where a third of the county, it was said, had recently suffered depopulation from enclosure, Major-General Whalley ordered that two-thirds of the arable land under dispute was for ever to remain in tillage. In a letter to the Council he hints that Nottinghamshire had been similarly affected by enclosure. See James, *op. cit.*, p. 124, and Appendix A, II, where the letter is given in full.

[2] Keith Feiling, *Hist. of the Tory Party,* p. 20.

[3] Mantoux, *Ind. Rev.*, p. 161.

ham's *Cheape and Good Husbandry* went through thirteen editions, and his *Way to Get Wealth* through fourteen,[1] while his *Farewell to Husbandry*, written in 1629, continued to reappear well into the second half of the century. He advocated a larger sequence of crops occupying ten or eleven years, of which three to four years were spent "lying at rest for grass". This breach with the accepted rotation of the open fields could hardly be practicable unless preceded by enclosure; it was especially suitable for the light soils of the Forest area, and may well have had considerable vogue in that part of the County. In any case, it forms an interesting transition from the old three-field rotation with its fallow, to the four-course rotation without fallow, the Norfolk rotation, which was adopted by the more enlightened farmers of the Forest district in the eighteenth century.[2]

Improvements in technique were accompanied by political action in favour of farmers and landlords which gave them a monopoly of the home market in grain and fat-stock and a bounty on the export of corn when the home price was at or over 48*s*. a quarter.[3]

From this time onwards enclosure is treated as a preliminary to agricultural improvement and the existence of open fields and especially common as a bar to progress. Grain farming now began to benefit from enclosure almost as much as pasture farming, and it only required the rising prices of the latter half of the eighteenth century to stimulate the enclosing landlords, the improving farmers and the more enterprising of the freeholders to overcome by means of parliamentary enactment the last resistance of the old system, and to banish common and common field for all practical purposes from the countryside.

[1] Brown, *Worthies of Notts.*, p. 168.

[2] See *Roy. Agric. Soc. Journ.*, First Series, Vol. VI, pp. 17 *et seq.*, and Ashley, *Bread of our Forefathers*, p. 32.

[3] For discussion of the political significance of the Corn Bounty Act, see Gras, *Evolution of Eng. Corn Market*, p. 254, and for influence of growing Metropolitan market, on agrarian improvements and legislation, pp. 125, 255.

This phase of the enclosure movement introduces us to a new method, the method of enclosure by Act, and it also opens a new chapter in the history of the freeholding peasantry. We have seen the effects of the earlier movement upon the position of the copyholder and other types of insecure tenantry; we have seen also that many of the townships enclosed in the Pasture area were apparently denuded of small occupying owners at the time of their enclosure. It would appear then, that the freeholders also in these parts were reduced in numbers, presumably by purchase; but elsewhere they still remained numerous, especially in the Clays.[1] Again, many villages were enclosed in the eighteenth century without parliamentary sanction, and in the majority of these, probably in 90 per cent., the small freeholder had apparently been bought out before enclosure took place. This, of course, was merely the continuation, possibly on a larger scale, of the progress that we have suggested was at work in the seventeenth century—the buying up of whole townships and even parishes by large proprietors. But there were many townships in which land was too subdivided for this to take place, and even if freehold proprietors in the open field could be absorbed, the owners of toft cottages with common rights attached might offer more difficulty. The Lord of Laxton, although he owns the open fields, is not complete master of the common, even now; a few freehold cottagers share with him the rights of common. In such cases, where property was in the form of open field farms or common rights, and was sub-divided among a numerous peasantry, enclosure was generally delayed; but assistance came to the larger owners in the form of enclosure by Act of Parliament, by which they were enabled to overcome the opposition of their smaller neighbours, to whom enclosure might well mean the forced sale of their tiny properties and the loss of the

[1] This may be shown by comparing the townships in which according to Thoroton there were numerous freeholders in 1612 and those which polled most heavily in 1722.

independence conferred by the enjoyment of the rights of common. Thus, by means of an Act of Parliament, opposition to enclosure could be legally overridden, whereas, until the adoption of this method, it had to be eliminated by purchase.

Enclosure by Act

It is necessary to state at once that there were exceptions to the rule indicated above and laid down so tersely by Mantoux in the words "All Enclosure Acts on the Statute Book without exception are evidence of so many cases when unanimous consent of owners could not be secured". Though this is certainly true in the great majority of cases, examples do occur in which the Act represents no more than a formal recognition of an agreement already arrived at by the owners.[1] Since the mere passing of an Enclosure Act cost from £180 to £300, and according to some authorities considerably more than that,[2] the parties to the enclosure must have had very good reasons for adopting so expensive a method, and it is difficult to see what the reason could have been except the existence of opposition that could not be overcome by other means.

We will now deal briefly with the procedure of enclosure by Act before considering its social effects.

The first step was the presentment of a petition praying for leave to bring in a Bill; and unless this was supported by the owners of four-fifths, or in some cases, three-fourths, of the area to be enclosed,[3] it fell to the ground. On the other hand, if a single individual had the necessary amount of land in his possession, he could carry the petition single-handed, although the rest of the land was sub-divided among numerous proprietors. In any case, the power of the larger proprietors was so over-

[1] See for instance Cotgrave, Screveton, Trowell, and West Leake.

[2] Mantoux, p. 171, quoting Lecky—for further and more detailed discussion of the whole cost of enclosure, see Hammond, *Agricultural Labourer*, pp. 76 and 98 and authorities there quoted. See also note 2, p. 178.

[3] For full treatment of the whole question, see Hammond, *op. cit.*, Chs. III and IV.

whelming that opposition rarely developed after the petition had once been presented, whilst its chance of success was infinitesimal. The work of drawing up the Bill was usually allotted to members with a local interest in the County, such as Lord Edward Bentinck, the Earl of Lincoln, Mr. Meadows, Mr. Willoughby, Sir George Savile. A pleasant story tells how the last of these saved by his own interference a poor and anxious opponent of enclosure who had walked all the way to London to be present at the Committee on the enclosure that was to decide his fate, and owing to the intervention of Sir George Savile, obtained an amendment of the Act by means of which he was "rescued from destruction".[1] In nine cases out of ten in Nottinghamshire Enclosure Bills went through without organised protest; commissioners were appointed and nothing more was heard about the matter. The Commissioners had to survey the ground, rearrange the allotments into enclosed fields, delimit the new farms, mark out the roads, see that the drainage and fencing and road making required by the Act were properly undertaken, and assess the claims for compensation for the loss of common rights. No human being could steer a course through this inextricable maze without defying the claims which someone regarded as his birthright. When the work was entirely in the hands of local landlords and large farmers the possibility of injustice was raised to its maximum. But they were usually assisted by one or two outsiders called in for their special knowledge and experience of the business of enclosure, whose names frequently recur in widely separated districts. Such men were experts in their task, and would be likely to moderate the tendencies of the local Commissioners towards an undue partiality for their own interests. Even so, it is interesting to note that Arthur Young, one of the strongest supporters of enclosure, utterly condemned the method by which it was pursued.

[1] Hammond, *op. cit.*, p. 54, quoting a speech by Lord Thurloe.

"Thus," he says,[1] "is the property of proprietors, and especially poor ones, entirely at their mercy (i.e. of the Commissioners), every passion of resentment and prejudice may be gratified without control, for they are vested with a despotic power known in no other branch of business in this free country."

Many Enclosure Acts included a provision to enable a person with a grievance to appeal against the Commissioners' decision to Quarter Sessions; but this was far from being an effective safeguard for the small owner, as the magistrates were themselves enclosing landlords and might even be interested in the enclosure upon which they had to adjudicate. Except where opposition emanated from powerful individuals, such as the lord of the manor or the tithe owner, it was entirely ineffective. At Mattersey, for instance, and Calverton,[2] a minority of the proprietors, most of them cottagers, who probably had little or no property beyond their house and rights of common, sent in counter-petitions to the enclosure; they were given the right to plead their cause by learned counsel, but in both cases the petitioners failed to take advantage of this expensive privilege. It is true that the Calverton opposition changed their minds and employed counsel in the end, but it need scarcely be said, without success. An interesting feature common to both these cases is that as soon as the opposing petition was presented and committed, the House ordered that "all have voices who come to the committee to whom the Bill is committed".[3] Mr. and Mrs. Hammond interpret this to mean that the supporters of the Bill were enabled to pack the Committee with their friends without limit, and so outvote the opposition. Such precautions were scarcely necessary against the four owners of cottages at Calverton, who constituted the opposition, and a similar handful at Mattersey, but it illustrates the overwhelming odds against which the opponent of enclosure was pitted.

[1] *Six Months' Tour through North of England*, 1771, Vol. I, p. 122, quoted by Hammond, *op. cit.*, p. 58; see also Mantoux, p. 174.

[2] *H.C.J.*, Vol. 32, p. 647, April, 1770; Vol. 37, p. 265, March, 1778.

[3] *op. cit.*, Vol. 32, p. 648; Vol. 37, p. 282.

From what we have said it will be seen that non-parliamentary enclosure proceeded without opposition, but that parliamentary sanction to enclosure in nearly all cases implied its existence, and was obtained in order to overcome it. The opposition, as far as we can see from the very few cases of which there is record in Nottinghamshire, came from the smallest freeholders; the support may have come from one or two very large proprietors; but in a large number of cases it appears to have come from the larger freeholders also. The following examples will illustrate this point:

	Resident Freeholders who Voted in 1722.	Enclosed.
Misterton	56	11 Geo. III
W. Stockwith	20	Same Act
Tuxford	28	39 Geo. III
Rampton	22	6 & 7 Wm. IV
E. Markham	42	48 Geo. III
S. Leverton	16	35 Geo. III
Laneham	14	12 Geo. III

In such cases enclosure by Act meant a struggle—not between peasants and landed magnates, as is sometimes assumed, but between peasants and peasants, the greater freeholders on the one side, the smallest on the other. For the latter enclosure involved the substitution of common rights by an allotment that required to be fenced within a stipulated time. Until the abnormally high prices of the war period came to his assistance, the cost of enclosure might be more than he could meet, and, as we have indicated elsewhere, the sale of his property might be forced upon him.

Summary

We are now in a position to summarise the chief phases in the decline of the peasantry in Nottinghamshire. First of all, copyhold tenure largely disappeared except on the lands of the Crown and the Church, its place being taken by other forms of tenure which would enable the landlord to raise the rent in accordance with changes in agricultural prices. That is to say, a large number of semi-proprietors became merely tenants.

Secondly, the number of tenants of all kinds was considerably diminished owing to the growth of pasture farming in the sixteenth and seventeenth centuries. Pasture farming led to an increase in the size of the farming unit and thus involved engrossing of farms and "depopulation", and we have given evidence that the displacement of population owing to the development of pasture farming, took place in numerous villages, especially in the south-east of the County. Moreover, freeholders as well as tenants seem to have diminished, and in many cases disappeared in the townships enclosed. We can only assume that if freeholders had ever existed in these townships, they had been bought out before enclosure took place. Thus larger tenants were being substituted for smaller tenants, and freeholders in many townships being bought out in the sixteenth and seventeenth centuries.

But as far as we can discover, this movement was confined, with a few exceptions, to the pasture district; elsewhere, especially in the Clays, the peasantry were numerous, as is shown by the lists of owners which Thoroton gives for village after village in this part of the County. But though the numbers of the peasantry remained steady, their property appears to have been liable to rapid change of ownership.

Mr. S. A. Peyton, who examined the Subsidy Rolls for a number of Nottinghamshire villages in the Bassetlaw division of the County, found that population had not altered appreciably between 1544 and 1641, but that its composition was constantly changing. Of the names which appeared in 1606, 37 per cent. had vanished in 1641, their places being taken by others.

"Names continually disappear, while new names are substituted," says Mr. Peyton, "these vanish, leaving one family running through the whole series of rolls . . . whatever the cause, these figures indicate a greater change than any due to ordinary chances of life. It is therefore possible to infer that the rural population was not permanently rooted to the soil." [1]

We may say, then, that in all districts land was changing hands in the sixteenth and seventeenth centuries, but only in the Pasture area did this result in an appreciable diminution in the number of occupiers and owners. In the eighteenth century, however, the other parts of the County began to be affected, the purchase of freehold properties both before and after enclosure took place rapidly. Mr. Davies, in his valuable study on the Small Landowner, from 1780 to 1830, could find no more than 930 occupying owners, including copyholders and lessees, as well as freeholders in the 158 parishes studied. He found that not only the old enclosed parishes, but those enclosed by other than parliamentary agreement, were largely denuded of occupying owners; we have shown that this was the case in all agricultural districts, and have suggested that the freeholders were bought out, as was the case with old enclosed parishes, in order to facilitate enclosure, i.e. before enclosure. This may well have been taking place in villages owned by the yeomen farmers as well as in landlords' villages. We have shown elsewhere that freeholders obtained Acts of Parliament to enforce enclosure upon a recalcitrant minority, and it is likely that in order to remove opposition of this kind, the larger freeholder was buying up his smaller brethren. It is worth noting in this connection that several villages which contributed largely to the subsidies of the seventeenth century had surprisingly few resident freeholders who went to the

[1] Peyton, S. A., Tudor Lay Subsidy Rolls, *Hist. Rev.*, Vol. XXX, pp. 246 *et seq.* Mr. Peyton's surprising contention is confirmed by the Leicestershire writer, Jos. Lee, already quoted. In his *Vindication of Regulated Inclosure* he says: "Few in common fields do keep their lands three generations." And he gives the example of his own village, Catthorp, in which only one estate had remained in the same family for three generations. He contends that enclosed estates changed hands less quickly than in the open field.—See Nichols, *History and Antiquities of Leicestershire,* Vol. IV, Pt. I, p. 97.

poll in 1722. Probably the absorption of the small freeholder had been going on in the grain-growing districts from the time of the Corn Bounty Acts of 1673 and 1688.[1] By the end of the century, according to the indications given by Throsby on his tour in 1790,[2] several villages which had numerous resident freeholders in 1722 were in the hands of a few large proprietors.

It would appear, therefore, that the freeholders as a class had definitely entered upon their decline in the Pasture district in the early phases of the agrarian revolution, i.e. from the end of the fifteenth century; that the decline spread to the other parts of the County before the end of the seventeenth century, when the profits of grain and cattle farming were assured by protective legislation, and that by 1780 they were reduced, in the phrase of Mr. Davies, to a mere remnant of their former strength.

After 1780, this tendency seems to have been checked; owing to the greatly increased price of grain and meat, even the smallest owner could hold his own, in spite of the expenses connected with enclosure, and instead of declining, his numbers actually increased. This is shown in the following figures compiled by Mr. Davies from the Land Tax Assessment in the Shire Hall Muniment Room:[3]

[1] For instance in Clarborough, Hayton-cum-Tilne, Clayworth, Gringley on the Hill, Walkeringham, Sutton-cum-Lound, N. Muskham, the number of resident freeholders was scarcely 10 per cent. of the number of seventeenth-century subsidy men. See S. A. Peyton, *op. cit.*, and Subsidy Rolls of 1689 published by G. Marshall, and Poll Book of 1722. It should be noted, however, that the Subsidy Rolls do not distinguish clearly between tenants, owners of land, and those who paid on their "stock". Again, it is impossible to say what proportion of the freeholders of the County went to the poll in 1722; the indications are that the poll was a heavy one, but only tentative conclusions can be drawn from these unsatisfactory sources. With the help of the Land Tax Assessments which are now being investigated, a more complete survey of the position of the peasantry will be possible.

[2] See for instance Rempston, Ruddington, East Stoke, Sutton Bonington, Orston, N. Muskham, etc.

[3] Davies, "The Small Landowner, 1780–1832, in the Light of the Land Tax Assessments," *Econ. Hist. Rev.*, 1927, Vol. I, No. 1, p. 106.

Number of Parishes studied, 158	Land Tax Under:									Over £20	Total.
	4*s.*	10*s.*	£1	£2	£4	£5	£8	£10	£20		
Estimated acreage.	4	10	20	40	80	100	160	200	400	400	—
No. paying Land Tax in:											
1780–2 . . .	219	308	154	116	70	18	22	10	10	3	930
1802	344	362	228	154	104	20	31	13	15	3	1,274
1832	410	352	222	132	94	18	33	9	18	6	1,294

We may conclude, then, that the steady prices of the eighteenth century enabled the larger and more enterprising yeoman farmers, as well as the large landowners, to consolidate their properties by buying out their smaller neighbours, but the high prices after 1780 and the artificial conditions of the war boom in agriculture enabled the smaller owners to recover their position somewhat. When Lowe wrote in 1794 he commented on the small size of many of the properties especially in the Clays. "The farms may in general be said to be small," he says, "few exceeding £300 per annum, and more being under £100 than above that sum, many (especially in the Clays) as low as twenty pounds or under."[1] Moreover, the yeomanry were by no means extinct by the middle of the nineteenth century; the Directories of 1832 and 1844, which give the names of all the chief inhabitants of all the villages in the County, indicate the existence of yeomen in many villages, especially in the Clays, and quote with embellishment (but without acknowledgment) the statement of Lowe given above as though it represented the existing state of affairs.

[1] Lowe, *op. cit.*, p. 14. The statement of Lowe is no doubt the basis of the remark of the writer on Nottinghamshire in the *Beauties of England*, Vol. XII, p. 24, when he says, "It is pleasant to see a whole county . . . in a high state of cultivation . . . inhabited by a respectable yeomanry and leasehold farmers" and then goes on to reproduce the figures given by Lowe. This is made an occasion for a tirade against large farms and a defence of the yeomanry by the compiler of the Directories of 1832 and 1844.

Thus the yeomanry, though a diminishing quantity, were certainly a surviving one until the middle of the nineteenth century. What was their subsequent position in Nottinghamshire we have not enquired; but as a possible answer to this interesting question, we may note the findings of Professor and Miss Gras after their investigation into the history of the yeomanry of a single parish in Hampshire.[1] "The Yeomanry," they say, "had been triumphant by 1850", having bought up the smaller properties, so that the village was shared among a small group of substantial yeoman farmers.

"By September 1902," Professor Gras goes on, "they had left the village or lost their status of yeomen. . . . How are we to explain their going? Locally it is said that the yeoman families died out. . . . Another explanation for their passing is the bad year of 1879 when wheat was brought in in cartloads 'sopping wet like manure'. . . . But the well-to-do yeoman farmers were able to withstand a single crop failure. What they could not do was compete with American wheat and Australian wool and mutton."

Whether this is true of the yeomanry of Nottinghamshire only further research will show.[2] The "black and populous cities", to use Mantoux's phrase,[3] which were growing up around them, may have given the yeomanry their *coup de grace*. On the other hand, they presented an opportunity for enterprise and adaptability which some at least would not let slip.

[1] Prof. N. S. B. and Miss Gras, *The Econ. and Social History of an English Village* (Crawley, Hampshire), p. 126.

[2] An investigation of 1877 gave the following figures for Nottinghamshire:

109	greater yeomen	owning	54,500 acres.
282	lesser yeomen	,,	47,940 ,,
3,838	small proprietors	,,	61,108 ,,
9,891	cottagers	,,	1,266 ,,

What was the proportion of yeoman farmers in the sense of occupying owners depending on their properties for the main part of their livelihood it is impossible to say. The numbers are large enough to indicate that the yeomanry had not declined appreciably, if at all, since 1832.—See Brodrick, *English Land and English Landlords*, p. 179. For interesting comparison between Notts. and Lincs. see *Journal of Roy. Agric. Soc.*, Second Series, Vol. XXIV, p. 512.

[3] Mantoux, *op. cit.*, p. 168.

PART III

SOCIAL CONDITIONS UNDER THE SQUIREARCHY

CHAPTER VIII

SOCIAL RELATIONS: THE POOR LAW

So far we have dealt with two aspects of local life: the evolution of the squire as the predominant figure in local administration and social life, and secondly the rise of a class of substantial manufacturers and farmers, employing considerable resources of capital and drawing upon the labour of those who were formerly independent or semi-independent peasants and craftsmen. This profound change in the structure of society involved equally important changes in social organisation and social relations, and it is to these questions that we must now turn.

The agrarian revolution, as we have seen, displaced the population in many villages in the south and east of the County; the growth of capitalist industry and national trade exposed the working population to the fluctuations that are inseparable from commercial enterprise; the monetary revolution of the sixteenth century lowered the real value of wages, and the dissolution of the monasteries had the double effect of reducing the means of relief while increasing the number of those who needed it. All these changes called for a thorough and drastic reconstruction if the alternative of armed revolt was to be avoided.

The first phase in the reconstruction was the sporadic growth of Poor Law institutions in the largest towns. London was the first in the field with compulsory poor rate, and discriminatory treatment for the impotent, the children, the deserving able-bodied and the idle. Other centres—Coventry, Norwich, York—followed; but the isolated efforts of the towns were rendered difficult, if not nugatory, by the fact that these regulated centres were invaded by the poor of other districts and destitution grew as fast as they relieved it.[1]

The only solution was a national system which would distribute the burden more equally over the whole country. Step by step the State followed in the wake of the towns; in 1536 the poor were differentiated into the familiar categories of impotent, deserving and undeserving poor, and were to be provided for in every parish by voluntary alms; in 1572 the collection of voluntary alms gave place to a compulsory assessment of a poor rate, fixed by the Justices and administered by a body of new officials, collectors and overseers; in 1576 Houses of Correction for the vagrant were ordered to be set up in every county, and every parish was to have a stock of material for the employment of those who were willing but unable to find work; in 1598 and again in 1601, these provisions were brought together in the great Poor Law of Elizabeth, and a comprehensive scheme of relief for all categories of poor and forced labour for the idle was at last in being.

Such was the answer of the Tudor State to the social upheaval of the sixteenth century. Actuated partly by fear of popular outbreak and partly by traditional Christian charity and common humanity, it tried to relieve the destitute, train the children, find employment for the workless and punishment for the work-shy. It went even further; it tried also to prevent as well as to relieve destitution by controlling, on behalf of the poor, the supply of food in times of scarcity. We have alluded in an earlier chapter to the work of the local gentry in distributing supplies of corn, controlling the markets, and protecting the poor from the evil effects of the speculator and monopoliser. The measure of success attending these efforts is, perhaps, a matter of dispute,

[1] The constables of Nottingham complained in 1556 of the poor people who daily came into the town and tarried there; and the Mayor was requested to find some redress as the town was unable to relieve them. Nottingham Borough Records, Vol. IV, p. 112.

but one result it had of great importance; it prepared the local government for the vigorous administration of the Poor Law under the powerful stimulus of Charles I's despotic government.

There is no doubt that in most counties, and certainly in Nottinghamshire, the Poor Law System was made to work at this time, particularly in regard to the provision of employment for the able-bodied; and practically every place, except the very smallest villages, had its stock of material for the unemployed to work on, a practice that was by no means wholly discontinued in the eighteenth century, as we show later on.

With the collapse of the central power and the total cessation of governmental supervision the parishes were largely left to their own devices. Moreover, the Civil War had dislocated the system of local government and had also released numbers of men from the anchorage of regular employment and cast them upon the highways and byways of a troubled world. How could the parish alone with the sporadic if beneficent interference of the local squire be expected to perform the complex functions of the Elizabethan Poor Law Code in an environment which was every day becoming more susceptible to social shocks owing to the growth of capitalist industry and foreign trade? Unanswerable as this question is, the Restoration Government chose this time to place upon the single parish the additional responsibility of the Settlement Regulations. Henceforward, the officers of the parish with the consent of a magistrate were enabled to remove any stranger who came into the parish *before* he actually became chargeable, unless he was possessed of sufficient means to satisfy the overseers, or could obtain a settlement by fulfilling certain very difficult conditions. The State had again adopted, as a national policy, the methods that were already in being in the towns and to some extent in the country districts, unmindful of the fact that in so doing the whole of the working population had been, in theory, immobilised.

The folly of basing a national system of poor relief upon the independent action of thousands of separate authorities was not allowed to pass without comment, but the remedy proposed—a union of parishes under Incorporated Guardians of the Poor—was vitiated by the ineradicable delusion that pauperism, if properly managed, could be made to pay. Numerous institutions were set up with the combined object of abolishing pauperism and making profit,[1] but though they failed, they led to the discovery of an important principle, the principle of the Workhouse Test.

It was now agreed that the poor would only work under compulsion; persuasion had failed, and only the spur of necessity would reconcile them to their duty of labour for the commonwealth. There was an outcry against the sins of the labouring class who were constantly accused of idleness, debauchery, insolence, dishonesty, and so on, an outcry that was too unanimous to be without foundation. It should be remembered that the commons were still open in the majority of Midland parishes and were able to yield the labourer or the artisan a supplementary income. Moreover, the labourer was only interested in maintaining a traditional standard of living, not in enjoying additional luxuries, hence in times of plenty and low prices—such as the period 1715–65—his efforts were apt to relax and a working week of three or four days was by no means uncommon. Indeed, it was frequently said that the labourer was as well off, certainly worked less hard, than some types of employers, such as the small farmer, who, according to Arthur Young, worked without intermission like a horse, and according to another writer was poorer than the day labourer he employed.[2] There is, therefore, some reason for Sir Thomas Parkyns' complaint that the true law of subordination was every day overturned by insolent labouring men, so that "by a notorious reverse of nature masters were vilely and contemptibly

[1] See later, p. 235.
[2] Cunningham, *Industry and Commerce*, Vol. II, p. 565n.

become the slaves of their servants and the equal of their slaves".

Moreover, the labourer held a specially important place in the commonwealth; he was regarded as the basis of the national effort, the chief if not the only source of wealth. His labour was essential to the well-being of the country in a fiercely competitive world. Idleness, therefore, was more than a nuisance; it was a crime. The persuasion or coercion of the labourer to perform his appointed task in society thus became an important function of the State, and Acts were passed to make idleness—even enforced idleness—both irksome and humiliating. By the Act 8 and 9 Wm. III, 30, the legitimate pauper, when he stayed in his own parish, was made to wear a large Roman "P" and the first letter of the parish to which he belonged on the right sleeve of his coat in order to distinguish him from the vagabond who continued to wear, no doubt, more indelible distinctions upon his back. He could not adopt the alternative of begging, as this was specifically repressed by the Act 12 Anne, 23; and the Act 9 Geo. I, 7, crowned the attack upon idleness by enabling parishes to set up workhouses and impose the workhouse test.

Besides these attempts to make idleness more distasteful than labour, the State, while protecting the labourer from actual fraud by the master, denied him any effective voice in the conditions under which his labour was performed. Combinations of workmen were severely repressed by the Act 12 Geo. I, 34, and any attempt to coerce masters by violent methods was punishable by fourteen years' transportation, while the wilful destruction of machinery, including the stocking frame, was punishable by death.[1] The law made some amends to the labourer by prohibiting the payment of wages in truck, but there was no attempt to put down

[1] The penalty of death was never imposed for frame breaking in the eighteenth century; towards the end of the century the penalty was reduced to 14 years' transportation by the Act 28 Geo. III, 55. The combinations of Masters were actually legalised by the Acts 17 Geo. III, 11; 24 Geo. III, 3. See Cunningham, *op. cit.*, p. 510.

the secret combinations of masters. When it is remembered that the labourer was liable to compulsory removal, even before he became chargeable, if he moved from his parish in search of work, it will be seen that the labourer, according to the law, was subject to a restraint that was scarcely distinguishable from a species of servitude.

If we had no further evidence than the Statute Book, we should be tempted to conclude that social relations under the squirearchy had reverted to those subsisting under the manorial system, with the Parish in the place of the Manor. But the inhumanity of the law was mitigated, partly by the inefficiency with which it was administered and partly by the action of the squires themselves, whose despotism, though absolute, was generally paternal. For instance, they frequently interposed their authority between a parish officer and the victim of parochial economy, as we show later; moreover, they signally failed to administer one part of the above code of repression, namely the Combination Acts. The Framework Knitters organised a powerful combination and in 1779 they went on strike; they broke machinery, hustled the hosiers, attacked their houses; every tile, window and door of hosier Need's house was smashed, and three hundred of his frames thrown into the street; the house of another was so damaged that he left it in ruins and set up his trade elsewhere, while another house was totally demolished. For most of these offences the death penalty could have been exacted, but juries, magistrates and Judge, before whom the offenders were tried, might have conspired to make a mock of the law. The highest penalty imposed was a fine of 6*s*. 8*d*. and three weeks' imprisonment, and a man who had wounded a Justice of the Peace with a stone was liberated on asking his pardon.[1]

The interest of the magistrate was not in industry,

[1] See Chap. II above based on Henson, *Hist. of Framework Knitters*; Sutton, *Date Book of Nottingham* and contemporary accounts in local press. For non-enforcement of Act regarding wearing of badges by paupers, see Webb, *Old Poor Law*, p. 161.

but in agriculture; above all it centred in his own parish where he ruled like a king; but the divinity that hedged him admitted the near presence of rustic courtiers, and it was by no means unknown for the magistrate and landlord to play the part of mine host and benefactor to the loyal subjects of his petty kingdom.

When, for instance, we read of Sir Thomas Parkyns, the Squire Western of Nottinghamshire, except for his greater learning, with his wrestlers, his charity schools, and his hospital for poor widows, or when we read of the celebration of Pancake Day at Aspley Hall [1]—where the villagers of Wollaton, Trowell and Cossal met in the Squire's kitchen to drink beer and toss pancakes and where large families were recommended by the Squire and his lady as a means of acquiring dexterity in the latter art—we are assured that though the law was inhuman, social relations, in the early part of the century at least, were tempered by friendly association of rich and poor and a hearty, if gross, liberality. But the last quarter of the century witnessed changes both for good and evil. On the one hand, there were many signs of a great social awakening; the terrible revelations of Howard and Hanway regarding prisons and workhouses; the well-intentioned Act of 1782 which allowed outdoor relief to the able-bodied in the Gilbert Unions; the attempt on the part of the Evangelicals to reform the public morals through a reformed local administration; on the other, there was the basic fact that the wages of the labourer were frequently insufficient to support him and his family, and that the granting of relief in aid of wages, a solution which had precedents going back to the seventeenth century, was adopted as a preferable alternative to raising them. The essentially servile position of the labouring class was now fully revealed; the labourer had a legal claim upon his parish of settlement, whether he had earned it or not; the employer had a claim upon his services whether he paid him a living wage or not;

[1] For account of this joyous celebration, see Sutton, *Date Book of Nottingham*, p. 71.

the parish was responsible for the pauper children born within its boundaries whether they were legitimate or not, and unmarried mothers obtained relief for their bastards from the parish officers or an offer of marriage or blackmail in return for silence from the fathers. There was a "monstrous incontinence" prevalent in English parishes;[1] indeed, during the last quarter of the century, the settlement of bastards cases was one of the chief items of public business, as may be seen from the Minute Book of Quarter Sessions.[2] By the end of the eighteenth century the labouring classes were sinking into a condition of unparalleled degradation, and among the causes none was more important than the Poor Law itself. It is necessary, therefore, to study the operation of the poor laws—the grand example of social planning by the aristocratic state—if the question of social conditions under the squirearchy is to be properly understood.

Relief of the Poor.

(1) The Impotent Poor

Organised relief for the impotent poor dates from the reign of Elizabeth, but as we have shown elsewhere the Government that did most for the poor by keeping a vigilant eye upon the administrators of the law was the government of Charles I. There is also evidence that the responsibility for poor relief which formerly devolved upon the manorial organisation had not entirely died out in Nottinghamshire, although only one example of it can be cited. In 1642 the Justices found that in the village of Epperstone "there is an ancient custome and course that the several lords have and doe usualie maintaine the

[1] Letter to J. T. Becher by J. W. Cowell, 1834, p. 8.

[2] According to Becher, bastardy affiliation orders had formerly been issued in petty sessions, but this does not seem to be borne out by the Minute Book of Quarter Sessions. Possibly Becher's statement is true only of the Liberty of Southwell and Scrooby for which the Minute Books are missing up to 1784. See Becher, "Letter on alteration and amendment of Bastardy Laws, 1834," p. 8. Mr. J. H. Meeds, who is investigating this subject, kindly informs me that the number of bastardy cases brought before Quarter Sessions for the period 1775–90 was 456. How many were settled outside Quarter Sessions it is impossible to say.

poore which happen upon those several lands", and therefore Mr. John Walker, one of the lords of the town, was ordered to pay the largest contribution to the maintenance of a pauper who formerly had her dwelling upon his land, but had moved into another parish and become chargeable.[1] This is probably a unique case; responsibility had by this time shifted from the individual to the group; but it is only necessary to glance at the cases cited by Mr. Hampton Copnall in his book of seventeenth-century records to realise that the responsibility was fully recognised, at least by the Justices of the Peace, who again and again fined parish officers "for neglect of duty", "not providing for paupers", "not allocating sufficient maintenance of paupers", etc., etc.[2] The Justices' own standards of relief appear to have been sufficiently low; 6*d.* a week for an impotent cripple in 1653; twelve pence a week for "a very poore man, very aged and past his work"; twelve pence a week "to Tingle being 100 years old". But they also ordered alternative accommodation to be found for people evicted by landlords, or rendered homeless by fire; the feeding and clothing of destitute children and the maintenance and education (apprenticeship) of an orphan boy. These, of course, are all cases of neglect on the part of the parish officers, who, without the stimulus of magisterial proddings, would have let the pauper shift for himself or starve. The report of the magistrates in the northern division of the County in 1623 is significant:

"Divers complaints by many poor people are daily brought to us at East Retford, sometimes at our dwelling houses, sometimes at any Sessions of the Peace, of want of maintenance and habitation by the negligence of Churchwardens and Overseers of the Poor, in all or most of the Constabularies in this division, leaving everything to the care and activity of the Justices of the Peace and doing nothing themselves, having more direct power than they.

[1] Hampton Copnall, *op. cit.*, p. 120. It may be noted that according to Thoroton the desire on the part of the Lords of the Manor to rid themselves of their poor relief obligations was one of the main motives for the emancipation of their servile tenants. Cf. Throsby's Thoroton, pp. xiv and 216.

[2] Copnall, *op. cit.*, p. 120.

The Chief Constables of the Wapentake of Bassetlaw were ordered to move the Churchwardens and Overseers of the Poor of each parish that they duly hold monthly meetings and see their poor parishioners so that henceforth there may not be just complaints in this case."

In 1636, thirteen years after the above complaint was made, we have the report of the Justices sent up to the Privy Council regarding their activities in this very part of the County, and a section of this report covering twenty-two villages in the North and South Clay and Hatfield divisions, has been published in Miss Leonard's *Early History of English Poor Relief*.[1] We have here a group of peasant villages, each a poor law unit in itself with its parish stock of materials and implements for the unemployed, a system of maintenance for the impotent, apprenticeship for the children and the whippingpost for the vagabond, and the local squire conscientiously supervising the whole under the eagle eye of the Privy Council. When Lord Clarendon wrote that under the beneficent rule of Charles I and his council the people of England "enjoyed the greatest calm and fullest measure of felicity that any people in any age for so long time together have been blessed with to the wonder and envy of all parts of Christendom",[2] he was not speaking without some justification.

During the Civil War relief continued to be distributed fairly generally and even in the besieged town of Newark the organisation appears to have continued without breakdown.[3]

The effect of the fall of the Stuart Monarchy upon the system of relief for the impotent poor is very difficult to assess. We have pointed out elsewhere that there appears to have been a marked decline in the willingness

[1] Leonard, *op. cit.*, p. 361.

[2] *Hist. of Rebellion and Civil Wars in England*, ed. 1888, Vol. I, pp. 93–5, quoted Webb, *The Old Poor Law*, p. 91. For very useful list of authorities on the subject of Charles I's paternal attitude towards social and economic relations, see Tawney, *Rel. and Rise of Capitalism*, p. 323.

[3] Hodgkinson, *Extracts from Records of Borough of Newark-on-Trent*, p. 37, and Hampton Copnall, *op. cit.*, pp. 115–19.

of the local magistracy to undertake the duties which still devolved upon them, and to that extent, the administration of the Poor Law would necessarily suffer; but after an inexplicable gap of a dozen years soon after the Restoration the records take up again the endless round of Poor Law litigation, reinforced now from the fertile source of the Settlement Laws.

In spite of the cessation of control by the Government, the Justices eventually take up again their round of poor law duties, though with far less energy; churchwardens and overseers continue to receive the stimulation of a prosecution and fine by Quarter Sessions, special cases of hardship are relieved, and an occasional freak of cruelty on the part of parish officers is punished. The following example shows the Justices in a specially solicitous mood:

"Upon a hearing between the inhabitants of Stanford and Sarah Goodby touching maintenance it is ordered that Sarah Goodby have four shillings a week for herself and two children until the overseers have found her a convenient house of two rooms, each room to be eleven feet square, and then to continue paying her three shillings a week and also find her a sufficient woman who shall take care of her." [1]

Letters like the following are frequently found among the records. "Widow Hill of Tuxford being in great want and having four children desires your worships will be so kind as to order the parish to allow her something to maintain her and her children"; and the sluggish machinery of poor relief was sometimes speeded up by appeals like the following: [2]

HON. SIR,

Let me humbly request the favour of you speedily to grant that the order to John Shepherd of Newthorpe, one of the Overseers of the poor of Greasly Parish, that he doo according to the

[1] MS. Quarter Sessions Minute Book, April, 1705. Orders were occasionally given by Quarter Sessions for building a house on the waste for an impotent pauper after having obtained the permission of the Lord of the Manor.

[2] MS. Session Rolls, no date, among documents for 1708.

order made pay Timothie Cocke weekly and every week the money ordered by yourself and Sir Francis Molyneux for yor servant

TIMI COCKE.

(Postscript) I have desired bearer to wait upon you for your letter and bring it to the Lady Dixie's at Selston for me that I may deliver it myself.

It is probable that the solicitude of the Justices was not infrequently misdirected. A case is cited by Mr. Copnall of a man receiving an allowance by order of the Justices on the grounds of lameness, but he unwisely boasted in the hearing of less fortunate villagers that he could walk thirty miles on a winter's day, through which indiscretion he lost his allowance.[1] Indeed, it seems highly probable that the Justices were somewhat out of touch with the opinion of the State, which took the lead in poor law matters from the large towns, and particularly London. At any rate, in 1722 it was deemed necessary to pass an Act to restrain them from indiscriminate granting of relief, no Justice being permitted to grant relief until the applicant had been refused by the Overseers, had shown cause for relief on oath, and the Overseers had given reason for refusing it. At the same time Sir Thomas Parkyns published his pamphlet "On Subordination or an Essay on Servants and their Wages", in which we get a somewhat belated echo of the policy so strenuously advocated by London writers such as Locke and Defoe, of increased severity to the poor,[2] but the impotent poor do not seem to have suffered in this campaign which was directed mainly against the able-bodied poor.

The Work of the Parish.

Important as the magistrate was, the man upon whom the chief burden of the Poor Law fell was the Parish

[1] *op. cit.*, p. 120; the most frequent form of fraud was the forging of counterfeit passes. See Minute Book, Jan. 15, 1745, etc.

[2] A small collection entitled "Queries and Reasons" by Sir Thomas Parkyns 1724—Nottingham Ref. Lib. *Cf.* Borough Records, Vol. VI, p. 165, and note.

Overseer. No one suffered more at the hands of contemporary criticism; perhaps no one deserved to suffer more; but in extenuation of the Overseer it should be remembered that he was the representative of the ratepayers, appointed by the vestry "to save the Parish as much money as possible in the management of the poor and to act as parish husbandman".[1]

In most parishes the resident paupers seem to have been treated fairly generously; it was the stranger, above all the stranger burdened with children, who suffered most at the hands of the parish officers. The most common form of relief granted by the overseers consisted of a small allowance of a few shillings a week in addition to gifts in kind. The Bleasby Overseer for instance paid Widow Roland 2*s.* a week; William Flint had 1*s.* 6*d.*; Widow Parke received £2 12*s.* 6*d.* for six months, and so on. Payments continue in some cases for several years. A pauper of East Bridgford received complete maintenance, including fuel, clothes' mending and washing for a period of over ten years.[2] Sometimes the parish contracted with individuals to board and lodge its permanent paupers at a stipulated charge "for the town's ease"; agreement was thus made between the churchwardens and overseers of the poor of Sutton Bonington on the one hand with Robert Bramley on the other to take Matthew and James Rower for one year for the sum of Five Pounds ten shillings; and if either of them fall sick he is to have five shillings extra; [3] Mary Briggs was paid Four Pounds Eighteen shillings and eight pence by the Overseers of East Bridgford for keeping Robert Howitt for 32 weeks,[4] an allowance which was sufficient to keep a working labourer in board

[1] Quoted from MS. Vestry Minute Book St. Peter's, Nottingham, 1718. For contemporary attacks on overseers, see *The Vestry Laid Open* by Jos. Phipps, 1739; *A Short View of Frauds and Impositions of Parish Officers* 1744 (Anonymous) in the Foxwell Collection of pamphlets in Goldsmith's Library, S. Kensington.

[2] MS. Overseers' Accounts E. Bridgford. Town Book Bleasby, etc.

[3] MS. Overseers' Accounts Sutton Bonington, Feb., 1753.

[4] MS. Overseers' Accounts E. Bridgford, 1745.

and lodgings. Relief was also given in kind, especially in the form of fuel and clothes. The entries for fuel generally occur in September and October when considerable quantities of coal were bought and distributed among the paupers, both regular and occasional. The following items occur in the Bleasby Accounts for September, 1769:

John Hans . .	30	hundred of coles	
Robt. Walker . .	6	" " "	
Elizabeth Wite . .	12	" " "	etc., etc.

Clothes were similarly distributed. Completely new wardrobes would sometimes be provided as the following entry shows:

> Pade for the stuf:
> Cote, weskat and Britches and Stockins
> and Stuf to mend the frock with a new Hat
> and two New Sherts and the making . £1. 4. 4*d.*[1]

It was more customary for clothing to be found or repaired as the need arose; shoes and coats were mended, new hats were provided; Widow Roland received a "pare of Stase and a Hanker Cheef"; two widows of East Bridgford were provided with two new shifts every year and so on.[2] Sometimes relief took the form of thatching of cottages and the payment of rent.[3]

It would seem further that the distinction between impotent and able-bodied poor was not clearly recognised for many recipients of relief in money and kind were also given raw materials from the parish stock.[4] Richard Howitt of East Bridgford, for instance, who was being maintained by the parish at a cost of 2*s.* 7*d.* a week and sometimes more, was also provided with an occasional pound of wool. The following account for Mary

[1] MS. Town Book Bleasby, Oct. 21, 1760.
[2] MS. Overseers' Accounts E. Bridgford, 1744, etc.
[3] MS. Town Book Bleasby, 1753.
[4] This is the case in the four parishes Bleasby, E. Bridgford, Sutton Bonington, Laxton.

Preston of the same parish shows that direct relief and employment were given indiscriminately:[1]

Mary Preston	7 hundred of coals . .	4. 8*d*.
„ „	5 yards of linnen cloth. .	4. 4*d*.
„ „	6 yards of woollen cloth .	7. 0*d*.
paid her for spinning		5. 7*d*.

And Widow Dunkin of Bleasby, besides a frequent grant of 1*s*. per week, was paid 3*s*. 6*d*. for spinning 6 lb. of flax.[2] The callousness of the parish officers which we alluded to above does not appear until we see them administering the laws of Settlement. Here there is no limit to the shifts and dodges they will practise to avoid the maintenance of a stranger, however sick or aged or helpless he may be. The blame should be put on the odious system they were compelled to administer, but the following cases cannot be recited without a shudder at the unbelievable inhumanity of village farmers in defence of their poor rate; each case, it may be noted, is the product of prosecution at Quarter Sessions: In 1681 the inhabitants of Stoke were fined 6*s*. 8*d*. "for removing a woman in her labour".[3] In 1720 Mary Mann, the mother of a bastard child, "was barbarously and unnaturally" carried by the Constable and other officers of Hickling before Sir Francis Molyneux, at least seven miles away, on January 13, 1720, in the hardest and severest weather, having lain in only a fortnight after giving birth to a bastard child. They did it "of their own heads and without any order from a magistrate, though they pretended they had an order from Sir Thomas Parkyns, for which slander they were bound over to good behaviour". During the examination regarding the paternity of the child, the mother had to be held up by two persons, "for which hard usage Mary Mann died".[4]

[1] MS. Accounts E. Bridgford, 1744. [2] MS. Town Book Bleasby, 1755.

[3] Hampton Copnall, *op. cit.*, p. 118.

[4] MS. Session Rolls, March 17, 1720–1. Another parish officer was indicted for "dropping a poor vagrant woman in a very sick condition in the public highway". Session Rolls, Oct. 1, 1719.

Poor Children.

One of the most important duties of the Parish Officers under the old Poor Law was the care of poor children. In the seventeenth century the work was not always left to the parish officers, but was shared by the corporation; on one occasion the Common Council of the town maintained a number of poor children at their own expense.[1] A more frequent method of relief was to provide a stock of tools and materials at the expense of the Corporation upon which the children were "ymployed, taughte and sette to work" on the business of wool combing and were paid according to their earnings.[2] But efforts of this kind on the part of the Corporate Body seem to have relaxed in the second half of the seventeenth century and to have ceased altogether in the eighteenth, and the work of providing for poor children was left to the operation by the parish officers of the Apprenticeship System as a method of poor relief. By the Act of William III,[3] masters were compelled to receive apprentices placed upon them by the parish officers under a penalty of £10, and parish apprenticeship henceforth became the most popular method of relieving the parish of its burden of poor children.

Long before this, however, compulsion of various kinds had been applied. In the early seventeenth century the method adopted by the Borough was for the Mayor and Common Council to issue a proclamation for the summons of certain specified persons to appear "att the Guildhall of the towne —— by eighte in the forenoon then and there to take apprentices" and if any neglected to appear or refused to take apprentices, they were to answer before the next General Quarter Sessions".[4]

[1] Nottingham Borough Records, Vol. V, p. 129.

[2] See later, p. 235.

[3] 8 and 9 Wm. III, 30, Section 5—the apprenticeship was supposed to last until the age of 24, but this was altered to 21 by 18 Geo. III, 47, although cases occur in the records in which the lower age limit was adopted before the Act was passed.

[4] MS. Nottingham Borough Records, per Mr. E. L. Guilford.

The choosing of a master for the apprentice was in the hands of the overseers and the choice was supposed to go by vote, but complaints of unfair discrimination frequently arose. Sometimes persons would plead their poverty, or escape the burden by making a money payment to the overseers. Everyone appears to have done his best to get the indenture cancelled and the apprentice discharged if any reasonable provocation could be pleaded; "he is a discomposed child and infirm—and many other larger farmers have not had any apprentice putt to 'em," pleaded one master; "she is inflicted with sores and incurable though great care hath been taken to cure 'em,"[1] said another, and a considerable number were discharged without any reason being entered into the Minute Book.

Many complaints were made in the seventeenth century that masters connived at the escape of their parish apprentices who incontinently reappeared before the parish officers in search of relief.[2] Towards the end of the eighteenth century an attempt was sometimes made to avoid these evils by compelling the master of a parish apprentice to enter into a bond of £20 to keep the parish secure from all charges respecting the child until he reached the age of twenty-one or gained a legal settlement elsewhere.[3]

The reluctance with which parish apprentices were taken by masters in the seventeenth and early eighteenth centuries is the more surprising in view of the premiums which were given with them. The preamble of the Act 7, James I, 3, shows that money was being left for the payment of premiums from the beginning of the seventeenth century and the returns of 1636 show the amount paid by the parish officers of the villages of

[1] MS. Minute Book, Vol. 24, p. 271 (1734), etc., etc.

[2] Hampton Copnall, *Notts. County Records*, p. 129.

[3] "Documents relating to Bleasby," Jan. 7, 1780, etc., etc. The discharge of an apprentice could only be effected at Quarter Sessions, though the consent of the Churchwardens seems to have been sufficient for transfer of an apprentice from one master to another—Quarter Sessions Minute Book, Oct. 2, 1721.

Nottinghamshire for this purpose.[1] £6 10*s*. was given with three poor apprentices in the village of Laxton; £7 10*s*. was given with two apprentices at East Markham, and so on. The amount of the premium seems to have varied with the age and ability of the apprentice. As much as £5 would be given with a helpless child; sometimes the premium amounted to only five shillings, or it might even be paid in house rent.[2]

The usual amount of the premium in the eighteenth century was from twenty to forty shillings, "not enough to get a good master".[3] It would seem also that the premium was a matter of private contract between the parish officers and the master, for in very few of the numerous indentures of parish apprentices found in the Quarter Sessions Records is mention of premium anywhere made. The amounts of the premiums were, however, entered into the parish book; the overseers of Bleasby, for instance, in the latter half of the century, usually gave £2 with their poor children; Sutton Bonington paid as much as £5 with a girl apprentice, and £4 with a boy.[4] It is probable that the premium went up towards the end of the eighteenth century, owing to the growth of population and the temporary excess of labour, as St. Peter's parish generally paid no more than fifteen to thirty shillings with its apprentices at the end of the seventeenth century.[5]

Besides the premium, the parish also fitted out its apprentices with a complete new wardrobe, which for boys consisted of the following items: one hat, coat, leathern breeches, stockings and new shoes.[6] The care of the parish overseers for a girl apprentice is shown in the following quaint document:[7]

[1] Given in Leonard, *loc. cit.*

[2] MS. Nottingham Borough Records, per Mr. E. L. Guilford.

[3] Report on Parish Apprentices—*H.C.J.*, Vol. 31, p. 249.

[4] "Documents relating to Bleasby", 1767, 1780, 1783, etc. MS. Town Book Sutton Bonington, 1758, 1763, 1784, etc.

[5] MS. Vestry Minute Book St. Peter's, 1691.

[6] MS. Town Book Sutton Bonington, 1795.

[7] MS. Overseers' and Constables' Accounts. Bleasby, 1755.

Paid for stuff to cure the lass of Itch . .	1*s.* 1*d.*
For stuff to make her two gowns and a Petecote and makeing	12*s.* 5*d.*
Paid for indentures to bind the lass . .	5*s.* 0*d.*
" " 3 yds of cloth to make her two shifts	5*s.* 0*d.*
For keeping the lass ten days before she went to George Belshaws	3*s.* 0*d.*
Paid to make the lass capps etc. . . .	5*s.* 1*d.*
For two pare of stockings	1*s.* 2*d.*

The apprentice once disposed of, the parish had no further interest in his fate. He might or might not be taught a trade; in the vast majority of cases his maintenance seems to have been regarded as a form of charity in return for which he was to serve his master in any capacity required. The condition of a parish apprentice under these circumstances must have been hard in the extreme. He could appeal in cases of cruelty to Quarter Sessions, but to enrage a brutal master by having him fined was highly inexpedient; the best that could be hoped for was a cancellation of the indenture, a proceeding more in the nature of a reward for the master than atonement for the ill-treatment of the child. But the system provided a cheap way of relieving the parish of a heavy burden, and was, therefore, very popular.

The later history of parish apprenticeship, when conditions of life had become still harder owing to the Industrial Revolution, does not concern us here, although there is ample evidence, both written and unwritten, that this county, no less than other more notorious manufacturing centres, owes its economic development to the exploitation of child labour. It is sufficient to advert merely to the graveyards of Papplewick and Arnold where apprentices were buried in scores, and to the incredibly horrible revelations of Robert Blincoe, of the condition of apprentices at Lowdham Mill,[1] for indication of the depths to which the institution of parish apprenticeship had fallen. Not all mills had the reputation of those

[1] Summarised in *Highways and Byways of Notts.*, J. B. Firth, p. 168.

at Lowdham, Papplewick and Arnold; the cotton and worsted mills at Cuckney, for instance, moved the pious Throsby to one of his characteristic asides:

> "Here are children from the Foundling Hospital, London, who are employed at the respective mills and are kept in excellent order, boys under one roof, girls under another. . . . They are trained in the duties of religion and fed plentifully. It is happy that these little aliens to kindred affection should, by the bounty of the good and opulent, be made such useful members of society and ornaments of philanthropy."

The treatment of parish apprentices by the Poor Law authorities has been the theme of many investigators, both contemporary and modern, and when it is realised that in the workhouses of London at the period of Josiah Hanway's investigations over 90 per cent. of the infants under five disappeared altogether—died of exposure, malnutrition and disease—it will be seen that the eighteenth-century workhouse might degenerate into a form of organised infanticide, more revolting even than the kind of factories described by Robert Blincoe. There is no evidence that the pauper children of Nottinghamshire suffered the fate of those of London; London was steeped in a squalor and decadence from which the Midlands were happily free. No account of the condition of the pauper apprentice in eighteenth century Nottinghamshire is available, but some indication is given by the known facts of the apprenticeship of non-pauper children. Complaints of immoderate correction of an apprentice or of refusal to provide him with sufficient meat and drink frequently came before the Justices. An apprentice to a "wyre drawer" at Caythorpe was found in 1617 to be black and blue "by reason of the intolerable correction" of his master. A husbandman and his wife at Eaton so misused an apprentice that "he dyed upon itt within the halfe yeare after", for which the two murderers were bound over to good behaviour![1] A Nottingham apprentice in 1633 appealed to the Mayor Recorded and

[1] Copnall, *op. cit.*, p. 128.

the rest of the Worshipful Brethren of Nottingham to be released from his master, William Graysom, butcher of Nottingham. The petitioner declared "He hath ever beene willinge to please and give content to his maister and Dame, with great extremitie being sent barefoot and bareledged in the could winter, and fasting about his mester's Business . . . and now he hath turned me away".[1] William Hutton, the Bookseller, had to endure two apprenticeships, one at Sir Thomas Lombe's mill at Derby, the other with his uncle a Nottinghamshire stockinger.

Writing of this period of his life he says, "I had just finished one seven years' servitude to enter another. In the former I was welcome to the food I ate; but now that it was more plentiful I was to be grudged every meal I tasted. My aunt kept a constant eye upon the food and feeder." On one occasion his master thrashed him with a birch rod with such vigour that he thought he would be broken in pieces.[2] He ran away, but hunger and exposure forced him back.

The case of Hutton is typical of a great number. The *Nottingham Journal* was constantly being used as an aid to the recovery of absconding apprentices. In almost every copy of the paper, which came out weekly, there were notices to the effect that two or three apprentices, usually in co-operation, had disappeared; minute description of their appearance and apparel were given, and a solemn warning was issued that no one was to give them employment under pain of prosecution. The practice of absconding became so common that a society was formed, with offices at the Bear's Inn, Nottingham, for reclaiming lost apprentices and for prosecuting those who harboured them.[3] It is clear that the condition of the ordinary apprentice, especially in poverty-stricken trades like framework knitting, was little better, if any, than of the pauper apprentice; in both cases masters

[1] Nottingham Borough Records, Vol. V, p. 157.
[2] *Autobiography of Wm. Hutton*, p. 29.
[3] *Nottingham Journal*, August 13, 1763.

could tyrannise over them with impunity, and the most effective escape for both was flight.

Lunatics and Distressed Debtors.

Lunatics and distressed debtors also came under the magistrates' poor law authority. The former might be taken up on a Justice's warrant by the parish officer, and if necessary, confined in chains; his maintenance, at the rate of 2*s.* 6*d.* a week, to be provided either by relatives or the parish of settlement.[1] In regard to distressed debtors, the following extract from the Records may be quoted as an illustration of their terrible situation:

"To the J.P.s at the General Quarter Session of Peace at East Retford, Petition from John Clarke, a poor distressed prisoner for debt in the County Gaol. Humbly sheweth . . . the said John Clarke aged 87 years, having suffered long and tedious imprisonment . . . has not whereby to maintain himself and must inevitable perish unless supported by Your Honour's Charities. . . ."

At the foot of the document was written: "Allow him County bread 1½*d.* per day and that the town of Walesby allow him 6*d.* a week".[2]

(II) Able-bodied Poor

The machinery devised by the Elizabethan Government to find work for the growing army of unemployed may be said to begin with the Apprenticeship Act of 1563 and its regulation of the whole industrial life of the country. Having dealt with the problem of the labourer in industry, the problem of the labourer unable to fit himself into the national scheme could next be considered. In 1576, and again in 1601,[3] Acts were passed to meet this difficulty and a new branch of the Poor Law was grafted upon the old stock of discipline and repression. By the first of these two acts, work was to be provided for those who wanted it; stocks of material were to be

[1] MS. Minute Book, 1732, April, Newark Sessions; *ibid.*, 1732–3, January, Shire Hall Sessions.

[2] MS. Session Rolls, undated, apparently 1708.

[3] 18 Eliz., 3; 43 Eliz., 2; 7 and 8 Jas. I, 4.

kept in all cities, towns and parishes for the use of the unemployed, by which means, it was hoped, all excuse of vagrancy was eliminated. This, it was thought, made it possible to distinguish between the deserving and undeserving able-bodied poor, and special treatment was meted out to the class known as "rogues, vagabonds and other lewd and idle persons", and Houses of Correction ordered to be built for their punishment. It is thus possible to divide the system of relief for the able-bodied poor into two parts, the first the provision of employment and relief for the deserving able-bodied poor of every parish, the second the treatment of vagrants.

The Deserving Able-bodied Poor: (a) *Parish Stock.*

It is difficult to say how far the provision for the maintenance of a parish stock by the overseers and churchwardens was carried out on account of the disappearance of parish records. But it seems certain that under the vigorous administration of the Stuart Privy Council, the law was observed in most parishes of Nottinghamshire.[1]

In the eighteenth century the system was undoubtedly maintained in many parishes as the following typical extracts from the records of four rural parishes clearly prove: [2]

Received 20 pd. of yarn—spinning the half year.	
Item 8 pd. of yarn—sold at 9*d*. per lb.	
Paid to Eliz. Wite for 3 lbs. of yarn . .	2. 0.
For washing and winding 13 yds. of linen .	1. 6.
1 lb. of spinning	1. 0.
Flax—23 lb. at 6*d*. per lb.	11. 6.
For a wheel and spinning	6. 0.

In connection with the parish stock the records of Bleasby are particularly interesting. After 1760 they swell to three or four times their former bulk, and in the single year of 1775 no less than 155 payments were

[1] See Leonard, *Early English Poor Relief*, Appendix XII.

[2] MS. Town Book Bleasby, 1755, etc. Overseers' Accounts East Bridgford, 1751, etc.; Sutton Bonington, 1750; Laxton, 1732, etc.

made to the poor for materials made up by them. The most favoured material was "Tow" bought from Mr. Oldknow of Nottingham, the father of Mr. Samuel Oldknow, the manufacturer of Lancashire fame.

From the extracts given above it seems plain that the parish stock far from having fallen into complete disuse in the eighteenth century continued to form part of the ordinary Poor Law administration of many country parishes. Apparently Nottinghamshire is somewhat exceptional in this respect, a fact which may be due to the very vigorous administration of the provisions for employing the poor by the justices in the period 1630–40. A tradition had taken root at that time and was far from having lost its force in the eighteenth century.[1]

Monetary relief was also given to able-bodied paupers, and from the following document, typical of a large number in the records, it appears to have been considered by the Justices as the ordinary alternative to the provision of employment.

"To the Constable and Churchwarden and others, the Overseers of the poor of the Parish of Burton Joyce,

Greeting:

Whereas complaint hath been made unto me Sir Thos. Parkyns Bart. one of his Majesty's Justices of the Peace . . . that Geo. Merston of your town who appears to Me to be an Inhabitant legally settled in your s^{d}. Parish is in Great need and Poverty and likely to perish for want of Employment to maintain himself and family.

These are therefore in His Majesty's Name to command you the Ch. Warden etc. . . . to set ye said George Merston on work or pay unto him Two shillings weekly forth and out of your Publick Levey for ye use of ye Poor made etc. . . . otherwise to come before me and show cause to the contrary. Hereof faill not at your peril." [2]

[1] Most writers take the view that the provision of work had given place to doles and pensions. See Webb, *Old Poor Law*, pp. 159 *et seq*. There is no doubt, however, that measures for finding employment continued to be taken in many Nottinghamshire parishes during the greater part of the eighteenth century.

[2] MS. Session Rolls, May 4, 1719.

It is interesting to note that the author of this letter was the first to raise his voice against the insubordination of serving men and insolence of paupers, whose refrain, he declared, had already taken the form of "the parish is bound to find 'em". From about this time, however, the problem of finding work for the unemployed is attacked from a different angle; in response to the Act of 1722, workhouses are slowly erected, though it is doubtful if the workhouse test was ever rigorously applied. In many districts, however, no workhouse existed within convenient reach, and labour or maintenance was found by the parish itself right up to the end of our period.

The Borough of Nottingham, on the other hand, was the scene of interesting experiments in the administration of relief to the able-bodied which show very clearly the change in the official attitude towards the problem, and will now be treated in some detail.

Relief for the Able-bodied Poor in the Borough.

The attempt on the part of the Municipality of Nottingham to employ the able-bodied poor, not simply on relief work, but on profitable manufacture, began very early. It would appear that, in this particular department of Poor Law business, the individual parish was superseded by the Town Council, and an attempt, backed by the authority, experience, and also finance, of the corporate body was made to utilise the labour of the unemployed without pecuniary loss to the town. It started with the setting up of a spinning school for children at St. John's Hospital, formerly a religious house, in 1627. Martyn Hill, with his assistants, including, apparently, woolcombers, are to give a month's training to children sent to them by the town, and after the training is complete he is to pay them "what they shall addle or deserve . . . according to the Manner of and usual rates of North Folke". For each child taken in hand in this way, Martyn is to receive from the Corporation 20*s*., but this is to be paid back again "att such convenient tyme as shall be fittinge".[1] What the other spinners and manufacturers of the town thought of this attempt to compete with them is not known, but the hopeful enterprise of making pauperism pay for itself does not seem to have been very successful, as a different system, involving a subsidy by the Corporation, was tried in 1636. In this case, children were to be taught the spinning and making of hair cloth, and carding and spinning flax for candlewicks, the material being found by the town; the cost of the children's food was to be borne by the Corporation at the rate of 1*s.* a week for each child and their parents were to find them lodging, the master of the school being paid for his instruction by the sale of the goods produced during the first month.

In 1649 the system of contracting with a master for the employment of the poor was made to include the able-bodied as well as the children. The Corporation undertook to supply a capital sum of £20 to the master, a quarterly subsidy of 27*s.* 6*d.*, and twelve spinning wheels. On his part, the master agreed to set the poor on the spinning of linen and woollen, and pulling out candlewick, and to pay the following rates of wages:

6*d.* per pound for cardinge and spinninge finest wool.
5*d.* ,, ,, ,, the second sort.
4½*d.* ,, ,, ,, ,, third ,,
1*d.* per leg (i.e. per skein) for linen spinning, the reel being 4 yards long.
½*d.* per pound for carding candlewick.
1*d.* ,, ,, ,, pulling out coarser part.
1*d.* ,, ,, ,, spinning candlewick.

It must have been obvious that by this municipal enterprise in subsidised labour unemployment would probably be made in one district as fast as it was unmade in another, but the experiment continued. In 1658 the town received a gift of £100 "to sett the pore on worke" from a wealthy resident, Lady Grantham, and another

[1] Borough Records, Vol. V, pp. 124 and 129.

£100 was added to it for the same purpose, and it was decided to lay the sum out in land worth £10 a year for setting the poor on work and apprenticing the children. In the following year 100 quarters of Dancks' Rye was bought as a common stock for the "releife of the Poor Inhabitants", and in 1659 the Corporation made over two considerable sums to the parishes of St. Mary's and St. Peter's for the relief of their poor.[1] In 1661 the method of providing employment and selling the product was again attempted when the chamberlains were ordered to buy enough flax to keep forty people at work and "to pay those poore people such somes of money as shall be allowed for theire laboure", but in this case the management of the scheme was kept in the hands of a committee of the Corporation. A sum of £50 was voted in 1663 and a "Trusse of Flaxe" was bought in 1675 for the same purpose, but by this time the relief of unemployment by the method of persuasion was proving ineffective; the laziness of the labourer was becoming a familiar theme of pamphleteers. By 1704 Defoe, following Locke, had discovered that the source of poverty was luxury, sloth and pride. Hence the next attempt to relieve the wants of the able-bodied poor took the form of a project for the erection of workhouses, where the poor would be kept at labour under the eye of a master appointed by the Justices of the Peace.

Workhouses.

In March, 1700–1, it was decided by the Corporation to petition for an Act of Parliament to erect workhouses in the town, but the project did not materialise until 1726, when land was leased to each of the three parishes of the town, St. Mary's, St. Peter's and St. Nicholas's, for the purpose of building workhouses. All three workhouses seem to have been well endowed with land at the expense of the Corporation, who charged only a nominal rent; St. Mary's had three acres on Gallows

[1] *Ibid.*, p. 305. It may be noted that the Corporation was at the same time paying the salaries of the lecturers (i.e. ministers) in these parishes, *ibid.*, p. 304.

Hill besides the ground on which the building stood; St. Peter's had six acres on "Gossy Close below Mapperley", and a committee was formed in 1742 to arrange for a lease of land in the same place to St. Nicholas's.[1]

The parish books of St. Peter's have survived and they throw interesting light on the organisation of the St. Peter's workhouse. The building itself apparently was not completed until 1732, in which year a committee of influential inhabitants and parish officers was formed to manage the newly erected workhouse. This body was elected in the vestry meetings annually and generally included at least one alderman among its members. Two overseers had the task of administering parish funds, and it is interesting to note that both made substantial payments for out-door relief as well as for the workhouse. The following extract is an example of the payments made:[2]

Mr. Seddon's Accounts:
Disburst for use of Parish
To Mrs. Redwood, Governess to Workhouse.

Towards maintenance of poor	£25.	12.	2½.
Outpayments to poor out of workhouse .	8.	15.	2.
For Cloaths & other payments and expenses incurred	23.	18.	6.
Towards paying off debt upon workhouse .	31.	0.	0.
Other expenses		2.	8.
Cravings allowed	2.	14	10.
A certificate		1.	0.
	£92.	4.	4½.

On the next page is Mr. Cock's account, the other Overseer for the same year:

[1] Borough Records, Vol. V, pp. 124 and 174.

[2] MS. Book Vestry Account Book St. Peter's, 1735. Abel Smith, the Banker, had advanced £50 for its erection in 1731. In Nov., 1786, it was noted that the Corporation had agreed to let the parish have another piece of land for the erection of a new workhouse, the former buildings having become a nuisance to the neighbourhood.

Disburst.			
To Mrs. Redwood, Governess of Workhouse,			
Towards maintenance of poor therein . .	34.	1.	9¼.
Outpayments to poor people & cloathes for ye poor in the Workhouse and for making new roomes in the Workhouse and other expenses	50.	14.	0¾.
Cravings	2.	4.	0.
Pd. with apprentice £2. 10. 0 a hat 1/3*d.* for cloathes 17/7— in all .	3.	8.	10.
	£90.	8.	8.

Then follows an account of receipts which, like expenditure, were given separately, thus:

Mr. Seddon . . .	£107.	6.	2¾.
Mr. Cocks	£116.	8.	3¼.

It would appear from this that the workhouse test was not applied to all classes of the poor; probably only the more recalcitrant pauper of the vagabond class was made to go in the house, as in 1739 all the workhouses of the town were turned into Houses of Correction, so that the trustees, "or any two of them . . . or their servant do Order and give the poor people that are put therein proper and reasonable correction if they misbehave themselves or refuse to work and be able to do so." [1]

Further light on the internal economy of the eighteenth century workhouse is given by the rules drawn up by the County Magistrates for the Mansfield workhouse, established in 1730.[2]

A book is to be kept wherein shall be regularly entered an account of all materials bought for the employment of the family and of the Gain of Manufacture.

The Master and Mistress are to keep the family at work in the summer months from six in the morning till seven at night and in the winter from seven till five;

[1] Borough Records, Vol. VI, p. 165, and note regarding similar entries for St. Mary's and St. Nicholas's.

[2] MS. Quarter Sessions Minute Book, Jan., 1729–30.

in summer the family is to rise at five and retire at nine; in the winter the hours are to be six in the morning and seven in the evening.

There are to be three meals a day, half an hour being allowed for breakfast and supper and an hour for dinner. Boys and girls are to be kept decent and clean and to have one hour a day for reading. No distilled liquors are to be allowed in the building and smoking is to be indulged in only by special permission.

Any inmate wishing to see a friend must get special permission from the master and the friend is to pay the master for the time lost on work set. If an inmate is hired out for the day, to work, his wages are to be paid to the master of the workhouse, who is to provide him with sufficient food for the day.

No person having goods or chattels shall be admitted unless he brings his goods and chattels with him.

Any who is heard to curse or swear or is seen to strike or use ill language towards another or disdain anyone for his infirmities or ridicule or scoff at anyone who hath been punished shall have no more than four oz. of bread and a pint of water a day until he shall acknowledge his fault and ask pardon of the whole family, and when the inmates are "pitched upon by the Master to help the Mistress in the Management of the House they are immediately to set about the same".

The omissions from this body of rules are more striking than its actual provisions. Nothing is said in regard to the segregation of the sexes, of distinguishing between the old and feeble and able-bodied poor; there is no mention of sick ward or children's quarters; all classes of paupers of all ages seem to be promiscuously lumped together, and ordered to be kept at labour for thirteen hours a day.

It is impossible that this inept regimen could have been seriously enforced by the master and mistress. For two people to attempt to keep a houseful of paupers at hard labour for thirteen hours a day on a meagre diet was a superhuman task. It is more than probable that the workhouse under such management often degenerated into a hotbed of corruption. The condition of Newark Workhouse was so bad that a contemporary townsman was stirred to a public exposure of its flagrant mismanagement.[1] The institution, he said, was in the hands of a single woman "who was utterly unable to serve the several ends of governing". Many were provided for who made no pretence of requiring charity, and of all the family these were the most stubborn and refractory, and most abounded in oaths and imprecations against the parish and its officers. Especially, they insulted and tyrannised over the aged poor and helpless children. The key of the street door was always in the lock, so that the inmates might go to the town at pleasure. They were not obliged to wear badges and on Sundays did not repair to church in an orderly manner with their mistress at their head but were left wholly to their own guidance and inclinations. "Such want of Regulation," the writer concludes, "must naturally excite many to get in to the Parish House who could comfortably provide for themselves in their own."

The building of workhouses managed by ignorant poor law officers and supervised by equally inexpert justices went on unchecked and by 1776 there were no less than eighteen workhouses, besides those of Nottingham itself, scattered up and down the county,[2] each usually serving a group of parishes. In the case of Nottingham, the parishes refused to unite for poor law purposes, and as there was no power to compel their cooperation, they continued to maintain separate and thoroughly inefficient institutions. Eden, in his report on St. Mary's Workhouse in 1795 on York Street, describes it as dark, verminous, ill-ventilated, and utterly

[1] An impartial Relation of some late Parish Transactions at Newark, 1751, p. 91. Gough Collection, Notts. II (3), Bodleian Library. A great reformation must have taken place before the end of the century, as Eden described it as "one of the very best in the country" in 1795. See Eden, *State of Poor* Vol. II, p. 572.

[2] Second Report of Committee to review Laws relating to poor given in first series of *Commons Reports,* Vol. IX, pp. 432 *et seq.*

unable to accommodate the hundred and sixty-eight inmates who crowded there for shelter.[1] Of these no less than seventy-seven were boys and girls under twenty. At the time of his visit it was suffering from a visitation of Spotted Fever. The absurdity of the system that divided the Poor Law administration of a single town among three parishes, frequently in a state of hostility with one another, each maintaining its own inadequate workhouse under its own incompetent management, was recognised by the vestry of St Peter's when in 1797 it made the wise suggestion to unite with St. Mary's and St. Nicholas's in the erection of a House of Industry common to the three under their joint management, on the model of the Shrewsbury Institution.[2] But the town was divided by political feuds and Eden, who had heard of a similar project a few years earlier, had little hope of its being accomplished.

Friendly Societies.

The failure of the workhouse system and the weakness of an organisation based upon the practical autonomy of the single parish was widely recognised, although there were some who, in order to obtain more effective control of the poor, found a remedy in making the unit still smaller.[3] The trend of opinion was expressed by Gilbert's Act of 1782 which permitted unions of parishes to be formed and handed over the duties of the generally abused overseer to a body of Guardians—lawyers, doctors, gentlemen and the like. Relief was to be given to the able-bodied in their own homes, the workhouse being turned into a poor-house for the sick and impotent. It was also the intention of the promoter of the Act to include provisions for the encouragement of Friendly Societies;[4] County Committees were to be formed with

[1] Eden, *State of Poor*, Vol. II, p. 573.

[2] MS. Vestry Minutes St. Peter's, Sept., 1797; for contemporary criticism of poor law system based on autonomous parish, see authors cited by Webb, *Old Poor Law*, pp. 264–76.

[3] See authors quoted by Furniss, *The Labourer in a System of Nationalism*, pp. 146–71.

[4] Eden, *State of Poor*, Vol. I, pp. 600 *et seq.*

the power to raise money for the purpose of supplementing the benefits of recognised societies and granting them other forms of financial aid. The development of Friendly Societies is an important feature of the social history of this period and shows that the labouring class were alive to the benefits of self-help institutions. In Nottingham there were no less than fifty-one Friendly Societies when Eden visited it in 1795; in Newark there were ten and even a small place like Hoveringham had a society of ninety-five members.[1] But promising as the movement was, it is doubtful if great advantage would have accrued from Gilbert's interesting proposals. They would not have altered the basic fact that, owing to the increase of prices, wages were dropping below subsistence level, and that the parish, not the employer, was expected to make up the difference. Under these conditions the virtues of independence and self-help, even with the help of the State, could not be expected to flourish.

The Subsidising of Wages.

In the country districts the overseers now began to adopt the method of letting out their able-bodied paupers "by houserow" to the chief farmers, who paid only a part of their wages, the rest being made up by a subsidy from the parish. The following extract[2] from the Parish Book of Sutton Bonington shows the system in being as early as 1783—twelve years before Speenhamland:

Feb. 7th 1783 Pd. John Mariot, H. Row		3.	0.	
„ William Wadkin, „ „		2.	0.	
To House Row men, viz:—				
Henry Hancock 12 weeks at 2/- per week .	1.	18.	0.	(*sic*)
Wm. Burrowes 13 weeks 3 days at 1/- per week		13.	6.	
Jno. Mariot 7 „ 3 „ „ 2/- „ „		15.	0.	
and ten more men Total £7. 10. 0.				

[1] *Ibid.*, Vol. II, p. 575.

[2] I owe these extracts to the kindness of Mr. W. E. Tate, Headmaster of the School, Sutton Bonington. For a good description of system, see Prior's *Forest Folk*, Ch. IX.

Later the method was somewhat altered; instead of the pauper's wage being made up by the parish, his employer appears to have paid him what he liked, and in return received a direct subsidy from the parish:

Feb. 11th 1803 Wm. Green goes to Fran[s]. Salmon to work and Salmon is to have 7/10 per week for his trouble.

By 1816, the subsidising of agricultural labour by the poor rate had reached a further stage, beyond which it would be difficult to go without reducing the labourer to the position of a parish chattel. It is described in the following letter by a Nottinghamshire farmer to the Board of Agriculture:[1]

"In some parishes in this neighbourhood a number of labourers would be out of employment except by the following means viz:—the overseer of the parish to which they belong calls a meeting of inhabitants on the Saturday evening at which meeting he puts up each labourer by name separately to auction; and they have been let generally at about 1/6 and 2/– a week; the farmer or other person finding victuals to the labourer for six days only. I was offered one of the labourers at 1/6 a week but refused to take him; he was a stout able married man 34 years of age; the family if any, is of course supported at the expense of the parish. The superfluous labourers in the parish in which I hold land are apportioned and allotted to each farmer for a certain time according to his rental and to his next neighbour afterwards around the parish; the farmer paying the labourer 8*d.* to 1/– per day and from 8*d.* to 1/– per day is given to him for maintenance of himself and family by the overseer of the poor."

It should be remembered only the settled or certified labourers would be subject to this system. The non-settled labourers would either have to maintain themselves by their own labours or be removed to their parish of settlement. It is worthy of note that the former alternative was not an impossible one; bad as the conditions were, there were non-settled labourers even in thoroughly pauperised parishes, who were able to main-

[1] Substance of replies to a circular letter sent by Board of Agriculture, 1816, p. 250.

tain themselves without recourse to the poor-rate. The explanation seems to lie in the fact that, as they were debarred from relief, they insured against destitution by their industry, reliability, possibly by their greater deference to masters, and certainly by the exercise of the virtues of self-help. These qualities, it was universally admitted, were rarely possessed by the pauperised settled labourer, whose legal right to security enabled him to dispense with them, and whose best endeavours were necessarily rewarded, under the circumstances of pauperism, according to a minimum standard, and that was the standard of a bare subsistence.

"Can it be expected," it was asked by Chief Justice Best, "that servants will have any respect for their masters when their masters do not pay them what they have earned, and when, if they are discharged from service and cannot get another master, they will be just as well maintained by the parish officers alone as by their masters and the parish officers jointly?" [1]

But while the parish continued to subsidise wages, farmers refused to raise them; when the parish did not subsidise them, as in the case of the non-settled labourers, farmers were willing to pay the full wage, such as it was, in spite of the competition of pauper labour. It was noted by the Overseer of Bingham that "non-settled labourers were industrious, their earnings were good, their habits and conditions in all respects contrasting favourably with those of the settled labourers. The poor law alone was the cause of difference." He determined, therefore, to administer the Poor Law in such a way as to remove this difference. The result was the famous experiments of Bingham, Southwell and Thurgarton, in which the labourers of those parishes were wrenched from their forty years of dependence on the parish, while there was no direct interference with wages. For a time the hardship was intense, but conditions gradually became adjusted, and when the Poor Law

[1] Address of Chief Justice Best to Grand Jury of Wilts, quoted Becher, *Anti-pauper System*, 1834, p. 30.

Commissioners came round to investigate, they were so impressed by the changes wrought by Mr. Lowe at Bingham, and Mr. Nicholls at Southwell, that they "recommended the Legislature to adopt, as the basis of future legislation, the simple principle (i.e. disagreeable workhouse tests) which those gentlemen have employed with such immense advantage".[1] How far this simple but disagreeable principle had been assisted in its operation by the organisation of Friendly Societies, Savings Banks, and the provision of credit at low rates, is a question that has not yet received the attention it deserves, but the Rev. J. T. Becher of Southwell leaves us in no doubt that in his opinion the Commissioners of 1834 were going only half-way to a solution of the problem of pauperism by placing their faith in a disagreeable workhouse without the accompaniment of these self-help institutions.[2]

(iii). Treatment of Vagrancy

In regard to the deserving able-bodied poor, we have been able to trace certain changes of attitude on the part of the Government of the day, moving from the paternal, but watchful solicitude of the Tudor and Stuart monarchy, through the growing severity of the Restoration to the deliberate harshness of the early Hanoverian Parliaments, back to the somewhat bewildered humanitarianism of the late eighteenth century. In regard to the vagrant, the oscillations of theory and feeling are less marked; certainly there is a reaction against the public flogging recommended by the statutes, and its alternative, incarceration in prisons that were admittedly among the worst in Europe. Apart from this, the vagrant continued as formerly, to be regarded as a dangerous person, a potential, if not actual, criminal, deliberately withdrawing his labour from the common

[1] Letter to Rev. J. T. Becher, second edition, 1834, with attack on Cowell and the basic principle of disagreeable workhouse test.

[2] See Becher, J. T., *Anti-pauper System, exemplifying the frugal and lawful administration of the Poor Laws*, 1835.

stock and living by his wits at the expense of his neighbours. It is not surprising, therefore, to find, as Burn tersely puts it, that "every punishment save scalping" had been tried at one time or another to intimidate him into finding employment or submitting to the parish economy we have described above. In spite of everything, an army of sturdy beggars, estimated by Gregory King at the end of the seventeenth century at no less than 60,000 families,[1] wandered at large and pestered town and country, and especially London, with an insupportable clamour and a haunting fear of fire, and, worse than all, plague.

The causes of this flagrant social evil cannot be investigated here; they lie in the economic and political changes we have described in the foregoing chapters. Contemporaries such as John Locke and Defoe and their many followers, found the cause in the simple but unexplained fact of a moral corruption that appeared to have descended upon the labouring poor like a blight. Locke, the philosopher, made a report to the harassed Board of Trade in which he attributed the problem of increasing pauperism and vagrancy to "relaxation of discipline and corruption of manners" and recommended as the first step in the relief of the poor "a restraint of their debauchery" by the suppression of superfluous brandy shops and alehouses.[2]

There is no doubt, however, that a proportion of the sins of the labouring class was the direct product of social action. Owing to the way in which the Poor Law had developed the unemployed labourer found himself faced with three alternatives, either of remaining in his parish in receipt of a pittance in money and sundry doles of clothes, fuel, and material to work on, or of asking for a certificate to permit him to move (a request which might very well be refused in the case of an energetic single man), or of taking the risk of stocks and whipping and setting out, a picker-up of uncon-

[1] Cf. Webb, *Old Poor Law*, pp. 356 *et seq.*

[2] Quoted Webb, *op. cit.*, p. 110; cf. also pp. 356 *et seq.*

sidered trifles, to see the world at the expense of his neighbours. There was, of course, the possibility of squatting unnoticed on the common; but parish officers and lords of manors were hot on the scent of the squatter; even the settled labourer had a difficulty in finding a cottage in many parishes; how much more precarious was the shelter of the unemployed labourer trying to establish himself unseen in the exclusive kingdom of the overseer and magistrate. It is not surprising, therefore, that a large number took the last of the three alternatives and joined the army of rogues and vagabonds that carried throughout the length and breadth of the land a fear of fire and plague, and on lonely roads where highwaymen could lurk, of sudden death.

In the seventeenth century, the simple methods laid down in the statutes for the treatment of the "valiant rogue" seem to have been vigorously enforced by the justices; he was seized, "stockt, stript, and whipt" by the parish constable and sent on from constable to constable to his last place of settlement. Mere loitering was treated in this way as the following case shows: four vagrant persons were taken in an alehouse in Carlton in April, 1655, upon suspicion of felony and stealing, but the charge was not proved and they were dismissed. Nevertheless, they were ordered to be "stockt, stript, and whipt at Lenton by the Constable and sent to their several places of habitation".[1]

The frequent presentment of constables for neglecting their duties and the orders and complaints of Quarter Sessions [2] suggest that the arrest of vagrants was often shirked by the parish officers even in the seventeenth century. Neither were the inhabitants anxious to endanger their skins in scuffles with sturdy rogues as the presentments of householders for not assisting the parish constable to apprehend vagrants plainly show. In 1656 the County authorities tried to enlist the support of the civilian population by offering a reward of

[1] Hampton Copnall, *Notts. County Records*, p. 114.
[2] *Ibid.*, p. 115.

two shillings for anyone who should apprehend a vagrant and carry him to the Constable. After being whipped, the vagrant was to be handed on from parish to parish to his last place of settlement, the two shillings being paid successively by the Constable through whose hands he passed.[1] By the Settlement Act of 1662 and the Act 13 Anne, 26, which overhauled the system of apprehending, punishing and passing on of vagrants, this bribe of two shillings [2] to the captor of a vagrant received statutory recognition, and by the Act 17 Geo. II, 5, was raised to five shillings for the arrest of a rogue and vagabond, and ten shillings for the capture of an incorrigible rogue. The effect was that the officer arresting the vagrant appeared in the light of an informer, fulfilling the law for the sake of a monetary reward, and the sympathy of the public was now transferred from the captor to the vagrant, and his arrest made more difficult than ever. Towards the end of the century the punishment of whipping fell into disuse and another unexpected result of the system of bribing the Constables to do their duty was seen. Arrest for vagrancy had now lost its liveliest terrors and cases arose in which vagrants actually arranged to get themselves arrested in order to share the reward with the parish constable.[3]

Besides the reward given for the capture of a vagrant, the cost of passing him on, and maintaining him on the way to his place of settlement, fell to the charge of the community. For passing him on the parish constable received payment from the High Constable and, from the provisions of the Statute of Anne, already quoted, it would seem that the parish constable had been making extravagant charges for this branch of his duties. Henceforth the Justices were to fix the rates of conveyance at their Easter Sessions; the allowance for each vagrant was to be put on the back of the certificate

[1] *Ibid.*, p. 117.

[2] The two shillings were paid by the Constable of the parish in which the rogue had last begged without being apprehended.

[3] See *History of Vagrants and Vagrancy, and Beggars and Begging*, by C. J. Ribton-Turner (1887), p. 229, and Webb, *op. cit.*, p. 370.

given to the petty constable so that no extra charge could be made, and to ensure the safe delivery of the vagrant, the petty constable in whose care he was placed had to bring a receipt of his safe arrival from the Constable of the parish next on his way before the allowance was paid. The rates for conveyance of vagrants were not often entered into the Minute Book, but the lists of 1744 may be given as typical of the few that have been found. Every vagrant above the age of 14 years, 4*d.* for a day and night; under the age of 14, 2*d.* for a day and night; for every horse necessarily employed in carrying them, 2*d.* a mile, and for every constable or other person going with them, 1*s.* a day.[1] The long, costly, and troublesome process of removing a vagrant from the place of his vagrancy to the parish of settlement is well illustrated in the following document taken from the Notts Quarter Sessions Records:

"Whereas Phebe Hood, widow, and her two children (seven and six years old respectively) were on the day of the date of these presents brought before me, one of her Majesty's Justices of the Peace of the City of aforesaid next residing to the Parish of St. Sepulchre, where the said Phebe Hood and her children were taken and in pursuance of a late act of Parliament. . . . I have carefully examined her, the said Phebe Hood: and it appears to me That her late Husband William Hood had served his Apprenticeship to his Father John Hood of the Parish of Attenborough in the County of Nottingham about twelve years ago, and I did not find that since that time he obtained any legall settlement elsewhere And I have excused the correction of the Aforesaid Phebe for good reasons to me appearing:

These are therefore in her Majesty's name to Will and Require you upon sight hereof to Remove the said Phebe Hood and her two children from the said Parish of St. Sepulchre, London, and conduct her out of the said city to the Parish of St. Sepulchre in the County of Middlesex which I think the most direct and proper way to the said Parish of Attenborough . . . to be from thence conveyed thither as the law directs.

Given under my hand and seal the 20th day of May Ano Dno. 1709.

[1] MS. Minute Book, July 20, 1744.

To the Constable of St. Sepulchre, London and to the Constable of St. Sepulchre in the County of Middlesex and to each of them and all others whom it may concern."

The various Justices into whose hands the unfortunate woman was thrust on her journey into Nottinghamshire endorsed the transaction on the back of the document as follows:

"To the Constable or Headborough of the Parish of St. Sepulchre in the County of Middlesex.
Convey persons within named to that part of the parish of Barnet which is in the county of Hertford to be from thence further conveyed as in the pass is therein written. Dated and signed this 21st day of May 1709."

"To the Constables of the Borough of St. Albans or either of them.
Convey the within mentioned Phebe Hood with her two children vagrants from out of the Borrough and the liberty thereof to Studham in the County of Bedford in order for Attenborough in the county of Northampton [*sic*] as the pass directs. Dated and signed 23rd day of May 1709."

"To the Constable of Studham cum Market.
Convey the vagrants within named to Little Brickhill in County of Bucks. Dated and signed 23rd May 1709."

"To the Constables of Little Brickhill.
Convey the within named to Passenham in the County of Northton (Northampton). Dated May 24th. 1709."

The document does not give the remaining stages of her journey, but on June 27 she was ordered to be conveyed from Attenborough to St. Mary's, Nottingham. This seems to have been her final resting-place as in July, 1709, the order for her removal there was confirmed.

A month was thus spent in sending a poor woman and her two children across the country to the place that had once been her husband's parish of settlement and with which she herself appears to have had no association at all; in order to effect this she was brought before six Justices, passed through the hands of six Constables, and maintained at the cost of the country for over a month.

But in addition to the convicted vagrant, taken up, and (if the magistrate was in the mood) stocked and whipped, and sent to his place of settlement, there was another class of migratory poor actually set in motion by the Justices themselves. These were "the men with a pass" so frequently met with in parish account books.

As the following extract from the records of Sutton Bonington shows, the system, intended originally for discharged sailors and soldiers, was used indiscriminately, and no doubt helped to restore many a beggarman and thief, as well as soldier and sailor, to his friends and relations:

Aug.	1784	Gave a man and woman with a pass	3*d.*
Dec. 21st	1783	Relieved 9 sailors with Mr. Charlton's pass	2. 6*d.*
Sep. 29th	1784	Relieved 5 sailors with a permit .	1. 0*d.*
Sep. 22nd	1802	Two women with a pass and being ill	6*d.*
Mar. 11th	1798	I p^{d}. to 2 poor sailors or soldiers with each one arm and a woman with them very ill to leave the Town (They wanted to stop all night)	1. 0*d.*[1]

Not only did the Justices license the movement of destitute wanderers, but they also continued the old practice of granting licences to beg, in other words legalising vagrancy in cases where the existing provisions of the Poor Law appeared for some reason inapplicable. For instance, we have found many instances of Justices granting licences to beg to anyone who could prove he had sustained loss through fire or the death of his cattle or any other calamity; the following explains the method adopted:

To all to whom these presents shall come, Hardolph Wasteneys, Bart. Issac Knight and Jonathan Acklom Esqs. . . . send greeting:

[1] I owe these extracts to the kindness of Mr. W. E. Tate, of Sutton Bonington. Many other examples could be given from other parishes. For the effect of these "free travelling facilities" on fluidity of labour, see Redford, *Labour Migration in England*, p. 81.

wee have at the petition of our neighbours (five names follow) upon it appearing to us upon oath that Thomas Wake the bearer hereof hath by the Great Losse that he hath lately sustained by the Losse of his cattle is become . . . an object of charity and compelled . . . to implore the reliefe of charitable people. WEE have therefore as much as in us lyeth Given Leave unto him to go from place to place within the said County to ask receive and take the Charity and Benevolence of all well disposed people towards Recovery of Said Losses . . . etc.[1]

This system gave rise to much abuse. Prosecutions for forgery—"for feigning dumb and counterfeiting a testimonial to get money"—were frequent and are illustrated by the following case: Joseph Taylor of Swettenham in Cheshire carried a licence, drawn up on thick parchment, but very creased and worn, which declared he had suffered loss to the amount of £140, and begging "Christian Charity upon the poor sufferers as we shall be ready to do the same to you upon the like occasion". He was found mixing with a set of rogues, taken up on a charge of forging his petition and ordered to be whipped till his body was bloody.[2] The following curt entry found at the foot of the Bleasby Overseer's accounts for 1750 is probably the outcome of unhappy experiences with bearers of licences to beg: "The Parish has agreed that nothing shall be pade to letter of Request nor losse by Fire."[3]

Assistance of a similar nature was given to persons who wished to pass through the County but by reason of some misfortune were too poor to take the usual means of travel; thus a pass was made out in Somerset to a man and his wife and children who had been shipwrecked and lost all their belongings and wished to travel to Whitehaven in Cumberland. It was signed by two Justices of Somerset and desired "all men to let them pass peaceably and officers of the parishes through which they travel to yield them such reasonable relief as you

[1] MS. Sessions Rolls, July 19, 1717.
[2] *Ibid.*, Nov. 4, 1718, Nottingham Sessions.
[3] MS. Town Book Bleasby, Overseers' and Constables' Accounts, 1750.

in your discretion shall think fitt". They were allowed six months in which to complete the journey.[1]

The evil arising from this constant circulation of a vagabond population, and the weaknesses of the system designed to meet them, were well known and the subject not only of complaint, but of frequent legislative action. The preamble of the Act of 2 Wm. III, 18, clearly recognises the futility of the existing system:

> " . . . many parts of the Kingdom are extremely oppressed by the usual method of conveying vagabonds from parish to parish in a dilatory manner whereby such vagabonds in hopes of relief from every parish through which they pass, are encouraged to spend their lives in wandering from one part of the Kingdom to another; and to delude charitable persons, frequently forge counterfeit passes, testimonials of character, whereby the charitable intentions of such persons are abused."

Henceforth, persons asking for relief with a pass were to be taken before a Justice for examination and the Constable himself was to convey them either to the House of Correction or to the next town on their way either by horse, cart or foot, according to the direction of the Justice. These very necessary precautions, later embodied in the Act 13 Anne, continued to form part of the vagrancy system of the eighteenth century and possibly checked the grosser forms of deception, but certainly did not put an end to the circulation of vagabonds by means of passes and permits indiscriminately given by Justices, anxious above all else to clear their district of the vagrant pest. Later Acts [2] tried to tighten up the system by grading the punishments, from forced labour to severe whipping, in the hopes that the punishments would be regularly and effectively imposed, but whipping was growing more and more out of favour, and forced labour was by no means easy to organise.

[1] Quarter Sessions Rolls, from bundle containing documents of Newark Sessions, April, 1721, and East Retford, July, 1721.

[2] 17 Geo. II, 5; 32 Geo. III, 45—by this act whipping was confined to men only. The flogging of women was finally prohibited altogether in 1819, 59 Geo. III, 12.

The policy of simply moving the vagrants on was far simpler, and it continued in spite of everything until the reforming movement of 1820–34.

This futile game of "general post" which the laws accomplished depended, for its continuance, upon the zeal and activity of the parish constables, who, by catching the vagrants, set it going, and kept it in motion by passing them on. But the parish constable was a busy man, and to escort a sturdy rogue, who in the towns could generally count on the sympathy of the crowd, on the next stage of his journey to his parish of settlement was not an enviable task. It is not surprising that parish constables appear to have been less active in the performance of these duties than they might have been.[1] Whatever the reason, the Justices took the work of conveying vagrants out of their hands and let it out to contractors, who conveyed and fed them for a stipulated sum. The following is the text of an agreement drawn up between the Justices of this County and a vagrant carrier:

> Whereas great number of vagrants passing from the Counties of Leicester, Rutland and Lincoln into the counties of Nottingham, Derby and Yorks. are apprehended by J.P.s of said counties of Leicester, Rutland and York and are ordered with passes and guides to be conveyed to the places of their respective residences and being frequently brought through Boughton-Sulney (i.e. now Upper Broughton, on border of Notts. and Leicestershire) and have been conveyed from constable to constable which hath been found a great charge and burden upon County of Nottingham. Therefore, to save expence it is agreed and contracted with John Bamston of Boughton-Sulney to convey all vagrants that shall be brought to him at Boughton Sulney to Nottingham or to other places in the said county through which they have to pass and shall be paid eleven pounds.[2]

There was also a vagrant carrier in the north of the County, no doubt working in conjunction with his fellow

[1] In this connection it may be mentioned that the Quarter Sessions Minute Book contains a number of presentments of constables for neglect of duty for letting a felon or vagrant escape.

[2] MS. Minute Book, Act 4, 1725.

in the south. They arrest attention by their frequent petitions for increase of salary, which were frequently acceded to by the Justices. In 1728, for instance, the vagrant carrier for the north part of the County received the unheard-of sum of £60 for his year's services, of which £20 was given him as a compensation for his great loss by reason of the extraordinary number of vagrants carried.[1]

Houses of Correction.

After the vagabond had been transported by one means or another to his last place of settlement he was put to labour by the parish officers or committed to the House of Correction.

The House of Correction for this County was erected at Southwell in 1611.[2] Here vagrants were to be whipped by the master according to the direction of the Justices and set to work on spinning, weaving of hair, cloth and sackcloth, Jersey woollen or linen yarns, and knocking hemp. The master was not to let anyone out of the House on any pretext save by a warrant from a Justice and not to release any save by the direction of two Justices. In 1653 a sum of £200 was levied upon the County for the erection of a new House of Correction, but the new building seems to have suffered acutely from a disposition to decay, as the County was put to fresh expense for its repair four times before the close of the century. This was no doubt due to the niggardliness of Quarter Sessions, an example of which is given in its order to the Master of the House to undertake the expense of repairs and the purchase of "boults, locks and shackles and dyverse ymplements" out of his meagre salary of £30 a year.[3] Further efforts to patch up the building were recorded at different times in the eighteenth century, but for a description of the place, it is necessary to go to the beginning of the nineteenth century, when a visitor described it in the following terms:[4]

[1] MS. Minute Book, May 1, 1728. [2] Hampton Copnall, *op. cit.*, p. 28.
[3] *Ibid.* [4] *Gent's Magazine*, Vol. 75, Pt. I, p. 169.

"In the floor of the room is a trap-door, from which are ten steps in to a loathsome hole or dungeon thirteen feet by ten by seven feet three inches high. There were three wooden bedsteads on which lay short dirty straw. The only ventilation is through an iron grating 2′ 10″ by only 8 inches and level with the court. In this place seven persons heavily ironed sleep every night. . . . There is no infirmary, no bath, no oven. Some of the prisoners are employed at cutting pegs for 2*d.* per thousand which the keeper sells at 4*d.* per thousand. Nothing can exceed the squalid wretchedness and filth and severity which are everywhere presented."

The Borough of Nottingham, owing to its small and compact area, was able to effect a more watchful supervision of the movements of the poor than was possible in the County. We have seen above how vigorously the Town Council of Nottingham set to work upon the problem of unemployment, and we shall deal fully with its equally effective measures for keeping out unwanted strangers, vagabonds or not, when we come to the question of Settlement Regulations. Hence it is not surprising that the evils of vagrancy do not figure with the same persistency in the Records of the Borough in the seventeenth century as they do in those of the County.

In the eighteenth century the annoyance had evidently grown to considerable proportions. In 1732 it was complained that the town was burdened with chargeable poor, vagabonds and sturdy beggars, which "some measure may be attributed to persons taking Lodgers and Inmates, and not giving notice thereof to the Overseers of the Poor". It was therefore ordered that in future the names of all lodgers and their last places of abode should be given to the overseers and churchwardens by lodging-house keepers twenty-four hours after their entry into the town.[1] In 1739 the workhouses were made into Houses of Correction [2] so that able-bodied inmates could be compelled to work when persuasion failed, a measure that would probably cause

[1] Borough Records, Vol. VI, p. 132. [2] *Ibid.*, p. 165.

the town to be given a wide berth by the vagrant population. Towards the end of the century, however, the system seems to have broken down, and the vagrant problem reached a critical phase. The peace of the town was so seriously interrupted by night outrages on the part of vagabonds and thieves that the citizens had to sit up in turns to watch their property.[1] By this time, it should be remembered, the penalty of whipping had fallen under the disapprobation of the new humanitarian movement; at the same time the Justices were questioning the utility of sending the casual vagrant to the moral and physical degradation of the gaols; hence the apparent increase of the evil should be taken partly as a sign of a greater laxity and humanity in the administration of the law. If the vagrant could be driven out by threats, warned off, or simply passed back to his settlement, the magistrate was fully satisfied.

Such was the system of apprehension and punishment of vagrants as it was applied in this County. Its main feature was the conveyance of the vagrant from the scene of his vagabondage to his parish of settlement. If the problem of the vagrant's employment had thereby been solved the system would have served a very useful purpose, but since the parish of settlement was no more able to provide him with profitable labour than the parish in which he had begged, his conveyance there was futile as well as expensive. The journey to his parish of settlement would almost inevitably be followed by his return at the earliest possible moment to the most profitable place of vagrancy. The system of conveyance thus tended to produce merely a state of perpetual motion among the vagrant population, and instead of the community being relieved of the burden of the vagabond, it was made actually to assist his peregrinations.

It remains now to sum up the effects of the Settlement System which was at the basis of the whole Poor Law organisation, and was at the same time one of the most potent influences in the social conditions of the time.

[1] Blackner, *Hist. of Nottm.*, p. 28.

(IV) SETTLEMENT SYSTEM

The growth, in the sixteenth century, of a general system of poor relief to which the members of each parish were pressed with more and more urgency to contribute, inevitably brought to a head the age-old question of a man's settlement and the precise responsibility for his maintenance. The position in regard to the vagabond was simple; he was a criminal, to be "stoct, stript, and whipt" and sent to his parish of residence for compulsory labour. But what of the artisan or labourer or evicted copyholder or tenant farmer searching for employment? Could he claim relief if he fell sick or destitute from the parish in which he happened to be, or was he a kind of criminal who must be returned summarily to his parish of origin from which he ought never to have moved?

These questions, like so many others, were left to be answered by the parishes themselves and especially the urban parishes, to which the uprooted countryman or the unemployed artisan tended to migrate. The answer seems to have been the natural but brutal one of closing the parish doors to all but the legal inhabitants. But it was impossible, and indeed undesirable, to keep out wandering labourers altogether, as their services were valuable in items of good trade; but lest they should make a permanent settlement, they were periodically hunted out and expelled, even after a residence of two years, although in so doing the municipal authorities were almost certainly exceeding their legal powers.[1]

The first recorded action of this kind in Nottinghamshire, not, by any means, the earliest in the country, was taken in 1613, when the Burgesses of the Borough complained that they were destitute of house room owing to the influx of foreigners, whom they prayed might be

[1] Only the impotent and indigent poor appear to have been legally subject to compulsory extrusion and removal to their native place. Cf. 1 and 2 Ed. VI, 3, and 3 and 4 Ed. VI, 16; also 5 Eliz., 3, and 14 Eliz., 5. In its final form in 1601, the Poor Law did not specifically authorise the removal of any kind of pauper other than the vagrant.

dispossessed of "their unjust tenures". From this time forth the unfortunate newcomers were harassed by the burgesses and trade companies, excluded from trading and even expelled the town; burgesses were forbidden under heavy penalty to erect houses, or to turn existing houses and barns into tenements, without special licence of Mayor and aldermen; neither were they to receive strangers, and those landlords who had tenants in their houses who had come in within the last three years were either to remove such tenants or be bound under £20 for each tenant to indemnify the town against their becoming chargeable. As Mr. Stevenson says:[1]

> "It is impossible to read the numerous orders against these poor people, and the general expulsion of them from the town without feeling that the rulers of Nottingham contributed something to the mass of cruelty and injustice that stain English History in the early part of the seventeenth century."

In face of this evidence it seems clear that the independent labourer was by no means free to settle outside his parish even before the legislation of 1662. The cases referred to above are those of "strangers", "foreigners" or "inmates", not vagabonds. "Inmates", Mr. Stevenson says, "were tenants and lodgers who were not burgesses of the town"; some of them had lived in the town for more than a year. Edward Slater, and his wife and child, were charged to leave the town within a month or go to the House of Correction after having lived in the town a year and a half. Thomas Johnson, cook, and wife and child had been in a year and a half; Richard Oker, hostler, his wife and two children had been in two years, but were ordered out within a month.[2] Yet according to the law, the right of extrusion could only be exercised against rogues and vagabonds. "Sir Francis Harvey, at the summer at Cambridge (in) 1629,

[1] Borough Records, Vol. IV, pp. ix, 305–6, 311. At a single sitting on May 7, 1613, 42 men, women and children were ordered either to leave the town, obtain sureties from their landlord for their maintenance, or go to the House of Correction.

[2] *op. cit.*, p. 311 n.

did deliver it that the Justices of the Peace (especially out of their sessions) were not to meddle either with the removing or settling of any poor, but only of rogues." [1] Nevertheless, the Nottingham Corporation in 1635, ordered that "everie Alderman shall, once in XIIII daies, with the assistance of some of his ward, walke his ward to see what strangers or Inmates doe come in, thatt some present coorse may be taken to avoyd them in tyme".[2] According to the letter of the law, there was nothing to prevent the independent labourer from settling where he liked; according to the practice of the towns, and possibly of the country districts also, he was liable to be "avoided" or denied shelter.

Whether the extrusion of strangers was followed by their removal to their parish of settlement is not easy to determine; since no mention of the lengthy and complicated business of settlement is made in the cases quoted above, it would appear that the municipality was content simply to close its doors to the wanderer; on the other hand, a case occurs in 1656, which shows that the process of removal was fully developed by the period of the Commonwealth, before its legalisation in 1662. Leonard Wood was charged with

"skulking here in our Towne of Nottingham and lately maryed one An Blankley, and now seekes a settlement here and may prove chargeable to our Towne. . . . And they confess that their last aboad and settlement was at Bridgford, these are therefore straitly to require you to conduct them to the said Bridgford, in his Highnes' name forthwith, there to be set on work and provided for according to the law. . . . To the Constables of Bridgford and the Overseers of the Poore there".[3]

The Act of 1662 marked a change in the legal, rather than the actual, position of the labourer and showed that legislation had been brought to the crude solution which the towns had already evolved. This Act subjected the entire body of manual-working population—nine-tenths

[1] Quoted Webb, *op. cit.*, p. 319.
[2] Borough Records, Vol. V, p. 174. [3] *Ibid.*, p. 290.

of the people of the country—to the indignity which had formerly, in law, been confined to the vagrant, criminal, and for a time, the indigent classes, of being liable to compulsory removal if they left their parish and failed to obtain a settlement elsewhere.[1]

Several Acts were passed during the next sixty years on the subject of settlement, but instead of being simplified and relaxed by this legislation, the difficulty of acquiring a settlement appears to have been definitely increased.[2] It would be a mistake, however, to argue that the working classes were in practice wholly prevented from moving from their parish of settlement; the legislation was confined to those who came for the purpose of "inhabiting" a parish, and therefore made no difference to labourers on tramp or the migratory Irish or Scotch, who, if they were interfered with at all, would be given a gratuitous lift on their road as vagrants; again, parish officers, with the consent of two Justices, could grant certificates enabling their own settled labourers to move, a liberty which, as we shall show later, was frequently utilised; moreover, removal cases were expensive, and with all the eyes of his neighbours on him, a parish officer would hardly involve his parish in the expense, and himself in the trouble of a removal, without adequate reason. The number of removals was likely, therefore, to be small; the figure generally given is two per annum per parish, and in some parishes it was probably far less—one every five or six years; but though the influence of the settlement system may have been proved by recent investigation to be less than was estimated by such contemporary observers as Adam Smith, its tyrannical nature has been no whit modified.

[1] The explanation in the preamble of the Act has recently been described as "a classic example of legislative mendacity" (Webb, *op. cit.*, p. 325) and its purpose seems to have been to give protection to London by immobilising the whole working population. Incredible as this may sound, it is confirmed by the history of the Bill itself, which is shown to have been the product of a committee under the management of the City Representatives.—Webb, *op. cit.*

[2] For full discussion of this question, see Webb, *op. cit.*, pp. 328–9, note and summary of legislation given in 1834 *Poor Law Commission Report* (Cmd. 2728), 1905, p. 153.

The fact remains that the Overseer could, and did, forcibly remove a man from his place of residence after obtaining a warrant from a Justice, to some other place, however distant, before any effective trial had taken place at all, and even without ascertaining the views of the parish to which he was being sent.

In a very large number of cases, as may well be imagined, the process of removal was not yet over. The parish to which the person had been removed would do its best to escape responsibility for maintenance, and on the least provocation would appeal to Quarter Sessions to have the order cancelled or "discharged". About fifteen such appeals came before the Notts. Justices in Quarter Sessions on an average every year in the early decades of the century, and of these about half were "discharged" and half "confirmed". It sometimes happened that cases of removal were so complicated that the Justices were unable to unravel them and they were left over for the Assizes, when the opinion of the Judge was sought. The following case not only illustrates the entanglements in which the Justices found themselves, but the carelessness with which the system was administered—as long as the newcomer was removed, it mattered little where he went. A person was removed from Plumtree to Burton; Burton appealed and the order was confirmed. But Burton then removed the person to Tollerton; Tollerton appealed and the order was again confirmed! The Judge to whom this case was submitted added, "Tho' Tollerton had no manner of right to the Person, the Justices cannot send him back to Plumtree, but it is a Misfortune upon the Parish unless they can find some other Legall Settlement elsewhere". Whether Tollerton took this broad hint to foist the unwanted stranger upon another parish does not appear; but as the law stood, there was no other remedy in a case of this kind.[1]

[1] MS. Sessions Rolls without date found in miscellaneous bundle for 1719. Note.—For a local dispute in King's Bench over a sum of 30*s*. for maintenance of a person during removal, see King's Bench 94, p. 353.

Not only carelessness but corruption was sometimes levelled at the Justices in their administration of the Settlement Laws; Henry Fielding writes: " . . . an appeal is almost certain to be made if an Attorney lives in the neighbourhood and it is almost as sure to succeed if a Justice lives in the parish".[1] It was certainly difficult for Justices not to allow their decisions to be influenced by their private interests. Sometimes they would refuse to commit themselves to a decision in cases which involved their own parishes, as is shown by the action of three Justices of Notts., Richard Sutton, John Thornagh and Andrew Thornagh, who did not give their opinion concerning an appeal brought against Worksop, "they having estates in the said parish of Worksop".[2]

Whatever the reputation of the Justices may have suffered through the Settlement Laws, there is no doubt that the Overseers and Churchwardens would stoop to any means, however base, to get rid of newcomers. Dr. Burn in a well-known passage says that the chief duty of the Overseer was to keep an extraordinary look-out to prevent persons coming to inhabit a parish without a certificate, and if he has one, to caution all inhabitants not to let him a farm of £10 a year and to take care to keep him out of all parish offices; to warn them to hire servants half-yearly, or if that is impossible, to pick a quarrel with them before the year's end and so get rid of them; to bind out all apprentices, no matter to whom, but to take especial care that the master live in another parish.[3] The following document, though belonging to a period later than that under review, shows the length to which Overseers and inhabitants of a parish would go in order to prevent the settlement of hired labourers:[4]

[1] Hen. Fielding, *Late Increase of Robbers*, 1751, p. 88.

[2] MS. Sessions Rolls, no date—in bundle marked "Michaelmas, 1722; Jan., 1722; July, 1722".

[3] Burn, *Hist. of Poor Law* (1764), p. 211.

[4] Taken from a bundle of papers in Bleasby Church Box entitled "Some old papers handed to Churchwardens by Captain Kelham, 1910".

"Articles of agreement made and entered into this 22nd day of October 1824 between the occupiers of lands or tenements in Parish of Bleasby and Church Wardens and Overseers of Bleasby.

Whereas the number of persons applying for relief to Parish of Bleasby has greatly increased. . . .

It is mutually agreed between the parties that if any of them hire any person to serve him for any period exceeding Fifty one weeks, or shall make any agreement by which any servant shall obtain a settlement in the Parish, then the person so hiring or making such agreement shall pay into the Churchwardens and Overseers the Sum of Ten Pounds to be used for the relief of the Poor."

There then follow the signatures of seventeen persons.

The helplessness of the labourer and his family when they were once in the meshes of the settlement law, and their dependence upon the will of petty officials and magistrates invested with despotic power over their movements, are well illustrated in the following case: a person was removed from Balderton to Long Connington in Lincolnshire; the Overseers of the latter parish at once took him before a Justice and obtained the opinion that he was not their legal inhabitant and must therefore have a trial at the next Quarter Sessions at Newark "in order to fix him according to law"; the Overseers then sent him with a letter to Balderton stating these facts with the following suggestion:

" . . . iff the said bearer and his famillie be settled on us we will pay all the charges that the said tryall shall leggarly cost and therefore do desayer you the overseers of Balderton to permit the bearer and his wife to live in their howse till then as a neighbourly kindness as we have doon to you by suffering Jo; Nutton and his famillie to live amongst us. . . ." [1]

The inexpediency of first removing a pauper and then enquiring whether the removal was lawful did not pass without comment; in 1819 a Bill was introduced to remedy this process by simply reversing it, but it was rejected, and the Commissioners of 1834 found it very difficult to offer reasons for obstructing so necessary a reform "unless we are to believe a tradition that it was

[1] MS. Sessions Rolls, Newark, Nov. 14, 1713, in bundle Jan., 1713.

defeated by a combination of persons interested in creating litigation and expense".[1]

Effects of the Settlement System.

It is unnecessary to say that the Settlement System, besides being futile and expensive, was heartlessly cruel. It made tyrants of magistrates and brutes of parish officers; there were cases of men in the agonies of death removed to save the parish the cost of their funeral; pregnant women, down to 1824, were hunted from parish to parish and even removed in their labour lest they should give birth to an illegitimate child; the steps of married men with families were dogged by the Overseer, while he cajoled the single man, if he could, into a marriage with the village harlot. A prisoner for debt "with no substance to keep him alive" and reduced to the last extremity, who must assuredly perish for want unless relieved, was awarded eighteen pence a week, but it was revoked on the application of the Overseers of Fiskerton "for as much as it is at present undetermined and very doubtful whether the last legal settlement of the said William Bush is in the town of Fiskerton or not".[2]

Perhaps the most sinister form of this parochial exclusiveness which the Settlement Laws engendered was the pulling down of cottages and putting obstacles in the way of building new ones in order to check the influx of strangers into a parish. During the first half of the seventeenth century the Justices kept the supply of houses in check in the County by enforcing with considerable vigour the Act of Elizabeth against building cottages with less than four acres of ground attached,[3] and in 1656 they ordered that no cottages were to be

[1] *Poor Law Commission Report*, 1834 (Cmd. 2728), p. 344.

[2] Hampton Copnall, *Notes of Quarter Sessions for* 1736–7, p. 8.

[3] 31 Eliz., 7, repealed 15 Geo. III, 32. For cases of prosecution under this statute, see Hampton Copnall, *Notts. County Records of Seventeenth Century*, pp. 125 *et seq.* A few cases occur in the eighteenth century, but no punishments were inflicted. See MS. Quarter Sessions Minute Book, Oct. 14, 1740, and July 20, 1744, etc.

built on the waste without the consent of the Lord of the Manor. We have seen above the uncompromising campaign waged by the Borough against the housing of strangers in the seventeenth century, but with the growth of the stocking industry the pressure upon the housing accommodation became greater and houses were divided and rooms let off to lodgers and inmates. Similar measures were taken in the County, and in two cases the owners were presented before Quarter Sessions for dividing their houses into a number of tenements and putting families in "to the great danger of ills and contagion and for depauperisation [*sic*] of the parishioners by overcrowding".[1] Both presentments occurred in small country villages near Newark; both were endorsed "True Bill" but exonerated. Possibly we have here an early example of the open parish surrounded by "close" parishes in which the labourer was not permitted to settle. Does that explain why the Justices exonerated the owners of the tenements in which overcrowding was taking place? They would certainly not be anxious to have their serene little kingdoms invaded by an army of evicted lodgers. As Eden said at the end of the century:

"One of the greatest evils that the poor labour under is the impossibility (in some parishes) of procuring habitation. Neither can the labourers who wish to migrate from their parents, although they have money to erect a cottage, always obtain permission from the Lord of the Manor to build one." [2]

Besides involving hardships upon individuals, the settlement was a source of great expense and infinite trouble to the country. Apart altogether from the legal expenses connected with appeals to Quarter Sessions and higher courts, there were the multifarious comings and goings which a parish officer thought necessary for the due and proper exercise of his office, all of which had to be paid for. The amount of parochial energy released by the operation of the Settlement Laws may be

[1] MS. Sessions Rolls, Oct. 1, 1706. [2] Eden, *State of Poor*, Vol. I, p. 361.

illustrated by the following extract from the records of Bleasby.

A Bill of Chearges for the Removall of Elizabeth Low to her Setement.[1]

Mar. 19.	Paid at Newark	0– 2– 2
	My chearges at Elton . . .	0– 1– 1
	Paid for warrant and examination .	0– 3– 0
	Chearges at Southwell	0– 1– 2
	John Hanes for going to Newark .	0– 0– 6
	for going to Newark & Elton .	2– 6
	Paid John Hanes	0– 0– 6
	for serving the Warrants . .	0– 2– 0
	Paid George Hodgkinson for going to	
	Southwell 3 times and chearges .	0– 2– 6
	for going to Nottingham . .	0– 2– 0
	and my chearges	0– 2– 3
	Paid for the wagin	0– 8– 0
	Chearges at Richard Horsepooles .	0– 3–10½
Mar. 22nd.	Servt. of the waginer	0– 0– 6
June 15.	Paid to Wm. Ward	2– 3– 0
	" " "	0–17–10
	Spent at Heselford	0– 1– 6
		4–14– 4½

How much of this was incurred in the legitimate pursuit of parish business and how much in pursuit of the Overseer's love of visiting neighbouring towns is a matter of speculation; it is difficult to believe so much running about was necessary, especially as he charged 2*s*. 3*d*. for going to Nottingham besides his expenses. We may rest assured, however, that the parish of Bleasby did not allow its officer to indulge in too many removals.

The above list of expenses does not necessarily close the account of the transaction. If the parish to whom the removed person was sent should appeal against the order, the case had to come before Quarter Sessions, and might even go up to King's Bench before it was settled, and the heavy expenses incurred by this further process,

[1] Entry in Parish Book, Bleasby, without date, apparently about 1750.

together with the cost of maintenance of the person concerned and possibly a heavy fine by the Justices for frivolous appeal, had to be met by the losing parish. Thus Bleasby had on two occasions to pay over £15 to the adjoining parishes, Fiskerton and Southwell, in expenses for unsuccessful appeals.[1] This point brings out one of the many weaknesses of the single parish as the basic unit of Poor Law and organisation, namely that many of the appeals settled by Quarter Sessions were actually brought up and fought out by contiguous parishes, as, for instance, Gedling and Carlton, Selston and Annesley, Tollerton and Plumtree, Hickling and Kinoulton, Beeston and Chilwell, etc., etc., and probably as many as 80 per cent. of contested settlements with all the expense, trouble and hardship which they involved were occasioned by disputes of parishes within the boundary of the County.[2]

It has been said, "An obvious method of restraining the ill effects of an ill-considered law is to make provision for its evasion".[3] In the case of the Settlement Laws this provision took the form of certificates of settlement issued by the parish officers with the consent of the Justices to permit a man or woman to migrate to another parish and be immune from removal until he or she became actually chargeable.[4] The certificate gave the name of the parish of legal settlement and of destination, and stipulated that in the event of his becoming chargeable the parish of settlement should be responsible, the document being signed by Overseers, Churchwardens, two inhabitants and two Justices. The following is typical of a large number to be found among the parish records of Bleasby:

[1] Documents relating to Bleasby. Receipts from Overseers of Southwell and Fiskerton. For a fine of £5 levied upon a parish for lodging a frivolous appeal see MS. Sessions Rolls, April 17, 1721.

[2] Average of period 1710–20 inclusive. These cases illustrate the prevalence of "short distance" migration in the eighteenth century. See further Dr. Redford's valuable monograph, *Labour Migration in England*, 1800–1850, Ch. IV.

[3] Mackay, *Hist. of Eng. Poor Law*, Vol. III, p. 342.

[4] See 14 Chas. II, 12, Section iii, and 8 and 9 Wm. III, 30.

Lib. tat de Southwell & Scrooby in Com. Notts.

To the Churchwardens and Overseers of the poor of the Parish of Bleasby Greeting.

We the ch.wardens & Overseers of the poor of the parish of Southwell in the sd. Lib. do hereby certifie that Joseph Alvy his wife & children are Inhabitants legally settled in our parish of Southwell & doe promise that if at any time they shall happen to become chargeable to your sd. parish of Bleasby to receive them back thay having gained no Settlement there. In witness we have hereunto set our hands & seals this 23rd day of June 1724.

Signed by 2 Churchwardens, 2 Overseers & attested by 2 inhabitants and endorsed as follows: We whose names are hereunto subscribed two of His Majesty's Justices for the said Liberty do allow of this Certificate.

Wm. Cartwright,
F. W. Becher.

In the rural parishes certificates appear to have been given fairly freely. The parish records of Bleasby, for instance, include a bundle of about forty certificates loosely held together by a string and therefore probably an incomplete collection; [1] the parish officers of Sutton Bonington entered the certificate of every newcomer into the Parish Book together with the name of the parish from which he had migrated. A complete list of new arrivals into the village and their parish of origin is thus available for the period 1698–1833, during which 118 certificates were entered and distributed over the whole period, the vast majority emanating from parishes within a radius of ten miles, and a large number from the neighbouring parishes of Kingston, Rempstone, East and West Leake, Gotham, etc. Assuming this to be a complete record, as it appears to be, the village was recruited by newcomers armed with certificates at the rate of one every fourteen months. During the same period there were twenty-eight removals, an average of roughly one every five years. It is worth noting, however, that the period when removals were most frequent was between 1829 and 1836, when no less than twelve

[1] Found among a collection of loose documents between two sheets of cardboard entitled "Papers relating to Bleasby" in the Parish chest.

cases are recorded, which reduces the average for the earlier period to one every eight years.[1]

The effect of the system of settlement upon the liberty of the labouring population seems to have been a matter of doubt even among contemporaries, the criticism of Adam Smith, who said that it turned the parish into a prison, being countered by the claim of Howlett and Eden,[2] that the effect was trifling. It is difficult to reconcile the latter assertion with the mass of litigation and enormous expense to which the system unquestionably gave rise, yet it is equally impossible to deny that the new populations of Sheffield, Birmingham and Manchester, as Howlett pointed out, were recruited from the rural labouring population in spite of the restrictions of settlement. It would seem that the effects varied according to the nature of the locality; in the towns where industry was flourishing and labour was in demand, the Settlement Laws were probably not enforced to the same extent as in the rural parishes where industry was tending to contract and labour was plentiful. It may be noted that in the printed records of Nottingham for the period 1700–60 not a single allusion to the settlement system is made,[3] yet there is no doubt that strangers were coming into the town as is shown by the following order of Quarter Sessions:

"... It is ordered by this court that all persons who take Lodgers & Inmates by the week or month or quarterly or yearly or divide their houses to lett out any Room or Rooms that they fail not to give in the true names Sirnames or last place of abode of such Lodgers or Inmates to the Churchwardens or Overseers of the respective parishes within this Town within Twenty four hours after their first coming." [4]

At the time of this order—1732—the framework knitting industry was rapidly expanding in the town and

[1] These figures were supplied by Mr. W. E. Tate.

[2] Eden, *State of Poor*, Vol. I, pp. 297 and 361.

[3] There is one case of conveyance of vagrant (Vol. VI, p. 170), but none of removal.

[4] Borough Records, Vol. VI, p. 132.

labour was required. It would seem therefore from the lack of reference in the printed records to Settlement litigation that the law was not put into operation against immigrant labourers because employment could easily be provided for them. When Eden visited Nottingham in 1794 at a time when trade was less flourishing and the town greatly overburdened with poor, the number of removals from St. Mary's Parish alone was fourteen or fifteen annually.[1] It is possible, then, that in Nottingham at least the Settlement Laws were alternately enforced and relaxed according to the lack or abundance of labour, their administration being for the most part in the hands of the employers of labour.

No doubt the existence of the Certificate System did something to modify the restrictions of the Settlement Laws (as far as they existed), but since it was similarly in the hands of men interested in maintaining the supply of reliable local labour, it was inevitably subject to discrimination according to the character for sobriety, or the reverse, which the applicant happened to bear. There is considerable evidence that single women, "enceintes" and widows could generally obtain certificates, while the granting of certificates to others appears to have depended mainly upon the condition of the local labour market.[2] By thus permitting the departure of undesirables and confining the reliable labourer to his parish, the power to grant certificates, while certainly facilitating the movement of labour, was also calculated to increase vagabondage, while the power to refuse them would bring the independent labourer another step nearer to a slavish dependence on his parish, where by the iron law of settlement his labour and maintenance were due.

On the whole there seems to be no doubt that the economic effects of the Settlement System, however

[1] Eden, *State of Poor*, Vol. II, p. 578.

[2] See Pinchbeck, *Women in Ind. Rev.*, p. 80. Hampson, "Settlement and Removal in Cambs.," *Cambs. Hist. Journal*, 1928, p. 286, and Marshall, *Eng. Poor in Eighteenth Century*, Ch. VI. For a case of a man refused a certificate and the effects upon him, see *Life of William Hutton*, p. 85.

irritating and wasteful, were insignificant compared with the moral effects. As we have seen, the supply of labour was not deeply affected by the Settlement restrictions; it was obstructed and probably manipulated, but not seriously curtailed. On the other hand, the moral effect upon the labouring class seems to have been profound. The stay-at-home labourer was discouraged from seeking work outside the boundary of his parish; the married labourer, if he ventured abroad, was never free from the haunting fear of removal, and often had the utmost difficulty in finding house-room; the single labourer could hope to escape its dangers only by the simple device of not marrying. These obstacles to marriage—lack of house-room and fear of removal—help to explain one of the most prominent characteristics of the social life of the time, the prevalence of bastardy. The part which it played may be seen from a glance at the Minute Book of the Peculiar of Southwell for the period 1784–1834, in which the bulk of the business before the Court in that entirely rural area consisted of the administration of the bastardy laws. It is an ironical commentary upon the progress of society that in 1580 the Archdeacons' Court at Nottingham is busily engaged in punishing the moral crime of incontinence by making the offender appear before the altar of his parish church in the white sheet of a penitent and declaring his fault before the congregation and craving forgiveness; in 1780 the local magistrates are amply rewarded if they can find or invent a putative father who can be made to pay.[1]

[1] Miss Hampson gives the following interesting figures relative to the increase of bastardy in Cambs. which she attributes largely to the shortage of houses and other difficulties placed in the way of the married labourer:

Between 1660–1749 there were 30 cases of bastardy before Quarter Sessions (65 years recorded).

Between 1757–1771 „ „ 37 „ „ „ „ (15 years recorded).

Between 1796–1830 „ „ 365 „ „ „ „ (35 years recorded).

It should be noted, however, that the second half of the latter period coincides with an increase of housing facilities owing to the policy of building cottages of which the rent was paid out of the poor rates. Early marriages were also

If the Settlement System favoured the single man, and penalised the married man, it was especially hard on the female wanderer; the widow who ran the risk of having her children taken away from her if she married again because they retained their mother's settlement while she took that of her second husband; and, in particular, the pregnant woman without home or husband.

"Coming up to town last Sunday," said an M.P. in 1774, "I met with an instance shocking to humanity; a miserable object in the agonies of death crammed into a cart to be removed lest the parish should be at the expense of his funeral. Other instances every day met with are the removals of women with child and in labour, to the danger of both their lives, lest the child should be born in the parish." [1]

In 1795 an Act was passed which prohibited the removal of persons until they actually became chargeable; but the only exception besides vagrants, to this important concession, was the unmarried pregnant woman, who could still be compulsorily removed to her own parish on the bare possibility of her becoming chargeable.[2]

encouraged by the allowance system, see Griffiths, *Population Problems at the Time of Malthus*, p. 137, and Pinchbeck, *Women in Ind. Rev.*, p. 81. After 1780 affiliation orders may have been made in Quarter Sessions instead of Petty Sessions. See "Letter on Alteration of Bastardy Laws" by J. T. Becher, 1834, p. 8. If this operated in Cambridge it would help to explain the great increase in the number of cases that came before the Quarter Sessions in the last period given above. See also p. 218, note 2.

[1] *Parl. Hist.*, Vol. XVII, p. 844 (Speech of Sir Wm. Meredith), quoted by Mantoux, *Ind. Rev.*, p. 445.

[2] 35 Geo. III, 101.

CHAPTER IX

WAGES AND PRICES, AND SOCIAL IMPROVEMENTS

BEFORE going on to study the actual level of wages and the conditions of life which they permitted it would be well to consider very briefly the position the labourer himself held in the social hierarchy. Although the labouring class in general was usually referred to as the "labouring poor" or "the poor" simply, whether they were able to maintain themselves by their own labour or not, the part which they played in the national life was regarded with the greatest importance. A contemporary proverb ran, "The labour of the Poor is the Treasure of the Rich"; or, as a speaker in the House of Commons said, "It is from their labour our quality derive their riches and splendour";[1] in one of his sprightly opening paragraphs Fielding alludes to them as "Those members of society who are born to furnish the blessings of life for the use of those who are born to enjoy these blessings",[2] and a writer later in the century said, "The poor in every country are the class of people of the first importance. Their industry is the only source of wealth in every country."[3] To use Professor Cannan's analogy, they were, in the theory of the time, the horses of the community, whose business it was to live, labour and procreate in return for subsistence.[4]

[1] For the proverb, see Marshall, *English Poor in Eighteenth Century*, p. 34, *q.v.* for the best summary of contemporary opinions on the subject. For the speech in the House of Commons, see *Parl. Hist.*, Vol. XV, p. 17, a most interesting survey of eighteenth-century social relations.

[2] *Tom Jones*, Vol. II, Ch. IX.

[3] Chas. Townsend, *National Thoughts*, 1767, p. 1, quoted by Furniss; *Position of Labourer in a System of Nationalism*, p. 22, *q.v.* for list of authors illustrating the same point of view.

[4] Cannan, *Review of Econ. Theory*, pp. 334–5.

The relation between the labouring poor and their masters was regulated in various ways by the State: in particular by the assessment of wages and by the supervision of contracts publicly made at the annual hiring and their enforcement in the Court of Quarter Sessions.[1] Thus the State, through the local government, undertook the task of supervising the relations of master and man so that the master had a remedy against the extortion of the servant when labour was scarce, and the servant was protected against undue oppression in the sale of the only commodity that was now left to him, to wit, his labour.

By the eighteenth century a good deal of this system of regulation had fallen into disuse; freedom of contract between master and man was not, in Nottinghamshire at least, directly limited by the action of the magistrates; they could, however, and possibly did, influence the supply of labour in favour of the employers by means of the Settlement and Certificate System, as we have shown above. But once the contract between master and man was made, it was vigorously upheld in the local courts. Indeed, judging from the very large number of prosecutions of masters in Quarter Sessions for withholding wages, this form of protection was very necessary and valuable. In 1723,[2] the magistrates went

[1] For the way in which the hiring and testimonial systems worked in the seventeenth century, see Copnall, *Notts. County Records of Seventeenth Century*, pp. 66–7.

[2] See pamphlet by Sir Thomas Parkyns, "A Method proposed for Hiring and Recording of servants in Husbandry offered to the perusal of his brethren the Justices of the Peace . . . containing also the rates proportioned of wages . . . for servants and artificers in Leicester and Notts," contained in a collection of his writings called *Queries and Reasons, etc.* (3rd edition, 1724). The Justices acted upon the suggestions of Sir Thomas and tried to restore the system of ordering the High Constables to take a record of all servants hired, and at the same time issued an assessment of wages for the County. The former may have been carried out; the latter almost certainly was not. In regard to eighteenth-century legislation on the subject of fixing wages the following Acts may be noted: 13 Geo. I, 23, which laid down the methods for paying piece-work rates in the Gloucestershire cloth trade; 29 Geo. II, 33, which temporarily revived the assessment of wages by Gloucestershire Justices; 13 Geo. III, 68, the Spitalfields Act, by which the wages of the silk weavers of Spitalfields were to be fixed by the magistrates.

further and tried to overhaul the whole system of regulation, including the assessment of wages; in all probability this assessment was never enforced, but it shows that the idea of regulation was by no means dead, while in some parts of the country, as is well known, it was revived or reorganised by special Acts of Parliament.

Thus, in the early part of the eighteenth century, wages were not wholly subject either to free competition or to State regulation or to any iron law of subsistence; they were governed far more by tradition. It should be remembered, the standard of the eighteenth-century labourer was practically static; his taste for luxuries, except the luxury of white bread, had not developed; so long as he could maintain a traditional standard of life he was satisfied, and in time of low prices a working week of four days would supply his wants. He extorted from his employer not higher wages but leisure, and his employers replied by abusing him for his drunkenness and sloth. As early as 1686 it was said that, when the framework knitters or makers of silk stockings were well paid, "they have been observed seldom to work on Mondays and Tuesdays, but to spend their time at the alehouse . . . The weavers 'tis common in them to be drunk on Monday, have their headache on Tuesday and their tools out of order on Wednesday." As Defoe said, the workmen would "hardly vouchsafe to earn anything more than a bare subsistence and spending money" because, since they had only a rudimentary taste for new luxuries, the stimulus to further exertion was lacking.[1]

Towards the end of the century, when prices rose, many types of labourers were scarcely able to supply their wants, even with most unrelenting toil, and the parish had to implement its guarantee of their subsistence; but while prices remained low and the commons remained open, the labourer was able to supply the

[1] John Houghton, *Collection of Letters*, p. 177, quoted Furniss, *op. cit.*, p. 121, and Defoe, *Giving Alms no Charity*.

necessaries of life while enjoying the leisure to pursue his pleasures; and these, as we show in our next chapter, included, to an extent that is not always realised, traditional forms of culture, particularly music, as well as the usual forms of vice and indulgence.

Wages and Prices.

The question of wages and prices did not assume any great importance in the County until the sixteenth century, when violent fluctuations in the value of money joined with the economic and social tendencies already at work to produce a situation of acute distress for the propertyless, and especially the workless sections of the community. We are told that the price of wheat, oats, and barley had gone up between two and three times between 1500 and 1580; the price of sheep had also gone up by about the same amount, and oxen by more.[1] Towards the end of the century the rise appears to have been even more marked, the price of such staples as wool and wheat being nearly six times as high as at the end of the previous century. The increase of wages during the period does not appear to have been more than twofold,[2] and although the relative position of wages and prices is not by any means fully represented in these rough comparisons, there is no doubt at all that distress was rife and in times of scarcity, dangerously acute.[3] The action taken by the State is embodied in the well-known clause in the Act 5 Eliz. providing for the periodical assessment of wages by Justices of the Peace in reference to the level of local prices. Numerous prosecutions took place in the County, in the first half of the seventeenth century, for giving and accepting higher wages than the assessment allowed,[4] which shows that the system was in active

[1] Tawney, *Agrarian Problem*, p. 198.

[2] *V.C.H.*, II, pp. 283–6.

[3] For efforts of J.P.'s to distribute corn and stabilise prices, see above, Chap. II.

[4] Hampton Copnall, *Notts. County Records of Seventeenth Century*, p. 65.

operation, and that the rates of the Justices were lower than many masters were willing to pay. George Fox went to considerable trouble to exhort the Justices of the Peace of Notts. to avoid oppressing the servants in their wages,[1] and from the records of a neighbouring county there is interesting evidence to show that the Justices' rates were very considerably below those which the more wealthy masters were accustomed to pay in order to retain skilled labour. Thus in 1611, only a year after an assessment was issued at Oakham, the Duke of Rutland is found paying his chief hop-grower the high wage of £6 13*s.* 4*d.*,[2] while the highest wage in the assessment was no more than £2 12*s.*[3] Again, he paid a cooper £4 10*s.* per annum, his materials being found for him; the man who looked after the swans "and who is to doe service when he is called" received £3 a year; the plumber and glazier had as much as a shilling a day in addition to his food, and when "he shoots and casts lead 2/6d a day",[4] while the estate rat-catcher had £2 a year and a horse to journey on.[5]

It would seem that the more powerful masters, like the Duke of Rutland, were able to overcome the shortage of really skilled labour in country districts by paying higher wages than the assessment allowed, as their social prestige would reduce, if not eliminate, the risk of prosecution at Quarter Sessions.

The following table is an attempt to compare the wages paid in Nottinghamshire with the figures given in the contemporary assessments for Lincolnshire and Rutlandshire. Two of the cases also show the Justices scaling down wages actually paid to the level of the assessment.

[1] *Journals of Geo. Fox* (edition of 1852), Vol. I, pp. 65–6.

[2] Hist. MSS. Com. 4 (*Rutland Papers*), Vol. IV, p. 483.

[3] *Archæologia*, Vol. XI, p. 200.

[4] The highest wage of artificers in the assessment was 8*d.* with food and 1*s.* without in the case of master carpenters and free masons, having charge over others.

[5] Hist. MSS. Com. 4, Vol. IV, p. 485.

MEN'S WAGES IN NOTTS.

Date.	Amount.	Remarks.	Corresponding Wages according to Assessments of 1610 and 1621 in	
			Oakham (Rutlandshire), 1610.	Lincolnshire[2] (1621).
Jan., 1606–7	26*s.* 8*d.*	Excessive for yearly wage of man under 21. Master fined £2 10*s.*[1]	29*s.*	20*s.*
			(Wages of a "meane" servant)	
Jan., 1620–1	11*s.* 6*d.*	For 23 days work, apparently standard rate for agricultural labourers in winter.	4*d.*–8*d.*	2½*d.*–5*d.*
			(Wages of thatcher, hedger, ditcher)	
Jan., 1627–8	4 marks	Excessive for a common servant, apparently the annual wages of a bailiff. Servant sent to gaol—master fined £1.[3]	52*s.*	46*s.* 8*d.*
			(Wages of a bailiff)	

In the above list the wages actually paid in Nottinghamshire between 1607 and 1627 seem to be midway between those established for Rutlandshire and Lincolnshire in 1610 and 1621 respectively. The figures incidentally indicate a considerable disparity between the wages of the North and South Midlands, the balance being in favour of the southern county, Rutlandshire.

It is clear from what we have said, that if the fixing of wages by the Justices had any definite effect, it was to depress them, but the majority of masters probably ignored the risk of prosecution and paid higher wages than the assessment allowed in order to obtain skilled labour. The institution appears to have fallen into decay by the end of the century,[4] but the gentry scarcely

[1] Copnall, *Notts. County Records of Seventeenth Century*, p. 67.

[2] Hist. MSS. Com., *op. cit.*, Vol. I, p. 460.

[3] Copnall, *op. cit.*, p. 67, evidently the winter wages of an agricultural labourer.

[4] Copnall, *op. cit.*

needed to fix wages by means of a formal assessment since, as we have seen in a previous chapter, they could control, to some extent at least, the supply of labour and hence the rate of wages, by the manipulation of the Settlement and Certificate System. Wages thus tended to remain at a traditional level according to the custom of the locality, and marked differences were observed in wages paid in parts of the country separated by comparatively short distances.

A guide to the wages paid in the eighteenth century is supplied by the assessment at Easter, 1723, the only one to be entered up in the Minute Book, and the well-known pamphlet of Sir Thomas Parkyns which preceded, and almost certainly prompted it. There is some ground for doubt, however, in regard to the intention of the Justices, and it may be that their real object was simply to overhaul the system of registering hired servants by the Chief Constables rather than to fix a legal maximum of wages. The figures of 1723 may be taken, however, as a guide to what the Justices thought were reasonable rates, while leaving the actual rates to the exigencies of the local situation.

The wages of the labourer who lived with his master may be taken first. The highest wage paid was that of the "chief servant to the husbandman" who usually received £5 per annum.[1] The second servant, according to the assessment, received £4; a manservant between the age of sixteen and twenty had £2; these figures seem to have been generally accepted in the County, as cases occur in the Quarter Sessions in which similar figures were quoted; John Bonnington of Hockerton received £2 16*s*.[2] per annum; Samuel Taylor of Hoveringham received £3 5*s*.[3] Certain minute additions in kind to these cash wages were frequently made, such as "taylors meat days" when the taylor came to make and mend the servants' clothes and was provided by the

[1] MS. Minute Book Wages Assessment, April, 1723, and Sir Thomas Parkyns, *op. cit.* The assessment was regularly confirmed for ten years.

[2] MS. Minute Book, Sept., 1725, Newark Sessions.

[3] *Ibid.*, 1728.

farmer with food; sometimes an amount of cloth was agreed upon, or wool for making hose.[1] Some landlords made substantial presents to their tenants at Christmas time, Mundy Musters giving two strike of wheat, a stone of beef, fuel and two quarts of ale "for their Christmas cheer" together with half a guinea on New Year's Day,[2] and it is unlikely that the farm-servants were altogether forgotten in thosc convivial times. For such wages as these the farm-servant worked his twelve hours a day in summer and "from the spring of the day until night" in winter, slept in garret or hayloft, and in comparison with the married day labourer, was economically in clover.

The day labourer, on the other hand, was the worst paid of all the labouring class except miners. This is clearly seen in the lists of wages drawn up by Sir Thomas Parkyns in 1721, who does not confine himself to wages in agriculture, but gives what he considers should be the maximum rate in all trades exercised in the County.

According to Sir Thomas, the agricultural day labourer should receive at the most 9*d.* a day in summer, 6*d.* in winter without food; while the assessment document of 1723 reduces the summer pay to 8*d.*; more skilled labour, such as thrashing, was paid at the rate of a shilling a day.[3] The carpenter,[4] on the other hand, got from a shilling to one and sixpence a day; a plumber 1*s.* 8*d.*; a mason 1*s.* 4*d.*; a millwright 2*s.* 9*d.* a day,[5] and in the amounts deducted for food, the difference between the standard of living of the agricultural labourer and the artisan is well seen. No more than 4*d.* a day was ever deducted from the wage of the agricultural labourer where food was provided; the mason and the millwright, however, cannot be fed under 8*d.* a day, and the plumber's wage was reduced by no less than 10*d.* a day when food was given.[6] The miner alone seems

[1] See interesting list given by Sir Thomas Parkyns, *op. cit.*

[2] *Nottingham Journal*, Jan. 22, 1763.

[3] Newdigate Diary, quoted by Granger, *Nottingham, its Streets and People*, p. 245.

[4] Borough Records, Vol. VI, p. 119.

[5] Sir Thomas Parkyns, *op. cit.*

[6] *Ibid.*

to have been considered on the same level as the agricultural labourer, his wages ranging between the same limits of 8*d.* and a shilling a day without food,[1] although according to a writer at the end of the seventeenth century, he worked no more than six or at most eight hours a day.[2]

At harvest-time, however, the wages of agricultural labour went up by about 50 per cent. in order to attract outside labour to the countryside. A mower of corn or grass received a shilling a day, a woman reaper of corn got as much as 8*d.* a day; "a haymaker, follower of the scythe, a hooker, a pitcher of a cart and a driver of a cart" each had 10*d.* a day, but a woman haymaker received only 6*d.*[3] Where food was given the wages were reduced by 4*d.* a day in the case of men, 3*d.* in the case of women.

Such appear to be the money wages of the agricultural day labourers in the first seventy years of the eighteenth century, before the rise in prices compelled a revision of these very low rates. A short comparison with the rates prevalent in the preceding century shows that the wages quoted above represent a scarcely perceptible increase on those of the earlier period in spite of the fact that during the seventeenth century prices had been rising steadily. For instance in 1621 a day labourer received 6*d.* a day;[4] in 1721 he received 8*d.*; women servants in husbandry received from thirty shillings to two guineas;[5] by the assessment of 1723 no advance was made upon this at all, although Sir Thomas Parkyns gives as much as £2 10*s.* per annum "to the best woman servant in charge of baking and brewing and kitchen and milkhouse".

Evidently little progress had been made in the advance

[1] *Ibid.* The actual wages may have been somewhat higher, from 1*s.* to 1*s.* 6*d.* Cf. Ashton and Sykes, *Coal Ind. of Eighteenth Century*, p. 135.

[2] *Eng. and Welsh Mines and Minerals discovered in some Proposals to the Honourable House of Commons for Employment of Poor, etc.*, 1699, by Moses Stringer, p. 16.

[3] Sir Thomas Parkyns, *op. cit.*, followed by Assessment of 1723.

[4] Copnall, *Notts. County Records*, p. 67.

[5] *Ibid.*

of wages; but conditions of life were considerably easier in the eigthteenth century on account of the lower prices prevailing from 1710–65. Moreover, while the open fields and common lasted, the labourer's wife and family could be relied on practically to keep themselves. Milch cows, calves, sheep, hogs, and poultry were among the supplementary sources of income which the labourer's family could utilise as long as they had the use of a plot of land or the open common, and by such means, a writer of 1785 states, "I have known instances of a wife's management of the live stock, together with the earnings of herself and her children in haytime and harvest, etc., produce nearly as much money in the course of the year as her husband by all his labour during the same time". [1] While the era of low prices and open commons remained, the labourer could live and bring up a family; in the parishes which were already enclosed his position must have been more difficult; but it should be remembered that here the control of the large farmer would probably be more effectual than elsewhere and the influx of labour from outside would be severely checked in the interests of the poor rates. There would thus be less competition for available employment than in the open villages in which cotters and squatters with their families were numerous.[2]

Cost of Living

Between 1715 and 1765 there were only five bad harvests—in 1727, 1728, 1740, 1756 and 1757.[3] Of these 1756 was the year of greatest severity, when wheat rose to seventy-two shillings a quarter at Mark Lane. Riots took place in different parts of the country, and Nottingham was the scene of considerable disorder, engineered by the infuriated wives of the Wollaton

[1] Enquiry into Consequences of Enclosing Waste, quoted Pinchbeck, *Women in Ind. Rev.*, p. 21.

[2] For figures of poor rate for all Notts. villages between 1776–84 see *House of Commons Reports*, Vol. IX, pp. 651–3. If these are compared with enclosure history, it will be found that the old enclosed villages were less liable to increase of poor rate than other types of villages.

[3] Tooke, *Hist. of Prices*, Vol. I, p. 39.

miners. Apart from these five lean years the period from 1715 to 1765 was one of successively abundant harvests and low prices. In 1742 a quartern loaf could be bought in Nottingham for 3*d.*; cheese was 2*d.* per lb., butter 3½*d.*; a Winchester bushel of malt cost 1*s.* 6*d.*, of barley 1*s.*, of oats 8*d.*[1] These prices are very low, and as they are taken from a political pamphlet written some sixty years later, they are subject to suspicion. The following "Assize of Bread" for the year 1758, showing a very small advance on the price for bread that is given above,[2] may be quoted for comparison:

1758.—Assize of Bread

The 2*d.* loaf [Mesling] consisting of 3 parts wheat and 1 rye to weigh 1 lb. 12 oz. 3 drms. The penny white loaf to weigh ¾ wheaten and so on in proportion through the table.

	lb.	oz.	drm.
1*d.* Wheaten loaf	0	11	2
1*d.* Household "	0	14	10
2*d.* Wheaten "	1	6	4
2*d.* Household "	1	13	4
6*d.* Wheaten "	4	2	12
6*d.* Household "	5	7	13
12*d.* Wheaten "	8	5	8
12*d.* Household "	10	15	8
18*d.* Wheaten "	12	8	3
18*d.* Household "	16	7	7

Note.—The table does not include pure rye-bread. Apparently its place had been taken by bread made wholly or partially of wheat.

At the same time, all forms of meat could be bought at a low price; beef, veal, mutton, lamb and pork were sold at 3*s.* a stone;[3] in other parts of the country the price appears to have been much lower.[4] Eggs were three or

[1] John Blackner, *Thoughts on Late Change of Administration*, 1802.

[2] Ayscough's *Nottingham Courant*, Oct. 28, 1758.

[3] Deering, *Hist. of Nottm.*, p. 70.

[4] Michael Combrune, *Enquiry into Prices*, pp. 81 and 82, says beef, mutton and veal were 1¾*d.* per lb. at Exeter in 1724; and that between 1706–30 the general price of beef and mutton was 1*s.* 8*d.* per stone; and of pork and veal 2*s.* per stone.

four a penny; fowls could be bought for 1*s.* 4*d.* a couple and ducks for only 8*d.*, a pig or Christmas goose cost less than half a crown, and rabbits were 3*d.* each. According to Gravenor Henson, a single man in 1730 could have board and lodgings for 2*s.* 6*d.* or 3*s.* 6*d.* a week and live comfortably.[1] Henson probably exaggerates the prosperity of the period in order to throw into greater relief the distress that followed. It would be safer to adopt the figure contained in all documents dealing with wages, and reckon the cost of a man's food at the very lowest at 4*d.* per day. This would permit of a diet of between two and three pounds of bread and half a pound of meat, or the equivalent in cheese, per day, with sufficient margin for drink, which was extraordinarily cheap; a gallon of small beer could be bought for 1½*d.*; the ale drunk by the Corporation, however, cost 1*s.* 6*d.* per gallon.[2]

Other expenses have to be considered, of course, before it is possible to estimate the labourers' real condition. The rent of his cottage was from 15*s.* to 25*s.* a year according to the amount of land, if any, which went with it; his complete outfit of clothes would cost, according to a recent estimate, £1 2*s.*, made up as follows:

A pair of breeches	4. 6.
A pair of shoes	4. 2.
Hat	1. 2.
Shirt	3. 6.
Pair of stockings	1. 6.
Gloves	6.
Frock and waistcoat	6. 8.
	£1. 2. 0.

Finally, there was fuel to buy, which seems to have cost about £1 or thirty shillings a year.[3]

The total annual expenditure of the labourer may now

[1] Deering, *op. cit.*, p. 70; Henson, p. 105.
[2] *Ibid.*, p. 70; Borough Records, Vol. VI, p. 59.
[3] Arthur Young, *Northern Tour*, Vol. I, p. 102; A. W. Ashby, *A Hundred Years of Poor Law Administration in a Warwickshire Village*, p. 180.

be calculated. A sum between £5 and £6 per year would find him in food; £1 2*s*. for clothes; £1 for rent; an indefinite sum for fuel and the cost of his tools. If the total is put at between £8 and £9 there will not be much danger of under-statement. An average wage of 8*d*. per day would just cover this sum if the labourer worked only for 300 days in the year, and leave him with a pound in his pocket.

Nothing is included here for the maintenance of wife and family, except the item of rent. The customs of the time, of course, demanded that women should take a large part in agricultural work, as is shown by the special provision made for them in all wage assessments. Children, too, were set to work at an early age, if only on the work of slaughtering sparrows,[1] scaring crows and minding sheep on the common; in the open villages there would be the family pig, goat, cow or poultry.

It will be seen, therefore, that the single labourer was comparatively comfortable—more comfortable possibly and certainly less hard driven than the small farmer who employed him. The married labourer with a family capable of earning could similarly make ends meet,[2] but the father of a small family too young to earn must have had a severe struggle, even in this period of low prices.

This is well illustrated by the following extract from Marshall:

"It always having appeared to me incomprehensible how a common labourer who perhaps does not earn more than 6*s*. or 7*s*. a week rears a large family, as many a one does, without assistance, I desired old George Barwell who had brought up five

[1] Churchwardens' and Constables' Accounts of East Bridgford; in 1743 forty-one payments for birds and eggs were made at the rate of 1*d*. per doz. birds and ½*d*. per doz. eggs. An entry for 1745 runs: Paid for 170 doz. sparrows 14. 2*d*., and for 1746 runs: Paid for 34 doz. sparrows 2. 10*d*.; 3 foxes and 2 Fullemartes, 3. 8*d*.

[2] Arthur Young gives the proportion of the family's earnings as follows: a wife's wages equal to quarter husband's; child of 15 equal to half his father's; child of 10 equal to quarter father's wage (*Farmers' Letters*, Vol. I, p. 196). See Pinchbeck, *Women in Ind. Rev.*, p. 21, in which the earnings of women and children where they had a plot of ground or access to a common appear to be regarded as rather more than the husband's yearly wage.

or six sons and daughters, to clear up this mystery. He acknowledges he has frequently been hard put to it. He has sometimes barely had bread for his children and not a morsel for himself having often made a dinner from hog peas. Since his children have grown up and able to support themselves the old man has saved by the same industry and frugality which supported his family in his younger days, enough to support himself in his old age! What a credit to the species!" [1]

The period of plentiful harvests and cheap living began to come to an end about 1765. The House of Commons was petitioned from many parts of the country, and a committee of investigation was appointed. Among the evidence submitted is the following list of comparative prices: [2]

	Old Price.	New Price.
Veal . . .	$2\frac{1}{2}$*d.* to 3*d.* per lb.	5*d.* to $5\frac{1}{2}$*d.* per lb.
Beef . . .	1*s.* 10*d.* per stone	2*s.* 4*d.* per stone.
Mutton . .	2*s.* 2*d.* " "	3*s.* 0*d.* " "
Pork . . .	2*s.* 0*d.* " "	3*s.* 0*d.* " "

In Nottinghamshire bread went up to $1\frac{1}{4}$*d.* per lb. (almost double the old price), butter was 6*d.* and cheese 4*d.*[3] A symptom of the new conditions was the outbreak in Nottingham of a serious riot; the transport of cheese to London via the Trent was stopped on account of the opposition of the populace, and the Mayor had to ask for assistance from the Government to restore tranquillity.[4]

This outburst expressed the popular resentment at a sudden and unexpected contingency; but what seemed a mere episode in 1766, the more unpleasant that it stood alone in a long period of plenty and low prices, was really the beginning of a profound change that rapidly reduced the agricultural labourer to a condition of great misery.

By 1770 the wage of a labourer boarded by his master had risen to £7 or £8, and in exceptional cases to £10

[1] Marshall, *Rural Econ. of Midland Counties*, Vol. II, p. 197.
[2] *H.C.J.*, Vol. 30, p. 787.
[3] Young's *Northern Tour*, Vol. IV, p. 451.
[4] *Home Office Papers*, Geo. III, 1766, Oct., 31, Nos. 301, 302.

per annum.[1] These wages, says Marshall, were not much more than half those paid in Yorkshire; but the disparity, he declared, was fully made up by the want of exertion and "an extravagance in keep, especially in beer", which characterised the servants in husbandry of the Midland Counties.

But the married day labourers, necessarily a majority of the class, were less fortunate. By 1770 the wages of the Nottinghamshire day labourer had risen to a meagre shilling a day in winter (without food); in hay harvest 10*d.* a day (with food), and in corn harvest a shilling, with food.[2] But the mere disparity between the real and face value of wages does not comprise the whole of the hardships added to the lot of the agricultural labourer at this time. The enclosure of common and common field brought its concomitant disadvantages to the labourer here as elsewhere. New methods of distribution of agricultural produce came in with large farms, and milk, eggs and potatoes which hitherto could be obtained from the farmers themselves, now had to be bought from the middlemen, who preferred to retail these goods at high prices in the towns.[3] In some parts of the country the labourer had to go to the mealman even for his corn for grinding; but in the Midlands the farmers still continued in most cases to let their labourers have their bread-corn at something below market price, especially in times of scarcity.[4] Finally, even the right of gleaning was taken away, and farmers now could warn off the women and children who, from the time of Moses, as Mr. and Mrs. Hammond remind us, had collected the stray ears from the gathered fields.[5]

[1] Marshall, *Rural Econ. of Midland Counties*, Vol. I, p. 97.

[2] *Ibid.*, p. 165. In some cases reaping was paid for by the "threave". The threave consisted of 24 sheaves, each of which measured a yard round the band, and the general rate was 4*d.* a threave plus beer; but if the crop was thin the price was raised to 5*d.* Professor Levy estimates rise in wages between 1760 and 1813 at 60 per cent. and rise in wheat prices at 130 per cent. *Large and Small Holdings*, p. 11.

[3] See Hasbach, *Agricultural Labourer*, p. 147.

[4] Marshall, *op. cit.*, Vol. I, pp. 165–6.

[5] See Hammond, *Village Labourer*, pp. 108–10.

Besides these economic difficulties there was a housing problem to face. Rather than build cottages farmers would employ men from distant parishes and so avoid the danger of adding to the poor rate of their own parish. Marshall writes: "Of six labourers I have in employ to-day, two have a mile, one has a mile and a half and three have three miles to walk home",[1] and, as we have seen, farmers would pledge themselves to refuse their labourers settlement and so prevent them from marrying and settling down in a permanent home near their work. Moreover, the class of cottagers and squatters from whom the day labourers were largely recruited were of all agricultural workers the worst hit by enclosure, which deprived them of the use of the common, and so reduced the earning capacity of the household, in some cases by half. Finally, it should be remembered that the settlement system made it difficult for the settled labourer to leave the parish in search of work, while if he was encumbered with wife and children it is difficult to see how he could move at all.

The cumulative effect of these conditions seems to have been a marked decline in the moral standing of the labouring class. The labourers of the Midlands, according to Marshall, were "much below mediocrity in regard to despatch and very deficient in honest pride of workmen. . . . Their slow pace was in no way accelerated at harvest time; no coming at 4 a.m.; no trotting with empty waggons; no personal exertion save such as is stimulated with ale as strong as brandy."[2]

He is particularly impressed by the inordinate quantities of liquor they consumed; moreover, it was liquor of special quality, small beer in the Midlands being equal, it was said, to the mild ale of many counties. In hay and corn harvest the customary allowance was a gallon of beer per man per day and "besides this mowers expect two quarts of ale and never have less than one". Even turnip-hoers had two quarts of beer and one of ale per day. One farmer allowed his labourers a gallon a day

[1] Marshall, *op. cit.*, Vol. II, p. 210. [2] *op. cit.*, Vol. I, p. 97.

per man both in summer and winter, and what they were unable to consume was to be taken home to their wives and children. He thinks this a better method than the more customary one of having a beer cask for the men to go to whenever they liked. It is not surprising to hear that it was no uncommon thing for men to get too drunk to work. "If the farmers had to pay for their malt, this custom would stop," he says. "It is only the practice of the farmers in malting their own barley at public malt-houses that persuades them to keep it up." [1]

The combination of these conditions—low wages, an abundance of strong beer, a lack of cottages, and a Poor Law system that put the most serious obstacles in the way of marriage—produced a condition of demoralisation that looks like the prelude to sheer decay. While the young man was discouraged by the Settlement System from marrying, the young woman found it an infallible means of obtaining either a husband or a dole, or payment for blackmail. Under the existing system a father of a bastard child must be found at all costs, otherwise the parish might suffer. The mother either helped the parish officer and had her reward by being escorted to the altar by her partner between the upraised sticks of the churchwardens —the "knobstick wedding" as it was called in Nottinghamshire—or she demanded the price of her silence in hard cash. In any case, her parish was bound to "find" her if she became destitute. Under the system we have described "incontinency became a passport to marriage", while systematised blackmail of reputed fathers by worthless women who made a trade of swearing their children to men who could best pay for them" [2] was the final achievement of the old Poor Law under conditions of economic change and social distress.

Wages in the Framework Knitting Industry

The change which the eighteenth century witnessed in the position of the labourer was not, of course, con-

[1] *op. cit.*, Vol. II, p. 44.

[2] Pinchbeck, *Women in Ind. Rev.*, pp. 81–2. Cf. also Witt Bowden, *Industrial Society in England towards the End of the Eighteenth Century*, pp. 262–3.

fined to the rural worker. The same tendency was at work in industry, and a skilled craftsman like the framework knitter, who at the beginning of the century could normally live in security, even in comfort, by the beginning of the next, found himself struggling ineffectually against the threat of pauperism. During the first thirty years of the eighteenth century employment seems to have been very regular and wages high. Henson states that the most skilled men, those employed upon fine silk work, earned from 2*s*. 6*d*. to 3*s*. 6*d*. a day, while as much as 5*s*. a day was paid for embroidered work, the most difficult of all.[1] The value of these wages was greatly enhanced by the low cost of living which permitted a man to get board and lodging for 6*d*. or 8*d*. a day. The complaint of Defoe and other pamphleteers, that the labouring class could earn enough in three or four days to keep them in idleness for the rest of the week, is thus seen to have been true of the better paid framework knitter. The main body of workers in this industry were, however, on a very different level. The worsted and coarse woollen goods could be produced at far greater speed and required far less skill and care, and wages were necessarily much lower. Distress began to creep into these inferior branches of the industry about the middle of the century. William Hutton writing in 1749 says that he had observed such penury among married stockingers that the idea of marriage was horrifying to him.[2] The painful experiences of Hutton as an apprentice and journeyman stockinger show very definitely that the industry, at least in its lower branches, had fallen on evil days even before 1750. Other evidence is not lacking that, although employment continued to be regular, and the industry was rapidly expanding, conditions for the bulk of the operatives were very unsatisfactory at this time.

In 1753 Edward Luck of Godalming employed nine journeymen, of whom three received relief from the

[1] Henson, p. 105.

[2] *Life of William Hutton*, p. 67.

parish.[1] On account of the poverty of the journeymen, the Company in 1752 forbore to ask for quarterage from "Poor Men, many of whom (though not Old) are scarce able to get Bread",[2] while the unskilled men and boys, nicknamed "Colts" in derision by the apprenticed journeymen, were said to be producing inferior hose (during their period of training, no doubt) at the price of 1½*d.* per pair.[3] It is no cause for surprise that the familiar comparison "as poor as a stockinger" was heard as early as 1750.

While prices remained low distress was not really acute. Even as late as 1768, when prices had begun to rise, a stockinger of the little village of Bramcote paid his master 3*s.* 6*d.* a week for board and lodging "and lived well".[4] The stockinger cited in this particular case seems to have been more fortunate than his fellows; he was able to build the house he lived in, with the aid of his son, who was also a stockinger, and contribute £40 to his club although his wages never exceeded twelve shillings a week. The wage of the average stockinger was considerably less than twelve shillings a week, and in some cases was no more than half that sum, so that the career of Felkin's old stockinger, whatever may have been his frugality and superior virtues, was hardly within the reach of the bulk of the operatives of the trade.

The breakdown of the apprenticeship regulations and the influx into the industry of cheap labour, together with the rise of the cost of living and the continuance of the system of frame rent and other deductions at the old rates, gradually brought about a state of intolerable distress among the workmen, and in 1776 they formed their "Association of the Midland Counties" to increase wages.[5] The great complaint of the stockingers was that the wages were subject to no known standard but only to the caprice of the masters. Unlike the Spitalfields weavers, with whom they were in close contact, they

[1] *H.C.J.*, Vol. 26, p. 783. [2] *Ibid.*, p. 794. [3] *Ibid.*, p. 780.
[4] Factories Enquiry Commission 1833, Vol. XXCI, p. 180.
[5] See Chapter III.

placed no faith in wage assessments by the local magistrates; they drew up, instead, an elaborate price list and petitioned that it should be incorporated in an Act of Parliament to make it legally binding upon the whole body of hosiers. It is impossible to say what the precise stipulations of the stockingers were, as the bill of rates has been lost, but some idea of their demands can be gained from contemporary statements.

One witness called before the Committee of the House of Commons asked that frame rent should be reduced by 6*d.* a week; another wished to have wages raised by 2*d.* in the shilling in worsted and 1*d.*–1½*d.* in silk; no advance was asked for in figured work. Others wanted the same price as was paid to workmen in Ireland, and many complained bitterly against the prevalence of "sham" work—that is to say, work which had the appearance of being of finer quality than it really was; it was sold at the rates of fine work, while the workman was paid at the rate of coarse work.[1]

The general level of wages is shown to have been extremely low. The following example [2] of the wages of a worker in the badly paid worsted branch is taken from the *Journals of the House of Commons*, but it surely represents the lower limit of wages, not the average:

The case of Mr. William Hallam of Nottingham:
He produced 12 pairs of worsted hose per week at 7*d.* per pair = 7*s.* 0*d.*

His expences were:

(1) Frame rent	9*d.*
(2) Standing room	3*d.*
(3) Needles	4*d.*
(4) For pulling worsted out of slips . .	2*d.*
(5) Fire and candles	5*d.*
(6) Seaming per doz.	7*d.*
Total expences . .	2*s.* 6*d.*
Net wage for food, clothes, house rent, etc., per week	4*s.* 6*d.*

[1] See *H.C.J.*, Vol. 36, pp. 740 and 742; Vol. 37, p. 372.
[2] *Ibid.*, Vol. 36, p. 740.

The more skilled branches, in which it was difficult, if not impossible, to introduce child labour as a rival to experienced workmen, were paid at a considerably higher rate. For fine worsted hose, some masters paid 16*d.* or 17*d.* per pair,[1] and for silk hose as much as 2*s.* 6*d.* per pair was paid.

The following table will illustrate the matter concisely.

Kind of Work.	Rate of Pay Per Pair.	No. produced per Week. Pairs.	Gross Wage.	Probable Net Wage.
Coarse worsted.	7*d.*–8*d.*	12	7*s.*–8*s.*	5*s.*–6*s.*
Fine worsted .	16*d.* or 17*d.*	8 or 9	10*s.* 8*d.*–12*s.* 9*d.*	8*s.*–10*s.*
Silk hose . .	2*s.* 6*d.*	4–5	10*s.*–13*s.*	7*s.*–10*s.*

Rates of pay having been reduced, the stockinger was compelled to protect himself against the rising prices by working longer hours. Shops were sometimes open from 5 a.m. till 10 p.m. and pauper apprentices were made to work until 11 or 12 o'clock at night to finish their tasks. William Calladine of Leicester declared he had to work fifteen hours a day for his net wage of 5*s.* 6*d.* a week. It should be remembered, however, that the stockinger worked harder at the end of the week, when he had to complete his task in order to take it into the warehouse, than at the beginning, when he was often held up for lack of yarn, or of inclination to make a start.

But the most interesting evidence came from the masters, who, in their arguments against the proposals of the men, showed up very clearly the current relations between employer and employed. The opposition was led by the wealthy hosier, Need, who had a factory in Nottingham, many frames in Arnold, and had helped to finance Arkwright. He said that a man could earn from 1*s.* 6*d.* to 2*s.* a day on coarse cotton hose by working twelve hours a day; his wife could earn 4*s.* at seaming; a child of 8 could earn 1*s.* 6*d.*; hence a man, wife, and family of two or three children could earn 20*s.* weekly.

[1] See Evidence of John Long of Tewkesbury, *Ibid.*, Vol. 37, p. 370.

Meagre as these figures are, they were vehemently denied by the operatives who later exacted a heavy penalty for this evidence. A London hosier considered it reasonably possible that a man, even without the assistance of his family, might maintain them by his own labour. It was stated by another Nottingham hosier that complaints had come only from the idle, and as an example of what could be done by the industrious, he instanced one of his own men, Cartwright, who earned 16*s*. 8*d*. in one week by working from five in the morning till eight at night, and sometimes from seven till eight. A master framework knitter of Nottingham, Sam Wilkinson, considered that conditions were a great deal better for the workmen than formerly, and thought it possible for a man to earn a comfortable livelihood in the trade by working six days a week and twelve hours a day. An additional advantage would be gained by having "an industrious wife who pulled the right way" and a family, at least after the children had reached the age of eight or nine.[1]

The evidence of the workmen confirms the statements of the hosiers regarding the long hours worked, but they are in more doubt than the hosiers about their capacity to maintain themselves. Edward Luck of Godalming stated that scarcely a single framework knitter in his parish could support a wife and two children without parish relief, and since the Parish Accounts had been kept for the previous twelve or thirteen years by himself, he was able to speak with some authority. Even the hosier, Wm. Muggleston of Alfreton, thought that a man would have to work very hard indeed—ten to twelve hours a day for six days—to earn a clear six shillings a week. For the great majority of framework knitters there was no escape from this life of drudgery, even by the most heroic degree of self-help. It is true men obtained frames of their own sometimes, either like Edward Luck, already quoted, through his wife's

[1] Hosiers' and Framework Knitters' examinations before Committee of House of Commons, 1780, in Derby Ref. Library.

money, or like Richard Rawson of Leicester, who married an industrious woman who pulled the right way, and after they had slaved for seven years managed to buy his first frame. But the possession of only one frame was useless, nay, worse than useless, to the stockinger, since the hosier and middleman would most probably refuse to give him work. This was the case with Matthew Poole of Sutton-in-Ashfield, one of the witnesses before the Committee already mentioned, who after buying a frame of his own found it necessary to pay a rent to a hosier in order to obtain work for it. Interesting evidence on the subject was given at the same time by the hosier Need, who said he had actually been offered rent by men who had frames of their own, but had never taken it, although he knew a man who had done so. Another hosier, M. Horton of London, made the interesting statement that he had never considered that rent was simply a charge for the use of the frame, or, as it was explained later, an insurance upon machinery let out to men in their own homes; he himself charged 2*s*. a week for frame rent, standing room, and work found. Here there is a definite admission that rent was in the nature of a commission paid by the workman to the employer for finding him work. There is no need to pursue the painful history of wages in the Framework Knitting Industry any further. It suffices to say that the attempt to obtain statutory sanction for a schedule of wages failed, and, after a period of fierce rioting, masters and men entered into negotiations which culminated in the wage agreement of 1787. With the closing of European markets in the Napoleonic War, and the introduction of cheap cut-up goods of inferior quality, wage agreements came to an end, and the industry lapsed into a condition of chronic distress that lasted until the rise of the factory with its by-products of an effective Trade Union and Board of Arbitration. No body of workers have more cause to be grateful to the introduction of steam power than the Framework Knitters of Nottinghamshire, who were relieved of the incubus of frame rent and the exactions of the bag master.

Social Improvements

From what we have said it would appear that by the end of the eighteenth century the labourer was both in theory and practice a drudge whose function was to toil and whose reward was economic security on a bare subsistence level. But at the same time, there were alleviations of the labourer's lot in the form of charitable and educational organisations which to some extent tempered the harsh winds of the new industrial society to the rising proletariate, shorn of the possession of industrial capital and agrarian "rights". An example of the voluntary organisation for charitable purposes was that founded in 1776 by Mr. Geo. Bott, a dentist of Bridlesmith Gate. It provided relief in the form of medicine, clothes, loans of money, fuel, etc., to those who could not be relieved adequately under the existing Poor Laws. Owing to the "free and liberal exertions of several medical gentlemen" maternity cases were treated, and orphans, widows and strangers were also cared for. Another organisation of a similar kind was the Benevolent Society connected with St. Mary's Church, founded in 1804; in the single year 1807 the first of these societies, according to Blackner, relieved 1,013 cases and the second 666.[1]

Another form of voluntary assistance of the poor organised by the middle class and the aristocracy was the General Hospital, established in 1781 on a site provided by the Duke of Newcastle and the Corporation jointly and supported by the contributions of the local gentry and tradesmen; in 1800 the vaccination of the poor was carried out free by a local practitioner, and in 1805 a public subscription was opened for paying surgeons to vaccinate the children of the poor free of charge.[2] At the same time, the provision of educational

[1] For constitution of Bott's Society, see Eden, *State of Poor*, Vol. II, p. 575.
[2] Blackner, *Hist. of Nottm.*, pp. 129 *et seq.*

facilities for the poor was advancing. Schools had been founded, mainly by the Church of England, in many villages of the County from the end of the seventeenth century onwards. With the appearance of rival religious organisations of intense vitality, in the shape of Wesleyan chapels, and above all, with the rise of the Sunday School movement, the voluntary organisation of education, largely supported by private charity and dependent upon gratuitous service, made rapid strides. It is impossible, of course, to measure the effects of these forms of social amelioration, but it is essential to consider them if a just estimate is to be formed of the conditions of life at the end of the eighteenth century. Modern students, looking back from the heights of contemporary amenities, are apt to see only shadows, unrelieved by the light of private benevolence and the growing scientific knowledge. Students of the epoch itself were less given to pessimism; it should be remembered, the worst time had still to come. Nottingham numbered less than 30,000 souls in 1801, and although by 1815 the town boasted of 300 courts, yards and alleys without proper illumination or drainage, slumdom was still in its infancy. There was room to breathe and space to exercise; the outskirts of the old town were splashed with green, and at crocus-time, with purple. The possession of this open ground moves Blackner to one of his quaintest flights;[1] after remarking with enthusiasm upon "our canal, where coal, timber, corn, iron, stone, slate, plaster, manure and tile wharfs abound, with their contiguous warehouses where industry sits laughing on the labourer's brow", he passes on, via the waterworks and the public baths, to the meadows, where he goes on:

"How pleasing it is to the contemplative philosopher when industry has laid down her implements to see her numerous off-spring both young and old rush into the meadows to have their toil relaxed with refreshing breezes of the evening; and while they inhale the odour of the flowering herbage or the new mown hay join in social conversation or in the sportive romp! While some

[1] *Ibid.*, pp. 23–29.

are sympathising over miseries brought upon mankind by the hand of oppression, the crush [*sic*] of emperors and the clang of arms; others are adoring the bounty of divine providence and others again are enjoying by anticipation the sweets of connubial love."

It does not appear that John Blackner, self-educated man of the people, radical editor of the *Nottingham Review*, and even suspected of complicity with the Luddite outbreaks, was unduly oppressed as he contemplated the Nottingham of 1815. Had he written thirty years later he would have found more material for "gloomy sensations" in the overcrowded slums, insanitary and disease-ridden beyond belief,[1] and in the unrelieved privations of the stockingers,[2] who differed from those of 1815 by being more numerous but not less poor.

[1] For the state of public health in Nottingham, see Health of Towns Commission Report, Appendix I, 1844, and the successive reports of Medical Officers in the Ref. Library at Nottingham. See also Hammond, *Age of the Chartists*, p. 86.

[2] The stockingers were too poor to buy stockings for themselves and their children! A witness before the Commission of 1845 said: "It is awful to contemplate the difference between the present and the past. When I was a young man you would scarcely see a person, man, woman or child, without stockings; now you can scarcely see a poor man's child that is not without stockings and shoes, and caps too. If these persons were supplied with them . . . the whole of the frames would be employed."—Report of 1845, Appendix, Notts. Evidence of Ben Humphreys, Q. 359. The people of Sutton-in-Ashfield (within the old limits of Sherwood Forest) had "not so much as *one acre* of common ground . . . for the use or amusement of the poor; not a bathing place to which the people have access without trespassing . . . and of the five thousand people, three thousand, owing to want of trade, have not had sufficient food for several years past. These poor stocking makers are now precisely as Lord Byron described them in the House of Peers, in 1811, "meagre with famine, and sullen with despair".—Spencer T. Hall, *The Forester's Offering*, 1841, p. 81. In 1860 conditions were even worse among children employed in the lace trade. A county magistrate is reported to have said in a meeting at Nottingham "that there was an amount of privation and suffering among that portion of the population connected with the lace trade, unknown in other parts of the kingdom, indeed, in the civilized world. Children of nine or ten years are dragged from their squalid beds at two, three, or four o'clock in the morning and compelled to work for a bare subsistence until ten, eleven, or twelve at night. . . . What can we think of a town which holds a public meeting to petition that the period of labour for men shall be diminished to eighteen hours a day". *Daily Telegraph*, January 17, 1860, quoted Marx, *Capital* (1920), p. 227. For description of conditions among Leicestershire stockingers in the middle of the century, see Felkin, *Hosiery and Lace*, p. 459.

CONCLUSION

CULTURE AND SOCIAL LIFE

We have now completed our survey of Nottinghamshire under the squirearchy as far as relates to the structure of local society and the development of economic life; and it might be more prudent to leave the investigation at the point it has now reached. But the topics we have treated—the form of local government, the development of industry and the conditions of the labourer's life—do not exhaust the sources of ascertained knowledge upon the social side of local history. Another source, of very great value but rarely utilised, is the history of local culture; and since this subject has received especially expert attention in the *Victoria County History* it is possible for the social historian to make use of it (in so far as it illustrates his special theme) without doing injustice to a highly specialised field of research.

The history of local culture is interesting to the social historian because it gives him evidence of profound changes in the mental life of the locality alongside the changes in economic and social organisation with which he is already familiar. A treatment of this unjustly neglected branch of social history enables him to approach one step nearer to a complete, and therefore true, picture of the past. It is very interesting, for instance, to find that the period of the squirearchy coincided with the fall of Classical studies in the local schools and a breakdown in the authority of the Church; the study of the three R's took the place of the Classics, and alongside the Parish Church rose the Dissenting Meeting Houses, and eventually the Wesleyan Chapels. These are changes of the greatest importance in the lives of the members of the society in which they took place, and some attempt should be made to place them alongside, and if possible to relate them with the changes already described in the more material aspects of life.

In his chapter on the Schools of Nottinghamshire,[1] Mr. Leach states that by the end of the sixteenth century there were endowed Grammar Schools at Nottingham, Newark, Southwell, Retford, Mansfield, besides an unknown number of smaller schools, relatively of the same status, in other places. The curriculum of the Grammar School can be indicated by reference to the Statutes of Retford School which, drawn up in 1552, have fortunately survived in their entirety. The boys of the first form were first to be taught to read and write accurately and then immediately to be put on to the declension and conjugation of Latin nouns and verbs, which "if it be done with diligence, a good and apt nature", it was said, could master in a year, while the more "prone natures" might spare some part of the year to study the less difficult epistles of Tully. The second form is to go on to the harder epistles of Tully, the Colloquia of Erasmus, Sallust, "Salern", Justinian's Institutes, and also the Old and New Testament. The third form is to study The King's Majesty's Latin Grammar, Virgil, Ovid, and more writings of Tully and Erasmus, and every day to turn a piece of English into Latin. The fourth form is to be taught prosody and the making of verses, and every boy is to produce an epistle in Latin every week, and the rudiments of Greek and Hebrew are also to be imparted by the schoolmaster "so far as his learning and convenient term will serve thereto".[2] The comment of Mr. Leach "that it is

[1] *V.C.H.*, II. See also Brown, *Hist. of Newark*, Vol. II, Ch. VIII, and Corner, "Education in the Middle Ages," a paper read before Thoroton Society, Feb., 1914.

[2] *Ibid.*, p. 240. The *Colloquies* of Erasmus, intended not only to teach boys how to speak correct Latin, but also to expose the vices of the age, is one of the most famous schoolbooks ever written. Condemned by the University of Paris, the College of Cardinals, and the Council of Trent, and also by Luther, it had a very wide sale, 77 editions being recorded between 1518 and 1533, of which two were English. Its keen satire of abuses and

sufficiently startling to find not only Greek grammar but also the Hebrew grammar in the fourth form, which was attained at the age of twelve or thereabouts" is certainly justified. The school started in summer at six o'clock and the first session lasted to 8 a.m. "and then the scholars to go to breakfast and to come again before 9 of the clock; at 11.30 to go to dinner". The afternoon session began at 1 p.m. and lasted till 3.30 "and then to go to their drinking", a sort of afternoon tea except that they drank beer. There was yet a final session from 4 to 6.

If it is astonishing to find so vigorous a curriculum in operation in the Grammar Schools of Nottinghamshire, it is no less astonishing to find that the education provided met with the cordial approbation of the people of the time. The Grammar School at East Retford, for instance, would have collapsed in 1548, but for the vigorous action of the bailiffs and burgesses and of "very many others of the whole country round" who petitioned the King for its continuance, while Mansfield School was not merely petitioned for by the inhabitants but actually maintained by them for a time, either by a

humbug, especially religious, and its robust humour easily account for its popularity, and also for the hostility which it aroused. In regard to "Salern", Professor Hewitt kindly informs me that it stands for "The Maxims of the School of Salern", an ancient medical school of Italy, which inculcated instruction in moral and physical well-being in the form of single lines in Leonine verse, such as *Si fore vis sanus, ablue saepe manus. Contra vim mortis, non est medicamen in hortis. The King's Majesty's Latin Grammar* was the Grammar produced by Colet, Erasmus, Lily and others in the early sixteenth century, and authorised by proclamation in 1540 "as the only Grammar to be used in schools", cf. Foster Watson, *English Grammar Schools to* 1660, Ch. XII. The effect of this interference by the new monarchy in educational methods is thus described, "With the increase of knowledge of the Renaissance, the boy of the post-Renaissance times compared with the Medieval boy had to undergo a martyrdom of despotism. . . . The post-Renaissance boy had to stop any impulse to reason and to simply get the Grammar known by heart, as preliminary to other work." *Ibid.*, p. 261. The Stationers' Company, which regulated the printing of the book, appear to have contemplated the sale of no less than 10,000 copies of the Grammar and Accidence annually. *Ibid.*, p. 255. For a satirical description of the teachers of the time who were "damned to thirst and hunger, to be choked with dust in their unswept schools, to wear out themselves in fret and drudgery", see Erasmus, *Praise of Folly* p. 115.

voluntary rate or by subscription, until an endowment was provided by two local landowners. Not only was the strictly classical education popular, it was at this time very largely free. A wealthy bell-founder, the husband of Dame Agnes Mellors, provided handsomely for the Free Grammar School of Nottingham; Thomas Magnus, ecclesiastic and civil servant, endowed the well-known Magnus Grammar School of Newark; and the landowners and tradesmen of East Retford and Mansfield made their schools free to local residents. Moreover, the standard of attainment appears to have been high; an intermittent stream of scholars was sent to the Universities from the five endowed centres, and they were drawn, it should be noted, from all social classes except the poorest. The mixture of classes referred to by Mr. Leach includes, he tells us, "not the destitute poor, the unsuccessful among the labouring classes, but the relatively poor, the sons of farmers and yeomen, of prosperous traders",[1] and in confirmation of this it is interesting to find among the first 22 names on the Register of Repton School (1564–1910) four sons of husbandmen, nine yeomen, two weavers, a carpenter and a tanner.[2]

The beginning of this vigorous local culture may go back to before the Conquest, to the misty origins of Southwell Grammar School; it was certainly flourishing in the time of Edward III when the Grammar School at Newark was favoured with the presence of a Scottish student in its ranks. This unique event gives rise to the intoxicating suggestion by Mr. Leach that Newark, like its neighbour Stamford in times past, was on the verge of becoming a University. Having inoculated the town with the University virus, the Scottish student appears to have departed North of the Tweed, leaving the Midlands (until the present time) in a state of perfect immunity.[3]

[1] *English Schools at the Reformation*, p. 109. See also Latimer's sermons, March 8, 1549. Everyman's Library, p. 86.

[2] Quoted by Tawney, *Agrarian Problems of the Sixteenth Century*, p. 135.

[3] I owe this suggestion to my friend and colleague, Mr. G. G. Neill Wright, M.A. (Edin.).

If the springtime of this local culture can be placed in the reign of Edward III and the summer in Elizabeth's reign, the autumn appears definitely to have set in by the Restoration. Indeed, the actual date may be hazarded; the year in which the last of the bona-fide Grammar Schools was founded. In 1669 a sum of money was left by a Lincolnshire landowner to endow a school at Tuxford for the instruction of children in "reading, writing, and casting accounts, and in Latin as the occasion should require".[1] Evidently the needs of Nottinghamshire are no longer fully met by reading the epistles of Tully and the poems of Virgil; the latter, no doubt, were read as occasion should require, since the school is known to have sent up one or two boys to Cambridge. But the "mental climate" has clearly changed. An earlier example of a Grammar School performing the function of an Elementary School may be cited, a straw to show the way the wind has been blowing since the beginning of the century. As early as 1615 a Grammar School was founded at Elston [2] which, says Mr. Leach, appears always to have been elementary in character. Thirteen years later, the first of the bona-fide elementary schools for teaching poor children to read and write was founded at Worksop; another followed at Ruddington in 1641, another at Sutton-in-Ashfield in 1669, another at Misson in 1693, others in 1695, '99 and 1700 and so on. From this time onwards, the founding of charity elementary schools "for teaching poor children to read and write", for the purchase of Old and New Testaments, to teach poor children to read the Bible; "for such as have been dipped," continued steadily so that by the end of the century there were over sixty free elementary schools, (excluding of course the Sunday Schools) covering about a third of the ecclesiastical parishes in the County.

The elementary school movement of the seventeenth century and early eighteenth century may be regarded, to some degree at least, not as a new thing, but as the

[1] *V.C.H.*, II, p. 250. [2] *Ibid.*, p. 252.

resuscitation of a former organisation which had suffered a violent death. Mr. Leach asserts very positively that existing elementary education, consisting of the Song Schools, was almost wiped out by the Reformation.

"The mischief was immeasurable", he says. "Of all the wealth of song schools which then existed outside the cathedrals, the Oxford and Cambridge Colleges, and Winchester and Eton, all have perished except the Song School at Newark . . . which escaped being endowed as a chantry and has survived, though in a mutilated form, to our own day." [1]

The Song School, it should be remembered, generally taught other things besides choir singing; reading necessarily, and writing sometimes, being included, and frequently playing "on the organs". At Newark the curriculum was to be "playne Song, pryk Song, descant, and to play at the Organs".[2]

There were besides small endowments for teaching children their letters or for reading or writing and probably a great many more of the Chantries were used for elementary education than has been recorded,[3] but no provision whatever was made for their continuance.

"It was mere robbery of the poor to abolish such foundations. What a chance they (the Protestant successors of Henry VIII) lost in not revising the policy of Henry and saving some of the Chantries for Elementary and the Colleges for Secondary Education! We might have had a singing people and an educated people three centuries ago instead of just beginning to be so in the nineteenth century." [4]

We shall try to show later that the skill in music, far from being dead, was the chief ingredient of popular culture in the eighteenth century, in spite of the ruthless slaughter of the Song Schools; but it was a skill acquired

[1] *English Schools at the Reformation*, 1896, p. 96.

[2] *V.C.H.*, II, p. 205. The meaning of "pryke song", etc., is thus given by Prof. Foster Watson; "to prick meant to write and was the term used to distinguish written music from sight singing, which was called 'plain' song". The study of "pryke song" probably included the copying of music. *op. cit.*, p. 208.

[3] Leach, *op. cit.*

[4] *Ibid.*, p. 97.

outside the walls of the new elementary schools. These, based upon the teaching of piety and the three R's, now carry all before them. Attempts are, it is true, made to stem the tide. The schoolmaster at West Drayton School, founded in 1688, was enjoined to teach "what he could of grammar learning"; the South Leverton School (1691) was nominally founded as a Grammar School; Bulwell Free School (1669), Walkeringham (1719), Sutton Bonington (1718) also included Latin in their curriculum; the master of Sir Thomas Parkyns' school at Bunny was to teach "so much trigonometry as relates to the mechanical and useful parts of mathematics"; moreover a prominent inscription over the door ran as follows, "Disce vel Discede", and lest the inscription should fail by reason of its not being comprehended, the energetic baronet wrote a *Practical and Grammatical Introduction to the Latin Tongue*, for the use of the school. But not even Sir Thomas Parkyns could keep the Classics alive;[1] they drooped in the older schools of Southwell, Newark and Nottingham and almost expired in the newer schools of Retford and Mansfield. Their place was taken by the three R's. In Newark where the Corporation had appropriated £290 of the school's annual income for paving and lighting the town and another £150 for a dispensary, the Classics, which of course were taught free, had to compete against more popular subjects for which fees could be charged.[2] The Nottingham school was described in 1816 as "a useful seminary for teaching boys English Grammar, reading, writing and arithmetic" and was practically monopolised by the members of the Corporation and their friends. "But its former celebrity in classical learning is at an end." East Retford School was shamefully pillaged by the Corporation which, in Elizabeth's time, had petitioned for its foundation; Mansfield School also had to fight for its endowment, but at least it was

[1] For an account of the Parkyns family, see *Proc. of Thor. Soc.*, Vol. VI, pp. 12 *et seq.*

[2] *V.C.H.*, II, 212.

spared the humiliation of East Retford, and the decrepitude of Southwell which, from 1858 to 1862, had to close its doors altogether. The case of Mansfield illustrates especially well the forces at work behind these interesting changes.

"Its present state," the commissioners of 1818 reported, "may be attributed . . . and more particularly because [*sic*] Mansfield is now more a *manufacturing* place than it formerly was; little classical learning being now unfortunately in requisition. The neglect of classical lore has evidently had a pernicious effect upon the manners and morals of the inhabitants. . . . At present there are no scholars with the Headmaster; and but few with the submaster, and these more for the purpose of receiving an English education in an adjoining room, which is paid for; seldom proceeding in the schoolroom further than the Latin Grammar." [1]

While the Grammar School was sinking into its grave, with "pernicious effects" upon the morals of the inhabitants, another institution was flourishing. This was the elementary school founded in 1784 with an endowment of about £100 a year for improving the education of the poor of Mansfield,[2] and with this was combined the legacy of Samuel Brunts, left in 1709 for putting to school poor boys of the parish so as to make them fit for honest trades. In 1831 forty boys and forty girls were being instructed in the three R's and the girls in needlework.[3] By 1891 the value of Brunts' endowment had risen to £3,800 and in that year the two charities were merged, and the modern Brunts' Technical School came into existence.

We have now seen the passing of the old system of Classical education in the lesser grammar schools and the rise of a new elementary education, based upon English and Arithmetic. The connection between the

[1] Quoted *Ibid.*, p. 248.

[2] *Ibid.*, p. 250. For outspoken attack on "ignorant, heedless, insipid schoolmasters with which this kingdom is overrun", see *Memoirs of Gilbert Wakefield* (1792), p. 34. The school which he attended at Wilford started, in summer time, at 5 o'clock in the morning and continued with two hours' intermission till 6 in the evening.

[3] *V.C.H.*, II, pp. 250 and 255.

rise of a commercial and urbanised civilisation and the rise of the new utilitarian education does not require to be emphasised. The connection seems to rest upon two facts; the decline of the yeomanry and independent craftsmen, who, in their heyday, had sent their sons to the local grammar schools; secondly, the commercialisation of agriculture, the growth of industry, and the development of internal trade through Nottingham and the postal towns which turned men's attention from learning to money-making, and for this a good supply of book-keepers with a sound knowledge of English, arithmetic and upright conduct has obvious advantages.

But however important were the economic reasons for the changes we have described, there are others which it would be fatal to neglect. They sprang from the break-up of religious unity and the development of sectarianism, individualism and anarchy in matters of faith. The grammar schools had sought to give, not only an intellectual training, but a moral discipline in orthodox religious practice. They were part of the authoritarian control exercised by the New Monarchy; "a national throne had donned the seamless purple",[1] and claimed to regulate the spiritual and intellectual as well as the secular lives of its subjects. Hence we find the Established Church enquiring not only into the lives of its own ministers and the moral conduct of the parishioners, but also into the conduct of the schoolmasters. The articles of enquiry at the visitation of Nottinghamshire in 1599 included the following, "Whether your Schoolmasters do teach their scholars catechism and do encourage them to love true religion." At the same time, it was ordered that the Sunday afternoon service in all the parishes of Nottinghamshire should take the form of "a catechising by question and

[1] Kennedy, *Elizn. Episcopal Organisation*, p. ccxvi. As a consequence of the despotic control of education by the New Monarchy, University teaching is said to have sunk into a lifeless tradition, and the only real development, especially in Science, took place outside. Cf. Parker, *Dissenting Academies*, pp. 14 *et seq.*

answer".[1] The more energetic clergy, it is said, divided their parishes into households, arranged the days and times for different groups and read out the arrangements publicly in the Church. Those who failed to appear for instruction were noted by the Churchwardens and presented every quarter at the Court of the Ordinary or the Archdeacon's Court.[2]

The Court of the Ordinary played a part in the common life of Tudor and Stuart England that has not received the recognition it merits. No more searching light could be directed upon the everyday life of those times than the twenty-odd volumes of Archidiaconal records recently made available to the Nottinghamshire student by the industry and generosity of the late Lt.-Col. Hodgkinson. They are the records of the Archdeacon's Court which sat every month, sometimes in Nottingham, sometimes in Mansfield, Newark or elsewhere, and dealt with such crimes as incontinence, blasphemy, usury, libel and defamation, refusal to maintain the church fabric and attend its services, working on the Sabbath, unlawful marriages, proving wills, breaking marriage troth. The degree of control exercised may be gauged by such cases as the following: a man of South Leverton was punished for taking an interest of 10 per cent. on a loan of £11 by being made to acknowledge his fault publicly in Church the following Sunday and by paying the large sum of £3 6*s.* 8*d.* to the poor box;[3] Mr. John Needham and his wife of Staunton excused their non-attendance at church on the grounds that the minister had such a pronounced impediment in his speech that they could scarce comprehend what he said;[4] Wm. Barnbye and John Bingham of Sturton were accused of playing football and fighting in the Churchyard, which they denied, especially the fighting, since Bingham's nose "fell ableeding of its own

[1] Kennedy, *op. cit.*, Vol. III, p. 317, and MS. *Register of the Archdeaconry of Nottm.*, Jan. 19, 1634–5.

[2] Kennedy, *op. cit.*, p. cx, quoting articles of Visitation of Chester, 1581.

[3] *Register of the Archdeaconry of Notts.*, March, 1583–4.

[4] *Thor. Soc. Trans.*, 1927, p. 124, quoting Register for 1639.

accord";[1] some had been seeking ducks' nests on the Sabbath; others had been throwing "clodes to one that was sleeping in the Church to wake him"; Bridget Rose had broken her troth to Edward Arden although she had received from him "a paire of sweete gloves and after that an English crowne of golde, in receavinge whereof she said unto the said Edwarde this golde hath wonn mine harte for ever and nowe I will never forsake thee" and even sent to him, by her fellow-servant, Jane Sharpe, "sixpence and a cluster of nuttes, and desired the said Jane Sharpe to tell him that as close as those three did stick together, so fast shoulde her harte stick to him". But as her father could not by any means be persuaded to give his goodwill, she claimed her freedom, which after a long succession of trials was at length granted her.[2]

Thus was the strait jacket of moral regimentation fitted on to the unresisting backs of Tudor and Stuart villagers. But there were many who, while heartily agreeing with the principle of authoritarian control of morals, objected to the form which it took. Hence the Puritans broke away, not for the sake of freedom, but in order to enforce their own kind of discipline. Its character, and especially its emphasis on the teaching of the young, is well brought out in the following description of a Puritan service in a Lincolnshire parish in 1614. The service was conducted by men in "Geneva clokes", and free from the Papistical distractions of the Established Church. It began with prayers and psalms, followed by Bible reading, and a two hours' sermon;

[1] *Ibid.*, p. 144, 1623.

[2] Reg. 5, March, 1592–Dec., 1593, pp. 132–4, etc. In the Borough of Nottingham it is interesting to note, this disciplinary activity had formerly been exercised by the town juries, which on the eve of the Reformation were most zealous in exposing all kinds of vices and abuses, being especially severe on priests and friars, and even on occasion censuring the Mayor and Aldermen. "The jurors," says Mr. Stevenson, "seem to have been most vigorous censors of the morals of the town, and in many cases became quite inquisitorial in their zeal." (Borough Records, Vol. III, p. xii.) The Reformed Church, therefore, was merely following the lead of the municipalities in exercising its ancient functions of moral control.

then came the roll-call of the youths of the parish, a long prayer, and an individual examination upon a set of questions propounded by the minister, followed by a further sermon of two hours, expository of the catechism already dealt with. "Their afternoone worship will be five howes, where, to my observation, there was as many sleepers as wakers, scarce any man but sometime was forced to wink or nod."[1]

During the Commonwealth Presbyterian ministers had been established in most of the Nottinghamshire parishes[2] with preaching as their primary function. The attempt to suppress them and the cause they served after the Restoration marks an important stage in the development of local education. From this point to the end of the century an unquenchable fire of Nonconformity burned in many parts of the County, and in 1672 when Charles II issued his ill-fated Declaration of Indulgence after a decade of persecution no less than thirty-three places, small villages for the most part, obtained licences for Nonconformist worship, and seventeen ministers received permission to conduct Nonconformist services at the same time. The fire was smouldering under the surface; occasionally it broke through and flared up into a fierce war of words, as may be seen in the pamphlets written to protest against the cruel persecution of the local Quakers. The leader of the attack on the Quakers is said to have been the historian, Thoroton, whose death in 1677 coincided with the cessation of a campaign which must have brought to ruin many a humble devotee of an unpopular, but inextinguishable sect.[3]

This period of mutual ill-will of the religious organisations necessarily led to the growth of dissimilar and

[1] Bishop Neale's *Primary Visitation*, Dioc. of Lincs., 1614, quoted in *Lincs. and Notts. Archæological Papers*, 1876–82, Vol. XVI, Pt. 1, p. 41.

[2] Cf. *V.C.H.*, II, p. 72.

[3] See *Ibid.*, pp. 74 *et seq.*, and pamphlets in Nottingham Ref. Library on persecution of Quakers by Dr. Thoroton. For list of Nonconformist conventicles during the Restoration, see Turner, *Original Records of Early Nonconformity*, Vol. I, pp. 153–8; Vol. II, pp. 715–25.

even hostile educational organisations. The Established Church, as we have seen, was mainly interested in the Charity School movement—the only organised effort, poor as it was, for village education of the time. The Nonconformists, on the other hand, whose main strength lay in the towns, and whose spiritual divorce from the Renaissance Grammar School and University had been made absolute by the Clarendon Code, began to form schools of their own, and were able from the start to strike out an independent line, unfettered by the rigid classical tradition of the older institutions. Being especially strong among the rising commercial and industrial classes,[1] it is not surprising that they went on from a foundation of classics and theology to build a more realistic conception of the changing world by means of such studies as mathematics, "natural philosophy", and modern languages.

It does not appear that Nottingham was fortunate enough to possess a school of this kind in the eighteenth century, but it is worthy of note that a vigorous intellectual as well as religious life centred round the Presbyterian—later the Unitarian—Chapel on High Pavement to which a Free School had been attached at the time of the Declaration of Indulgence in 1672. In 1717, it is said, the congregation of the High Pavement Chapel numbered no less than 1,400, probably a sixth of the population of the town. But the greatest period of High Pavement Chapel was yet to come. In 1774 a new assistant minister was appointed in the person of the Rev. George Walker, a noted mathematician, a Fellow of the Royal Society, a friend of Price and Priestley, and well known even to Adam Smith; and for twenty-five years—the happiest years of his life, as he himself said—he held sway in Nottingham, the acknowledged leader of its religious and intellectual life. His political speeches on the subject of Parliamentary reform

[1] See especially Ashton, *Iron and Steel in Ind. Rev.*, for importance of Quakers in early iron industry. See also *Quakerism and Industry before* 1800, by J. Grubb.

were compared by the Duke of Portland to those of Cicero, to the disadvantage of the latter, and the red-hot petition sent by the Corporation to the Government of Lord North on the scandalous mismanagement of an unjust war, protesting against the political evils which "devour the public Treasure, defeat the National Efforts, degrade the spirit of Englishmen into a sordid avarice, subvert the independence of Parliament and act with a malignant influence upon all that is dear to our country", could scarcely have come from any other pen. Four years later he was joined by another great spirit of revolt, Gilbert Wakefield, who came back to his native town in 1784, and formed with Walker and others, a literary club which met for discussion at the houses of the members. It is flattering to local pride to read that "The members of the club were generally of a description superior to what most provincial towns were capable of affording"; more than this, it shows that Nottingham may claim to have made a worthy contribution to the stream which, rising from the rich source of Dissent, fed the intellectual as well as the industrial world with some of its finest leadership.[1]

But the intellectual work of the Dissenting movement, admirable as it appears to have been, could affect only a fraction of the population, and these mainly of the tradesman or upper artisan class. What of the isolated village communities and the growing numbers of labour-

[1] For the part played by Nonconformity, and especially the High Pavement Chapel, see *Early Presbyterianism in Nottingham*, by Rev. B. Carpenter, 1862, and a very interesting article in *Trans. of the Unitarian Hist. Soc.*, Vol. I, Pt. 1, April, 1917, entitled "Early Records of a Presbyterian Congregation", by G. C. Warren. For later history of High Pavement Chapel with occasional references to the school, see *High Pavement Chronicle* (six vols.). There were Presbyterian congregations at Blidworth, Bulwell, Calverton, Selston, East Leake, Normanton, Widmerpool, Normanton-on-the-Wolds, of which some disappeared between 1717–30. For the relative importance of Presbyterians and Congregationalists in the early history of Unitarianism see *Transactions, etc.*, Vol. I, Pt. 2, May, 1918, article entitled "An Apology for Nonconformist Affairs of the Eighteenth Century", by F. J. Powicke, Ph.D. For the petition to the House of Commons quoted in the text, see *H.C.J.*, Vol. 37, p. 581, Feb. 8, 1780. See also *Memoirs*, by Gilbert Wakefield, Vol. I, Ch. II, XI, XIV, etc., for influence of Nonconformists upon education.

ing poor in the towns and the industrial villages? Is it possible to assess the level of their mental lives? Perhaps not; but such evidence as exists, and it is not wholly inadequate, shows that important changes were at work here as elsewhere, for as we have seen, about sixty village schools were founded, mainly by ministers of the Established Church or members of that communion.

What was the character of this education? The old Grammar Schools, with all their teaching of Ovid and Cicero, were also intended to be seminaries of good manners and good morals; "Syr," said the trustees to the Schoolmaster at Newark in the seventeenth century, "ye be chosyn to be maister instructeur and precepteur of this scoole and to teche chyldern repayryng to the same not only good literature, gramer and other vertuous doctrine, but also good maners accordyng to the ordynance of Maister Thomas Magnus."[1] Schoolboys, after all, were to become citizens in a godly society, and for this something more was needed than a knowledge of Latin grammar. The new elementary school went further and tried to train its scholars for the actual part and station which the godly society allotted them. The basis of the commonwealth was labour, the labour of the poor, and it was the part of the charity school to train the poor in those principles and habits which would most effectually reinforce that basis. A writer on Charity Schools points out that "men who are to remain and end their days in a laborious and Tiresome and Painful Station of Life, the sooner they are put upon it at first, the better they will submit to it for ever after".[2] One method, of course, was by means of apprenticeship, and as we have seen in the treatment of Poor Relief, the Corporation of Nottingham spent considerable sums of money in the seventeenth century on this object and throughout the eighteenth century money continued to be left for apprenticing poor boys to crafts. In 1706,

[1] *V.C.H.*, II, p. 206.

[2] Mandeville, *An Essay on Charity Schools*, 1723, p. 329, quoted Marshall, *Eng. Poor in Eighteenth Century*, p. 24.

however, an interesting innovation took place. In that year the Nottingham Charity School was founded for the instruction of fifty poor children in the "principles of religion, spelling and reading", and was "supported by the contributions of the Corporation and others". Its objects may be seen in the following extracts from its rules and orders, published in 1793:

"The master shall teach the children the true spelling of words and syllables and stops, which are necessary to true reading. They shall also be taught to write a fair and legible hand and the rudiments of practical arithmetic, viz. the first five rules. And the mistress shall teach the girls to mend their own clothes, work plain work, and to knit. And both boys and girls shall be taught to sing psalms and a mannerly behaviour towards all persons; all of which being duly performed, will the better fit them for service or apprenticeships."

Here we have a definite transitional case; the municipal provision for manual training is giving place to a semi-municipal elementary school, still designed, however, to give a training "for service or apprenticeship". The same can be observed in the country districts, as, for instance, at South Wilford and Clayworth, where part of the money went in prizes to the best ploughers and reapers or in the provision of apprenticeships; and at North Muskham where the girls were to be taught sewing in addition to the Church Catechism.[1] These, like the Blue Coat School, are transitional cases, a bridge between the old and the new approach to popular education. The three R's, however, easily obtain supremacy, not only over the classical studies of the Grammar Schools but also over the technical training of the old apprenticeship system. Education, even popular education, is clearly moving with the times, a tendency which

[1] See *V.C.H.*, II, pp. 255 *et seq.*, and also *Abstract of Returns of Charitable Donations for Poor Persons*, 1786, pp. 940 *et seq.*, included in *Notts. Charities* in Nottingham Reference Library. For an account of the Blue Coat School, see Deering, pp. 158–9, and Blackner, p. 122. For a survey of the background from which the eighteenth-century Charity School sprang, see Trevelyan, *Blenheim*, Ch. III.

did not pass without comment by a number of acute and critical observers.

"The Charity School", said a writer in 1763, "is another nursery of idleness; nor is it easy to conceive or invent anything more destructive to the interests and very foundation principles of a nation entirely dependent on its trade and manufactures than this giving an education to children of lower class of her people that will make them contemn those drudgeries for which they were born." [1]

About the same time another writer expressed similar doubts:

"These poor children (who learn to write) are taken out of that rank and order wherein providence has placed them . . . what must be the consequences should this mistaken charity prevail universally? Who will be left to do the drudgery of the world? The principle of any plan to employ the children of the poor should be to inure them to the lowest and most early labour." [2]

Towards the end of the century Thomas Ruggles, in his *History of the Poor*, stated the position with admirable clarity and honesty: "The art of writing is not necessary to a performance of the duties of the poor. . . . There must be in society hewers of wood and drawers of water; if all are good penmen where are those who will contentedly live through a life of toil?" [3]

The experiment of teaching the labouring class to write and reckon was continued in spite of these objections, and it enormously extended its range when the Sunday School movement began to sweep large numbers of the urban children off the streets of the rapidly growing towns in the last quarter of the century. The pioneer of the movement locally, according to Blackner, was William Hallam, a framework knitter, educated at East Retford, who is said to have conducted seminaries for those who could pay and in addition to have taught

[1] *Considerations on the False Effects to a Trading Nation of the Present Excess of Public Charity*, Anonymous, Lond., 1763, p. 25, quoted Furniss, *Position of Labourer in a System of Nationalism*, p. 168.

[2] *An Enquiry into Management of the Poor*, Anon., London, 1767, pp. 15–16.

[3] Ruggles, Vol. II, p. 180, quoted Furniss, *op. cit.*

the children of the poor gratis on Sundays from 1781, when he opened a school at Mansfield. The Methodists of Nottingham opened one at Hockley about the same time, where they taught arithmetic on one evening in the week, and other subjects on the Sabbath. From this time the growth of educational institutions went on rapidly so that by 1815 there were forty private academies and smaller schools besides the larger institutions organised by the Chapels and Churches. The Corporation, it should be noted, also took its part and made a grant in 1810 of a piece of land for the erection of a new Lancastrian School.[1]

As in the case of the charity school, the implications of the Sunday School went further than the assumptions upon which it was founded. The moral condition of the poor was the object of widespread apprehension in the second half of the eighteenth century, and the Sunday School movement was fostered as a means of combating the degeneracy which to many at this time constituted a very real social danger.[2] The part played by the Sunday School at this crisis in the social morals of the country is well explained by the Archdeacon of Nottingham, Dr. R. Kaye, in 1787.[3] He speaks first of the growing depravity of the poor, their extreme licentiousness, not only in the Metropolis, but in the most distant towns and villages, and sorrowfully refers to the youth and even infancy of many of the criminals. To combat this deplorable tendency a society had been formed to spread the knowledge of Sunday Schools, and within six months more than two hundred had been founded and six thousand children provided for. The objects of Sunday School he sets forth as follows: to rescue children of the poor from ignorance, vice and idleness; to inculcate duties of industry and subordination so as to qualify them for the several relations of society; the preservation of health by habits of cleanliness and decency; and last, to be taught to read. The

[1] See Blackner, *Hist. of Nottm.*, pp. 115 *et seq.*

[2] Furniss, *op. cit.*, Ch. V.

[3] Copy in Ref. Library, Nottingham.

effect, he says, was instantaneous. Not only were children seen "to change their mode of conduct, to curb the wildness of their tempers, and increase the respect due to superiors, but also to exert a salutary influence on the mode of life of their parents, and all this by methods free from undue severity or corporal punishment".

These desirable effects do not seem to have been as lasting or as widespread as the Archdeacon hoped. After thirty years of further effort a Derbyshire clergyman still found occasion to upbraid the poor for their lawlessness and base ingratitude for all the charities that had been showered upon them and exhorted them to

> "avoid the Company and Doctrine of those who act in defiance of lawful authority. Remember the angels . . . who wanted to be equal or perhaps greater than their author or governor. Speak not evil of rulers or Dignities who have dominion over you; they are in the hands of the Almighty appointed for the correction of the bad and the encouragement of the good." [1]

Two years after this seasonable advice had been written the Pentrich Revolution occurred. A band of deluded and desperate framework knitters thinking "the lads of the North" would be there to join them, fell into the infamous trap of a government spy and marched upon Nottingham, plundered the farms of firearms, murdered a farmer and surrendered to the Dragoons. Three of their leaders "having been seduced by the instigation of the Devil to make war on their King" were hanged outside the gaol at Derby.[2] The vision of social harmony evoked by the Archdeacon of Nottingham from the vasty deep of popular education had clearly not been realised.

The measure of success attained by the new educational organisation may be ascertained, to some extent at least, by a study of the actual writings of the self-

[1] *Seasonable Advice or Antidote to the Poison of Disaffection*, by the Rev. Wm. Cantrell, Derby, 1815.

[2] For a full account of this tragic episode, see Hammond, *Skilled Labourer*, pp. 360–71.

educated leaders whom the industrial struggle of the time threw up. The framework knitters, for instance, almost invariably expressed themselves both accurately and eloquently and their evidence reported in the *Commons Journals* of 1776 and 1779 and in the pamphlet their leaders published afterwards, is a clear statement of a complicated case; their occasional letters to the Company's officers in London, or to the local papers, are entirely free from any sign of illiteracy. The leader of the Leicester stockingers, besides being a brilliant orator, was a poet and a wit; the Nottingham stockingers, in addition to their many less prominent leaders, produced Gravenor Henson, the author of what is still the chief historical source of the industry, and John Blackner, who defended the Luddites in his paper, *The Nottingham Review*, and wrote a very valuable history of the town. Entirely by his own efforts he had escaped from utter ignorance to a state of knowledge and mental freedom which to him seemed celestial. "Man without education", he wrote, "would be little better than the beast of the field . . . to the noble qualities which exalt the soul and harmonise the mind he would be a stranger." The nascent working-class movement did not have to wait for compulsory elementary education to produce capable leaders; the best products of the Charity School and the Dame School and the Sunday School will challenge comparison with those of a later system.

We have so far been speaking only of the leaders, who, of course, did not appear until the latter half of the century, when the industrial problems began to be acute. What of the rank-and-file, the farmers and labourers and craftsmen in the villages, the tradesmen, artisans, labourers, loafers of the towns? The evidence of popular culture among these classes is scarce; if the modern tendency to identify culture with a capacity for reading and writing be correct, then probably it *was* scarce; after all, in that form it was not necessary. Skill in handling tools, in ploughing a straight furrow, making a stack, hedging, and ditching, fashioning a stocking on a forty-gauge frame, and helping with voice, viol or fiddle, to swell the chorus in the village church, this was the kind of skill required in the early eighteenth century; and if a man really wanted to learn to read, it would appear that he could do so. At least there was always someone of humble station in the parish who could both read, write and reckon. Otherwise how are we to account for the voluminous parish records that were everywhere kept, often enough by the rough hands of a village husbandman, sometimes, as at Laxton, by a skilled penman who took an artistic pride in his work? The fetish of intellectual pursuits for all had not yet come in; and skill of hand and eye had not yet gone out.

Again, just as their skill sprang from contact with the soil, so their pleasures smacked of the raw earth. The brutality of the eighteenth century is well known, but if men liked to see animals fight and suffer, as for instance in the sports of cock-fighting, cock-shying, bear-baiting and bull-baiting, they delighted equally in fighting and inflicting suffering upon one another. There is no need to advert to the barbarities practised in the name of the Poor Law, the whipping of men and women vagrants, the removal of women in labour, the beating of apprentices, the unimaginable squalor in which lunatics were kept, and the scandalous conditions of many workhouses and most gaols. As late as 1765, a man who had committed suicide at Nottingham was buried in the public highway, with a stake driven through his body. Again, according to Fielding, to drink and to fight together were almost synonymous terms with the lower people of England. Not that there was anything ungenerous, unfair, or ill-natured in this, he says, "nay it is common for the combatants to express goodwill for each other even at the time of the conflict; and as their drunken mirth generally ends in a battle, so do most of their battles end in friendship".[1]

For this species of friendship, no period could have

[1] *Tom Jones,* Vol. I, p. 131, Everyman's Library. For the burial of the suicide, see Sutton *Date Book,* Pt. II, p. 68.

offered greater facilities than the eighteenth century, and few towns as many as Nottingham, whose ale was so delicious that London brewers were fain to borrow the glamour of its name to sell their own, and poets praised its virtues in unimaginably bad verse. The light variety might be had for a 1½*d.* a gallon; fine strong ale cost one and fourpence. It was consumed enormously on all possible occasions, both public and private, but being healthy as well as stimulating it was never associated with the ghastly effects of the contemporary gin orgy of London. The taste of Nottingham was healthier and humbler, and received confirmation from the rulers of the City. The Mayor and Corporation drank and smoked copiously at the town's expense as often as possible; and in the circle of their gratuitous potations they occasionally included the Members of Parliament and the citizens at large. A substantial *pourboire* of "Thirty Gallandes and an hogs-head" was sent to the Parliament men in 1705,[1] wine of the better sort and ale for the poor were provided to stimulate the loyalty of the townspeople at the Coronation of Queen Anne,[2] and elections were made the occasion for an incredible amount of swilling and gorging, which was not wholly omitted even when there was no contest.[3] In order to prevail upon that "debauched" borough, Newark, £1,000 to £1,500 had to be expended, and Lord Howe's success in the Nottingham election of 1754 was partly due to an original method of electioneering which took the form, we are told, of a prolonged and sumptuous entertainment at his seat at Langar Hall for some time before the election, with the result that a number of his guests had the misfortune to die soon afterwards, but not, it would appear, before registering their votes. Even the Archbishop of York was not free from the prevailing weakness, and scandalised the Vicar of St. Mary's by regaling himself after a Confirmation service with a flagon of ale and pipes of tobacco in the vestry.

[1] Borough Records, Vol. VI, pp. 29 and 31. [2] *Ibid.*
[3] *Nottingham Journal,* Dec. 18, 1762.

Other opportunities for these amiable indulgences in the intervals of elections, coronations and Confirmation services could not be lacking in a town of 10,000 inhabitants that boasted of 132 inns and alehouses, besides facilities for private brewing possessed by most houses of size, and a number of Bacchanalian clubs. One of these, it is said, met at the unusual hour of 4 a.m. and exacted a heavy penalty from any of its members who had not emptied his quart pot by six.

But the supremacy of ale, even in the affections of the lower orders, was being challenged by tea. The change is announced without approval by Deering as follows:

"People here are not without their Tea, Coffee, and Chocolate, especially the first, the Use of which is spread to that Degree, that not only Gentry and Wealthy Travellers drink it constantly, but almost every Seamer, Sizer and Winder will have her Tea in a Morning . . . and even a common Washerwoman thinks she has not had a proper Breakfast without tea and hot buttered white Bread. . . . I could not forbear looking earnestly and with some Degree of Indignation at a ragged and greasy Creature who came into a Shop with two Children and asked for a penny worth of Tea and halfpenny worth of Sugar," and said she could not live without drinking tea every day.

As in the habit of ale-drinking, popular sports and amusements began to show some slight indications of change towards more modern standards. Alongside the usual notices of cocking-matches, race-meetings and prize-fights, announcements for monthly assemblies for dancing and cards occur—one for the "better sort" and one for the tradesmen. The barbarous sport of bull-baiting seems to have entirely decayed in Nottingham before the middle of the century, a demise that no one will regret who reads the lively description of the sport given by Houghton as follows:

When he is full grown and strong he is baited almost to death, for that great exercise makes his flesh more tender; and so if he is eaten in good time (before putrefaction, which he is more subject to than if not baited) he is tolerable good meat, although very red.

"A collar is put about his neck fastened to a thick rope about 3 or 4 yards long hung to a hook fastened to a stake in such a way that it will turn round. The bull circulates to watch his enemy, a mastiff with a short nose so that his teeth may take better hold; this dog will creep upon his belly to take the bull by the nose. I have seen a dog tossed by a bull 30 if not 40 feet high. The man in charge strives to catch the dog lest it is injured.

"The famed dogs have crosses or roses of ribbon stuck with pitch on their foreheads; and such the ladies are very ready to bestow on Dogs or Bulls that do valiantly. The true courage is to hold the Bull by the nose until he roars, which a courageous bull scorns to do. Not only the baser sort, but the greatest lords and ladies delight in this sport. . . . Men are often tossed as well as dogs."

In the County the sport lasted till towards the close of the century, a bull being baited in Newark market-place to the great enjoyment of many hundreds of spectators in the streets and at the windows as late as 1781.[1]

But this hearty grossness was not entirely unrelieved by gleams of higher things; although there was probably little reading and less writing being done, and the circulating library and the cinema were missing, the humblest member of the community in town and village still had consolation for his spirit. There was music, for instance. The history of popular music at this time is an obscure subject; but there are hints here and there that a thorough investigation might lead to the discovery of hidden treasure. The song school at Newark, as we have said, appears to have been the only one outside Cathedrals and Collegiate Churches to survive the ordeal of the Reformation; but the long training in choral music and even the copies of the music sung would not disappear in a day. The churches continued to require

[1] For subject of Notts. elections, ale-drinking and bull-baiting, see Bailey, *Annals of Notts.*, pp. 1223 and 1182; Surtees Soc. Publications, 1860, I, *Rotheby Memoirs*, p. 55 n.; Sutton *Date Book*, p. 15; Borough Records, Vol. VI, p. 83; Deering, pp. 72 and 95; John Houghton, *Collection for Improvement of Husbandry and Trade*, 1693, p. 108; Brown, *Hist. of Newark*, p. 291. For mention of 115 alehouses in town of Nottingham in Eliz. reign see *S.P. Dom.*, Eliz., Vol. CXCVIII, p. 51. In the eighteenth century the common alehouse licence cost £20 to all but Burgesses. Cf. Borough Records, Vol. VI, p. 90.

instrumental as well as choral skill, and the great revival of Churchmanship in the Elizabethan and Stuart period would do much to counteract the deadly effects of the Reformation. Puritanism, with its "singing i'th nose", (it is still practised in its original purity in remote hamlets of North Holland) may have given it a setback, but the century of Handel was certainly musical from top to bottom of the social hierarchy. The Corporation of Nottingham paid again and again for its "waits"; [1] concerts and musical parties and picnics to St. Anne's Well shared with cards and gambling the primacy of indoor amusements; later in the century, at a time when industrialism was spreading in the towns and pauperism eating into the villages, there were Handel festivals lasting a week, and at a small country town like Ashby-de-la-Zouch, local talent was equal to a production of that quintessence of the Augustan Age, *Acis and Galatea*, besides other works of the same master. And if it be objected that these examples of musical skill and enthusiasm belonged only to the rising middle and professional classes, it is only necessary to turn to the vivacious record of the Leicester stocking manufacturer, William Gardiner, whose roseate account of the eighteenth-century stockinger's life makes pleasant reading.

"Every village had its wake", he says, "and at this time the lower orders were comparatively in a state of ease and plenty. When the wake came the stockingmaker had peas and beans in his snug garden and a good barrel of humming ale . . . but more than all he had leisure, which in summer time was a blessing and a delight. The year was chequered with holidays, wakes and fairs. . . . The artisans had their amusements at home. They were members of the village choir and on the Wake Sunday everyone that had a voice and could lend a hand with the hautboy, bassoon or flute repaired to the singing loft in the Church to swell with heart and voice the psalm or anthem. Those harmless recreations were for everyone." [2]

[1] See Borough Records, Vols. IV, V, VI, for numerous references.
[2] The works produced were said mainly to be those of Arnold, Knapp and Bishop.

There were also travelling instrumental bands.

"A band of two viols and a bass, playing trios of Kamell and Lampugnani, went to the wake every year at Ratby—the last of the itinerant minstrels—and joined the choir on Wake Sunday and with assistants from neighbouring villages produced what was called a grand 'crash' that never failed to fill the Church.

"At Christmas the choir of Shepshed with voices and instruments took circuit round the town and performed the carols at the principal houses and sang also the best of our English glees. . . . How changed are the circumstances of this class of society. Since the introduction of machinery, which in every case lowers the price of labour, the slow hand is obliged to be increasingly at work to provide for his family. . . . There is no leisure for music and in place of the viol and flute at the wake you have nothing now but noise and vulgarity with swearing and drunkenness. . . . That simplicity of character which the same people possessed (before coming into the towns) is now gone, and were it not for efforts made to educate them they would soon be found in a state of complete demoralisation." [1]

In the new economy of large-scale production there was no time for flute or viol, but if this source of consolation was cut off, one other, which cost no money and little time, was not ruled out. This was religion. Pope had said earlier in the century:

> Religion blushing veils her sacred fires
> And unawares morality expires.

There were, however, occasional signs both of heat and light in the local annals of religious life. About 1730 the Presbyterian Chapel on High Pavement was rapidly moving to the Unitarian position which it has since held, and the horror of the Congregationalists, expressed in Saturday night lectures by their earnest young pastor, James Sloss, led to a lively passage of arms with one of his own congregation, who was charged among other things with going round the alehouses of Nottingham asking the following questions: Are there three persons

[1] Gardiner, *Music and Friends,* Vol. I, pp. 43, 47, 85.

in the Godhead, and are these three one God, the same in substance and equal in all Divine Perfection and Glory?[1] It is interesting to think that among the 132 inns and alehouses of Nottingham[2] there were some in which questions of this kind could be discussed. There is no doubt that the religious life of the Presbyterian Chapel, though rent by schism, was very active during the early as well as the later years of the eighteenth century, and in 1717 is said to have had a congregation of 1,400, of whom 335 were voters. Later on, as we have shown above, they could boast of a figure of national distinction in their minister, the Rev. George Walker, but his influence was felt at least as much in the intellectual and political sphere as in the religious. Similarly, the Church of England had its local notabilities. Bishop Warburton, who was born and educated at Newark; Archbishop Secker, who came from Cuckney, and Samuel Halifax, Bishop of Gloucester, who came from Mansfield.[3] But the native product who really mattered in the local life, and struck the imagination not only of the outer world, but even of his birthplace, was Gilbert Wakefield. His contemporary, Blackner, did not deny himself the pleasure of introducing him with appropriate éclat; Gilbert Wakefield, he says, "was one of those transcendant luminaries that the Almighty in the plenitude of His wisdom sometimes favours the world with

[1] Narrative of case of Jos. Rawson by Jas. Sloss, M.A., Nottingham Ref. Library. For further history of this episode, see authorities quoted p. 314 note 1 and for a brilliant survey of the disruptive tendencies of eighteenth-century Dissent until the arrival of Wesley.—See Halévy, *Hist. of the English People in* 1815, pp. 354 *et seq.*, and Bibliography, pp. 550 *et seq.*

[2] Deering, p. 95.

[3] Mellors, *Men of Nottingham and Nottinghamshire*, p. 131. For much interesting information on Church life of Notts., see *Acct. of Benefices and Population, Number and Condition of Glebe Houses and income of all benefices not exceeding £150 per annum.*—Accounts and Papers, 1818. The unbelievable decrepitude of many of the glebe houses—"built of mud", "a miserable hovel", "built of stud and mud"—helps to explain the absenteeism and lack of pastoral care which were prevalent. Many of the industrial villages had hopelessly outgrown existing provisions for religious life. See *Accounts of Population of certain Benefices or Parishes with capacity of their Churches and Chapels.*—Accounts Papers, 1818.

for a season, for the purpose of unfolding to mankind the obtruse [*sic*] operations of nature".[1]

But a luminary of far greater magnitude, from a parsonage in Lincolnshire, had preceded him: John Wesley. He alone had the key to the hearts of the new England that was growing up in the towns and industrialised villages. The intellectual approach of Anglicanism and Presbyterianism had lost its hold; the force of Calvinistic logic, while it produced fierce and futile schisms, was as powerless with the growing population as the voice of Anglican authority; the disciplined devotion which had formerly been attracted by theology or the lore of the Schools was being directed to the pursuit of Science, but above all to Business and the money-making arts, and the strength of religion now lay in its hold over the imaginations and emotions of the populace. This was unexplored territory and ripe for occupation. A framework knitter in receipt of a wage of 6*s.* a week could not be expected to attend with rapture to a prolonged exposition of a Presbyterian catechism or to the tepid homilies of the Anglican Church. Even the Baptists, that "small handful of the unworthy dust of Zion",[2] have little to record but the maladministration of charitable funds and the disputes between Congregation and Pastor; [3] but Wesley from the first obtained a hearing and, towards the end, a mastery which was unique. Josiah Tucker, Dean of Gloucester, spoke of the unparalleled brutality and insolence, debauchery and extravagance of the poor; they had become a reproach to the nation, he said.[4] But Wesley found after many tribulations that they would at least listen to the word of Salvation, and to the promise—the incredible promise—of honour and glory for the likes of them. On his first visit to Nottingham in 1741 he found the room in which he had to preach only half full, and that the congregation

[1] Mellors, *Men of Nottingham and Nottinghamshire*, p. 340.
[2] Godfrey and Ward, *History of Friar Lane Baptist Church*, p. 7.
[3] *Ibid.*, pp. 11, 23 *et seq.*
[4] Quoted Furniss, p. 231.

far from evincing any form of devotion chatted negligently before the service began and listened to his opening prayer in the most indolent posture they could assume.[1] Later, when he addressed a multitude in the open air he had occasion to reprove a number who behaved lightly and one who contradicted and blasphemed. Thirty-six years later, when the growing burden of long hours, low wages and high prices had become wellnigh intolerable, he notes a marked change in their demeanour:

> "There is something in the people of this town", he says, "which I cannot but approve of; although most of our Society are of the lower class, chiefly employed in the stocking manufacture, yet there is generally an uncommon gentleness and sweetness in their temper, and something of elegance in their behaviour, which when added to solid vital religion make them an ornament to their profession." [2]

At this time, it may be remembered, the framework knitters were organising an association of the Midland Counties to petition Parliament on the subject of their wages, which frequently fell as low as 6*s*. a week per man. They had entered upon their seventy years' sojourn in the wilderness—the nineteenth-century domestic system—and the Promised Land was already fading into celestial distances. Nothing short of downright starvation could exceed the miseries which they suffered at one time or another on this apparently endless journey; until at last the power-driven factory, with its concomitants of Trade Union, State Inspectors and Arbitration Boards, mercifully opened its doors to them. The part played by the religious revival in their enfranchisement was to train the rising democratic movement in the arts of oratory and leadership; it also taught with tireless emphasis the "sad science of renunciation" in a transient world, and in so doing helped to build the

[1] Wesley's *Journals*, edited by Curnock, Vol. II, p. 464.
[2] *Ibid.*, Vol. VI, p. 156.

barrier, none too stout, which separated Sidmouth's England from the vengeance of Ned Ludd.[1]

[1] Cf. Halévy, *History of the English People in* 1815, p. 371, in which the political effects of the evangelical movement are thus summed up: "Society might easily have lapsed into anarchy had there existed in England a bourgeoisie animated by the spirit of revolution . . . had the working classes found in the middle classes leaders to provide them with a definite ideal, a creed, a practical programme. But the élite of the working class, the hard-working and capable bourgeois, had been imbued by the Evangelical Movement with a spirit from which the established order had nothing to fear . . . with their passion for liberty they united a devotion to order and the latter finally predominated."

APPENDIX I

EXPLANATION OF TECHNICAL TERMS USED IN CHAPTERS ON FRAMEWORK KNITTING

IN THE ORDER IN WHICH THEY OCCUR IN THE TEXT

Frame.—Originally the wooden framework upon which Lee fixed his first row of needles inserted firmly in a piece of wood—used afterwards as a general name for the whole mechanism.

Needle.—A long barbed hook with a groove in the stem in which the tip of the needle (the "beard") is pressed to allow the loops to be brought over.

Presser Bar.—A wooden bar. used to press down the beards of the needles to allow the loops to be brought over.

Sinkers.—Thin plates of iron made to pass between the needles in order (i) to make the loops across the needle stems; (ii) to bring them under the needle beards and the web already made to the needle stems in the same action; (iii) to bring forward the web over the needle beards; (iv) to take the web back.

Treddles or Treadles.—Three treddles placed side by side operated by the feet; the two outer ones for the purpose of "drawing the jacks", i.e. causing the sinkers to fall by drawing the slur-cock along their "tails", the middle one to force down the presser bar.

A course.—The fabric consists of a series of loops each of which is called a course and for the formation of each course eleven different operations are required.

A narrow frame—has 150–600 needles, according to the gauge.

A wide frame.—Anything up to 1,500 needles.

Gauge.—Signifies number of needles, sinkers or sometimes jacks (needle leads) in a given space. There were three types of hand-frames: (i) *coarse frame* having one needle in every jack—called a "split frame"; (ii) *ordinary frame* having two needles in every jack—called a "solid frame"; (iii) *silk frame* having three needles in every jack—called a three-needle frame. In order to illustrate the meaning of the term *gauge*, an example of each kind of frame will be given:

A 24-gauge coarse frame has 24 needle leads (jacks), 24 needles and 24 jack sinkers in 3 inches (8 needles per inch). This was probably the size of Lee's first frame.

A 24-gauge ordinary frame has 24 needle leads, each containing 2 needles, 24 jack sinkers and 24 lead sinkers in 3 inches (16 needles per inch).

A 24-gauge silk frame has 24 needle leads, each containing 3 needles, 24 jack sinkers and 48 lead sinkers in 3 inches (24 needles per inch). This was the coarsest type of silk frame used (Henson, p. 44). For detailed account of hand-stocking-frame see Quilter and Chamberlain, *Framework Knitting and Hosiery Industry*, Vol. I, pp. 132–68.

APPENDIX II

A List of the Civil Parishes, Townships and Principal Hamlets of the County of Nottingham, with a note of the area of each Parish, a brief account of their Enclosure History, and a guide to the whereabouts of the Enclosure Awards

By W. E. Tate

(*Headmaster, Council School, Sutton Bonington*)

Note.—Owing to lack of space it has been found impossible to give particulars of the enrolment or whereabouts of Enclosure Acts, or the numerous sources used in making this compilation. A full Bibliography will be published separately elsewhere.

ABBREVIATIONS

w.P.s. = without Parliamentary sanction.

P.C. = Parish Council.

P.M. = Parish Meeting.

S.H. = Shire Hall.

U.D.C. = Urban District Council.

(G.A.) = General Act.

(M) = Enclosure of Meadow.

(W) = Mainly or entirely enclosure of Waste.

Curtis = *Topographical History of Nottinghamshire* (*c.* 1844).

Thoroton = *History of Nottinghamshire* (1677) with additions by Throsby (1798).

Lowe = *Agricultural Report on Nottinghamshire* (1798).

Acreage given in Column 4 is taken from the Award except where it is marked * when it is taken from the Enclosure Act.

Name of Place.	Land Area (Acres).	Date and Manner of Enclosure.	Area Enclosed. A. R. P.	Award in Possession of
Adbolton .		In Holme Pierrepont, q.v.		
Alverton . .	445	44 Geo. III, 42	410 0 0	Lost.
Annesley .	3,111	1,200 acres were enclosed and emparked in 1661. Another enclosure as follows: 48 Geo. III, 1.	582 3 13	Apparently lost.
Arnold . .	4,610	29 Geo. III, 57.	2,848 0 20	U.D.C.
Askham . .	1,311	6 & 7 Wm. IV, 115 (G.A.) Complaints of enclosure were made in 1639 and according to White there was further enclosure of arable in 1832 without Parliamentary sanction.	305 0 34½	P.C.
Aslockton .	1,269	20 Geo. III, 1 (with Scarrington).	1,996 0 16 (in the two)	Vicar of Scarrington.
Attenborough		In Toton, q.v.		
Averham .	2,120	Probably before 1700.		
Awsworth .	361	Probably before 1700.		
Babworth *including* Morton Ranby	6,321	In Morton there was enclosure and conversion to pasture in 1512, but the greater part of the parish (Babworth and Morton) was enclosed from the Forest w.P.s. shortly before 1797 (*c.* 4,080 acres) Ranby was decayed in Thoroton's time.		
Balderton .	3,780	6 Geo. III, 89.	3,077 0 5	S.H.
Barnby-in-the-Willows	1,845	Complaints of engrossing farms in 1608 point to enclosure before 1700.		
Barnby Moor with detached portion	1,294	47 Geo. III, 57.	1,276 2 13	Rector of Blyth.
Bilby	684	260 acres of waste enclosed w.P.s. just before 1798.		

Name of Place.	Land Area (Acres).	Date and Manner of Enclosure.	Area Enclosed.	Award in Possession of
			A. R. P.	
Barnstone .		Included in Langar, q.v.		
Barton-in-Fabis	1,560	32 Geo. II, 55 (with Clifton).	1,541 3 37	Rector of Barton.
Basford . .		In Nottingham, q.v.		
Bathley . .	1,245	11 Geo. III, 62 (with N. Muskham and Holme).	3,000 0 0* (in the three)	Chairman P.C. (North Muskham).
Beckingham .	2,663	16 Geo. III, 62. According to Curtis a portion was enclosed by agreement in 1730.	2,900 0 0*	P.C.
Beesthorpe .		In Caunton, q.v.		
Beeston . .	1,582	46 Geo. III, 52.	821 2 33	U.D.C.
Besthorpe (M. W.)	1,288	6 & 7 Wm. IV, 115 (G. A.). Curtis refers to an enclosure apparently of waste "more than a century ago".	210 0 12	?
Bestwood Park	3,723	An old Royal Park empaled temp. Ed. III and largely divided into farms before Thoroton's time. Remainder divided into 13 farms *c.* 1778. Granted temp. Chas. II to Nell Gwynne.		
Bevercotes .	734	Apparently all old enclosure.		
Bilborough (W.)	1,097	48 Geo. III, 34 (with Strelley).	400 0 0* (in the two)	Chairman P.M.
Bilby . .		Detached portion of Barnby Moor, q.v.		
Bilsthorpe .	1,579	Partially enclosed w.P.s. between 1778–98.		
Bingham .	3,069	w.P.s. 1778–98.		
Bleasby . .	1,509	17 Geo. III, 129.	447 2 39	Vicar.
Blidworth (M. W.)	5,465	9 Geo. III, 112; 45 Geo. III, 32; ratified by 54 Geo. III, 50.	1,508 0 32 2,329 3 9	S.H.

Name of Place.	Land Area (Acres).	Date and Manner of Enclosure.	Area Enclosed.	Award in Possession of
			A. R. P.	
Blyth (W.) .	1,320	Apparently partially enclosed before 1700. Township enclosed as follows:		
Including most of Nornay .		54 Geo. III, 53. Enclosed under Styrrup Act of 1802, q.v.	113 1 15	Church chest.
Bole . . .	1,333	Apparently very late example of enclosure w.P.s.		
Bothamsall .	2,462	w.P.s. *c.* 1772.	(*c.* 1,016 acres).	
Boughton (W.)	1,374	Largely enclosed w.P.s. *c.* 1772: some under 30 Vict., 20 (Annual General Act).	138 0 0*	S.H. and Vicar.
Bradmore .	1,254	w.P.s. *c.* 1778.		
Bramcote (W.)	1,062	11 Geo. III, 57 (with Stapleford)	968 1 19 (in the two).	S.H.
		8 & 9 Vict., 118 (G. A.)	41 2 34	S.H.
Brinsley (M. and W.)	954	15 Geo. III, 71.	300 0 0*	Lost.
Broadholme (W.)	640	According to Throsby it was enclosed before his time, but a portion was enclosed under 42 Geo. III, 95 (with Harby, Notts, and Saxilby, Lincs).	1,200 0 0 (in the two Notts townships).	Vicar of Saxilby.
Budby . .		See Perlethorpe.		
Bulcote . .	648	8 Geo. III, 52 (with Burton Joyce).	1,174 1 23 (in both).	S.H.
Bulwell . .		In Nottingham, q.v.		
Bunny . .	2,135	37 Geo. III, 86.	More than 1,000.*	Lost.
Burton Joyce	1,357	*Vide supra* Bulcote.		
Calverton .	3,418	19 Geo. III, 79.	2,334 2 26	P.C.
Carburton (W.)	2,242	w.P.s. 1770–1798.		
Carcolston .	1,642	Enclosed in Thoroton's time.		
Carlton (near Nottingham)	1,452	32 Geo. III, 64 (with Gedling and Stoke Bardolph).	3,555 3 10 (in the three)	Gedling Church Chest. Another copy in S.H.

Name of Place.	Land Area (Acres).	Date and Manner of Enclosure.	Area Enclosed.	Award in Possession of
			A. R. P.	
Carlton in Lindrick	4,033	Complaints of enclosure and depopulation in 1639, but see also 7 Geo. III, 49.	2,530 3 27	Rector.
Carlton on Trent	904	5 Geo. III, 7.	852 3 3	Lost.
Caunton *including* Beesthorpe, Knapthorpe	3,104	35 Geo. III, 42.	803 1 20	Clerk to P.C.
Caythorpe .	314	5 Geo. III, 29 (with Gunthorpe and Lowdham).	2,500 0 0* (in the three).	Vicar of Lowdham.
Chilwell . .	1,421	w.P.s. before 1790. Possibly enclosed in Thoroton's time.		
Clarborough *including* Welham	2,215	16 Geo. III, 71.	802 0 24 354 1 2	P.C.
Clarborough Moorgate		Now in E. Retford, q.v.		
Clayworth .	2,124	30 Geo. III, 42.	1,092 0 12	P.C.
Clifton-with-Glapton	1,886	32 Geo. II, 55 (with Barton).	1,541 3 37 (in the two).	Rector of Barton (some pasture was excluded from the Act and is open to-day)
Clipston (on the Wolds)	938	45 Geo. III, 47 (with Plumtree).	1,228 2 11 (in the two).	S.H.
Clipstone .	4,007	Wood emparked temp. Hen. II. Other enclosures took place in 18th and 19th centuries.		
Coddington .	1,968	33 Geo. II, 46.	1,869 2 39	S.H.
Colston Bassett	2,447	Enclosed in Thoroton's time.		
Colwick . .	1,271	Probably enclosed before 1700.		
Cossall . .	971	Probably enclosed w.P.s. before 1800		

Name of Place.	Land Area (Acres).	Date and Manner of Enclosure.	Area Enclosed.	Award in Possession of
			A. R. P.	
Costock . .	1,688	According to Curtis, the "High Fields" estate here was open in his time, but see: 33 Geo. II, 40.	710 0 0*	Chairman of P.C.
Cotgrave *including* Straggle-thorpe	3,704	30 Geo. III, 25.[1] Given by Lowe separately from Cotgrave as enclosed before his time, evidently w.P.s.	2,365 0 0*	
Cotham . .	1,350	Enclosed in Thoroton's time, though Lowe gives *c.* 1778–98.		
Cottam . .	599	Probably enclosed before 1700.		
Cromwell .	1,388	13 Geo. III, 11.	1,342 1 23	Rector.
Cropwell Bishop with	1,602	42 Geo. III, 26.	1,286 3 3	S.H.
a detached portion .	36	Probably enclosed with Cropwell Butler 1787, q.v.		
Cropwell Butler	1,877	27 Geo. III, 41.	873 0 0	S.H.
Cuckney . .	1,110	w.P.s. 1768 (Curtis).		
Darlton . .	1,506	Some enclosure in late Middle Ages. Mainly w.P.s. 1765. Possibly small portion enclosed by Dunham Act 1803, q.v.		
Dunham .	1,059	43 Geo. III, 42 (with Ragnall) (see also Darlton above).	1,500 2 6 (in the two).	Chairman of P.C. (Dunham).
Eakring . .	2,567	Mainly enclosed w.P.s. in 18th century. About one-fifth still remains open including arable, meadow and waste.		
East Bridgford	1,899	36 Geo. III, 105.	1,302 1 16	S.H.
East Drayton	1,555	59 Geo. III, 10.	913 1 3¼	Vicar.
Easthorpe .		In Southwell, q.v.		

[1] Act merely confirms agreement made "somtime since".

Name of Place.	Land Area (Acres).	Date and Manner of Enclosure.	Area Enclosed. A. R. P.	Award in Possession of
East Leake .	2,510	38 Geo. III, 11. (An attempt at enclosure appears to have been frustrated by Sir Thos. Parkyns in 1781.)	2,408 1 27	Clerk of P.C. Kept in Church chest. A copy at S.H.
East Markham	2,754	50 Geo. III, 137.	1,635 0 0	Clerk of P.C.
East Retford (W.) *including*	4,656	6 & 7 Wm. IV, 115. (G.A.)	45 1 3½	Town Clerk.
Clarborough		39 Geo. III, 77.	85 3 39	Clarborough Parish chest.
Moorgate (W.)				
Bolham and Little Gringley		Probably enclosed w.P.s. in 18th century.		
Ordsall		40 Geo. III, 71.	410 0 0*	Town Clerk.
West Retford		14 Geo. III, 9.	876 3 27	Town Clerk.
East Stoke .	1,654	35 Geo. III, 101 (with Elston).	2,704 3 0	Vicar.
Eastwood (W.)	923	31 Geo. III, 34.	148 0 0*	U.D.C.
Eaton . .	1,519	49 Geo. III, 131.	796 0 0*	S.H.
Edingley .	1,755	17 Geo. III, 117 (with Halam).	?	Chairman of Parish Meeting (Halam).
Edwalton .	831	"All or most enclosed" in Thoroton's time.		
Edwinstowe (mainly W.)	5,989	58 Geo. III (Crown Award). (There was also much non-Parliamentary enclosure before this.)	1,487 0 0	S.H.
Egmanton .	2,217	1 & 2 Geo. IV, 8 (with Walesby and Kirton). Three awards, one for each parish.	1,033 1 23	Chairman of P.C.
Elkesley (mostly W.) *including* Normanton	2,645	19 Geo. III, 99. Act confirming agreement already made. Extensive enclosures made (apart from this Act ?) by D. of Newcastle prior to 1798.	1,358 0 0*	Lost.

Name of Place.	Land Area (Acres).	Date and Manner of Enclosure.	Area Enclosed. A. R. P.	Award in Possession of
Elston . .	1,605	36 Geo. III, 10 (with E. Stoke).	2,704 3 0	Vicar of E. Stoke.
Elton . .	989	47 Geo. III, Sess. 2, c2.	906 0 12	Lost ?
Epperstone .	2,500	8 Geo. III, 50.	1,027 3 37	A copy at S.H.
Everton *including* Harwell	3,795	32 Geo. II, 46.	3,636 0 5	S.H. Schoolmaster has a copy.
Farndon . .	1,830	7 Geo. III, 90.	1,696 0 1	Lost ?
Farnsfield . *including*	4,555	17 Geo. III, 55.	2,714 0 22	Vicar.
Hexgrave .		Formerly in Southwell. Originally a park attached to the Archbishop's palace ; probably divided and cultivated in or before 17th century.		
Felley . .	413	Probably old enclosure; partially enclosed with Selston (q.v.) in 1865.		
Fenton . .		In Sturton, q.v.		
Finningley .	2,396	14 Geo. III, 72 (including Blaxton and Auckley in Yorks).	1,904 0 39 (in Finningley).	S.H. Copy at custody of Rector.
Fiskerton-cum-Morton	1,547	6 & 7 Wm. IV, 115. 2 & 3 Vict., 3.	1,499 2 16	"Lately with the Overseer."
Flawborough	976	Enclosed and depopulated in Thoroton's time.		
Fledborough	1,448	Apparently w.P.s. in 18th century.		
Flintham .	2,169	15 Geo. III, 2.	1,959 0 0	Chairman of P.C.
Fulwood . .	178	The wood was enclosed by the Prior of Lenton as early as 1246.		
Gamston .	1,966	48 Geo. III, 70.	1,628 0 0*	?
Gamston (nr. Nottingham)	442	Probably enclosed in Thoroton's time.		
Gateford . .		In Worksop, q.v.		
Gedling . .	1,917	See Carlton.		
Girton (W.) .	1,045	8 & 9 Vict., 118 (G.A.).	611 1 12	S.H. and Clerk to Parish Council.

Name of Place.	Land Area (Acres).	Date and Manner of Enclosure.	Area Enclosed.	Award in Possession of
			A. R. P.	
Glapton . .		See Clifton with Glapton.		
Gonalston .	1,342	By agreement 1768.		
Gotham . .	2,563	44 Geo. III, 21.	2,287 2 39	Rector.
Granby *including* Sutton	2,310	33 Geo. III, 15.	2,113 3 37	S.H.
Grassthorpe .	710	39 Geo. III, 83.	307 2 10	Vicar (of Normanton).
Greasley *including* Bagley	5,363	39 Geo. III, 83.	332 2 6	S.H.
Newthorpe and Watnall (W.)		Enclosed probably in Tudor times.		
Gringley-on-the-Hill	4,335	36 Geo. III, 98.	3,000 0 0*	P.C.
Grove . .	1,324	Probably enclosed before Thoroton's time.		
Gunthorpe .	1,124	5 Geo. III, 7 (with Caythorpe and Lowdham).	2,500 0 0* (in the three)	Vicar of Lowdham.
Habblesthorpe		Now in Leverton, q.v.		
Halam . .		See Edingley.		
Halloughton	988	Probably old enclosure.		
Harby . .	1,229	See Broadholme.		
Harwell . .		See Everton.		
Harworth (W.)	4,007	39 Geo. III, 74.	1,285 1 22	Clerk to the P.C.
with detached portion,		5 Geo. III, 85 (with Tickhill).	1,600–1,700 (mainly in Tickhill).	Vicar of Tickhill.
Serlby . .	507	Probably old enclosure.		
Haughton .	1,000	Probably old enclosure.		
Hawkesworth	693	33 Geo. II, 26.	639 3 20	Vicar of Scarrington; also S.H.
Hawton . .	2,168	Enclosed and depopulated in Thoroton's time.		
Hayton *including*	2,391	33 Geo. II, 28.	1,192 1 35	P.M.
Tiln . .		Probably enclosed w.P.s. 18th century.		
Haywood Oaks	677	Probably enclosed at an early date.		

Name of Place.	Land Area (Acres).	Date and Manner of Enclosure.	Area Enclosed.	Award in Possession of
			A. R. P.	
Headon . .	2,347	55 Geo. III, 2.	792 3 31	S.H.
Hexgrave .		In Farnsfield, q.v.		
Hickling . .	2,855	15 Geo. III, 68.	2,601 0 7	S.H.
Hockerton .	1,386	Probably w.P.s. in 18th century.		
Hodsock (W.)	4,211	The park was enclosed before Leland's time.		
Holbeck . .	1,291	Enclosed before 1832. Date unknown.		
Holme . .	1,090	See Bathley.		
Holme Pierrepont *including* Adbolton	2,198	Old enclosure.		
Hoveringham	900	Probably w.P.s. in 18th century.		
Hucknall-under-Huthwaite (W.)	1,999	34 Geo. III, 97 (with Sutton-in-Ashfield).	3,092 0 34 (in the two)	Clerk to U.D.C. (Sutton-in-Ashfield).
Hucknall Torkard	3,276	8 & 9 Geo. III, Sess. 2, C. 91.	1,032 1 10	U.D.C.
Kelham . .	2,072	Possibly enclosed before 1700.		
Kersall . .	669	18 Geo. III, 66.	800 0 0*	Apparently lost; recently in custody of P.M.
Keyworth .	1,438	38 Geo. III, 23.	1,500 0 0*	Vicar.
Kilvington .	491	Some enclosure in 1590. Also by agreement 1750–1760.		
Kimberley .	838	Probably old enclosure.		
Kingston-on-Soar	1,312	Old enclosure; temp. Henry VII.		
Kinoulton .	3,077	By agreement in 1770.		
Kirkby-in-Ashfield (W.)	5,811	36 Geo. III, 79.	2,023 2 37	U.D.C.
Kirklington .	1,977	Largely enclosed w.P.s. in 18th century.		
Kirton . .	998	1 & 2 Geo. IV, 8 (with Walesby and Egmanton).	154 1 5	Rector.

Name of Place.	Land Area (Acres).	Date and Manner of Enclosure.	Area Enclosed.	Award in Possession of
			A. R. P.	
Kneesall . .	2,311	Probably w.P.s. after 1798.		
Kneeton . .	962	Enclosed in Thoroton's time.		
Lambley (W.)	2,174	32 Geo. III, 63.	660 0 0*	Rector.
Laneham .	1,588	12 Geo. III, 115.	1,073 2 37	P.C.
Langar-cum-Barnston	3,868	Old enclosure.		
Langford .	2,179	Partly enclosed temp. Elizabeth.		
Laxton *including* Moorhouse (W.)	4,007	Arable fields and common still open. 11 & 12 Vict., 27. (Annual G.A.)	113 2 14	S.H. and Vicar of Laxton.
Lenton . .		In Nottingham, q.v.		
Linby (W.) .	1,481	16 Vict., 11.	151 0 0	S.H.
Lindhurst .	885	Apparently w.P.s. in 19th century.		
Littleborough	345	2 & 3 Geo. IV, 8 (with Sturton).	218 3 26 (in Littleborough).	Chairman of P.C.
Lound . .	2,362	15 Geo. III, 74 (with Sutton).	3,545 2 0	Vicar of Sutton.
Lowdham .	1,687	See Caythorpe.		
Mansfield (W.)	7,032	13 Vict., 8. } (Annual G.A.s)	2,360 0 0*	S.H.
Mansfield Woodhouse (W.)	4,820	12 Vict., 7. }	1,200 0 0	S.H.
Maplebeck .	1,196	Enclosed w.P.s. in 1780.		
Mapperley .		In Nottingham, q.v.		
Markham Clinton	1,064	48 Geo. III, 62.	?	P.C. See also Tuxford.
Marnham .	2,305	Probably enclosed w.P.s. in 18th century.		
Mattersey .	2,440	10 Geo. III, 91.	1,720 0 28	P.C.
Meering . .	463	Formerly an extra-parochial liberty consisting of a single farm. Probably enclosed before middle of 17th century.		
Misson . .	6,133	33 Geo. II, 50.	3,760 0 0*	Clerk to P.C.
Misterton .	4,262	11 Geo. III, 100 (with W. Stockwith).	3,142 2 7 (in Misterton).	Clerk to P.C.

Name of Place.	Land Area (Acres).	Date and Manner of Enclosure.	Area Enclosed.	Award in Possession of
			A. R. P.	
Moorgate .		Formerly in Clarborough, now in E. Retford, q.v.		
Moorhouse .		See Laxton.		
Morton . .		See Fiskerton.		
Morton . .		In Babworth, q.v.		
Nether Langwith	1,292	Enclosed before 1832; period unknown.		
Newark-on-Trent	1,900	40 Geo. III, 44.	423 1 33	Town Clerk.
Newstead .	3,209	Partly enclosed by Prior of Newstead in Middle Ages and partly w.P.s. after 1793.		
Newton Oldwork		See Shelford.		
Normanton .		See Elkesley.		
Normanton-on-Soar	1,440	10 Geo. III, 91.	1,195 2 23	S.H.
Normanton .		See Southwell.		
Normanton-on-Trent	1,208	40 Geo. III, 18. The Act gave the proprietors the option of enclosing the meadows or leaving them open, and ordered the "Holme" to be stinted.	750 0 0*	P.C.
Normanton-on-the-Wolds	803	Enclosed in Thoroton's time.		
Nornay . .		See Blyth.		
North Clifton	1,097	33 Geo. II, 48 (with S. Clifton).	1,979 1 4 (in the two) .	Messrs. Smith, Wooley & Co., N. Collingham
		31 Vict., 31 (with S. Clifton)(Annual G.A.)	43 0 0* (in the two).	S.H.
North Collingham	2,449	30 Geo. III, 76. Cow pasture enclosed under deed poll executed by proprietors 1790.	1,590 2 1	P.C. (see above).

Name of Place.	Land Area (Acres).	Date and Manner of Enclosure.	Area Enclosed.	Award in Possession of
			A. R. P.	
North-Lever-ton-with-Habbles-thorpe	2,404	35 Geo. III, 76.	1,488 1 14	R.D.C.
North Musk-ham	1,165	See Bathley.		
North Wheat-ley	2,192	6 & 7 Wm. IV, 115.	1,214 0 19	P.C.
Norton . .	1,591	Nothing definitely known.		
Norwell *including* Willoughby	2,568	6 & 7 Geo. IV, 15. (G.A.) Some enclosure in Tudor times	1,300 0 0*	P.C.
Norwell Wood-house	455	Probably old enclosure.		
Nottingham	10,801	2 & 3 Vict., 28. 2 & 3 Vict., 32. 7 & 8 Vict., 7. 8 & 9 Vict., 7.	34 0 0* 18 0 0*	Town Clerk.
including Basford (in-cluding Mapper-ley)		32 Geo. III, 67. Assorting here from time of Ed. I. Throsby gives it all old enclosure "except that part belonging to the Forest." Some enclosure 1797.	1,491 0 12	Town Clerk.
Bulwell .		Some medieval enclosure; partly enclosed under 42–3 Vict. cciv; partly open to-day.		
Len-ton } (W.)		7 Geo. III, 36.	665 1 17 (Lenton). 551 2 17 (Radford).	Town Clerk.
Rad-ford } (W.)		36 Geo. III, 114.	276 1 37 (in the two).	Town Clerk.
Sneinton .		36 Geo. III, 42.	787 3 0	Town Clerk.
Wilford .		See South Wilford.		
Nutthall . .	1,333	Nothing definitely known. Open fields temp. Ed. III.		
Oldcotes . .		See Styrrup.		

Name of Place.	Land Area (Acres).	Date and Manner of Enclosure.	Area Enclosed.	Award in Possession of
			A. R. P.	
Ollerton (W.)	1,760	18 Geo. III, 91.	500 0 0*	?
Ompton . .	614	Enclosed w.P.s. since 1800.		
Ordsall . .		See East Retford.		
Orston . .	1,953	33 Geo. III, 67 (with Thoroton).	2,156 0 27 (in the two).	Said to be in custody of Chairman of P.C. of Orston.
Osberton .		See Worksop.		
Ossington .	2,403	6 & 7 Wm. IV, 115 (G.A.). Most of this parish enclosed w.P.s. 18th century. See also Sutton-on-Trent.	54 1 38 125 0 0	?
Owthorpe .	1,639	Probably before 1700.		
Oxton (W.) .	3,611	12 Vict., 7 (Annual G.A.)	1,139 0 0	S.H. and Vicar.
Papplewick .	1,979	About 1,000 acres seem to have been enclosed w.P.s. since 1793.		
Perlethorpe (with Budby)	3,845	About 1,217 acres by Royal Grant in 1723. A good deal of the rest since 1832.		
Plumtree .	1,859	See Clipston.		
Radcliffe-on-Trent	2,147	27 Geo. III, 40.	1,647 0 10	Clerk to P.C.
Radford . .		See Nottingham.		
Ragnall . .	1,201	See Dunham.		
Rampton .	2,160	6 & 7 Wm. IV, 115 (G.A.s) 2 & 3 Vict.	1,392 2 0	Clerk to P.C.
Ranby . .		See Babworth.		
Ranskill . .	1,311	42 Geo. III, 67 (with Scrooby).	1,300 0 0* (in the two). 971 1 21 (in Ranskill).	Clerk to P.C.
Ratcliffe-on-Soar	1,122	Enclosed before Thoroton's time.		
Rempstone .	1,579	8 Geo. III, 12.	1,355 2 27	S.H.
Rolleston .	1,627	Probably w.P.s. in 18th century.		
Ruddington .	2,987	7 Geo. III, 34.	2,781 0 20	S.H.

Name of Place.	Land Area (Acres).	Date and Manner of Enclosure.	Area Enclosed.	Award in Possession of
			A. R. P.	
Rufford . .	9,910	*c.* 1,860 acres by Saviles 1776–98. A good deal probably after 1800.		
Saundby . .	1,412	Probably w.P.s. in 18th century.		
Saxondale .	684	Enclosed in Thoroton's time.		
Scaftworth (W.)	1,069	12 Geo. III, 17.	427 2 6	?
Scarrington .	932	See Aslockton.		
Scofton . .		See Worksop.		
Screveton .	1,152	16 Geo. III, 83. The Act confirms an already existing agreement.	350 0 0*	
Scrooby . .	1,591	15 Geo. III, 23.	1,350 0 0*	Vicar of Scrooby.
		42 Geo. III, 67 (the latter with Ranskill).	1,300 0 0* (in the two).	P.C. (Ranskill).
Selston (W.) .	3,316	52 Geo. III, 42 (with Pinxton, Derbyshire). (Very small part of Selston, which is now owing to rectification of boundary probably included in Derbyshire.)	24 3 25 (in the two).	S.H.
		28 Vict., 39 (Annual G.A.)	704 3 17	S.H.
Serlby . .		See Harworth.		
Shelford *including* Newton Oldwork	3,128	Possibly old enclosure. Partly w.P.s. about 1778–98. Partly by Agreement *c.* 1760.		
Shelton . .	845	Enclosed in Thoroton's time, though Lowe says 1778–98.		
Shireoaks .		See Worksop.		
Sibthorpe .	951	It may have been partially enclosed temp. Henry VIII and again 1778–98.		
Skegby (W.?)	1,465	48 Geo. III, 65.	259 0 32	Vicar of Marnham.

Name of Place.	Land Area (Acres).	Date and Manner of Enclosure.	Area Enclosed.	Award in Possession of
			A. R. P.	
Sneinton . .		See Nottingham.		
Sookholme .	988	Nothing known.		
South Clifton (W.)	1,290	See North Clifton.		
South Collingham	3,017	Probably enclosed before 1700. See also North Collingham.		
South Leverton	2,201	35 Geo. III, 77.	1,549 1 33	Mr. J. White, S. Leverton.
South Muskham	2,730	Probably enclosed at an eary period.		
South Scarle	1,093	Probably enclosed w.P.s. in 18th century.		
Southwell .	4,922	The parks in Southwell were enclosed at a very early date.		
including:				
Westhorpe (W.)		14 Geo. III, 30.	?	
Normanton		15 Geo. III, 3 (both of these include part of Southwell proper).	426 2 37	Clerk to P.C. (?).
Easthorpe (W.)		6 & 7 Wm. IV, 115. (G.A.)	116 1 34	
South Wheatley	645	Probably in 17th century.		
South Wilford *with*	1,472	5 Geo. III, 67.	1,167 2 34	P.C.
detached portion	1	(The Shire Hall).		
Spalford . .	1,043	53 Geo. III, 154 (with Wigsley).	480 3 21 (in Spalford).	Vicar of S. Scarle.
Stanford-on-Soar	1,500	Probably enclosed before 1700.		
Stanhope .		Given by Leadam as the place in Thurgarton Wapentake where *c.* 30 acres were enclosed in 1504. Site of village now unknown.		
Stanton-on-the-Wolds	1,406	Enclosed in Thoroton's time.		
Stapleford .	1,247	See Bramcote.		

Name of Place.	Land Area (Acres).	Date and Manner of Enclosure.	Area Enclosed.	Award in Possession of
			A. R. P.	
Staunton .	1,371	32 Geo. II, 5. This enclosure did not include the Manor of Staunton Haverholme (Lowe's *Staunton-cum-Orston*) which was formerly monastic property and probably early enclosed.	918 2 23	Cannot be traced.
Staythorpe .	651	Probably enclosed w.P.s.in 18th century.		
Steetley . .		See note under Worksop.		
Stoke Bardolph	1,086	See Gedling and Carlton.		
Stokeham .	604	Probably enclosed w.P.s. in 18th century; but see Throsby on E. Drayton.		
Stragglethorpe		See Cotgrave.		
"Le Strete" .		According to Leadam *c.* 90 acres were enclosed here 1494–1504; he suggests it may be situated on the Roman Road between Littleborough and Doncaster. Perhaps it may be Steetley, q.v.		
Strelley . .	1,065	The Award for the Bilborough Act of 1808 which covers Strelley states there were no open lands in Streley. Probably Strelley was enclosed w.P.s. in 18th century.		
Sturton-le-Steeple *including* Fenton	4,034	2 & 3 Geo. IV, 8 (with Littleborough). *Note.*—Above Act gives only 455 acres to be enclosed in Sturton and Fenton. I cannot account for difference between this and Award figure.	1,940 0 9 (in Sturton and Fenton).	Destroyed by fire 1901. Parish has typewritten copy.

Name of Place.	Land Area (Acres).	Date and Manner of Enclosure.	Area Enclosed.	Award in Possession of
			A. R. P.	
Styrrup . .	3,040	42 Geo. III, 78.	2,296 3 5	Clerk to P.C.
Sutton (near Granby)		See Granby.		
Sutton (near Retford)		See Lound.		
Sutton Passeys		Vanished village; site occupied by Wollaton Park.		
Sutton Bonington	2,158			
St. Anne's		14 Geo. III, 27.	1,163 3 8	Clerk to P.C.
St. Michael's		16 Geo. III, 71.	875 0 1	Clerk to P.C.
Sutton-in-Ashfield (W.)	4,810	34 Geo. III, 97.	3,092 0 34	S.H.
Sutton-upon-Trent	2,588	43 Geo. III, 81.	1,158 0 14 (excluding about 125 acres in Ossington).	Clerk to P.C.
Syerston . .	768	32 Geo. III, 49.	510 1 33	Vicar of E. Stoke.
Teversall .	2,721	Enclosed w.P.s. at an unknown period.		
Thorney . .	2,248	Possibly w.P.s. in 18th century.		
Thoroton .	782	See Orston.		
Thorpe (by Newark)	713	Largely enclosed in Thoroton's time; but *c.* 180 acres waste said to have been enclosed w.P.s. in 1792.		
Thorpe-in-the-Glebe	863	Enclosed temp. Henry VII.		
Thrumpton .	979	Enclosed in Thoroton's time.		
Thurgarten .	2,572	Enclosed by agreement *c.* 1772.		
Tiln . . .		See Hayton.		
Tollerton .	1,211	Partly enclosed at time of Civil War; also by 43 Geo. III, 29.	435 3 20	Rector.
Torworth .	1,377	Enclosed 1801–8 by agreement of proprietors.		
		1801	165 3 31	Vicar of Blyth.
		1801	478 1 21	Vicar of Blyth.
		1808	324 0 4	Vicar of Blyth.

Name of Place.	Land Area (Acres).	Date and Manner of Enclosure.	Area Enclosed.	Award in Possession of
Toton	1,332	Enclosed in Thoroton's time.		
including Attenborough		Enclosed in Thoroton's time ("Few houses and no fields"—Thoroton).		
Treswell	1,570	6 & 7 Wm. IV, 115. (G.A.)	567 3 15	S.H. A copy lately with Overseer.
Trowell	1,602	27 Geo. III, 23. Agreement confirmed by Act.	1,597 0 11*	
Tuxford	2,847	39 Geo. III, 100.	1,648 3 11 (including some lands allotted to Markham Clinton).	Vicar.
with detached portion	46			
Tythby	583	Apparently enclosed before Thoroton's time.		
Upper Broughton	1,902	33 Geo. II, 39.	2,000 0 0*	P.C. cannot trace.
Upton (near Retford)		Included in Headon, q.v.		
Upton (near Southwell)	1,488	35 Geo. III, 41.	1,436 2 8	Clerk to P.C.
Walesby	1,473	1–2 Geo. IV, 8; 280 acres probably enclosed from "Walesby Warren" w.P.s. before 1798.	894 3 30	Vicar.
Walkeringham	2,994	42 Geo. III, 105.	1,930 0 0	P.C. cannot trace.
Wallingwells	601	Partly enclosed in Tudor times; partly under Act for Carlton in Lindrick, q.v.		
Warsop	6,162	About two-thirds of this parish was enclosed by agreement in 1775. See also:		
		58 Geo. III, 5. Varied in 1858 by an order under the Act of 1845.	1,779 0 31*	Clerk to P.C.
Watnall		See Greasley.		

Name of Place.	Land Area (Acres).	Date and Manner of Enclosure.	Area Enclosed. A. R. P.	Award in Possession of
Welbeck . .	2,669	Largely enclosed from waste by 3rd Duke of Portland.		
Wellow . .	1,000	6 & 7 Wm. IV, 115. 2 & 3 Vict., 3 (G.A.)	274 1 28	S.H. and P.C.
West Bridgford	1,115	Probably enclosed before Thoroton's time.		
West Burton	954	Probably enclosed w.P.s. in 18th century.		
West Drayton	672	Probably enclosed w.P.s. in 18th century.		
Westhorpe .		See Southwell.		
West Leake .	1,603	Two agreements confirmed by Act in 1742 and 1754. The Act of 1742 is in Nottingham City Library. I have not seen the Act of 1754.		
West Newark	222	No data; probably an early enclosure.		
Weston . .	1,740	36 Geo. III, 88.	1,082 0 16	Clerk to P.C.
West Retford		See East Retford.		
West Stockwith	686	See Misterton.		
Whatton . .	1,754	29 Geo. III, 20.	1,700 0 0*	Mr. Stokes of Aslockton has a certified copy; Mr. Matthews of Whatton also; minus the plan.
Widmerpool (W.)	2,102	43 Geo. III, 1.	1,795 1 18	P.C. cannot trace.
Wigsley . .	1,233	53 Geo. III, 154.	718 2 10	P.C. cannot trace.
Willoughby .		See Norwell.		
Willoughby-on-the-wolds	2,103	33 Geo. III, 83.	1,695 0 22	S.H.

Name of Place.	Land Area (Acres).	Date and Manner of Enclosure.	Area Enclosed. A. R. P.	Award in Possession of
Winkburn .	2,371	Enclosed w.P.s. in 18th century (?).		
Winthorpe .	630	17 Geo. III, 40.	329 3 21	Rector.
Wiseton . .	1,045	By agreement of proprietors *c.* 1760.		
Wiverton Hall	1,023	Enclosed before Thoroton's time.		
Wollaton *including* Sutton Passeys	2,064	Enclosed "long before" Thoroton's time.		
Woodborough	1,944	35 Geo. III, 92.	1,266 0 19	S.H.
Woodhouse Hall	333	Formerly property of Welbeck Abbey; probably early enclosed.		
Worksop *including*	17,754	43 Geo. III, 68.	10,801 2 20(?)	
Gateford, Shireoaks		36 Geo. III, 33.	461 3 36	
Osberton, Scofton and possibly formerly including a little of Steetley, now entirely in Derbyshire. See above, "Le Strete."		According to Lowe, *c.* 1,350 acres were enclosed here w.P.s. from the Forest borders shortly before 1798.		
Wysall . .	1,553	40 Geo. III, 69.	1,375 1 36	Chairman of P.C.

INDEX